International African Library 30
General Editors: J. D. Y. Peel, Colin Murray and Suzette Heald

ISLAMIC AND CASTE KNOWLEDGE PRACTICES AMONG HAALPULAAR'EN IN SENEGAL

The *International African Library* is a major monograph series from the International African Institute and complements its quarterly periodical *Africa*, the premier journal in the field of African studies. Theoretically informed ethnographies, studies of social relations 'on the ground' which are sensitive to local cultural forms, have long been central to the Institute's publications programme. The *IAL* maintains this strength but extends it into new areas of contemporary concern, both practical and intellectual. It includes works focused on problems of development, especially on the linkages between the local and national levels of society; studies along the interface between the social and environmental sciences; and historical studies, especially those of a social, cultural or interdisciplinary character.

International African Library
General Editors
J. D. Y. Peel, Colin Murray *and* Suzette Heald

Titles in the series:
1. Sandra T. Barnes *Patrons and power: creating a political community in metropolitan Lagos*
2. Jane I. Guyer (ed.) *Feeding African cities: essays in social history*
3. Paul Spencer *The Maasai of Matapato: a study of rituals of rebellion*
4. Johan Pottier *Migrants no more: settlement and survival in Mambwe villages, Zambia*
5. Gunther Schlee *Identities on the move: clanship and pastoralism in northern Kenya*
6. Suzette Heald *Controlling anger: the sociology of Gisu violence*
7. Karin Barber *I could speak until tomorrow:* oriki, *women and the past in a Yoruba town*
8. Richard Fardon *Between God, the dead and the wild: Chamba interpretations of religion and ritual*
9. Richard Werbner *Tears of the dead: the social biography of an African family*
10. Colin Murray *Black Mountain: land, class and power in the eastern Orange Free State, 1880s to 1980s*
11. J. S. Eades *Strangers and traders: Yoruba migrants, markets and the state in northern Ghana*
12. Isaac Ncube Mazonde *Ranching and enterprise in eastern Botswana: a case study of black and white farmers*
13. Melissa Leach *Rainforest relations: gender and resource use among the Mende of Gola, Sierra Leone*
14. Tom Forrest *The advance of African capital: the growth of Nigerian private enterprise*
15. C. Bawa Yamba *Permanent pilgrims: the role of pilgrimage in the lives of West African Muslims in Sudan*
16. Graham Furniss *Poetry, prose and popular culture in Hausa*
17. Philip Burnham *The politics of cultural difference in northern Cameroon*
18. Jane I. Guyer *An African niche economy: farming to feed Ibadan, 1968–88*
19. A. Fiona D. Mackenzie *Land, ecology and resistance in Kenya, 1880–1952*
20. David Maxwell *Christians and chiefs in Zimbabwe: a social history of the Hwesa people c. 1870s–1990s*
21. Birgit Meyer *Translating the devil: religion and modernity among the Ewe in Ghana*
22. Deborah James *Songs of the women migrants: performance and identity in South Africa*
23. Christopher O. Davis *Death in abeyance: illness and therapy among the Tabwa of Central Africa*
24. Janet Bujra *Serving Class: masculinity and the feminisation of domestic service in Tanzania*
25. T. C. McCaskie *Asante identities: history and modernity in an African village*
26. Harri Englund *From war to peace on the Mozambique–Malawi borderland*
27. Anthony Simpson *'Half-London' in Zambia: contested identities in a Catholic mission school*
28. Elisha Renne, *Population and progress in a Yoruba town*
29. Belinda Bozzoli, *Theatres of struggle and the end of apartheid*
30. R. M. Dilley *Islamic and caste knowledge practices among Haalpulaar'en in Senegal: between mosque and termite mound*

ISLAMIC AND CASTE KNOWLEDGE PRACTICES AMONG HAALPULAAR'EN IN SENEGAL

BETWEEN MOSQUE AND TERMITE MOUND

R. M. DILLEY

EDINBURGH UNIVERSITY PRESS
for the International African Institute, London

To the memory of EM
and to Donna

© R. M. Dilley, 2004

Transferred to digital print 2009

Edinburgh University Press Ltd
22 George Square, Edinburgh

Typeset in Plantin
by Koinonia, Bury, and
Printed and bound in Great Britain by
CPI Antony Rowe, Chippenham and Eastbourne

A CIP record for this book is available
from the British Library

ISBN 0 7486 1990 9 (paperback)

The right of R. M. Dilley to be
identified as author of this work has been
asserted in accordance with the Copyright,
Designs and Patents Act 1988.

For other publications of the International
African Institute, please visit their web site at
www.iaionthe.net

CONTENTS

List of figures viii
Preface ix
Note on transcription and orthography xiv
Maps xvi

1 The Mosque and the Termite Mound 1
   Islam and caste 1
   Islam in Senegal 3
   'Popular' Islam 4
   Conceptions of caste 6
   Conceptions of Islam 7
   Islam in stratified societies 9
   Islamic 'magic' 12
   The territory 14
   The people 16
   The Islamic community 20
   Caste, power and knowledge 22
   The mosque and the termite mound 23
   An ambivalent adventure 25

2 Ranks and Categories: The Emergence of a Haalpulaar
   Social Division of Labour 27
   Social divisions among Haalpulaar'en – social ranks 27
   Social divisions among Haalpulaar'en – social categories 30
   Social categories of the men-of-skill (*nyeenyɓe*) 38
   Bondsmen and women 46
   Patronyms 48
   The hierarchical relations of political economy 49
   Discussion 53

3 Historical Origins and Social Pedigrees of Craftsmen and
   Musicians: Genealogies of Power and Knowledge of the Wild 57
   Historical origins and sources 57
   A history of men-of-skill categories 59
   Local histories 63

The social division of knowledge: men-of-skill and the wild	67
Characterisations of social ranks	77
Gandal and the social division of knowledge and power	79
History and hierarchy: a reprise	83
The fetishisation of production	85

4 The White and the Black: Ideology and the Rise to Dominance of the Islamic Clerics — 89

A brief history of Islam in the Senegal river valley	90
Formation of the *tooroɓe* social category	93
The construction of *tooroɓe* Islamic ideology	99
The Muslim reformism of Al-Hajj Umar Taal	101
Umar Taal, the 'mystical warrior'	106
Concluding remarks – Islam and the Other	110

5 Accommodationist Sufi Islam and Rites of Passage: Tensions and Ambiguities — 114

The ideological configuration of accommodationist Islam	114
Ritual specialists and rites of passage	117
Ambivalence in religious thought	122
Islam and the reinterpretation of myth	125
Discussion	128

6 The Witch-Hunter and the Marabout: Competing Domains of Knowledge and Power — 131

The black arts and fields of knowledge	132
The witch-hunter and the marabout	140
Discusssion: a social division of healing	152
Nyeŋgo and spiritual tutelage	155
Summary	157

7 The Power of the Word: The Oral and the Written — 160

Proverbial sayings and the denial of agency	161
The vocabulary of speech and language	163
The potency and danger of names	164
Praise-songs, poetry and prayer	167
The patterns of language	169
Spells, protective verses and incantations	171
Discussion of spoken 'magic'	175
Writing and the order of things	178
The prose of the world	188

8 Islamic Reformers, Islamists and the Muslim Community — 192

'Book magic'	193
Developments in the field of education	195

Islamic reform movements	197
The renegotiation of Islam and social exclusion	200
The changing nature of caste and Islam	204
Afterword	214
Notes	220
Bibliography	249
Index	266

LIST OF FIGURES

2.1	A *mabu* weaver on the streets of Dakar	38
2.2	A *lawɓe* woodcarver making domestic utensils	39
2.3	A *sakke* leatherworker in St Louis making leather amulets containing Qu'ranic verse or parts of animals etc.	41
2.4	A *baylo* smith at his forge in Fuuta Toro.	42
2.5	Seydu Gisse (Seydou Guisse), a *mabu* weaver and praise-singer now living in Tiaroye	44
6.1	Two vendors selling the raw materials for amulet-makers	145
6.2	The old house of the local imam and site of the Qur'anic school, in the village of Dumga, Fuuta Toro	148
7.1	A Haalpulaar healer/marabout's market stall in Rufisque	181
7.2	The Rufisque healer/marabout with his 'magical' 'weather-vane'	182
7.3	A *haatumeere* or 'magical' design written by a healer/marabout	183
7.4	An example of a *haatumeeje* or 'magical' design written by Cheikh Tall	185
7.5	A further example of a *haatumeeje* or 'magical' design written by Cheikh Tall	186

PREFACE

The process of arrival in a foreign place and of adjustment to anthropological fieldwork has been described as one involving a series of 'cultural disorientations' (Lienhardt 1987). The task I am faced with here is to achieve the opposite sense in the course of interpretation and analysis. This task entails, initially at least, orienting a reader to the object of study; from the outset, to plot a series of coordinates that refer to a locality, a set of people and a network of social relations. This task also refers to a set of coordinates in time and history. I am concerned with the western-most region of West Africa, an area in part covered by the present-day nation-state of Senegal, a one-time French colonial possession held as part of a swathe of territory across sub-Saharan Africa known as *l'Afrique Occidentale Française*. The period I attempt to embrace begins back in the late eighteenth century and connects with my own fieldwork in Senegal in the 1980s and mid-1990s. I am also concerned with a body of religious thought and practice – namely, Islam – that is confined neither to one place nor one ethnic or 'tribal' group. The object of my study, therefore, reaches across time and space, and is not limited by the conventional parameters of traditional anthropological analysis.

The historical presence of a world religion – Islam – in an ethnographic area poses intriguing problems: the analytic strategies of a number of disciplines converge on the issue of Islam, and the analyst situated at the confluence of these many interests may be swept in a number of directions. The pull of these many intellectual currents is strong. The question is: how to avoid potentially conflicting sets of analytical imperatives? For example, comparative religionists and scholars of Islamic studies would urge an emphasis on the analysis of forms of religion and religious institution in different locations, perhaps compared to a pure or parent type of the religion. Or again, historians of religion might recommend the tracing of patterns of diffusion of the faith and its evolution and adaptation within specific contexts. There are at least two competing perspectives here: one examines Islam in Africa, the other 'African Islam' (Evers Rosander and Westerlund 1997). From an anthropological point of view, the particularities of each cultural milieu have to be meshed with the sense of historical development and the possibility that cultural knowledge is not necessarily contained within social boundaries that are conventionally recognised by analysts.

Evans-Pritchard's work on the Sanusi of Cyrenaica (1949) is instructive in this regard. In his case, the Sanusiyya, a Sufi Muslim brotherhood, represented a pan-regional movement with historical and cultural connections in the western Maghreb and with religious lodges (*zawiyas*) situated throughout north-east Africa and the Hijaz. Yet, his analysis was focused on the establishment of this brotherhood among the Bedouin of Cyrenaica, a region of present-day Libya. His was a study of history, of place and of cultural connection. Evans-Pritchard developed his views about history in the Marett Lecture of 1950, when he argued that the imperatives of historical analysis and those of anthropology are not necessarily opposed; indeed, they meet at the crossroads of interpretation. This present project is concerned with the strands of Islam found within a network of local West African communities; it is concerned too with how these communities intertwine to form a broader fabric of social and cultural life. Islam is not, however, a static entity, but is dynamic and has developed over time. This investigation thus involves a grasp of history and of historical transformation, and a sense for anthropological interpretation that together form points of orientation for the analysis.

This book is an attempt to marry history and anthropology. It is consequently neither a standard historical text nor is it a conventional anthropological monograph. If anthropology involves the interpretation of the lives of human beings situated in different spaces from the one we occupy, then history involves the interpretation of the lives of human beings situated in different times from our own. A union between these two perspectives is thus the challenge of this present work. I am primarily trained as a social and cultural anthropologist, and the historical dimension I have developed in the course of my research has been in response to the increasing realisation that synchronic perspectives alone are inadequate to the task of complex analysis of social process and transformation. In order to trace the genealogy of relationships that people forge in the course of their lives, and that in turn inform the contexts in which the lives of future generations are played out, a method of historical ethnography is required. The relationships I am concerned with revolve around the question of 'what it is to be a Muslim' in Senegal from the eighteenth century through to the present day. This question is not confined to issues of theology or religious doctrine, but concerns social identities of living communities of human beings who divide themselves up into different categories of people. What has been referred to as 'caste' in West Africa is one such way of dividing people into different categories. The history of the question 'what it is to be a Muslim' is also a history of responses from indigenous interpreters who attempt to negotiate their way through an array of possible social identities. I attempt to show that in some respects answers to this question from people living within the Senegambian region show a remarkable consistency across time.

This work does not constitute an original piece of archival research since most of the historical sources I have used derive not from primary archives but from secondary published works. I examine these sources with a view to piecing together information and data scattered across a body of literature that allows for only a partial and fractured image to emerge of the relationship between members of caste groups and the religion of Islam at different historical periods. The sources, both primary and secondary, tend to focus on the dominant social groups of the region, those in positions of political authority or of religious ascendancy. To plot the traces of more marginal social groups of artisans, entertainers and musicians (the 'castes') is to plot the history of 'muted', 'subaltern' groups that have often been overlooked by commentators, chroniclers and others. Sources are often silent, gaps and lacunae appear, and inevitably only partial clues and traces are there to be detected and tracked down. The task of historical reconstruction is frustrating and sometimes incomplete, and it is at such moments that a historical and an anthropological imagination are drawn upon in order to fill out bolder connections between partial traces. All one can do is admit to this methodological device and to highlight its use at points in the text where it has been deemed appropriate. The responsibility for this imaginative engagement with historical material is mine alone.

This book builds upon my earlier social anthropological analyses of craftsmen, in particular weavers, as one among a set of social categories that are present in Fuuta Toro, the northern-most region of Senegal that runs along the south bank of the Senegal river. I have now broadened the perspective to embrace a more synthetic analysis of these social categories, and how they articulate a set of social relationships over time. The concept of caste, like that of the religion of Islam, does not constitute an essential category of analysis, but for me it brings to mind a set of social relationships of inclusion and exclusion, a set of dividing practices that have operated, *mutatis mutandis*, within the river valley over time.

The conventional anthropological focus on a specific place and the people who inhabit it does not adequately describe the movement contained within the present analysis. I begin my historical investigation by focusing on an Islamic revolution in Fuuta Toro in the late eighteenth century, and examine how this had implications for social relationships within the river valley. In some senses this might be considered a somewhat arbitrary starting point, but I take it also as a convenient and indeed crucial moment at the outset of this analysis, for I argue that it has importance for the redefinition of relations between an emergent group of ruling Islamic clerics and those with other social statuses. As the investigation develops, the compass of the study widens such that by the final chapter I examine relationships between Islam and caste within the general area of Senegal. This analytical movement reflects a historical movement of people and ideas out from Fuuta Toro into neighbouring territories during the course of the nineteenth and twentieth centuries. Indeed, the changes that occurred in Fuuta Toro in the eighteenth century were not the result of an immaculate conception, but were rather the product of a set of complex social and historical process from an earlier century that connected the region to the Moors and Berbers further to the north: a kind of 'Senegalo-Mauritanian' Islamic space. The people and ideas that subsequently moved south and east from Fuuta Toro into Senegambia and beyond in the period succeeding the revolution brought a version of Islam and consequent social upheavals through jihad or through passive means to existing kingdoms, chiefdoms and other polities of the area. The shift in anthropological focus of this work thus attempts to capture the shift in historical development of ideas and practices as they leached south and east from the river valley.

My own field research too mirrors in an inverted image this historical movement of people and ideas from Fuuta Toro. Early fieldwork between 1980 and 1982 and again in 1995 plotted a course from Dakar and the Cap Vert peninsula, where many weavers were then working, to Diourbel and Kaolack – two towns some 100 kilometres or more to the east and the south-east, both centres of cloth production and trade – and eventually back to Fuuta Toro, the place of origin of many of these craftsmen. Migration from Fuuta Toro and changes within the social and economic relations of cloth production formed an early focus of this research. Conceptions of social identity and questions of cultural difference became part of the study as the nature of 'caste' group membership emerged as a salient issue during fieldwork. What has subsequently become labelled as 'multi-sited' field research was for my part a pragmatic response to the attempt to trace networks of individuals moving across space over time. The historical impetus behind this present work might be construed as a counter-movement to the momentum set up by the dynamic of field research, reconstructing the flow of people and ideas from a period prior to the synchronic snapshot of one individual's fieldwork.

Fieldwork in Senegal from 1980 to 1982 was funded by a studentship and field-research grant from the ESRC (then the SSRC), to whom I am grateful for their support. A return trip in 1995–6 was funded in part by a Research Grant from the Carnegie Trust and by the University of St Andrews Travel Fund, and I would like to acknowledge with thanks the grants they both provided. A period of library and archive research in Paris in 2000 was generously funded by the British Academy (No. SG-31014) and a period of research leave enabling me to write a first draft of this work was supported by an AHRB Research Leave Grant (No. RLS-AN703/APN11649). I gratefully acknowledge their support too.

Early forays into the analysis of aspects of my ethnographic material were presented to a number of colloquia organised under the direction of Richard Werbner in Satterthwaite, Lake District, and my thanks go to him and the many participants who commented on those presentations. Furthermore, large sections of this book were presented at All Souls College, Oxford in the form of the Evans-Pritchard Lectures in 2001. It was a privilege to have been elected to this lectureship, which provided an important spur towards the completion of this project. In particular, I would like to thank for their helpful and constructive comments on those lectures John Davis, Warden of All Souls, Wendy James and David Parkin along with a number of Fellows of the College. I should too like to acknowledge the profound influence on my work as an anthropologist of my Oxford DPhil supervisor, the late Peter Lienhardt.

The period of research spent in Paris was enlivened by my association with the CNRS ERASME *équipe de recherche*, at whose seminar some of the ethno-historical material was presented. My thanks to the participants of that seminar, in particular to the late Daniel de Coppet, to Cecile Barraud and André Iteanu. To the staff at the *Centre d'Etudes Africaines* and at other libraries in Paris I give acknowledgement for their assistance and guidance. Louis Brenner read the manuscript through in early draft form, and I am grateful to him for his helpful and encouraging comments, as well as for those of the two readers for IAI. The patience, persistence and continued encouragement of J. D. Y. Peel merits a warm note of thanks, as do the kind efforts of Richard Fardon, Catherine Alès and Jean Chippiano in helping me realise aspects of this project.

In Senegal more people than I can mention have helped in bringing form and giving content to this project. With especial warmth I thank Seydou and Bomma Guisse, my teachers in the arts of the *maabuɓe* weavers, and all *Dumganaaɓe*, whose cooperation and friendship made my research both pleasurable and absorbing. Omar Athie and other members of the Athie family helped me at numerous points in my work, and Assane Lô and family must be remembered for their warm hospitality, friendship and help in more ways than can be described briefly here. To M. Ndiaye, then *Le directeur*, and his staff at *Les Archives Nationales*; to M. Papa Massèn Sene, M. Fode Conde, M. Samba Demba Bah and M. Mammadou Sané of *Les Archives Culturelles*; to M. Abd el Kader Agne and M. Diaw; to Dr Mammadou Kanji and Abdou Gaye, I express my gratitude for their cooperation and valuable assistance lent to me.

Finally, but not least, to the members of my family who have journeyed with me to Senegal, either in person or through their imaginations by virtue of my continued fascination with things Senegalese; I thank them for their warmth, patience and forbearance, and for their indulgence of my intellectual obsessions.

NOTE ON TRANSCRIPTION AND ORTHOGRAPHY

The system of transcription adopted in the text follows the conventions of the international system of Bamako, a slight variant on the official Senegalese transcription in which 'ñ' replaces 'ny'.

TRANSCRIPTION OF SOUNDS IN PULAAR
Vowels

Short vowel sounds are transcribed as single vowels – a, e, i, o, u.
Long vowel sounds are transcribed by a doubling of the letter, such as 'aa', 'ee', 'ii', 'oo', 'uu'.
The last 'e' of a word is always sounded, and resembles an 'é' in French.

Consonants

c – as in '*ch*urch'
g – as in '*g*arage'
j – as in '*j*am'
k – as in '*c*at'
ŋ – as in 'so*ng*'
ny – as in the Spanish 'ma*ñ*ana'
ɓ, ɗ and y – are glottalised consonants

Transcription of Arabic words has followed a simplified system and attempts not to overcomplicate spellings by the strict or exact use of all diacritical marks etc.

ORTHOGRAPHY OF PLACE AND PERSONAL NAMES

The orthography of place names in Senegal varies according to author, as well as with respect to the historical period in which they were recorded, and to the spelling conventions of the language in which they are transcribed. Not only are there French and English spellings, but more recently orthographic systems have been developed that reflect more closely the specifics of local vernaculars, in particular Pulaar in this case. I have often used the most common forms of spelling, although on close inspection they are not necessarily consistent with the demands of the new orthographic systems. I often note in brackets alternative spellings widespread throughout the literature in the hope that this may help comprehension.

One particularly problematic area is personal names, many of which are now inscribed in a specific form through the procedures of the Senegalese state with respect to birth, marriage and death certificates, and so forth. However, the transcription of personal and place names in the French literature is often not consistent from one author to another. For example, the patronym 'Cam' or 'Caam' in Pulaar is rendered as Thiam, Tyam and even Chiam in French orthography. I have adopted where possible spellings that follow the vernacular systems, although in the case of many well-established names or names of contemporary persons I have also noted the conventions set by French spelling, for to do otherwise would be to introduce confusion at the expense of orthographic exactitude. To avoid confusion in certain cases, I indicate in parentheses alternative spellings according to different orthographic systems.

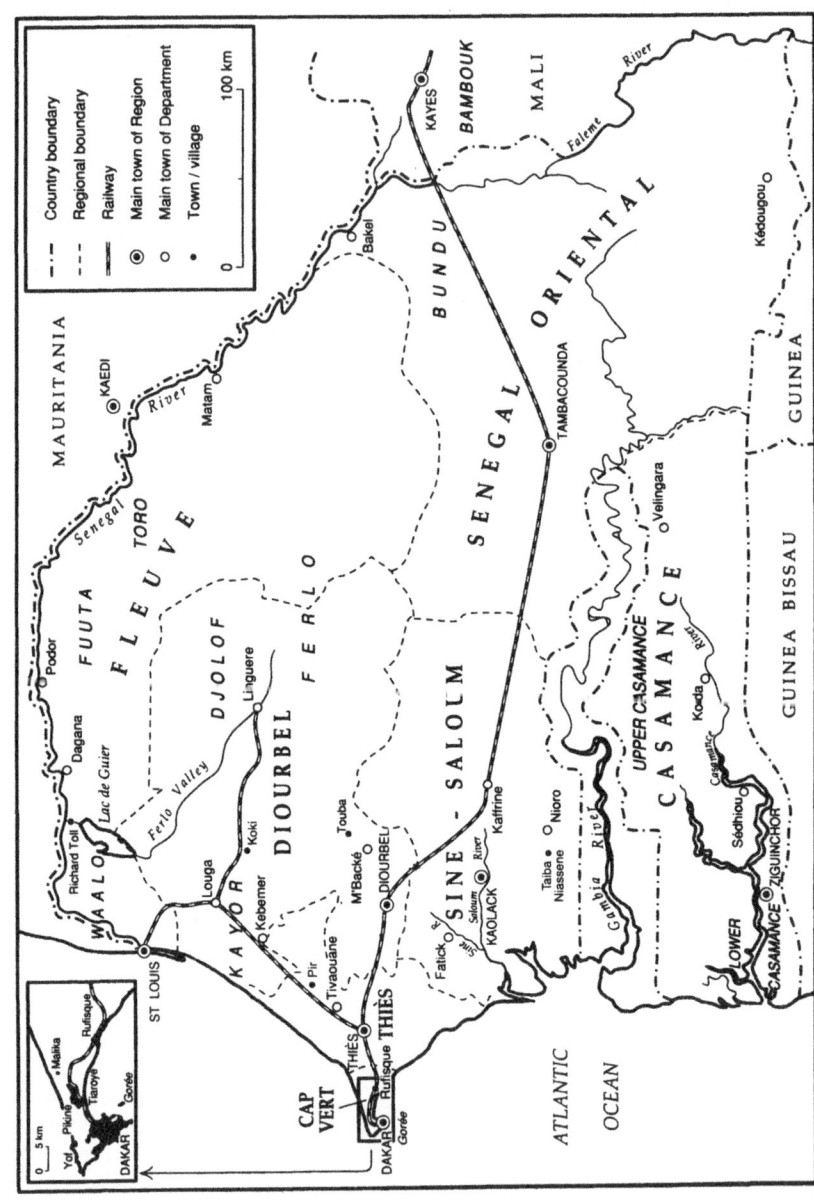

Map 1 Senegal, showing regions, towns and other features

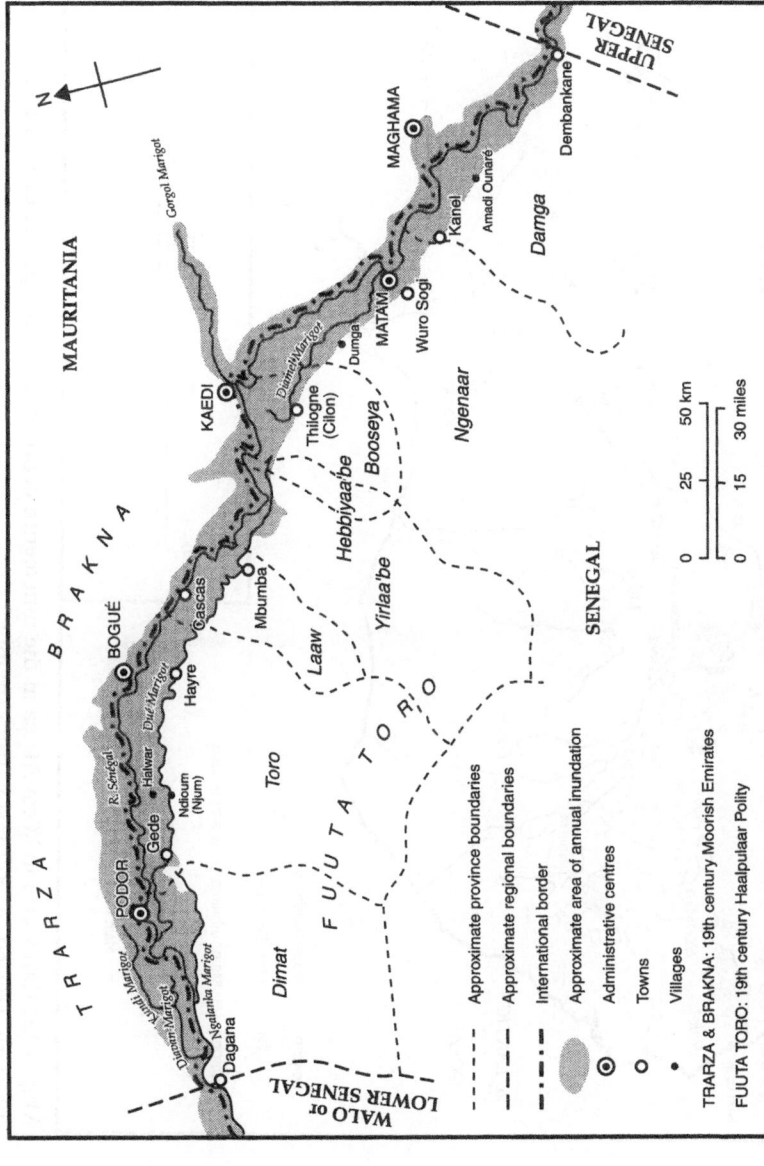

Map 2 The Middle Valley of the Senegal River, showing the provinces and significant towns and villages. (Based on Robinson 1985 (map 2.4) and Schmitz 1998 (carte 2, p. 65).)

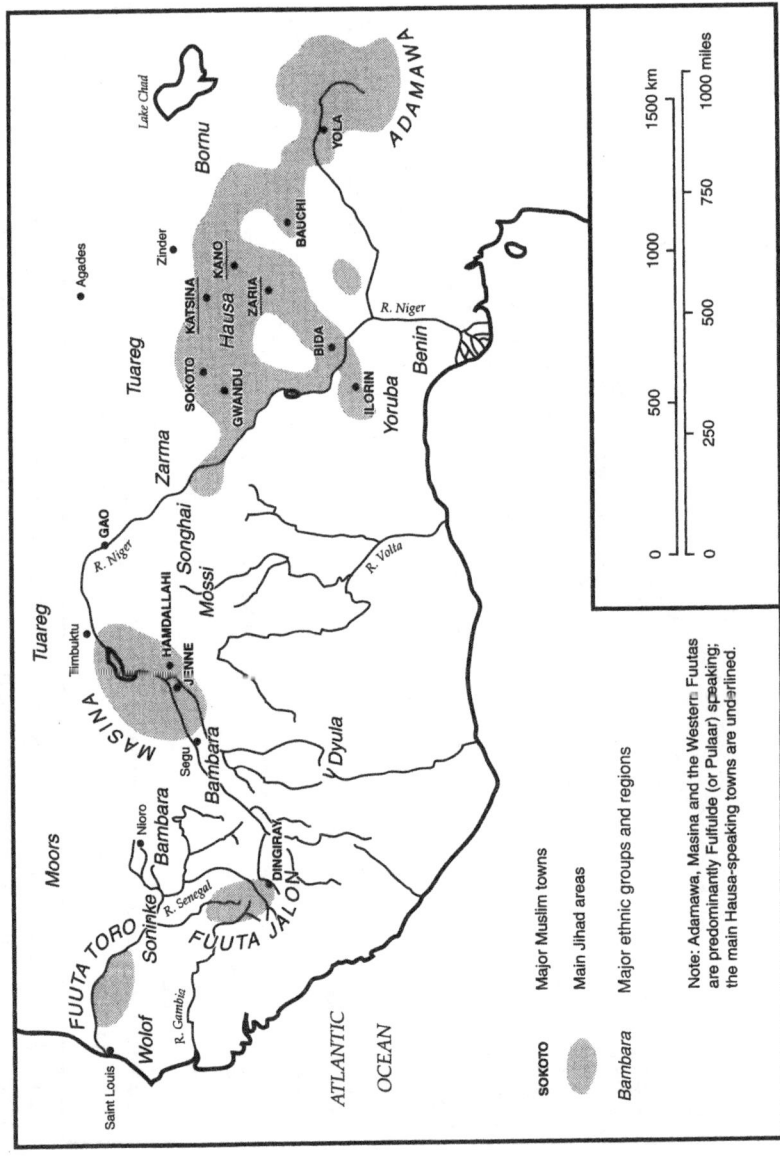

Map 3 Muslim states in West Africa in the nineteenth century. The Haalpulaar or Fulfulde diaspora. (Based on Robinson 1985 (map 2.2).)

1

THE MOSQUE AND THE TERMITE MOUND

ISLAM AND CASTE

Islam and caste are two terms that are central to this book, but they are also both problematic in certain respects with reference to West African history and ethnography. The concept of Islam has been inspected, more generally, within the literature on the anthropology of Islam, wherein discussion has focused on how best to approach a religion that is at once recognised historically across many regions of the world, and that is at the same time always localised within specific cultural contexts. The concept of caste too has been the subject of some debate with regard to certain West African societies, specifically in relation to the occupationally specialised groups of artisans, praise-singers and musicians found predominantly in the savannah and sahel zones of the region, stretching from Senegambia, through Guinée and Mali, and into parts of Nigeria, Cameroon and beyond.[1] While I have argued elsewhere (Dilley 2000) that the term 'caste' is something of a misnomer, specifically in view of comparisons made with analytical concepts derived from ethnography of the Indian subcontinent, and also in view of detailed interpretation of indigenous West African conceptions of how the social and cultural divisions so described look to those who live within such 'caste systems', I retain the term here simply as a shorthand gloss. It refers to members of those occupationally specialised groups of artisans, praise-singers and musicians who are labelled and marked out as 'nyeenyɓe' among speakers of Pulaar, the Halpulaar'en. Similar social categories are found among neighbouring Wolof, Serer and Mande speakers but are referred to by other labels.[2]

Islam and caste provide two points of reference for a series of social and cultural relationships that exist within the changing milieu of the Senegal river valley. I examine these relationships with respect to two axes. The first involves an investigation of the 'genealogy' of the relationship between Islam and caste, taking as a convenient starting point the Almaamate Muslim revolution of the late 1770s in Fuuta Toro in northern Senegal. This book traces the way in which *nyeenyɓe* artisans and musicians have been positioned socially in relation to the emerging form of dominant Islam from the eighteenth century until the present day. This genealogy examines the relationships between marginalised 'caste' groups and the dominant freeborn groups, especially the Islamic clerics, initially in terms of the political economy of Fuuta Toro and the historical and cultural origins of these various social categories in Chapters 2 and 3.[3] It also examines the position allocated by clerics[4] to members of caste groups within the local community of Muslims (*jama'a* – especially those followers congregating around a particular Shaykh), and how the shape of these communities varies over time and according to different conceptions of Islam that have taken hold in the region. The question is posed: to what extent do historic hierarchical distinctions within a stratified society have a bearing on full membership of and participation within the Muslim *jama'a*? Genealogy is a tool, therefore, used in the examination of historical relations between caste and Islam, but it is also used in a descriptive sense to examine the claims to origin of different social categories. The putative genealogies recounted by members of different status groups might also be read as genealogies of knowledge and power (see Chapter 3).

The second axis of analysis is developed from Chapter 5 through to Chapter 7, and this involves what might be called an 'archaeology' of the relationship between knowledge and power.[5] By means of this axis I examine the ways in which competing bodies of specialist lore (Islamic and craft) construct ideas about potencies and powers that lie behind esoteric practices; I also attempt to indicate under what conditions these conceptions of lore and practice become possible. This archaeology seeks to uncover the ideological sediments in the construction of knowledge and power relations at different historical junctures.

In Chapter 8 I consider 'fundamentalist' or better 'Islamist' and other reformist conceptions of the Muslim *jama'a* in order to investigate why these forms of Islam have been more attractive to members of artisan and musician groups compared with the older established cleric-dominated Sufi brotherhoods. The answer, I suggest, lies in the nature of the changing relationship between competing forms of knowledge and power. A cultural debate has been taking place since the eighteenth century about the relative positions of caste and Islam, and this historical conversation has a genealogy that can be traced. This debate too provides Islam in West Africa with a dynamic of its own: it revolves around the issue of how to accommodate members of craft and musician groups as full participating co-religionists within the Muslim *jama'a*. The debate addresses questions such as: is Islam blind to caste status? to what extent is it possible for a Muslim brotherhood (*tariqa*) to treat as equal, believers who are drawn from social categories set within a historically rigid hierarchical society? Could Islam bleach the traces of tainted caste status from its believers? These questions, I argue, have fired a historical conversation among Haalpulaar'en, and has provided local Islamic communities with a dynamic of their own.

Another way of referring to this dynamic articulates around the question:

what is it to be a Muslim? What is necessary for a person to be a full member of a local community of Muslims? These are not necessarily questions of a theological or doctrinal nature, the answers to which might be found in the writings of local theologians and scholars; instead they are issues that involve 'non-religious' matters and broader social identities such as social status (caste), gender and even ethnicity (see Launay 1992). These are squarely anthropological concerns that relate to issues about cultural belonging and about the social processes of membership of categories and groups, and the interrelations between members.

The two axes of this analysis, the genealogical and the archaeological, are reflected in the way the book is structured. Chapters 2 to 4 are concerned with origins and the development of ideology and discourse while Chapters 5 to 7 comprise ethno-historical material relating to an accommodationist conception of Islam, a characteristic and predominant variant in the period up to the mid-twentieth century. Chapter 8 seeks to meld both genealogy and archaeology in considering more contemporary conceptions and movements of the faith in Senegal.

C. Coulon (1983) describes *une dynamique de l'islam au sud du Sahara*, a religion that is in movement. The point of articulation of this movement is for him, however, the way in which Islam has the capacity to resist the power of the centre, of centralised political authorities such as the state.[6] The dynamic I describe below, by contrast, is an internal dynamic surrounding questions of knowledge and power central to the conception of what constitutes proper religious practice and what should be demarcated as illicit practice. Coulon goes on to argue that Islam is the *contre-culture* of subaltern groups vis-à-vis *le Pouvoir*. I argue, however, that the subaltern groups within local Islamic brotherhoods are caste groups, whose genealogies, histories and conceptions of their own identity are often 'muted', by virtue of the idea that they can be construed as a challenge to the knowledge and powers of the dominant position of Muslim clerics within these brotherhoods.

ISLAM IN SENEGAL

A vast body of literature has been produced by a large number of scholars on Islam in Senegal. A comprehensive review of this work would be beyond the scope of this present book, but a number of themes can be indicated within this literature. Sufi brotherhoods (*tariqa*, pl. *turuq*) have attracted most attention, from the widely studied Murids (Mourides) through to the Tijaniyya and the lesser studied Qadiriyya. One of the most striking themes is the role of marabouts – charismatic Muslim leaders – within these orders, in terms of the internal organisation of the brotherhoods.[7] Also their role in the articulation of brotherhoods and the structures of state power, either in traditional polities or with the nation-state, has been the focus of other studies.[8] Leading marabouts have attracted especial attention as key political figures in colonial and post-colonial regimes. Marty's numerous studies (1915–16 and 1917), encouraged by the French authorities, were a major survey of Islam in the area during the early colonial period, and they examined the personages and personalities of the dominant Muslim leaders of the time. More recently Robinson and Triaud's collection (1997) focuses on the prominent figures and main currents within maraboutism in West Africa, and numerous studies of the careers of individuals have also appeared (such as Creevey 1979; Monteil 1969; Sanneh 1987). The focus on individual leaders, jihadists, reformers and political reactionaries is apparent, whether they be marabouts or princes, chiefs or clerics, saints or politicians.[9] These constitute in the main the leading figures of an elite Senegalese Muslim establishment.

Schmitz (1983b), in a critique of the way in which much of this literature is analysed, argues that the examination of historical persons by reference to a dichotomy between temporal power and authority and spiritual power and authority is misplaced; indeed it reproduces categories derived from the French colonial administration. He goes on to show through an examination of the lineages of clerics and of the ancient aristocracy how they are often intertwined, and that relations of social reproduction of these two social categories are so complex that a distinction between them becomes blurred.[10] Any analysis of maraboutic society should start from a conception of Islamic clerics as constituting a 'class', Schmitz argues, a class conceived, however, not in orthodox Marxist or Weberian terms. Instead, clerics constitute a class that is defined around the acquisition, control and reproduction of a form of knowledge-power (*savoir-pouvoir*), the *gandal* of Haalpulaar'en or the *Khamkham* or *Xamxam* of Wolof-speakers (Schmitz 1983b). This profound insight has been hitherto little developed as a factor in the composition of the Islamic clerics as a social group or 'class' of persons.[11] My own earlier research has emphasised the importance of lore or knowledge-power for caste groups,[12] and it is my present aim to examine the social categories that make up Haalpulaar society by reference to the acquisition, control and reproduction of competing forms of knowledge-power (*gandal*).

'POPULAR' ISLAM

This book endeavours to shift the focus away from marabouts and the literate elite to a consideration of other religious and spiritual figures in a more broadly populist perspective on competing forms of specialist religious practice within the region. The concept of 'popular Islam', as discussed by Peel and Stewart (1985), is important in that it reminds us of a level of religious practice beyond a literate mainstream. This concept should not serve to introduce a misleading dichotomy between 'popular' and 'establishment' Islam, but is suggestive of a dynamic, dialectical process that helps to illustrate how 'popular practice and belief serve to define and legitimate the literate mainstream' (Stewart 1985: 367). Part of popular religious thought and practice I consider here are the specialist practices of artisans and musicians, who offer a range of secondary ritual and religious functions; also considered here is how their activities serve to define and legitimate a literate mainstream dominated by marabouts and clerics. These latter, in turn, define caste activities in terms of a distance they see between their own maraboutic practices and those of caste specialists.

The relationship between Islam and caste has been a subject little studied in any systematic or sustained manner within the body of literature on Senegalese Islam. While some authors have considered Islam in relation to traditional social structure (see, for example, Sy 1969 or Markovitz 1970), few have developed leads about this relationship left scattered through various works. Cruise O'Brien (1971), for instance, notes that Murid clergy were keen to attract craftsmen to their newly settled lands for the practical skills they offered, but at the same time they were often considered unsuited for Islamic education and were 'left to observe the cults associated with each craft' (Colvin 1987: 60); also musicians and *griots* or praise-singers were largely unwelcome in many clerical establishments (Monteil 1980). Work on caste groups in Senegambia has tended to focus on *griots* (Diagne 1982; Diop 1995; Irvine 1978; Wright 1989) rather than other specialist artisan occupations, and until very recently their relationship with Islam has been largely overlooked.[13] Weavers, blacksmiths and other artisans have also received some attention (Diouf 1983; Kyburz 1994; Morice 1982), and some discussion of the question of Islam and caste has been raised. I attempt to draw some of these sources together in a more sustained treatment of this question; indeed any consideration of popular Islam has to have regard for how the range of caste groups are integrated or not within Muslim practice and conceptions of the Muslim community.

In relation to Fuuta Toro specifically, extensive work has been carried out on the political history of the region (Johnson 1974; Robinson 1975a, 1975b), but the focus has been primarily upon the clerics and religious leaders as motors of political and religious development. Wane's 1969 ethnography of *la société toucouleur*, while discussing the range of social categories and castes among Haalpulaar'en, takes very much a clerical perspective on aspects of cultural difference. Similarly analyses of the political, economic and geographical constitution of individual villages in Fuuta Toro by Schmitz draw close attention to the *tooroɓe* clerics and other freeborn social groups as the major landholders (Schmitz 1986, 1990, 1994). The position of craftsmen and musicians has been largely unexplored. My aim here is to seek to address these lacunae and piece together the fragments of the history of subaltern caste groups, with the aim of linking them to the developments put in train by Muslim *tooroɓe* clerics.

CONCEPTIONS OF CASTE

Given the caveats entered above regarding the use of the concept of caste, some further brief clarification is necessary. I take the term 'caste' to refer not to an essentialised or reified object independent of history or social context (Amselle 1998), but instead to the product of a set of dividing practices, to a form of cultural politics involving the exclusion of particular members of a community from certain economic resources, from political office and from specific religious functions within Islam. Tamari (1997) has plotted from the fifteenth and sixteenth century onwards the historical presence in West Africa of artisans and musicians who have been marked out and set apart, being treated differently from freeborn agriculturalists. There seems to be something enduring in the repeated manifestation of exclusion of members of these social categories, many of whom bear the same caste names as contemporary ones. One cannot of course say with any certainty what the ideological reasons were for social separation, or what the cultural values were that attached to these social statuses in earlier times. This is apparent for the period prior to the Muslim uprising of the late eighteenth century in Fuuta Toro, for which the sources are often patchy, uneven or indeed often silent on what the relevant cultural distinctions were founded upon. However, with the rise of the Muslim Almaamate regime, caste occupations became marked by local commentators as an obstacle to achieving cleric status. These commentaries are suggestive of the fact that caste became a culturally salient issue that had profound implications for participation in the reforming Islamic community of the period. Indeed, a tension was produced between the supposed brotherhood of the Sufi orders that took root, and the form of social hierarchy that supported a conception of radical social and cultural distinctions between the diverse inhabitants of villages along the middle Senegal river valley.

The analysis which follows argues that the reasons for the exclusion in the late eighteenth and nineteenth centuries of members of caste categories revolve around the issue of the kinds of knowledge and power each specialist group controls in the pursuit of their respective occupations. This brings them into a contested relationship with Muslim clerics, who have variously denigrated and devalued the occupations caste members practise by virtue of the bodies of knowledge and power they routinely draw upon. These are bodies of knowledge and power that lie outside the domain and reach of the clerics. If caste is anything, it inheres in the relationship of knowledge and power controlled by different social categories of persons among Haalpulaar'en. While analytically I approach caste as the outcome of a series of social relationships between categories of persons and ideas, this will be seen below to be in marked contrast to indigenous conceptions of such cultural distinctions: from this point of view it is regarded as an essentialist form of difference.

CONCEPTIONS OF ISLAM

How have analysts, and anthropologists in particular, conceived of the religion of Islam? There are at least two aspects to the problem of the analysis of Islam. First, it is at once a world religion as well as, in any instance of it, a form of practice located within a local context (Eickelman 1982). Second, as a set of practices and body of knowledge, Islam is subject to differing interpretations and manifestations in the hands of the faithful in any particular context. Klein (1968) introduced the idea of 'conceptions of Islam' to denote the particular variants of Muslim thought and practice that may be found in any specific location. This idea has been developed more fully in Launay's work on Islam among Dyula in Ivory Coast (1982 and 1992). Different conceptions of Islam, for him, are so many different interpretations of Islam as embodied and practised within a setting of specific social relations, identities and forms of cultural politics (Launay 1992).

The first aspect of the conception of Islam relates, therefore, to how analysts have handled the problem of 'the one and the many' (Launay 1992) in the study of the religion; the second aspect concerns how to approach the question of diversity and the politics of religious practice within any one specific setting in terms of the 'conceptions of Islam' held by local practitioners.

Analytical approaches to the anthropology of Islam

Launay makes the point (1992) that for an anthropology of Islam to be a meaningful enterprise it must presume the 'reality' of Islam as more than simply a label for a variety of phenomena found in diverse social contexts that have little intrinsically in common with each other; that is Islam is not like totemism, an invention of western academics and anthropologists. Without wishing to fall into the trap of representing Islam as a set of universalistic principles, as a seamless historical essence that has profound and enduring effects on social life, how can the diversity of religious thought and practice labelled as Islamic across a vast array of different social contexts be construed as referring to a common object? Islam is not the product of any singular or specific social context, but yet it must always be approached in relation to contexts of practice.[14]

The 'potential for misleading reifications' (Eickelman and Piscatori 2001: 20) must be tempered by an anthropological insistence on the interpretation of 'how Muslims conceive of and experience "Islam" and the communities in which they live' (ibid.: 3). This should not lead to the view that anthropologists simply label under one heading all those heterogeneous items, activities and forms of religious thought that have been designated as Islamic by local informants (Asad 1986). Asad himself advocates a perspective on Islam by starting from the point that Muslims do: 'from the concept of a discursive tradition that includes and relates itself to the founding texts of the Qur'an and the Hadith' (Asad 1986: 14). Islam as 'discursive tradition' involves a kind of genealogy relating discourses about the past and the future as well as Islamic practice in the present. The proper theoretical beginnings, Asad argues, are instituted practices, set within a particular context and having a particular history, 'to which Muslims are inducted as Muslims', practices which are 'authorized by the discursive traditions of Islam' (Asad 1986: 15).

The authorisation of practice by reference to discursive traditions involves a relationship that establishes an orthodoxy, and that relationship is one of power (Asad 1986). Argument and conflict over the form and significance of practices are part of any Islamic tradition, and it is the anthropologist's task to describe and analyse those processes and contestations. The power relations I attend to here are those implicating Islamic *toorobe* clerics, who attempt to define an orthodoxy, and those members of caste social categories who often lie outside that orthodoxy and whose presence historically has engendered debate and discussion about the proper constitution of the local Muslim community.

Localised conceptions of Islam

Local debate among Muslims about what are corrective or normative interpretations of Islam generate different conceptions of Islam. 'The crucial issue', Eickelman insists, 'is to elicit the implicit and explicit criteria as to why one interpretation of Islam is considered more normative than others ...' (Eickelman 1982: 12). The kinds of conception of Islam we will meet in the context of Fuuta Toro are those inspired by the Qadiri and Tijani brotherhoods at different points in history. Indeed, how these conceptions have influenced the views of *toorobe* clerics is also of central importance. The rise of the Tijaniyya in the nineteenth century challenged the Qadiriyya as a dominant variant in the region, and with such challenges came other readings from non-cleric Muslims of what the Muslim community might entail.

I am not so much concerned in any detail with doctrinal and theological differences embodied by differing conceptions of Islam in Senegal, but my concern is rather more with the social consequences that different conceptions have had on the make-up of the Muslim community. This perspective gives not so much a window into the divine cosmos and the universe, but more a view of the social world and the processes and relationships among the faithful. With respect to the relationship between Islam and caste, the focus of my analysis, Launay sums up a perspective that serves this purpose well:

> Different conceptions of Islam must either in some ways legitimize these distinctions [ethnic, class, age, gender – and one might add caste], refuse to acknowledge that such distinctions can legitimately

be made by Muslims, or pass over these distinctions in silence on the grounds that they are ultimately irrelevant to Islam. (Launay 1992: 31)

Each of the possibilities Launay raises will be seen reflected in how different conceptions of Islam in Fuuta Toro do or do not recognise or legitimate the issue of caste. Moreover, this enquiry into conceptions of Islam among Haalpulaar'en follows Launay's important insight among Dyula Muslims: 'Questions about Islam are questions about the nature of communities and of their relationship to how individuals define their own identities and those of their neighbours' (1992: 229).

ISLAM IN STRATIFIED SOCIETIES

The hierarchically organised society of Fuuta Toro composed of social ranks or estates and numerous social categories, some of which are referred to as castes, poses a series of questions about the social distribution of Islamic learning among them. What social cleavages did the distribution of knowledge cement? What were the forms of authority and legitimacy that each category sought to draw upon? What meanings can be placed upon Islam in a society that is characterised by divisions into strata (Gilsenan 1982)?

From within the rank of the freeborn there emerged in the eighteenth century a new status group of Islamic clerics. Those individuals who acquired knowledge of the religion of Islam through Qur'anic study established themselves as part of a new cleric 'class'. Not only did they look to scriptural sources as the basis of their authority, but genealogy became an important resource in order to establish lines of descent to points of origin outside the immediate region of Fuuta Toro.[15] Furthermore, the construction of chains of transmission of knowledge (*silsila* and *isnad*) provided additional means of legitimating the positions of authority that the clerics were in the process of claiming. The Qur'anic school and seat of learning at Pir Sagnakhor in Kayor holds a unique place in the memory of *toorobe* clerics of Fuuta Toro. An education at Pir appears to have been another plank in the platform of legitimacy the clerics constructed, for as Johnson states, 'ascribing education at Pir Sagnakhor to a man is comparable to his inclusion within a Pantheon of great Muslim heroes of Futa' (Johnson 1974: 491).[16]

This educated elite, which might be considered to constitute the local *ulema*, or group of scholars, developed a 'scriptural Islam' or what Launay calls a 'theological' or better a 'public' form of Islamic learning that involves the practice and interpretation of the Qur'an and Muslim law (Launay 1982: 37 and 1992: 152; see also Sanneh 1997: 26). Another form of Islamic knowledge developed by *toorobe* clerics is what Launay refers to in a Dyula context as 'magic' or better 'private and secret learning' (1982: 37

and 1992: 152), an esoteric form of knowledge concerned with divination of and/or the manipulation of affairs in this world for personal and social purposes. This form of knowledge is linked to a Sufi conception of reality: that behind the appearances of religion is a concealed domain, *al-batin*, that can be known through a series of mediative, devotional and spiritual disciplinary exercises (Gilsenan 1973).[17]

The Sufism of West Africa differs in social character from that of, for example, the slums of Aswan, Egypt or in the *bidonvilles* of Morocco, as Gilsenan points out, for in these places *baraka* and *karamat* (divine blessing and miracles or 'grace-acts') became 'a dream in which one finds refuge', 'a dream of the poor' (Gilsenan 1982: 95 and 111–15). Instead, he notes, *baraka* in Senegal 'is the key ideological transformer' specifically in relation to the Murid brotherhood, wherein *baraka* is 'a basic legitimating concept to an institution' that is religious as well as highly organised as a political and economic unit (ibid.). The centrality of *baraka* is evident too among *toorobe* clerics, and is manifest in virtue of the worldly renown and spiritual achievement of great marabouts. These are the signs and manifestations of grace (Cruise O'Brien and Coulon 1988; Sanneh 1997). Divine grace goes hand-in-hand with an immersion by an individual in esoteric Islamic knowledge (*gandal sirru* or 'secret knowledge-power', cf. Launay's *siru karamogoya* for the Dyula (1992)).

The forms of legitimacy, authority and sources of power of social groups laying beyond the exclusive boundaries of the clerics are differently construed. There are multiple sources of authority and influence within Haalpulaar society, and these sources are investigated in depth in Chapter 3 below, especially with respect to caste groups. One of my tasks here is to retrieve a sense of what those forms of legitimacy, authority and power were and are for members of caste social categories. 'Historical documents give only inadequate and scattered accounts of what ordinary people are supposed to believe' reports Gilsenan, 'and then only as seen through the eyes of literate specialists' (Gilsenan 1982: 13). This is the case for Fuuta Toro, and particularly so regarding Haalpulaar castes, whose history is 'often disregarded in the narrative of events' (ibid.: 21).

Social stratification within Fuuta Toro is not to be found, then, between the religion of the rural masses in the form of ecstatic Sufi brotherhoods versus an austere, urban, educated elite *ulema* (Gellner 1981); instead social distinction inheres in the definition of competing esoteric domains of knowledge-power (*gandal*) which are the specialisms of caste-like groups, among which one could include the clerics in this regard. Furthermore, the dichotomy perceived elsewhere in the Muslim world between an urban elite associated with scholarship and adherence to Shari'a law on the one hand, and a rural population associated with popular religious practices and customs on the other, is blurred in Fuuta Toro. Here there was a development of rural Islamic scholarship, and this development, it has been argued, was among the preconditions for the Muslim uprising of the eighteenth century (Levtzion 1987). The clerics played an important role in appropriating agricultural surpluses of the river valley produced by a large servile population. This provided the economic base for Islamic scholarship, in the absence in Fuuta Toro of a merchant class upon which many other Muslim communities have depended (ibid.). The growth of a rural tradition of scholarship differed in organisation to that of urban or commercial Muslim communities (see Launay 1982 on Dyula, and Sanneh 1979 and 1989 on Jahkanke). Based on large servile populations attached to each freeborn – indeed caste – homestead, the labour of those in bondage was not only controlled by their masters but other conditions applied to them. In accordance with a general rule in Islamic law, slaves could not assume the office of imam, although some schools of thought were more liberal, such as the predominant Maliki school in West Africa. This latter might allow a slave to lead public prayers provided the function carried no juridical or similar responsibilities (Sanneh 1997: 60). Slaves were also excluded from leadership roles within *majlis* or *dudals*, namely Qur'anic schools.

The Fulani jihad in Sokoto involved, as in Fuuta Toro, the articulation of groups within a stratified social system. However, caste did not have a prominent role here, although caste interests may have played a part in selecting among the Tuareg the allies of the Shaykh Uthman (Last 1967b: lxxviii). One of the Fulani Muslim clans to play a part in the establishment of the Sokoto Caliphate was called Toronkawa, comprising *toorobe* clerics originally from Fuuta Toro in Senegal (Last 1967b). The Fulani Caliphate articulated three ethnic groups – settled Fulani, Tuareg and Hausa – into an overarching social system in which the Hausa were to play the role of agricultural peasant farmers whom both the Fulani and Tuareg despised, labelling them 'blacks' or *al-Sudani*. By contrast, many of the freeborn cleric families in Fuuta Toro were themselves simple peasant farmers, under whom worked a body of servile labour, and whose rights in land gave them extra income from rents, tithes and so forth.

The case of Dyula of Ivory Coast illustrates another means of articulating social groups within a broadly stratified social setting (Launay 1982, 1992). Characterised in the colonial period as a trading community, the Dyula population were divided into three major social categories: *mory* scholars – Muslims typically following the Suwarian conception of Islam; *tun tigi* warriors who were local chiefs not known for their piety or Islamic learning but who increasingly came to adopt the conduct of the scholars; and traders who were drawn from the other two categories but predominantly from the scholars. Muslims of a *mory* Suwarian persuasion appear to be characterised by their passivity and political quietism, in stark comparison with the *toorobe*/Fulani jihads in other parts of West Africa. What is striking in the

Dyula case is that the migration and insinuation of traders into areas of northern and central Ivory Coast in the seventeenth century (Launay 1982: 14) was effected in such a way that relations with Senufo inhabitants of the region seem not to have been marked by domination and subjugation. Senufo, considered as 'pagans' in contrast to the Dyula who were considered as virtually Muslim by definition (Launay 1982: 18), coexisted in a nexus of social relations with Dyula migrants who concentrated on trade and avoided farming. Senufo were the local agriculturalists, among whom craft specialists or castes worked (see Richter 1980). Dyula traders appear to have been uninterested in state-building, a consequence of which was that neighbouring groups of clients and agriculturalists were left in a relatively uncontrolled social space. *Toorobe* clerics in Fuuta Toro, by contrast, intent upon building an Islamic state, appear to have been eager to incorporate all social groups and categories into the apparatus and ideologies of the state, drawing in craft specialists as marginalised others.

ISLAMIC 'MAGIC'

Chapters 6 and 7 below deal with topics that would conventionally be classified under the rubric 'magic': that is 'the purported art of influencing the course of events through occult means', means that are hidden, esoteric and mysterious (Willis 1996: 340). I examine in those chapters the 'magical' practices of witch-hunter/magicians (*wileebe*) and the procedures practised by clerics that are often referred to by many commentators as 'Islamic magic' (for example, Goody 1968a; Hamès 1997; Marty 1915–16, 1917). These latter procedures include what Launay admits to as a misleading translation of the Dyula *siru karamogoya* as 'magic', and which he amends to 'private and secret' knowledge later (1992: 152). Sometimes known as 'maraboutage' in Senegal, the magical procedures of marabouts and learned clerics comprise such practices as writing amulets and talismans using Qur'anic script, numerology and astrology, and forms of divination based on techniques derived from Islamic occult sciences. These practices are held in an ambivalent position by many Muslim commentators and interpreters; indeed, Last, for example, has discussed the attitudes of Shaykh Uthman or Usman and his son during the nineteenth-century Sokoto jihad towards the 'supernatural' and the workings of charismatic powers (see Last 1967a, 1988). He reports that the Shaykh and his son Muhammad Bello strongly disapproved of almost all magic foretelling the future, condemned all protective magic except for charms using the words, names or attributes of Allah and special prayers (Last 1967a: 8). Such doctrinal debate is not unknown among certain *toorobe* clerics of Fuuta Toro, who attempt to make a distinction between magic and occult powers on the one hand, and miracle and spiritual authority on the other. The former are often referred to by the derogatory label *sihr*, while a shaykh's miracles are referred to as *karamat*, or better 'grace-acts' or wondrous events, the workings of wonders through prayer. A person possessed of *baraka* or 'divine grace' is in a position to bring about wondrous acts that fill people with amazement.

To practise *sihr* is to perform 'black magic', condemned often as pagan or pre-Islamic practices which consist, according to orthodox Muslims sources, 'essentially in a falsification of the reality of things and actions' and is both reprehensible and allied to falsehood (Fahd 1997: 567). The genealogy of the term 'magic' in Europe and the Christian world has similar connotations, and is defined in relation to orthodox and normative religious practice. What theologians attempt to do is to separate falsity from truth by labelling one set of practices as 'magic' and the other set as 'religion' (Tambiah 1990).

More distant from the writings of literate theologians are the popular conceptions and practices of the majority of local believers. At this level, the distinction between miracle and magic, between licit wondrous acts and illicit ones, is not so clear. Indeed, my argument below is that the activities of marabouts and of other specialists such as witch-hunter/magicians, craftsmen, diviners and so on are all regarded in some respects as wondrous, enchanted acts that derive their efficacy from different domains of knowledge-power – each the expertise of a different body of specialists. The tendency to condemn and devalue some practices and to see others as legitimate and positively valued is an act of cultural politics that links to the processes of social differentiation of one category of experts from another. Last coins the phrase 'a culture of power' (1988) to describe the competing forms of charismatic power derived from different sources in northern Nigeria (sources such as Allah, local cults, ancestors, sorcery, witchcraft, etc.). This concept is useful to think of the way in which different conceptions of knowledge-power permeate the activities of Haalpulaar specialists, as well as the conceptions of those who experience the consequences and results of specialist practices.

Chapters 6 and 7 also examine the 'technologies of power' of different specialists in Fuuta Toro. The analysis seeks to avoid the use of the term 'magic' to describe any of these technologies and activities, perferring instead the neutral, non-value-laden description of them as 'knowledge-power (*gandal*) practices'. Ibn Khaldun described the difference between miracle and magic as residing in the fact that miracle is the effect of a divine force which confers upon the soul the power to exert influence over beings. Thus the miracle-worker is supported in his actions by the Spirit of God, while the magician realises his project through his own resources, through his own psychic force and sometimes with the assistance of demons or jinn (Fahd 1997: 570). This takes us to the heart of the matter: namely the existence of competing domains of knowledge-power such that in Fuuta Toro the domain of Islam is regarded as a 'white' form of *gandal* (*gandal danewal*), and that of other religious activities as 'black' *gandal* (*gandal balewal*).

My argument below is that this dichotomy, an ideological distinction that has its roots in the rise to dominance of *toorobe* clerics in the eighteenth century, is an attempt to impose an order on the array of specialist practices of clerics as opposed to those of craftsmen and other experts. This ideological distinction runs through the 'culture of power' that informs Haalpulaar conceptions of the world, and is a central thread in the analysis that follows. While this dichotomy is primarily ideological, it also reflects the separation of practices among specialist practitioners situated in different social categories and castes. However, what I also seek to show is how in terms of the technologies of power there is much in common between the practices of these competing domains of knowledge-power; indeed, these shared elements are the consequence of a long historical 'conversation' between sections of Haalpulaar society. The argument is that both sets of technologies and practices of power share a common epistemology regarding the relationship between words – written and spoken – and the order of things in the world. This idea of a common epistemology overlaps with Brenner's concept of an 'Islamic Religious Culture', 'a single conceptual framework for the way in which Muslims have understood, practised and expressed their religion'; it also embraces religious pluralism in that it provides a frame of reference within which can be viewed heterogeneous practices and '*all* cultural manifestations defined as Islamic by Muslims themselves' (Brenner 2000a: 144). The practices of clerics and castes have been formed in the context of a long historical conversation, and to regard them as forming two distinct and historically separable domains is to disregard their mutual interconnections.

THE TERRITORY

The region of Senegal to be examined in the following series of chapters is the Senegal river valley in the northern part of the country. This valley delimits the frontier with present-day Mauritania to the north. Indeed, the stretch of the river valley that is of particular interest here lies between the town of Dagana in the west to Bakel in the east, that is the section known as the 'middle valley', which sweeps its course from south-east to north-west in an arc that makes its way to the Atlantic Ocean via its mouth at the port of St Louis, the original colonial capital of the territory of French West Africa. This is, or certainly was, Senegal's fertile crescent, a valley of agriculture, and the cradle of early Islamic political aspirations. The focus of numerous important political developments, this area has seen the establishment of the Takrur empire ruled by one of West Africa's earliest recorded Muslim leaders, Jar Wabi, at the turn of the first millennium, and this was followed much later by the rise of the Deniyaŋke dynasty in the mid-sixteenth century. The Deniyaŋke rulers, *satigi*s, were overthrown at the hands of militant Muslim reformers at the end of the eighteenth century, and they installed an Islamic polity, the Almaamate regime, the rule of *al-imam*. This regime lasted until the French colonial conquest of the area from the mid-1800s onwards, after which time the grip of Muslim rule weakened (Johnson 1974). The last Almaamy was elected in the late 1890s, by which time the political office was largely ineffective and the polity unstable and fragmented (Robinson 1975a).

The economic significance of the middle valley hinges on the fact that the river flows through a wide flood plain that starts to the north of the town of Bakel and continues north-westward past Dagana, a town over 100 kilometres from the coast and the port of St Louis. The importance of this geographical feature is summed up in the local phrase, *Fuuta ko feetal jabaaji*, that is, 'Fuuta Toro' – the local name for the middle valley – 'is a double-barrelled gun', a reference to the two harvests that could be obtained each year. The first harvest was produced on stretches of land (*jeeri*) standing high above the river and was watered by rains during the wet season, July to October. The second harvest was cultivated on the flood plain (*waalo*) which was inundated each year. Cultivation of these lower tracts of land, composed of a mozaic of small flood basins (*kolangal* in Pulaar or *cuvettes de décrues* in French), took place each year once the waters receded in November. The allusion to a double-barrelled gun suggests that if one harvest should fail there was always a second one to rely upon. Fertile, productive and highly prized, the flood basins have always been a key resource over which social groups have competed throughout the history of the area. Today, a system of dams, one towards the mouth of the Senegal river and another further upstream at Manantali in Mali, built in the 1980s, has shifted emphasis in local agriculture away from reliance on the annual inundation following the rains to a managed system of water usage involving irrigated plots (*périmètres*) for the production of rice rather than the customary millet and sorghum. The system of agriculture in the valley is now in flux, and the one that I describe here refers predominantly to the pre-dam set-up. In Chapter 2, I examine this system, the political economy of the river valley and the way in which a complex social division of labour emerged. The hierarchical relations that developed within the political economy have their cultural underpinnings, and this is the subject of Chapters 3 and 4.

If the label 'middle valley' describes a geographical zone, the name Fuuta Toro refers more to a political space inhabited by a broad range of social groups. The population of the whole valley, from the lower reaches of the river up to Bakel, is in excess of 800,000 inhabitants, and for the middle valley the figure is nearer half a million (see *Recensement Général* 1976 and 1988). Today Fuuta Toro is part of an administrative region made up of seven provinces (*diiwal*) on the south bank (*worgo*) of the river. In the past, the region included settlements on the north bank (*rewo*) too, in present-day Mauritania, and the communities on both banks constituted a single system of social relations. Post-independence, the region of Fuuta Toro has, since 1964, been divided into two *départements*, which comprise in total seven provinces: Dimat, Toro, Laaw, Yirlaaɓe and Hebbiyaaɓe, Booseya, Ngenaar, Damnga. The adminstrative centre of the western *département* is the town of Podor and of the eastern one is the town of Matam. While Dagana is the town that stands at the region's most westerly limit marking the territory of the ancient Wolof-speaking kingdom of Waalo, travelling east, a territorial division forty kilometres from Bakel marks a linguistic and geographical boundary between a predominantly Haalpulaar or Pulaar-speaking territory and Soninke-speaking areas beyond. In the past, this boundary was marked by the Njorol valley, but now it is the village of Dembankane which stands at the meeting point of the *départements* of Matam and of Bakel, and it delimits an administrative as well as a sort of cultural boundary. The region of Fuuta Toro extends for some 450 kilometres following the path of the Senegal river valley, making it over time a difficult corridor of territory to administer.

THE PEOPLE

That I began by locating a physical space is intentional, for the simple reason that the description of the middle valley as a unified ethnic territory is difficult to sustain. To the north are the Moors, Arab-Berber populations whose presence on the right bank has been variously constructive and formative or tense and antagonistic over time. Relations of Islamic learning and scholarship reach back very far in history, and they run from north to south connecting Fuuta Toro with Moorish *zawiyas* or lodges and other centres of Muslim learning in the Maghreb, north-east Africa and eventually extending into the Middle East. Competition over land and other resources, by contrast, made Fuuta Toro's relationship with its northern neighbours both tense and competitive as groups struggled for control of the flood plain. To the west are Wolof-speaking populations whose kingdoms in the fourteenth century rivalled the position of Takrur, which was eventually brought under the influence of the Djolof state immediately to the south. And to the east was the Empire of Mali, the supreme power in the Western Sudan by the thirteenth century whose influence, at the height of its splendour, extended into the Senegal valley.

A collective label widely used to denote the inhabitants of Fuuta Toro, especially those of the south bank, is 'Tukulor'. This term is used to distinguish the inhabitants from the Wolof to the west and south, and also from the Arab-Berber Moors to the north. However, this is not a term they use to describe themselves and it is thought to be a deformation of a Wolof pronunciation of Takrur, the name given to the early empire on the river in 1000 CE (Monteil 1939; Al-Naqar 1969).[18] Tukulor, or Toucouleur in French orthography, as a 'tribal' or ethnic term became established in the French literature in the late nineteenth century (Robinson 1985).[19] This French usage became standard, despite the occasional lone voice such as that of Anne Raffenel, the sea captain and nineteenth-century explorer, who spoke out against its continued use. He claimed 'that this etymological fantasy, on which many false assumptions have been hung', existed only in the minds of its European creators (Willis 1989). An early example of an orientalist critique perhaps, Raffenel went on to point out that the riverine populations refer to themselves as *al-Poular* or *Torodo*. *Torodo* is (a version of) the singular of the plural term *toorobe*, denoting those of Islamic cleric status associated with the eighteenth-century Almaamate regime. This title is said by some analysts to denote either a 'caste' or a 'status group' (e.g. Wane, 1969, or Schmitz, 1983a, among others), but I prefer for the moment to retain the general and neutral term 'social category' for this and other specialist cultural and occupational identities. *Torodo* was, Raffenel reported, one of the preferred forms of reference for certain categories of local people when they spoke of their own sense of social belonging and cultural identity. As we will see, there were many more such labels, but there was none that denoted a collectivity in the conventional sense of a 'tribal' or an ethnic group. The social categories and ranks of belonging will be discussed at greater length in Chapter 2, and their historical origins and putative lines of ancestry are examined also in Chapters 2 and 3.

Al-Poular is Raffenel's rendering of *Haalpulaar'en*, a term meaning literally 'the speakers of Pulaar', the local vernacular. It is perhaps significant that the area's inhabitants see language as a common denominator, and not common ancestry or to a lesser extent common territory. The label *Fuutankoobe*, the 'people of Fuuta', is sometimes used to denote those who live in the middle valley. But this label is neither ethnically nor linguistically specific, in as much as members of neighbouring language groups such as Wolof or Soninke living in the region could refer to themselves as such. The collectivity of Haalpulaar'en or Pulaar-speakers is an important one, but it is not geographically bounded, for there is a Pulaar-speaking diaspora across West Africa. In particular, there are important Pulaar-speaking communities whose members originated in, or were closely connected with populations of, the Senegal river valley, and they have settled in, for instance, Fuuta Jallon in Guinée or in Masina in Mali. This Pulaar-speaking diaspora is connected to the spread of Islam throughout the region, particularly during the nineteenth century to the east into present-day Mali. Vincent Monteil (1980: 286) repeated the well-known dictum in Pulaar that states that 'the language was born in Fuuta Toro, grew up in Masina, and grew old in Fuuta Jallon'. Furthermore, Pulaar is one dialect of a much broader language grouping known as Fulfulde, a language spoken by pastoralists throughout West Africa, who reach as far as Cameroon and Chad in the east. In Nigeria, these groups, some of whom have settled, are known as *Fulani*, a Hausa word derived from Arabic for this social category. Fulani is now established in the English literature to refer to such groups.[20]

Pulaar-speakers living in Fuuta Toro might, therefore, refer to themselves as Haalpulaar'en in contra-distinction to other language speakers in the valley. Or they might refer to themselves as *Fuutankooɓe* ('inhabitants of Fuuta') if they wanted to distinguish themselves from Pulaar-speakers elsewhere beyond the region. Monteil suggested that *poulophone* or Haalpulaar society defined itself as an *anti-ethnie*, an 'anti-ethnic' or tribal group, which has had the ability over time to absorb within itself groups of different language and culture, ordering them anew as so many status groups or social categories after they adopt the new language (see Schmitz 1983a and 1986: 359, quoting Monteil). Indeed, each of these constituent social categories bears a resemblance to a kind of ethnic group in itself. Haalpulaar'en trace no common ancestor from whom they are considered to descend so as to form a cultural sense of a unified people or collective identity. Moreover, each social category has its own line of ascent to an apical ancestor of one sort or another; in the case of Muslim clerics it is to putative Arab-Berber forefathers who point towards Middle Eastern origins; in the case of some craftsmen groups, it is often to mythical origins, to semi-divine, half-man half-spirit originators of their respective occupations. Members of these different social categories represent themselves, moreover, as different breeds or stocks, even as different races (*leyyi*, whose singular is *lenyol*, a word translated by some as 'caste', e.g. Wane 1969).[21] This is an issue I deal with in Chapters 3 and 4. Indeed, the historical processes involved in the formation of the *tooroɓe* clerics reveals much about the constitution of other more marginalised social categories, namely those of the craftsmen and musicians.

A number of occupational groups have been highly mobile throughout the region during the course of history. Connections were established by Islamic clerics across the Western Sudan and beyond, but other groups such as Woodcarvers and Weavers have long been itinerant, moving in search of outlets, markets and economic opportunities. Indeed, communities of these craftsmen, including smiths, have sprung up in other language-speaking areas far afield from Fuuta Toro, and sometimes they have ultimately been assimilated by them. The mobile nature and relative cultural autonomy of some of these social categories contribute to the difficulty in construing a global collective identity – a single ethnicity – that embraces a range of such categories. However, the sharing of a common territory in Fuuta Toro has fostered sets of social, economic and political relations between diverse social categories that were set within a division of labour, and the occupation of a common tract of land has engendered sentiments of attachment to place and a variety of cultural evaluations of those who inhabit the area together. They are linked in a cultural discourse of mutual evaluation of themselves, their fellows and neighbours.

These various reflections invite us to loosen our conception of what has been conventionally construed as a global entity called 'Tukulor' society. There are two aspects to this conventional concept of 'society' in anthropological usage. One aspect is the extent to which it is a useful analytical category. Here I suggest that as a nexus of social relations, in this case centred on Fuuta Toro, an initial and useful object of investigation is constituted. However, that object is neither discrete nor bounded tidily, for that nexus is part of a wider set of historical and regional relations that spread out in ever-decreasing networks of influence and across diasporas of cultural displacement. The first aspect of the concept of society concerns, therefore, the ultimate open-endedness of networks of social, economic and political relations that are arbitrarily bounded for the sake of anthropological and sociological analysis.[22] There is a second aspect, however, and this concerns those cultural categories to which people envisage themselves as belonging. 'Society' might be construed as much a local native category as it is an analytical one. This is what Benedict Anderson (1983) called 'imagined communities' – how people see themselves as belonging to collective entities. Each of the individual Haalpulaar social categories imagines itself in some respects as a kind of cultural collectivity, which historically became assimilated into that assemblage of peoples that speaks Pulaar today. It is this history of social association and cultural identification which forms part of the project I wish to investigate over the course of this book. Moreover, it is the extent to which links can be traced between forms of social association and processes of cultural identification that provide the theoretical thrust of this project.

I start this analysis, then, by means of a historical and ethnographic focus on Fuuta Toro. This focus progressively widens in the course of analysis to encompass parts of the Pulaar diaspora made up of networks of co-religionists established at nodes throughout Senegambia. The spread of Islamic ideas in the hands of *toorobe* clerics who settled in different locations across the region gave a structure to this diaspora. In brief, reformist Muslims initially agitated for political control among groups of Moors on the north bank of the Senegal in the seventeenth century. Muslims from Fuuta Toro, influenced by these reformist ideas, first established an Islamic polity in Bundu to the south-east of Fuuta by the late seventeenth century under the leadership of the self-proclaimed *almaamy* Malik Sy (*c.*1640–1700); further waves of Muslim political activity eventually led to the founding of an Islamic polity in Fuuta Jallon, Guinée, by the mid-eighteenth century, and afterwards the Almaamate regime took root in Fuuta Toro in the late 1770s. Movements of *tooroɓe* clerics rippled out from Fuuta Toro in subsequent decades and were the impetus behind the formation of many other polities in Senegambia, especially in the nineteenth and twentieth centuries. Fuuta Toro was the source of marabouts who started Qur'anic schools in many other areas, and they spread the ideology of Muslim revolution (Klein 1968: 68). Clerics of Futanke origin 'played a disproportionately large role in the Islamization of Western Senegal' (Robinson 1975b: 220), but they came not as leaders of jihad in every case, but also as reformers and teachers who settled in new territories and became indigenised or Wolofised. Notable examples include: Ma Ba Diakhou (1809–67), born to a Futanke family now settled in Rip on the northern shore of the Gambia river, who conquered Wolof and Serer states in central Senegal; Amadu Bamba Mbacke (1850–1927), founder of the Murid brotherhood, whose father of Futanke origin was part of the court of Ma Ba; Malik Sy (1855–1922), from Dagana but raised in Wolof country, who set up the main Senegalese Tijani lodge at Tivouane; Saidou Nourou Tall or Taal (*c.* 1890–1981), grandson of the great jihad leader Umar Taal, and until his death the head of the Dakar branch of the Tijanis. This Futanke diaspora provides a point of reference for the broad discussion of contemporary currents in the articulation of Islam and caste in Chapter 8 below.

THE ISLAMIC COMMUNITY

West African Muslims tend to speak their own vernacular languages rather than Arabic. The speaking of Arabic, while prized as an ability among the educated clerical elites, is not widespread among the general population. Indeed, for some Haalpulaar scholars, the Pulaar language itself has come to take on a sacred quality akin to that of Qur'anic Arabic.

One concept through which local Pulaar-speakers have organised a sense of their own social and cultural belonging is derived from the Muslim faith, a religion well established throughout all levels of Haalpulaar social life for over two to three hundred years. The notion of the *umma* or 'community of believers' is one form through which a collective identity has been crystallised. As a cultural category, however, the *umma* is neither ethnically, linguistically nor necessarily geographically specific. It lends itself to the conceptualisation of a community of the faithful either at the level of Muslim settlements within the river valley or through links to settlements of co-religionists in Fuuta Jallon, Mali and elsewhere; indeed, it can be extended ideologically to embrace the global community of believers. Haalpulaar'en are predominantly attached to the Tijaniyya, a Sufi brotherhood that spread particularly through the proselytising efforts and jihads of the nineteenth-century marabout and military leader Al-Hajj Umar Taal, born to a family in Fuuta Toro. The Qadiriyya is a longer-established Sufi brotherhood found throughout West Africa that was largely overtaken by the Tijanis, while the other major Muslim order in Senegal is the Muridiyya, virtually exclusive to the Wolof. Both of these brotherhoods are also linked more or less loosely to the notion of the *umma*, despite the rivalries and tensions that exist or existed between them. The *umma* is, then, a primary imagined community, for its members can be thought of as belonging to a collective entity. As members, they are involved, and can imagine others to be involved, in similar kinds of activity and practice at similar times of the day and month. This sense of belonging can also be bolstered by pilgrimage on the Haj.

A second Islamic concept, the *jama'a*, is also a relevant focal point of cultural identification. More specific than the *umma*, the *jama'a* is the immediate community of believers around a religious leader, and it also takes on the sense of a 'daily place of prayer', in contrast to the mosque (*juma'a*) used on a Friday. Both of these concepts – *umma* and *jama'a* – furnish the means by which inhabitants of Fuuta Toro could and still do imagine themselves as a collectivity in the absence of any totalising designation or a principle of cultural connection among the diverse social groups and categories. Indeed, the ambiguity or elasticity in these concepts, particularly as to the limits of the *umma*, render them useful to a population that is historically contingent and geographically mobile. The question of the constitution of the *jama'a*, and of who can claim a full and recognised position within it, throws up significant issues about the dynamics of Haalpulaar social life. What is it to be a Muslim in a specific local community? What constitutes criteria for membership and have those criteria changed over time? These are questions to be raised in later chapters. Indeed, the issue is raised of whether a contradiction exists between the culturally perceived differences among members of distinct social categories or 'castes' on the one hand, and the ideal recognition of equality among the Muslim faithful within a Sufi brotherhood on the other. The fraternity of the Muslim faith could be seen to rub against the cultural distinction of caste. This issue is addressed more fully in Chapter 4, and returns again in Chapter 8.

A concern over Muslim fraternity and caste exclusion is addressed in local Futanke discourse, to the extent that some indigenous commentators have called for a reinterpretation of the Muslim *jama'a*, which conventionally excluded people of caste ancestry from positions of religious authority. Instead, they proposed the model of an age-set (*fedde*) for the Muslim community, a broadly egalitarian social group among whose members distinctions in social status were to be minimised. The differing visions of the constitution of the Muslim community raise questions about the exclusion of specialised occupational groups of craftsmen and musicians in particular. It also throws up the issue of how over time Muslim revival movements linked to Fuuta Toro have attempted to include or alternatively further marginalise craftsmen and musician groups. The notion of the *jama'a* has thus furnished Haalpulaar social thinkers with a concept that can carry the burden of a collective identity; it was also a means to construe and subsequently to remodel the nature of the relations between the variety of social groups and categories. The issue of who does and does not belong fully to the Muslim community is an enduring theme throughout much of what follows.

My starting point, then, is a place – Fuuta Toro – inhabited though not exclusively by one language-speaking group whose members have settled throughout the region. Fuuta Toro and its communities have been subjected to forms of knowledge and power that have their roots planted in soils outside the region; Fuuta Toro is also a place whose inhabitants have been the active agents in the pursuit of these forms of knowledge and power; they have, moreover, been equally adept at making those forms their own. Fuuta Toro is not ethnically homogeneous; but neither are ethnic groups necessarily culturally homogeneous. Brenner makes the following acute observation: '... [local] religious experts themselves were quite prepared to cross supposed religious and cultural boundaries in their search to expand and deepen their own esoteric knowledge and powers.' But then, perhaps, they 'did not necessarily conceptualize of their own knowledge as being contained within bounded cultural or religious systems' (Brenner 2000a: 163). In this context of social and cultural fluidity, the concept of the Islamic community, either in the form of the *umma* or of the *jama'a*, furnished the means for many co-religionists to imagine an entity to which they could belong.

CASTE, POWER AND KNOWLEDGE

In the chapters that follow, I am interested in the historical position and social organisation of a set of traditional Senegalese artisans, poets and musicians. They are set apart by members of the majority agrarian community – and also within the contemporary urban populations – as being different in character and 'caste'. They are often described as being 'despised and scorned' by the majority population, but this stereotype – while true in some respects – is both simplistic and partial. The cultural and religious history I investigate is carried out with a view to uncover the perspective of the non-dominant, minority craftsmen and musicians, and especially their relation to cleric-dominated Muslim communities. This approach contrasts with that of other scholars who have worked in the area, for they have concentrated on the views of the dominant Islamic cleric group. This present investigation comprises what has been called in other contexts the recovering of 'subaltern histories', those which have to be reclaimed from the margins of history; they are in one sense 'muted', to use Ardener's term (1989). One emerging theme will be, therefore, the way in which local forms of Islam have interpreted and conceived of creative arts and craftwork, and how these activities were drawn into an Islamic cosmology in a manner that was complex and ambiguous.

An earlier generation of historians of Islam in West Africa saw the practitioners of specific arts and crafts as adhering to 'pre-Islamic' traditions. What requires further investigation, therefore, is the complex connection between bodies of knowledge associated with a range of activities, from craftwork, music and poetry on the one hand, to the Islamic sciences and Sufi mysticism on the other. The pre-Islamic/Islamic distinction is an oversimplification of a complex history of accommodation of the creative arts within a local Islamic orthodoxy, and does not allow for a view of the dynamic and shifting nature of indigenous cultural dialogue and debate. The labels 'pre-Islamic', 'pagan' and so forth have been used by local Muslim reformers as part of a rhetorical strategy within their religious and political projects. It is this sense of a continuing cultural debate between different sectors of Haalpulaar society that is to be the focus of much of what follows. The muted voices of the artisan and musician groups are heard sporadically, and they cannot be explained away as the re-emergence of some sort of pre-existing 'pagan tradition'. What the Islamic establishment views as orthodox belief and practice has developed in a mutual conversation with popular belief and practice, and the evocation of the concept of a pre- or non-Islamic sphere by local interpreters must be set in the context of indigenous cultural politics. The two are intimately linked and they mutually inform each other. Jack Goody (1968b: 204) used the phrase 'a state of dynamic disequilibrium' to describe the situation of constant interaction between Muslim and local cosmologies in West Africa. This phrase 'dynamic disequilibrium' captures well the push and pull between different kinds of religious knowledge and power in Fuuta Toro.

The cultural debate among members of different Haalpulaar social categories about issues of cultural and religious identity, knowledge and power, and so forth, came to a head it will be argued around 200 years ago with the Almaamate uprising. This cultural discussion has continued, *mutatis mutandis*, up to the present day. It has passed through the stage of the flowering of militant Sufi Islam in the mid-nineteenth century under Al-Hajj Umar Taal (discussed in Chapter 4), and through the emergence of a new branch of a Sufi order in the early twentieth century to the more recent Islamist critiques of Sufi mysticism in Senegal over the last twenty years or so (discussed in Chapter 8). These latter attacks target the long-established accommodationist West African Sufism.

THE MOSQUE AND THE TERMITE MOUND

A weavers' song (*dillere*) I worked on some years ago (Dilley 1987b) involved two singers, a pair of brothers, the youngest of whom sang a lyric based around the theme of the 'able-man' (*baawo*), a person endowed with a range of powers and abilities to bring about all manner of effects. The eldest brother interrupted this rendition from time to time with *cefi*, words of power and protection for their recitor and for those people he wished to embrace under his protective mantle. The elder brother recited his verses and incantations in part in a language few ordinary people understood, at other times in words of everyday Pulaar. The unintelligible words of power – 'the language of the spirits' (*haala jinne*) he said – spoke of his claim to be himself an 'able-man' who held in his possession fearful and dangerous potencies with which few folk would want to be associated. He sang of his explicit intention to flout the usual taboos of contagion by associating with places infected with spirit power, and to flaunt his own mysterious gifts in asserting with pride this arrogant expression of hubris. In a series of suggestive images he invoked an identity between himself, as an able-man, and potent spiritual forces: 'those who walk with the jinn', he sang, 'leave me with the jinn'; 'those who walk by the termite mound, leave me by the termite mound' (*jahoowo e jinne, miin e jinne; jahoowo e waande, miin e waande*).

He finished his incantation by invoking the name of Allah and his envoy. Thus, in the course of one protective verse, the singer moved from the termite mound to the mosque. He shifted from an association with the spirits of the bush that dwell in features of the natural environment – the termite mound – to a link with an institution – the mosque – at the heart of the local social and religious community of Fuuta Toro. He laid claim to charismatic powers of different orders. These forces are connected not only to the *baraka* or divine grace from Allah that is thought to surround West African Muslim 'saints' (*wali*s) or 'friends of God' or holy-men; they are also the potencies of the wild and of the bush (*ladde*) which the singer, as a member of a specialised, hereditary, occupational social category or 'caste', is routinely brought into contact with. Here are two images of different orders of power: the bush and village; the termite mound and the mosque. Indeed, there are, in addition, other competing sources of power and knowledge – witchcraft, sorcery and magic for example – that sit in an ambiguous and ambivalent relationship with the dominant religion of Islam. Processes of rivalry and contestation between members of different social categories over access to a variety of sources of power and knowledge become crucial at specific social junctures. Some of these sources are regarded as being more appropriate to members of certain social categories than to others. These processes revolve around concerns to do with the politics of knowledge and with the 'culture of power' among Haalpulaar'en.[23] The two images of the mosque and the termite mound capture, therefore, the idea of different indigenous notions of power and knowledge, of the range of technologies of power and the social processes of knowledge; that is, two culturally defined domains occupied by different orders of expert who are seen to compete and contest one with the other.

To talk of power here is to refer to it as an enabling and creative potency, not only as a constraining and dominating presence.[24] These forces of creativity and enablement, however, derive as Michael Jackson (1982) puts it, from beyond the ordered world of social rules and norms, and instead from the bush, from the domain of the wild. It is power that is at once potentially fertile and fruitful, but it is also potentially threatening and dangerous too. It has to be contained and hedged around with social convention. There is more to this issue of power than cultural and metaphysical questions. If it is to be contained, it becomes an issue of worldly politics. Local cultural notions of power are linked, therefore, as much to matters of political office and authority, and to political economy, as they are to notions of social agency – and it is here that the analysis begins in Chapter 2 with a study of the changing pattern of historical relations and social organisation in Fuuta Toro.

AN AMBIVALENT ADVENTURE

An anecdote taken from the ethnography by the late Jean-Marie Gibbal on the Ghimbala cult from the area of the Niger bend, to the east of this present study, illustrates well a range of key themes for this book. It highlights the idea of competing domains of power, of the cultural politics of knowledge – the ambiguities and ambivalences it entails – and the exercise of political authority in attempting to impose a definition of social reality. The Ghimbala possession cult is founded upon invoking the presence of spirits or jinn, often associated with the River Niger, and they take possession of the priests, officiants and participants in cult ritual. The relationship between cult members and local Muslim authorities varies from tense and antagonistic to an attitude of tolerance and indulgence – the latter attitude is struck in view of the cult's therapeutic successes.

Gibbal (1994), in his book *Genii of the River Niger*, relates a story about an early nineteenth-century Muslim ruler, Shayku Amadu, and a magician, Waada Samba. The Shaykh had ordered that all traditional priests should renounce their beliefs as a part of a policy to eradicate the remaining traces of paganism in the state of Masina. Waada Samba refused and was set a test by the Shaykh to see how his powers measured up against those of his marabouts and Muslim scholars. As part of the test, the Muslims and the magician each had an opportunity to divine what animal had been hidden beneath an upturned calabash. The magician predicted a hare, the Muslim marabouts a bird. On lifting the calabash a hare appeared, only for the anguished Shaykh to cry out and exort his Muslim advisors: 'Do something to make him appear to have lied, so that white triumph over black', that is that Islam be victorious over paganism. In one version of the story, the hare is then magically transformed into a bird before it disappears into the bush, now reverting again to its original form as a hare. The gathered assembly of onlookers watched in amazement and, finding the whole affair amusing, they collapsed with laughter on the ground. The magician Samba finally won favour with the Shaykh, whose daughter he cured of an affliction brought on by a spirit attack.

This story represents a local interpretation of the origins of the Ghimbala cult, with its ambiguous status and ambivalent relationship to Islam. That Islam was strongly connected to political authority and was used as an arm to impose a definition of reality – however fleeting – is highly pertinent to the situation following the eighteenth-century Muslim revolution in Fuuta Toro. That the onlookers are at once amazed and amused by the antics of these ritual specialists captures both the mood of serious power-play at stake, as well as the sense of ambivalence and ambiguity they experience. Their laughter also suggests a sense of bewilderment and a resistance to take these ritual specialists too seriously. The story illustrates local conceptions of knowledge and power as 'white' and 'black', of Islamic clerics and of traditional experts – one a possession of the politically dominant group, the other a possession of a more marginalised group of practitioners. This motif of the white versus the black will be met again in what follows below. The cultural atmosphere of Fuuta Toro society was similarly as complex and polysemic as that of Masina. Here too can be heard many voices – some, however, call louder than others. It is my aim during the course of these chapters to capture something of this multilayered nature of social and religious life among Haalpulaar'en.

2

RANKS AND CATEGORIES: THE EMERGENCE OF A HAALPULAAR SOCIAL DIVISION OF LABOUR

This chapter attempts to plot some of the contours of Haalpulaar social divisions, their social ranks and social categories. It will first describe the three broad social ranks or 'estates' and will then move on to consider the constituent social categories. The aim is to analyse these distinctions in terms of a division of labour, from an initial perspective of political economy.

SOCIAL DIVISIONS AMONG HAALPULAAR'EN – SOCIAL RANKS

Pulaar-speakers of Fuuta Toro are divided into three social ranks (sometimes called 'estates') and a large number of social categories. The literature is littered with attempts to shape these groupings into one or more type of conception familiar to European ideas. In his monograph on *Les Toucouleurs du Fouta Tooro*, the Senegalese sociologist Yaya Wane employed a bewildering array of concepts drawn from a variety of ethnographic and theoretical traditions: social orders, social strata, social classes and even castes, each of which denoted a particular level of social division, and all of them were supposed to be present in one social system. Analysts of neighbouring societies have deployed a comparable range of concepts, including that of 'the estate', for the three broad social divisions that are characteristic of many sahelian societies of the western Sudan.[1] I prefer in general to avoid such labels that come with particularly strong cultural or theoretical overtones, whether they be from the Indian caste system or the European feudal system.[2] Where on occasion I do use terms such as 'caste' or 'estate' it is in a restricted sense or a shorthand or gloss rather than to point out any profound level of comparative analysis. They will not be used at the expense of trying to squeeze one form of social organisation into the preconceived categories of another.

I prefer instead to employ the neutral term 'social rank' for the three conventionally labelled 'estates' or 'orders', and 'social category' for the constituent groupings often referred to as 'castes' or, much better, 'status groups' in a Weberian sense. Indeed, 'estate' will be used only in the sense of a category of people forming or regarded as forming part of the body politic, and only with respect to the analysis of political economy. The three social ranks or estates among Haalpulaar'en are *rimɓe*, *nyeenyɓe*, and *jeyaaɓe*. *Rimɓe* is a term that can be translated as 'those without stain' or more frequently as the 'freeborn' comprising free men and women. The linguistic root *rim* means 'pure, free of all stain', from which is derived terms referring, for instance, to thorough-bred horses, precious stones and noble metals.³ The second rank, or *nyeenyɓe*, includes craftsmen, musicians and praise-singers, and the indigenous label could be translated as 'those of skill' or the 'skilled ones'; indeed, it is derived from the verb *nyeenyde* meaning 'to ornament' and 'to carve', or alternatively 'to flatter' or 'to praise'. This verb captures succinctly a range of *nyeenyɓe* occupations and its substantive *nyeenyal* means 'skill'. Bousso (1957) gave a meaning to the verb as 'to refine' or 'to render beautiful', and so the name of this rank could be glossed as 'the beautifiers', or 'those who render beautiful' both things and sounds, whether they be craft objects or the words and music of praise-songs or poems. Although the indigenous term is gender neutral – in the sense of 'the skilled ones' – there is implied a male emphasis in that the most publicly recognised *nyeenyo* occupations are performed by men, and so I retain the translation 'men-of-skill'. There are, nonetheless, some allied female occupations, particularly pottery, hair-styling and body ornamentation carried out by the womenfolk – the 'women-of-skill' or *nyeenyɓe rewɓe* – of various *nyeenyɓe* categories.⁴ The third rank of *jeyaaɓe* comprises all those of slave and servile origin, that is 'those that are owned', a translation derived from the Pulaar root *jey*, to express a relation of ownership. This rank was composed in the past of trade slaves, not usually part of a household retinue, and of serviles, namely bondsmen and bondswomen who were counted as members of the domestic sphere.

It is the minority rank of men-of-skill, and in particular the social category of weavers, that has been the focus of my attention for a number of years, and it is my contention that a study of such minority groups reveals at least two important features about Haalpulaar social life: first, it uncovers 'marginalised' perspectives on, or 'muted' voices telling of, forms of social organisation that have hitherto received little ethnographic attention; second, the unique social position of these 'marginal' groups paradoxically reveals much about the social and cultural processes of those at the 'centre', if this is the correct metaphor to use. Those beyond whose grasp lie the reins of power often unveil the lineaments of that power and the processes by which the 'centre' gains domination.

Each of these three ranks or estates can be regarded from the perspective of the body politic and division of labour. The rank of the freeborn included all the major landholding groups, all those who occupied political office and performed the major religious functions within Islam.⁵ It also comprised the 'primary economic producers' of animal herders, fishers and agriculturalists. Members of the second rank or estate held neither political office nor land in Fuuta Toro (apart from the unique exception in one specific village, Hamadi Ounare, to be reviewed below) and were debarred from occupying

Islamic religious offices. They were free in a sense, but their social condition was constrained and they were dependent upon freeborn patrons for access to resources and land. These patrons also commissioned craft objects or other services that men-of-skill offered. Men-of-skill were politically subordinate, seen as inferior in terms of the Muslim religion and were dependent upon freeborn landholders for access to cultivable plots, particularly to the highly prized and productive flood basins adjacent to the river. Those who belong to this second rank primarily provide services to freeborn families and can be considered as 'secondary producers', exchanging goods and services for subsistence items. They were and still are referred to by their patrons as *nyaagotooɓe*, 'those who demand', 'those who solicit favours' or even 'beg' from their superiors.[6] Cultivation did, nonetheless, play a part in subsistence strategies of the men-of-skill households, although few relied solely on it for a livelihood.

The freeborn composed around 70 per cent of Haalpulaar'en, those of servile origin, the bondsmen and women, approximately 20 per cent of the population, and the remaining 10 per cent or less are men-of-skill.[7] Boutillier reports in the 1960s that servile families were three times more likely, and men-of-skill one and a half times more likely, to have to rely on rental arrangements for access to cultivable land than freeborn households. Furthermore, while serviles held virtually no land as *jowre*, or inherited family lands, some freeborn social categories held seven times the amount compared with men-of-skill.

One of the most important politico-economic offices in Fuuta Toro was that of *jom leydi*, or chief or master of a territory, that is the cultivable land – both rainy-season and flood-plain fields – connected with each settlement. The office was usually held by the dominant or longest-established family within a village, and its functions lay in the area of assigning plots to individual households, collecting taxes and land fees, and generally supervising land usage especially in the flood basins. A complex set of fees were levied on land use, including an initial payment for cultivation rights (*coggu*) on a field for a period of usually not more than five years, and an annual payment for access to plots in the flood basin of an entry fee (*njoldi*), the size of which varied according to the position and height, as well as extent, of each individual plot within the basin. In addition, a renewal fee (*cottigu*) was charged by the *jom leydi* on the death of a holder of cultivation rights in a plot, and failure to do so meant the land reverted back to the chief. One of the most onerous of land rental arrangements was sharecropping (*rempeccen*) that demanded the surrender of up to half the agricultural yield on a plot to the title-holder of the land. In addition to these fees, all cultivators had to pay a tithe or *asakal* (a deformation of the Arabic *zakat*), a tenth part of the harvest given to the village authorities. This store of food was reserved for communal activities, the upkeep of the poor and needy, and for the entertainment of guests and foreign travellers. In 1890, the French authorities decided that this Muslim tax should be paid to the village chief rather than what they misconstrued as being the 'owner' of the land, the *jom leydi* (Boutillier et al. 1962). This tax was initially imposed by the eighteenth-century Islamic regime on local cultivators, and indeed the land that they controlled in the valley was redefined as *leydi bayti*, land held by the Muslim community (from the Arabic *bait al-mal*, the public Muslim treasury).

An analysis of the three ranks, therefore, reveals a hierarchy of sorts in relation to the control of material resources and agricultural means of production in Fuuta Toro. The second and third ranks were progressively alienated from the means to economic and political dominance. They were also excluded from religious office. The control of the cultivable areas of the flood plain (*waalo*) was important for two reasons: first, it is the key to understanding the dynamic of Haalpulaar history and social organisation in Fuuta Toro; second, social hierarchy is manifested with respect to title to land. Indeed, at the level of each individual flood basin (*kolangal*) which made up a village territory (*leydi*), a sort of miniature, inverted model of the social hierarchy was apparent (Schmitz 1986, 1994). The lowest plots within the least elevated flood basins above the river, namely those inundated year after year, were cultivated by the territory chief, the founder of the settlement and the original settlers, that is freeborn families almost without exception. Plots lying up the sides of the basin, namely those less certain to be inundated, were cultivated by later arrivals in the village, men-of-skill and finally bondsmen and women. Any unused plots in favourable positions within a basin would be offered for rental, but the terms of the contract would vary according to whether the cultivator be a freeman, a man-of-skill or a bondsman. The more onerous contracts fell on those lower in the social hierarchy. In short, the higher the social position of a family, the lower the plots of land they controlled relative to the river. By contrast, the rainy-season lands (*jeeri*) on bluffs and ridges high above the river were less controlled, for the soil was less fertile, title to land was less rigidly defined and a pattern of shifting agriculture was practised. This was a mode of livelihood open to anyone living in a settlement.

If we now turn the analysis to examine the social categories that comprise each of the three ranks, then a finer-grained picture emerges of the division of labour and the historical processes of domination by specific social categories.

SOCIAL DIVISIONS AMONG HAALPULAAR'EN – SOCIAL CATEGORIES

An earlier generation of sociologists tended to investigate *la société toucouleur* from the reference point of the *tooroɓe*, the category of Islamic clerics (see especially Wane 1969). They excluded, in particular, one geographically and socially marginal group from their purview, namely the Fulɓe pastoralists or cattle-herders. It might also be added that few analysts have attempted to integrate fully the perspectives of the minority groups of craftsmen and musicians. More recent studies have attempted to decentre the earlier analytical gaze on the self-consciously strident cleric category by reincorporating the cattle-herders as integral to an understanding of social relations in Fuuta Toro (Kyburz 1994; Schmitz 1986, 1994). Such a perspective allows for a richer appreciation of the historical developments in the region, but it must not detract, I will argue, from an understanding of the dynamics set in train by a reforming Muslim faith and the attempts by clerics to establish an Islamic state in the course of the late eighteenth and early nineteenth centuries. But first, a short description of each of the social categories.

Fulɓe

Those who call themselves Fulɓe are of two types: first, transhumant pastoralists, and second, those who have abandoned cattle-herding and transhumance for a sedentary lifestyle in the villages of Fuuta Toro. Sedentarised Fulɓe are not a new phenomenon, for in the mid-sixteenth century a Fulɓe leader named Koli Tengella led an invasion of the valley from the east, ended Jolof domination of the area from the south and west, and established the Deniyaŋke dynasty which ruled the middle valley for over two hundred years. The Deniyaŋke regime was overthrown by Muslim *tooroɓe* clerics in the 1770s, for whom the old regime was viewed as 'non-Islamic' in the eyes of many of the faithful.[8] Fulɓe cattle-herders progressively abandoned pastoralism as a mode of livelihood from then on, becoming increasingly sedentary and adopting Islam as a religion. These acts in effect brought them into close association with the rank of the freeborn (*rimɓe*) and indeed many were assimilated into the category of *tooroɓe* clerics. Those that were not assimilated as clerics retained their Fulɓe identity and claimed freeborn status. These settled Fulɓe still hold a range of political offices in parts of Fuuta Toro, especially where the Deniyaŋke regime had been the strongest, namely in the eastern provinces of the region. They retain today around 33 per cent of the agricultural territories (*leydi*) across Fuuta (Schmitz 1994).

Those Fulɓe who have remained as pastoralists retain few landholdings of importance. They have established symbiotic relations with sedentary agriculturalists especially with respect to access to pasture after the harvests and to the exchange of cattle products for grain. Access by cattle in November time to the wet season lands on stretches of higher ground is first negotiated with agriculturalists, and this is followed by entry of herds (*nyaaŋgal*) into the cultivated flood basins arranged for specific times in April. A complex set of relations and social mechanisms have developed to govern access to cultivable plots. This is particularly the case with entry into the flood basins, where movements of cattle have to be closely supervised, an issue which can be the cause of much tension between herder and cultivator. These tensions are often exacerbated today with the newly developed irrigated rice plots (*périmètres*), on which cattle can inflict serious damage if allowed to graze unattended. The association of herding with wet-season agriculture, however, establishes a more relaxed cycle of the exploitation of pasture and the fertilisation of the soil, and this is of benefit to both parties. For the remainder of the dry-season, up until the onset of the following wet season, herders take their beasts south away from the river valley to the hinterland (Ferlo) in search of pasture. They make use of pools and waterholes, near to which they make their dry-season camps. A cycle of transhumance is therefore established between the savannah plains to the south and west and the river valley, with herds following paths of movement that run perpendicular to the river.

Fishermen

The *subalɓe* Fishermen constitute a social category among the freeborn. They occupy villages perched high along the banks of the river Senegal and its many branches which trace their way over the valley floor. Despite their close proximity to the river, they also cultivate plots, especially on the shoulders of the river banks (*falo*) around their settlements. Fisher villages are often located near to places (*tufnde*) where easy access can be gained to the river, and here they act in a double capacity as ferrymen, transporting people and goods across the waters. This role brings them into close association with Fulɓe cattle-herders, who take their herds after the harvest to isolated fields surrounded by the many minor branches of the river (*marigots*) that criss-cross the middle of the flood plain. Ferrymen levy a toll for carrying herders across the river in their dugout canoes, while the cattle have to take their chance in the water.

Fishers exploit a number of exclusive methods for catching fish at different times of the year. They include establishing barriers in backwaters and channels in the wet season to prevent fish from returning to the main water course, or in the dry-season the use of nets and lines in the permanent branches of the river. They hold political office in many of the riverine villages, and have control over 5 or 6 per cent of cultivable territories (*leydi*) in Fuuta Toro (Schmitz 1994). They are regarded by some Haalpulaar'en as an anomalous category among the freeborn, for they exercise an occupation that other freemen and women conceive as being easily assimilated to those of the men-of-skill (see also Wane 1969: 46). They are no doubt allotted freeborn status due to the fact that they control land and occupy political office in a significant number of villages in Fuuta Toro. I will return to the connection between fishing and craft occupations later.

Warriors

The third social category that comprises part of the freeborn rank is that of the *seɓɓe*, or 'warriors', of whom there are at least two different types: the *seɓɓe worgankooɓe*, 'warriors of the south bank of the river' (*worgo* means 'south bank'); and the *seɓɓe Koliyaaɓe*, 'warriors of Koli Tengella', the conquering founder of the Fulɓe Deniyaŋke regime in the sixteenth century. The 'south-bank' warriors are believed to be of Wolof descent and are linked to some of the earliest settlers in the region, prior to the Deniyaŋke invasion. The second type were throne slaves of the Deniyaŋke rulers who held the title 'satigi', and they are know also as *maccuɓe satigi*, the '*satigi*'s bondsmen' or 'slaves of the ruler'. They did not suffer the same social conditions as trade slaves or those held by ordinary families, but instead enjoyed the relatively privileged status of a body of armed men held in the service of the ruling Fulɓe dynasty. They were settled in villages along the river and, after the collapse of the Deniyaŋke polity, they enjoyed more autonomy and served as military support for the new Islamic regime founded by the *tooroɓe* clerics, for whom they acted as defenders of the south bank against raids from the north by predatory Moorish groups.

Warriors have a reputation as fierce and fearless fighters, with an indomitable courage, temerity and a supposed indifference to physical pain. They are thought to know the secret of physical invulnerability (*tunndaram*) to metal, that is to swords, knives and bullets, and this quality is inherited from father to son as well as nurtured by the ingestion of specific medicines. They came late to Islam, converting only after the founding of the Almaamy-ship, and consequently retain a wild and unruly reputation, being little inclined to piety (Wane 1969). As a social category, they control around 12 per cent of the cultivable territories (*leydi*) in Fuuta Toro (Schmitz 1994), and thus represent an important authority within the valley.

Courtiers and counsellors

The *jaawamɓe* are the fourth social category of the freeborn rank, and their title is often glossed as 'courtiers and counsellors'. As a social group, they have very few members, most of whom live in a small number of settlements concentrated particularly in one area of Fuuta: they make up large neighbourhoods in a least four villages, but occasional families can be found scattered in villages throughout the valley (Schmitz 1994; Wane 1969: 43). They were allied to the former Deniyaŋke rulers and their court, but seem to have switched their allegiance from Fulɓe to *tooroɓe* in the late eighteenth century. Claimed to be of Fulɓe extraction, they sometimes keep cattle although they are thoroughly sedentarised. They were some of the first to join the *tooroɓe* cause and, today, a number of them have developed maraboutic or Islamic cleric practices. Yet they still jealously guard their sense of cultural difference from the *tooroɓe* clerics, whom they served as diplomats and advisors. They are held to possess a fine intelligence and patience, and are gifted with etiquette and manners in order to insinuate themselves into the noblest of company (Wane 1969). They control very little land, no more than 1 per cent of the territories in Fuuta, and all of that within a very tight circle of neighbouring villages in the most easterly province of the valley (Schmitz 1994).

Tooroɓe Islamic clerics

The last social category to be considered among the freeborn is the most recent to be established. It is the tooroɓe[9] and is connected especially with the rise of the Islamic Almaamate polity ('rule of the imam') in the late eighteenth century, which overthrew the Fulɓe dynasty started by Koli Tengella. The widespread presence of marabouts,[10] or Islamic scholars, teachers, clerics and the practitioners of Muslim esoteric arts, nonetheless, is recorded much earlier: for instance, in the mid-seventeenth century European travellers described their activities in villages throughout the region. They were observed to dispense justice in local disputes, to carry out religious duties such as leading Muslim prayers, teaching the Qur'an, washing the dead and naming the newborn, as well as healing by means of amulets, talismans and Qur'anic script-potions (*aaye*). These potions, called 'erasures' elsewhere,[11] are medicines derived from the ink (*dahaa*) of Qur'anic script that is written onto wooden tablets (singular, *alluwal*) and washed off to provide a potion that is drunk or administered to the body as a washing lotion. Some specialist marabouts also provided services such as divination by means of dreams (*listikaar*) and they also conducted retreats for spiritual guidance (*khalwa*). These, together with other arts, are deemed by many in the Muslim community to be part of an Islamic tradition, although local clerics have debated these issues from time to time. The duties performed by marabouts have, moreover, changed little in the intervening 350 years or more since they were first recorded (see also Hamès 1997; Kyburz 1994).

The nature of the *tooroɓe* as a social group, however, has without doubt changed from a loose network of Muslims attaining Qur'anic knowledge and practising Islamic arts in the seventeenth century to a powerful political movement that wrought social change in Fuuta in the eighteenth century. The criteria of membership also seem to have changed over this period, and the status was transformed from one which anyone with the relevant Islamic learning and ability could claim, to one that was closed and exclusive to those linked by particular lines of putative descent and marriage (see Robinson 1975b, 1985; Schmitz 1983a, 2000a; Willis 1979, 1989). The social category thus came to resemble something akin to a 'caste-like' group, offering an appearance close to that of the men-of-skill categories. I will elaborate more on this transition and the ideological transformations that accompanied it in a later chapter.

The question of the origins of the members of this social category is an issue fraught with difficulty and is likely to touch on social sensitivities. A self-regarding group whose sense of their own self-importance and superiority over other social categories is difficult to match elsewhere in Fuuta Toro, they regard questions about their possible lowly social origins with disdain. (The *jaawambe* Courtiers come pretty close to the *toorobe* with respect to their own self-regard (Kyburz 1994).) They claim Arab-Berber ancestry and trace putative lines of descent to the Middle East and to the times of the Prophet himself or to one of his companions. More than probably any other group, they have established links well beyond the region, across West Africa, up into North Africa and the Maghreb, and east into Arabia. Those clerics of Qadiri affiliation were part of a local network of learning and an exchange of ideas linking Fuuta Toro with scholastic communities (*zawiya*) in Mauritania and with the Kuntas of Timbuktu;[12] those of Tijani affliliation, some time later, were connected with Fez, the city of the founder of the brotherhood, al-Tijani (Abun-Nasr 1965). Their long-established connections to an international Muslim community have been developed through journeys to Mecca and through periods of study abroad in far-flung centres of Muslim learning.[13] Their origins are perhaps less illustrious and noble than many of them claim, and it seems that the early Muslim converts in the seventeenth and eighteenth centuries in particular were a mixed bunch, being recruited from all levels in society (see Kamara 1998; Kyburz 1994; Robinson 1975; Schmitz 1983a and b; Willis 1989). What drove the ideological transformation from humble origins to putative Arab-Berber descent was the attempt by the clerics to seize and maintain their hold on power following the decline of the Deniyaŋke dynasty. I will inspect these transformations at greater length in Chapter 4.

The majority of the *toorobe* were and still are agriculturalists pure and simple who hold rights to land gained through their connections to the founders of villages or the original settlers in an area. Those who hold land and concessions but occupy neither political nor religious office are called *aldube*. In the past, these lands would have been worked as much by those they held in bondage as by their own hands. Those *toorobe* who are simple farmers lacking landholdings, great wealth, influence or authority are called *miskineebe*. The social category as a whole holds almost half the cultivable territories (*leydi*) within the valley, although these rights are concentrated in the hands of a relatively small number of families (Schmitz 1994). Recruited from specific *toorobe* families are those (*seerembe*) who hold religious office (such as imam of the local mosque) and carry out religious functions in virtually all of the villages in Fuuta. Separate from the religious office-holders are those *toorobe* who provide the political leaders (*laambe*) at local level, especially village and territory chiefs. Where the offices of village chief (*jom wuro*) and religious leader, that is secular and sacred authority, are occupied by members of the same lineage within a single settlement, then two separate lines of succession are often defined down which pass entitlements to the relevant positions. The overarching office of Almaamy, above that of village chief, was conceived at the outset of the Almaamate regime as an attempt to introduce not only religious reform but political change too; the political authority laid the foundations for an Islamic state in the river valley. The Almaamy, at this level, might be seen to represent a fusion of both aspects of authority, the political and religious, which was often separated within village polities.

If the *toorobe* dominate the offices of religious authority throughout Fuuta Toro, then the same cannot be said of their control of other political and economic positions. With respect to the latter, the two key offices are *jom leydi* and *jom wuro*, respectively chief of cultivable territory and village chief, a leader with authority over people rather than land. Historically, they managed to seize control of only 46 per cent of the territories in the valley, that is over half the territories are in the hands of other social categories (Schmitz 1994). In those villages where *toorobe* have come to dominate all positions of authority, then such settlements are most likely to have been established after 1776 following the Almaamate revolution. These new settlements (*sincaan*) were founded on uninhabited stretches of land, and permission to settle them was usually granted by the Almaamy, the central office of authority in the region. The areas where the *toorobe* failed to establish themselves as dominant tend to coincide with pockets of strongly rooted and well entrenched inhabitants, whether they be the rump of the Deniyaŋke Fulbe dynasty predominantly in the eastern most province of Damnga, or in the Fisher- and Warrior-dominated villages immediately alongside the river.

In Schmitz's view (1986, 1990, 1994), the Almaamate 'revolution' was at best partial, for the distribution of social categories across geographical space is not uniform, and the division of offices among them is complex and varied across the valley. One conseqence of the *toorobe* seizure of power, no matter how partial, was the emergence of a distinction in status between those leading families who provided or were involved in selecting religious and political office-holders on the one hand, and those who did not and were excluded from such processes on the other. The leading families that brought about the overthrow of the Deniyaŋke rulers elected one of their number to the office of Almaamy, the first being Abdul Qadir Kan, originally a scholar of renown but who became a Muslim military figure. He helped organise, alongside Suleyman Baal, a long campaign lasting many years against the *ancien régime*. Kan held power for thirty years until 1806 when he was killed in battle, and after his death the Almaamyship never again saw such long-term stability. In the course of the nineteenth century, a string of Almaamys was elected for short periods of office by a group of *toorobe* families that were to become known as the 'electors' (*jaggorde*). They chose an Almaamy from one of a number of different leading *toorobe* families, the *laamotoobe* or *laambe*, 'the eligibles', and a series of complex marriage alliances and exchanges developed between the two groups, such that riches received as bridewealth were later recirculated in the form of prestations made and then distributed at the enthronement of a new Almaamy (Schmitz 1985a). This occasion signalled also the obligation on the part of ordinary village chiefs to organise prestations to the newly elected leader. Outside this elite circle of electors and eligibles was the vast majority of *toorobe*, who stood at some distance from what some writers have labelled an Islamic cleric 'nobility'. One thing they all had in common was a self-conscious adherence to a revived form of Islam that was historically associated with the Almaamate regime.

The Almaamate never achieved its goal of implanting a strong centralised Islamic state in Fuuta Toro. Political developments closer to this ideal were realised during the mid-nineteenth century further east in present-day Mali under the leadership and inspiration of a *toorodo* from Fuuta Toro named Al-Hajj Umar Taal (Robinson 1985). Too many competing claims for authority existed in Fuuta Toro for the Almaamate to be effective, and the French authorities manipulated the situation so that conditions militated against stable, centralised Islamic rule – one development the colonial powers feared the most. An anti-dynastic ethos worked against the concentration of power in one person or family, and one of the reasons for Abdul Qadir Kan's decline was such a reaction to his extended occupation of office.[14] Competition engendered among the numerous eligible cleric families meant that the Almaamy was rarely much more than a symbolic leader who gained material benefits while in office. The Almaamyship was occupied for periods as short as one or two years, and in some cases only a few months, before the incumbent was unseated and another was elected with a view to receiving the customary prestations (*ndoodi*) from local 'village republics' headed by neither elector nor eligible families.[15] These prestations were passed on at least in part to those electors who had supported the successful candidate. Power was perhaps ironically more in the hands of the dynasties of the grand electors than in those of the persons elected as Almaamy.

The overall picture of political organisation in the nineteenth century is of a network of village republics, at the nodes of which were micro-states each with their own territory of cultivable land (*leydi*), their own village and territory chiefs and local councils (*batu*) made up of lineage elders (Schmitz 1994). The morphology of these village republics comprised members of a range of social ranks and categories, a dominant freeborn group (clerics, fishers or warriors), together with an assorted bunch of craftsmen, praise-singers, musicians and finally bondsmen and women, who were dependent on freeborn patrons and landholders in varying degrees. Village composition was heterogeneous and not exclusive to one particular social category or another.

THE SOCIAL CATEGORIES OF THE MEN-OF-SKILL (*NYEENYBE*)

Each of the social categories of the men-of-skill rank is identified with a socially recognised occupation or trade. There are four manual occupations (*golle*) whose male practitioners are classified as men-of-skill, and these are Leatherworkers (*sakkeeɓe*), Smiths (*wayluɓe*), Weavers (*maabuɓe*) and Woodcarvers (*lawɓe*) (see Figures 2.1–2.4).[16] The women of these categories (*nyeenyɓe rewɓe*) may engage in a range of parallel manual trades, but they are not regarded as forming separate categories on that basis. They specialise in pottery (potters are *buurnaaɓe*) and are renowned coiffeuses (*mooroɓe*). The women of the leatherworker category often tattoo lips and gums (*fesde*), a bodily ornamentation considered to enhance a woman's beauty, and carried out as part of a girl's initiation. They also carry out female excision. Woodcarver women are experts in the arts of seduction and produce perfumes and sweet-smelling woods (*cuuray*) for that purpose. By contrast, the wives of freemen are not expected to partake in any home industry which might be assimilated to the craft occupations of the *nyeenyɓe*, and it is beneath their dignity and discretion to dance, sing or play a musical instrument. Dancing is thought by many to be an expression of sexuality, public displays of which are frowned upon, especially by the clerics.

2.1 A *mabu* weaver on the streets of Dakar

2.2 A *lawɓe* woodcarver making domestic utensils, In the background, others work on building a fishing boat.

In addition to the four male manual occupations, there is also a category of entertainers, namely the *wambaaɓe* who play a five-stringed lute (*hoddu*) and a category of Praise-singers, that is the *awluɓe*, otherwise known in the French literature as *griots*.[17] A number of branches of other men-of-skill social categories are also praise-singers for a variety of freeborn groups. While the *awluɓe* sing the praises of any family, whether of the leading *tooroɓe* families and older nobility or of men-of-skill, two branches of the Weavers' category sing the praises of the *jaawamɓe* Courtiers and of the Fulɓe respectively, and one branch of the Woodcarvers eulogise the *seɓɓe* Warriors (see Figure 2.5). Each freeborn category has, therefore, a corresponding set of men-of-skill specialists, and these are versed in the histories, genealogies and noble deeds of their respective patrons. These specialisms perhaps developed historically as each of the freeborn categories emerged as politically significant in Fuuta Toro, such that, for example, the Woodcarver praise-singers of the Warriors could well have formed relatively recently following the liberation of their patrons from service to the Deniyaŋke rulers (Kyburz 1994). The one exception to this are the Fishers, who themselves specialise in a form of song (*pekaan*) which lauds the exploits and broadcasts the praises of their own brothers-in-trade. This is yet another point of similarity between the Fishers and the men-of-skill.

The practice of one's socially allotted occupation does not in itself define membership of a men-of-skill category; instead, membership is ascribed through birth, status being hereditary and irrespective of what occupation is practised. A Weaver is a Weaver whether or not he weaves. Men-of-skill occupations are exclusive to their specific categories and it is held to be dangerous for a non-member of a category to practise a craft which he or she was not born into. This is particularly the case for a freeman who might be inclined to take up a men-of-skill occupation. This, however, is a very unlikely prospect since these trades are despised by the freeborn. While membership of a category passes predominantly through the male line, it is possible in the case of mixed men-of-skill marriages for a child, usually one who is orphaned, to take up the occupation of his mother's brother. Such people are called *fanyiiɓe*, artisans who have changed trades.

While some men-of-skill categories are subdivided into branches specialising in singing and entertainment, others are subdivided according to trade specialism. These specialisms often carry a symbolic colour coding. The Smiths, for example, are divided into blacksmiths (*wayluɓe ɓaleeɓe* – literally 'smiths who are black') specialised in forging and working iron (*njamdi ɓaleeri* or 'black metal'), and jewellers (*wayluɓe sayakooɓe*), those who fashion gold (*kaŋŋe*) and silver (*cardi*) into items for personal decoration. From the freeborn perception, there is little difference in the social condition of these two subdivisions, both are considered together as dangerous, maleovolent and shunned occupations (Wane 1969). From

2.3 A *sakke* leatherworker in St Louis making leather amulets containing Qu'ranic verse or parts of animals etc.

2.4 A *baylo* smith at his forge in Fuuta Toro.

within the category, there seems to be an emphasis on social differentiation, but this is perhaps more ideological rather than practical. It is reported that jewellers who claim Fulɓe descent consider themselves to be red (*wojji*, 'to be red') in skin colour and reject in marriage the Smiths who are 'black' – both in the sense of working iron and skin colour (Kyburz 1994). In practice, this distinction seems difficult to sustain, for Smiths do change their specialisms over time, and branches of the same family specialise in both arts.[18] A similar distinction is made between two sub-branches of Leatherworker, 'those who are red' (*wodeeɓe*) – again of supposed Fulɓe descent – who make sandals and other goods for cattle herders; and the *alawɓe*, also known as 'black leatherworkers' (*sakkeeɓe ɓaleeɓe*), who are held to be of Soninke origin and practise leather tanning and shoe-making (Kyburz 1994). Again, it is reported that the 'reds' reject the 'blacks' in marriage, although cases of such intermarriage are reported. Also, the Woodcarvers are divided into canoe builders (*lawɓe laade*) and those specialising in domestic utensils (*lawɓe worworɓe*). The former work closely with fishermen, making the dugouts they use for fishing and ferrying as well as fabricating fishing accessories. The latter produce such items as pestles and mortars, calabashes and spoons. Again, a distinction is make between these two sub-branches such that the canoe-builders hold themselves to be superior to the domestic woodcarvers, and will take wives from that group, although this exchange is not reciprocal. Despite these subdivisions among men-of-skill categories and the colour-codings they carry, as a whole craftsmen and women do marry between social categories. This is an idea particularly espoused by the Weavers, who will recite lines of descent and links of intermarriage as proof of their claim. The one exception to all of this is the *awluɓe* Praise-singers, who stand apart from the other five social categories, being rejected by them in marriage and being seen as inferior to the rest.[19]

The term 'caste' is frequently used to refer specifically to the men-of-skill social categories. This is a borrowing from the Indianist literature rather than from an earlier European sense of the word derived from Portuguese usage indicating 'species, race or lineage' (Pitt-Rivers 1971). The application of this term in the Indianist sense is problematic for a number of reasons, although the broader original European sense of 'race' and 'lineage' do come closer to the Haalpulaar conception, I have argued elsewhere (see Dilley 2000). Social groups that are conventionally labelled 'caste' in the West Africanist literature are specialised, occupational groups whose separation one from another is marked to some extent by endogamous marriage practices. But endogamy is much clearer at the level of the rank of men-of-skill as a whole relative to the freeborn rank. As Mollien reported in 1818, 'even a slave will not marry a woman from a family which has exercised one of these [men-of-skill] professions' (Mollien 1818: 59), and much the same can be said today. It is very rare for freeborn–men-of-

2.5 Seydu Gisse (Seydou Guisse), a *mabu* weaver and praise-singer now living in Tiaroye

skill marriages to be contracted, and it used to be the grounds for annulment of a contract if one party had attempted to hide his or her social origins from the other during the period of engagement. Such marriages are still scorned upon by both families, who as a mark of opposition have been known to boycott weddings, and fathers have failed to exchange the customary speeches of alliance, a prerequisite to the pronouncement of a formal marriage ceremony presided over by a marabout. They are considered something of a mismatch, a miscegenous union that is indeed thought to bring together different types, even different races, of people. Resulting offspring, thought to be susceptible to physical deformity and mental problems, often take their status from the lower ranked partner. If the mother of a child is a woman-of-skill and the father a freeman, the offspring will usually follow the occupation and have the same status as the woman's family. The convention runs contrary to the preferred principle of patrilineal inheritance of occupation and status, and is often cited as one reason why such unions are to be avoided. This runs counter also to the convention that applies even to those cases of concubinage, in which offspring born of a bondswoman will take the status of their freeborn father rather than the mother.

Rather than the social category, it would seem that social ranks fit better the description of castes as endogamous groups, but few if any analysts have suggested that ranks or 'estates' be labelled as such. Other social categories are rarely if ever referred to as 'castes', and the assumed articulation of the various social units as a system remains problematic. Can there be 'castes' without a caste system? The issue of hierarchy is also problematic, given that it appears to be present in terms of political economy at the level of rank or estate rather than of social category. And, moreover, the principles on which anything resembling a Haalpulaar system might rest would appear to be very different from those of Hindu India.

Another twist in the tail of Haalpulaar relations is that it is more acceptable for a freeman to have a relationship with a bondswoman than with a woman-of-skill. For bondswomen might be taken as concubines (*taara*) and relations between the two parties governed according to a set of Islamic principles considered to be part of Shari'a law. The offspring of such a union would eventually be manumitted. By contrast, while marriage contracts of whatever sort between the freeborn and men-of-skill are difficult to envisage for both parties, sexual relations between them are charged symbolically. Women-of-skill bear the cultural marks of alterity. For example, sexual relations with a Woodcarver woman are thought to be positively beneficial for a young man – indeed he cannot find a better partner for his first encounter, it is thought – whereas relations with Smith women are thought by many to be potentially dangerous and contaminating to the man. Sexual relations between freemen and women-of-skill appear always to be culturally charged with value; they are rarely neutral. The same kind of marking does not seem to apply to relations between freeborn women and men-of-skill. The cultural construction of difference in the case of women-of-skill is perhaps an example of the 'orientalising' of an already 'orientalised other'. If the rank of craftsmen and musicians as a whole is already construed as culturally different, then the women-of-skill within that rank would appear to be further marked out symbolically. Women-of-skill seem to bear a double burden of cultural separation. This issue will be returned to later, but I turn now to complete the description of the social ranks and categories by considering the bondsmen and women.

BONDSMEN AND WOMEN

The third rank or estate of *jeyaaɓe* included various categories of slave, bondsmen and women or serviles. The gender-neutral term *jeyaaɓe* means 'those who are owned',[20] and is one of a number of terms referring to servile social conditions. There is some variation over the meaning of these terms in the literature, although I will not go into those differences here.[21]

Jeyaaɓe is the general term that I take to mean all those who were in slavery or in bondage, and included specifically trade slaves who were not regarded as part of a master's household. Up until the nineteenth century such slaves were traded locally within the region, and they constituted as well part of trans-Saharan and transatlantic commerce (Curtin 1975; Klein 1998). Captives were counted as part of a family's wealth, and moreover they worked for a household to produce wealth. They might be traded against cattle or cloth, or even given as part of marriage prestations in alliances between two households. As captured or purchased slaves they had few legal rights, in contrast to those slaves born in captivity who were accepted as members of a master's household. Members of this latter category of bondsmen and women were referred to sometimes as *rimayɓe*, 'those of the freeborn', who were adopted into domestic bondage after the birth of the third generation in a master's household. They were then incorporated into the family, but were not free and had to work for the household. They could not be sold and now enjoyed the right to purchase their own freedom, thereby being released from all obligation to the master's house (Gaden 1931: 104). Two other commonly used terms, both gender-specific, denote bondsmen (*maccuɓe*) and bondswomen (*horɓe*).

Those in bondage were also labelled 'dependents', *halfaaɓe*, who relied upon their masters for the means to survive. They held little or no land in Fuuta Toro, controlled few economic resources, and had no access to political or religious office within village social organisation. The *jagodin*, an honorific title for the head bondsman, was charged with general surveillance of work and the allocation of tasks among his fellows. The office-holder remained in bondage, although after long and loyal service, he might be repaid by his master with the gift of manumission. Bondsmen cultivated their master's fields on specific days of the week, and they were allocated rights to cultivate land themselves for their own subsistence. These plots were granted under the most onerous of contracts. Sharecropping arrangements, involving the surrender of up to half the harvest, were often imposed by freeborn landholders on bondsmen cultivators, and this rent was in addition to the *asakal* tax or tithe payable to the village or territory chief. Furthermore, they were often required to perform *doftal*, a form of service involving an obligation to work one or two days in clearing and sowing land for the title-holder.

A bondsman was expected to be able to acquire any skill required by his master, and he would often carry out a range of activities including woodcutting, the slaughtering and butchery of animals, and carpentry and stonemasonry. He would also be charged with caring for domestic animals, and he was a groom and stable-lad as well as a bodyguard and all-round handyman.[22] He was commonly thought to possess a universal competence, and the popular conception of the bondsman was that he was strong in the arm but weak in the head (*muddo*) (Wane 1969). Bondswomen would be expected to deal with many of the routine domestic tasks from collecting water and cleaning the homestead to spinning locally grown cotton and helping with the harvest. Wane articulated the freeborn view of serviles when he wrote that 'slaves were not so much like humans, as they might appear, but overall more like beasts' (Wane 1969: 32).[23]

A bondsman was given authority by his master to cultivate a small plot of land, a *njeylaari*, by means of which he might be able to raise sufficient resources to purchase his own freedom. He would henceforth become a *cotiido*, a person who it was said had 'bought his own head' (in the infinitive: *soode hoore mum*) and would now no longer be dependent upon his master nor obliged to give him service. Another means by which slaves, usually men, could be affranchised was through Islamic study, and this privilege was extended by a master to favoured or bright young bondsmen. Manumission was achieved at the completion of Qur'anic schooling, which could take many years, and the affranchised bondsman would be referred to as a '*daccanaado* Allah' or 'one released by Allah'. A means through which bondswomen might be manumitted was to bear as a concubine the master's child. Although local Islamic Maliki orthodoxy suggests that a concubine and her children should have had exactly the same status as a freeborn wife (Fisher and Humphrey 1970), in practice this privilege was not extended until after the third generation, once the concubine had become a grandmother.

The means by which bondsmen and women were able to achieve release from servitude were well defined, as were the rules governing the capture of slaves in the past from neighbouring pagan peoples, although this does not mean deviations from them were unknown. A justification for slavery by slave users and traders could be found in Islam, while at the same time the recognition of the institution by the religion led to restrictions on the conditions under which people were held (Klein 1998). There was what we might call the 'rule of law', informed at many points by Islamic principles, concerning the capture of prisoners of war and the emancipation of slaves. Moreover, freeman and slave were legal statuses and relations between the freeborn (including here the men-of-skill – *nyeenyɓe*) and those in bondage were defined with respect to those statuses.[24] The notion of Muslim law was also extended into the area of the agricultural economy, which was subject to Islamic conventions and taxes. Within the political economy, relations between the freeborn and serviles in particular were defined in relation to the 'rule of law'. By contrast, as I will argue later, relations between the freeborn *rimɓe*, specifically the *toorobe*, and the men-of-skill were governed by the 'rule of lore', that is lore in the sense of a body of knowledge, whereas those between servile and the rest of society were governed by the rule of law, that is principles drawn from Islamic law.

In 1909, following the earlier abolition by the French government of slave-trading in its colonies,[25] the institution of domestic slavery, *captifs de case*, was also abolished throughout its territories. Ties between those in bondage and their master's household loosened, although they were still not completely broken. Ex-slaves are viewed today as occupying a lowly and degraded social position, one that many try to hide if they move to an urban area. Stories are still told of how up until recently masters removed all the property from a dependent's home, including the cooking pot (*barme*), the symbol of material security. Bondsmen cultivators remain in a subordinate position regarding access to cultivable land. This has changed a little with respect to recent development schemes in Fuuta Toro that have put in place irrigated rice fields (*périmètres*), access to which has been open to all irrespective of social status. These schemes have nonetheless generated a good deal of debate about the forms of organisation imposed as a condition of development by outside agencies (Adams and So 1996; Knight 1994). Beyond the rural economy of Fuuta Toro, still dominated to a large extent by freeborn families, a bondsman may simply lose touch with his ex-master, and is referred to as a *tayabogol*, 'someone who has cut the relation' between himself and master. Despite these developments, urban *jeyaaɓe* often remain concerned to rid themselves of the stigma of bondage and of the threat of future obligation to their master's household by purchasing their own freedom with cash payments.

PATRONYMS

A *yeetoode* or patronym is a term that is more properly translated as 'that which bestows honour on the person' (Gaden 1969). Some patronyms are specific to individual social categories and they can be used to identify its members, particularly in the case of the men-of-skill groups. The *maabuɓe* weavers, for example, have eleven patronyms that are exclusive to them alone, and the *jaawambe* courtiers also sport exclusive names. Other social categories have clusters of patronyms which occur more frequently although not exclusively among them, while some others share them across a diverse range of groups. This fact can be taken as supporting evidence of the claim that at various historical periods some categories were more open than others, and this is particularly so for the *tooroɓe*.[26] The situation is complicated, however, by what appears to be cases of families changing patronyms on the adoption of new social statuses, again especially *tooroɓe* identity. I will return to this issue later. The rank of bondsmen and women illustrates another process of naming, whereby serviles newly integrated into the households of their masters would often adopt the master's patronym. Many of them, therefore, bear the names of the freeborn. Some, however, retained what must have been their original clan names from the neighbouring peoples from whom they were captured, for they bear patronyms that are not Haalpulaar ones but which suggest Bambara or Sarakole descent, such as Kamara, Keyta and Kulibaly. These names were retained perhaps as an act of defiance or a statement of cultural identity by captives from neighbouring regions in the face of processes of Haalpulaar assimilation.

A patronym is used almost as an honorific title in the elaborate scheme of greetings exchanged between two Pulaar-speakers when they meet, such that a name will often be repeated as a response to the lengthy string of enquiries about health and well-being of the respective families and so on. That names are also suggestive of social standing is clear from examples such as the reaction of many freeborn in Fuuta Toro to the news in the 1980s that a new Minister in the Diouf regime, following President Senghor's retirement, was a man named Thiam (Cam) who bore a patronym frequently found among Smiths. A body of local opinion in the river valley took this elevation to high office of someone who bore a men-of-skill patronym as a deeply worrying and indeed almost sinister development. While a patronym claimed by a family may have been subject to change over time, these names nonetheless can give clues to family origins, and are indeed recognised in such a way by people who live in Fuuta.

THE HIERARCHICAL RELATIONS OF POLITICAL ECONOMY

Relations between the three ranks or estates were, and still are to some extent, structured hierarchically with respect to access to land, political and religious offices, and to other economic resources in Fuuta Toro. This hierarchy was, however, 'tangled' (*enchevêtrées*, Wane 1969: 74) in many respects with regard to the relative positions of social categories within those ranks. Indeed, the position of certain categories was, and still is, disputed by some people, such as the freeborn status claimed by those of Fishermen origin. Some *toorobe* clerics argue that Fishers are more appropriately conceived as men-of-skill (*nyeenybe*). Once we come to investigate in the next chapter the issues of the attribution of cultural value and the politics of value, then the idea of a simple hierarchy might not be sufficient. But this point anticipates later arguments.[27] In terms of the political economy of the river valley, however, the processes by which hierarchical relations were established can be illustrated by reference to two case studies. One focuses on the one exception so far recognised in the region to the general rule of men-of-skill categories not holding land or office of *jom leydi*, master or chief of the territory; the other involves the creation of a settlement (*sincaan*) in Fuuta Toro in the late eighteenth century following the Almaamate revolution. The first case illustrates the processes of displacement of an established group by Islamic clerics that occurred with Islamisation, the second case the installation of hierarchy at the outset of the creation of a village (*wuro*).

The case of Hamadi Ounare

Hamadi Ounare is a village located between the towns of Matam and Bakel in the easterly province of Fuuta Toro, namely Damnga. The present-day population is around 2,500 inhabitants comprising mostly Haalpulaar'en, but also Soninke, a neighbouring people from further east. The village is named, according to local tradition, after a hunter and fisherman, Hammadi Hunaare (Kamara 1998), who came to this uninhabited spot to catch game in the forests and to fish in the river that runs close by. He later installed his family in the area, and these first inhabitants were pagan hunters who set up home initially on the banks of the river and then on higher ground further away. These ancestors are said to have formed the original *maabube* or Weavers' quarter (LeBlanc 1964). The Weaver clan Kundul holds the original title of *jom leydi*, chief of the territory, whose authority today extends over a large swathe of cultivable flood plain abutting a forest. It would appear that they are the inheritors of the status of the original settlers in the area, the *Edinaabe* (LeBlanc 1964), hunters and fishers turned Weavers.[28]

Two of the remaining quarters in the village are *toorobe* neighbourhoods associated primarily with two leading cleric families, the Dems and the Tallas.[29] The third quarter is occupied by a Soninke clan called Jaawara, who settled in the village towards the end of the Fulbe Deniyanke dynasty, and were instrumental in its downfall towards the end of the eighteenth century (Kamara 1998). The *toorobe* Dem family is thought to have arrived around much the same time, and both groups are said to have received permission to settle from the first Almamy, Abdul Qadir Kan, under whose jurisdiction much of the land of Fuuta Toro was nominated as *leydi bayti*, territory of the Muslim community. All of the leading Muslim families that came to settle in the village were allocated land by the *maabube* chief of territory in exchange for instruction in the religion of Islam, and today each of the four quarters of the village hold specifically demarcated territories, each with its own chief or master.

We know little of the circumstances that led to the establishment of the original settlement or why it became the unique example of a place in which men-of-skill hold title to land.[30] The later historical process of encroachment by Muslim families is much clearer. The ways in which marabouts are known to have established themselves in settlements in the eighteenth century are echoed in the example of Hamadi Ounare. Muslim clerics would be invited by village authorities to settle in a particular place, and land and concessions were made over to them in exchange for instruction in the faith. The hand of a girl might also be offered in marriage to the marabout, who would be exempt from the customary bridewealth payments. There is no evidence of intermarriage between the Weaver Kundul clan and the incoming clerics, and it would seem highly unlikely to have taken place. Shaykh Musa Kamara, native of Fuuta and author of one of the historical accounts of the village, betrays in his writings on Fuuta Toro something of the contempt held by *tooroɓe* clerics towards the men-of-skill. Reporting on the *maabuɓe* of Hamadi Ounare, he describes how the men were weavers and cultivators, while the women were potters, adding that 'they are considered communally to be a vile people, base, avaricious and mendicant' (Kamara 1998: 259, my translation).

The *tooroɓe* Dem family seems to have been granted some of the best and largest tracts of land, with the weavers retaining an adjacent set of fields close to the river, bordering a forest. Whether the exchange of land for Islamic instruction was deemed equal by both parties, or whether it was forced upon the original *maabu* inhabitants by the clerics and the central authority of the Almaamy is unclear. Islamic clerics have in the interim established a strong religious character to contemporary social life in the village, stopping for example dancing by the young at night and trying to exclude women from certain parts of the marabout quarter. Whatever the exact nature of the social and political processes at the end of the eighteenth century, the example of Hamadi Ounare illustrates, nonetheless, how the original settlers were alienated from part of their claim to land on the founding of the Almaamate regime. If this case represents the fracturing of a long-standing settlement, then the second case study reveals the processes of the establishment from new of a *tooroɓe* village.

The case of Dumga Rinjaow (Doumga Rindiao)[31]

Dumga Rinjaow takes its name from a town on the north bank in Mauritania, from where the family of the founder claims to have come. The village is situated in Damnga's neighbouring province further to the west, namely Ngenaar. It was settled by Eliman Mammudu Acc (Athie) and a number of his companions who accompanied him to the site on which the village was eventually built. Created sometime around the turn of the nineteenth century during the early years of the Almaamate regime, Eliman Mammudu brought with him other *toorobe* to help clear the land for cultivation, and the process was carried out with the use of Islamic amulets attached to the trees that grew in the area. The tree would be found dead some days later, it is claimed, and could be easily uprooted by the settlers. This practice is, therefore, firmly situated by village oral historians within a local Islamic tradition, and is not cast in terms of the expertise of men-of-skill, such as the *lawbe* Woodcarvers, who specialise in the felling of trees for their craft. Trees are thought to be the dwelling places of nature spirits (*jinn*) who can harm the unskilled or the unwary. The first *toorobe* settlers are represented as clearing the land using their own Islamic expertise, and they were followed by the client families of the men-of-skill and serviles, who came from a number of diverse villages. The Acc family took the offices of village and territory chief, as well as the post of imam in the village mosque, which stood at the centre of the original settlement. A Qur'anic school also operated from one of the Acc homesteads, and still does today. The later arrivals set up home on the periphery of the nucleus of original homesteads, such that the geographical plan of the village reflects an image of centrality focused on the mosque and with the homesteads of the late arrivals on the periphery. This could be taken as a spatial metaphor of the relations between the ranks and categories that make up its population.

A story tells of how Eliman Mammudu gained permission from the first Almaamy, Abdul Qadir Kan, to settle on a site close to the present one. The Eliman had, however, preferred another spot, on land controlled not by the Almaamy but by a pagan Fulbe leader, Ardo Moodi Kah of Kawil Jalube, a settlement just to the south on the edge of the Ferlo. The Almaamy is reported to have been undergoing problems of his own at this time and had decamped from his original seat at Cilon (Thilogne) to Kobilo. This claim, if correct, would date the village to the early years of the nineteenth century, just prior to the Almaamy's death in 1806, a period in which tensions generated within the new political regime under Abdul Qadir began to emerge fully. These tensions were to lead to the first Almaamy's eventual demise.[32]

Perhaps exploiting this weakness, Eliman Mammudu went against a plan hatched between him and the Almaamy to bring the Ardo to justice and enslave him as a pagan captive. Instead, the Eliman struck a deal with the Ardo that he should be granted the land he desired and that he should hand over the Fulbe leader to the Almaamy, not, however, as a pagan but as a brother in the Muslim faith. The Eliman converted the Ardo to Islam and the latter, now as one of the faithful, thus escaped the bondage awaiting him at the hands of Abdul Qadir. Having acquired the land in this manner, the Eliman divided it up among the families that accompanied him when he returned there to set up home. Some of his companions received wives from the Acc family, so creating a network of affinal relations among the newly-settled households; the Ardo's family was, however, excluded from this tight circle of affinity. Soon to follow were the households of the Warriors, Courtiers, Weavers, Blacksmiths and serviles, the descendants of whom still live in the village today. The serviles were either brought along with other household chattels on the establishment of the patron's household, or were acquired through exchange relations set up with neighbouring villages. In recent years, the village comprised around 80 households and had a population of around 1,000 inhabitants, having risen from a figure of about 200 in 1904. Some of these households arrived in the last fifty years or so, and at least one of the original settler families has died out.

Among the early settlers was the Gisse (Guisse) family of Weavers, who trace their ancestors to Hamadi Ounare, to an era that merges with mythic time before the establishment of the *maabuɓe* proper. The first ancestor in the line of weavers, some eighteen generations ago, came from Hamadi Ounare, they claim. Five generations later they are believed to have moved to a neighbouring village, and then seven generations ago their ancestors settled in Dumga Rinjaow, after a brief stay in an adjacent settlement. If *maabo* genealogists are correct, seven generations back in time would take us to the late eighteenth or early nineteenth century as the period when Dumga was most likely established. These early men-of-skill settlers did well out of the division of prize flood basin plots, for the Gisse family have rights to cultivate land in some of the lowest basins adjacent to the river. These plots are among the first to flood and are the most reliable for regular cultivation after the waters recede. Not all men-of-skill families did so well, many of the late arrivals having to settle for plots higher up the sides of the flood basins. The gift of cultivation rights of these plots to the Gisses is remembered in a weaver's song (*dillere*) sung today by members of the family.[33]

DISCUSSION

The example of the post-Almaamate village of Dumga Rinjaow illustrates the more common and widespread pattern of the distribution of cultivation rights among men-of-skill in Fuuta Toro, compared to the exceptional case of the long-established settlement of Hamadi Ounare. It illustrates the processes of the distribution of land controlled from the outset by *tooroɓe* clerics at the creation of a new village. This is part of a process known locally as *feccere Fuuta*, the 'division of Fuuta' at the end of the eighteenth and early nineteenth centuries on the founding of the Almaamate regime. Not allowed access to large tracts of land nor consistently to well-located plots within the lowest flood basins, men-of-skill are 'secondary settlers' – just as they are secondary producers – following in the wake of freeborn patrons who lay a prior claim to a territory and to the important offices of the village polity.

All those of the rank of the *rimɓe* are primary producers, or more strictly they control the primary means of agricultural production: either they are major landholders or they are engaged in cultivation, or they are occupied in provisioning society with a basic food stuff such as fish or cattle products in the case of Fulɓe. They are in Thurnwald's terms 'primary producers' (1965). The men-of-skill, by contrast, although involved in agriculture were never major land-holders nor did they ever control sufficient land to make subsistence agriculture alone a viable option. Craftsmen frequently had a dual mode of subsistence, gaining a living through the production of craft goods and services as well as through some cultivation (Boutillier 1962, 1963; Dilley 1986b). The agrarian economy of Fuuta Toro provided agricultural surpluses to allow for the development of non-agricultural specialists, but the resulting division of labour was subject to differential cultural evaluations of its constituent parts. The attribution of inferiority to those engaged in secondary activities, that is the degrading of those who do not produce directly their own subsistence but have to exchange manufactured goods or services for nourishment, is a common pattern in many agrarian systems.

Mary Helms, in her book *Craft and the Kingly Ideal*, discusses the connection between the control of craft production and of long-distance trade with the development of political authority of elite groups. Both trade and craft industries are the means of 'creating or acquiring the tangible objects that embody intangible powers' she asserts (1993), and they confer honour and prestige upon their possessors. If this was the case in Fuuta Toro, then part of the processes leading to the control of craft production also involved the devaluation of those persons who produced the embodiments of power and authority, namely craft objects. As we shall see in the next chapter, however, the situation in Fuuta does differ in some important respects from the general picture painted by Helms. In particular, the crucial element in craft products is not the powers and energies from the cosmological gods or heroes that objects embody, as Helms claims, for these are dangerous forces that many local Muslim consumers wished to distance themselves from. They laid claim instead to other forms of power and energy that lent support to their authority, and they did not want to be associated with those connected with craft production. To anticipate a later argument, it is not objects that are fetishised – to use a term coined by Marx – but it is production itself that is the object of a vivid cultural imagination and set of symbolic elaborations.

The freeborn refer to all men-of-skill by the epithet *nyaagotooɓe*, meaning 'those who beg, solicit, or sponge', that is men-of-skill are considered to be beggars or spongers who live off the generosity of their freeborn patrons.

This label refers to the way in which all men-of-skill clients used to demand gifts in return for their goods and services, and for performances of eulogies to their patrons in the rural economy. A system of delayed, generalised reciprocity developed in the rural economy during the nineteenth and twentieth centuries whereby men-of-skill were not immediately rewarded for goods or services (see Dilley 1986b). Instead, as part of a continuing set of cliental relations that linked craftsman or musician to a patron household, they could demand rewards over a period of time before and after a commission or musical performance. Some men-of-skill claim to recognise benefits in this system compared to a market-based form of exchange, suggesting that it was possible to receive more for a craft product exchanged within a system of patronage than if it were sold directly at market.

The system of economic interdependence between the various Haalpulaar social categories and ranks in the river valley is conceived through different idioms according to the social position of the local interpreter. While men-of-skill construe benefits in the old system of village patronage, they also articulate a different perspective on the emergence of this form of exchange. They talk in terms of a division of labour (*fecciram golle*) generated far back in time when there were only herders (*ayaaɓe*) and fishermen (*awooɓe*), two occupations simply referred to by descriptive labels and not social category titles.[34] To these two initial groups were added progressively those specialists who performed services and made goods for them, and so the division of labour emerged. The interpretation of this emergent system was that each party benefited from the mutual exchange and economic interdependence until such time as greed (*ndeereeru*) and deception (*naafigaagu*) appeared in the evolution of human life, and so mistrust and competitiveness were introduced into the relationship between exchange partners. This vision that men-of-skill articulate might be set against the freeborn view of the division of labour, in which it is freeman generosity that supports the system in the face of seemingly endless men-of-skill demands. What is important to recognise is that in both accounts the question of power enters as a key to understanding the division of labour in society.[35] This is a theme to be pursued below.

From the perspective of political economy, which has been the focus of the above, it is clear that the *toorobe* clerics attempted to take control of the primary agricultural resources, namely the highly productive river basins and flood plain (*waalo*), although they were only partially successful in this regard. Agricultural production was carried out by freeborn cultivators who were supported to a large extent by a sizeable proportion of the population who were held in bondage (up to 25 per cent in some estimates (Boutillier 1962; 1963)). In many respects the system of agricultural production probably changed very little in its essentials with the Muslim uprising in the eighteenth century. What it did introduce were new forms of tax on agricultural produce, and a conception of land as being, theoretically at least, under the control of the Almaamy and local cleric village chiefs. It also instituted aspects of Shari'a law that governed family and household social relations. The new regime appropriated religion to itself as an instrument of power and authority (Gilsenan 1982: 52) in order to bolster the cleric's position of authority within a rural agricultural Islamic state. They consolidated their authority through a monopoly on education, through their role in legal matters and as 'guardians of revelation' (Gilsenan 1982: 23). One key set of social relations that was cemented more firmly by the application of Shari'a law were the principles that governed those held in bondage, who constituted an important source of agricultural labour. Agricultural production and the social reproduction of this large group of bondsmen and women were now defined with reference to the authority of the Qur'an and Muslim legal texts. These were part of the political and ideological conditions that were necessary to secure production as well as the reproduction of social relations of bondage within the new Islamic state (Asad 1980). Crucially, the relations between those in bondage and those who controlled access to land were regulated by principles defined in Islamic law. The appropriation of agricultural surpluses in a rural economy by a scholarly elite, allied to their roles in education, in the legal system and so forth, combined as factors that constituted a complex web of authority and of potential power of some signficance. The authority of *tooroɓe* clerics, moreover, inhered not only in an economic and political sphere, but it revolved too around controlling access to knowledge and ensuring its transmission within a social group that progressively came to resemble an artisan's caste (Schmitz 1983a and b). Islamic lore, knowledge and power (*gandal diine*) was restricted eventually to those of cleric status, and members of slave, servile and caste groups were generally excluded from it. Caste groups controlled their own exclusive bodies of lore and knowledge (*gandal golle* or 'occupational lore'), and the social reproduction of these social groups with respect to their specialised bodies of lore became socially significant. If relations between the freeborn and slaves were governed by the *rule of Islamic law*, then it might be suggested that relations between *tooroɓe* clerics and caste groups were governed by the *rule of lore*. This is a topic to which I now turn.

3
HISTORICAL ORIGINS AND SOCIAL PEDIGREES OF CRAFTSMEN AND MUSICIANS: GENEALOGIES OF POWER AND KNOWLEDGE OF THE WILD

This chapter deals with the men-of-skill from the point of view of the social division of knowledge and charismatic power. In dealing with the division of labour and the political economy of agriculture in Fuuta Toro in the last chapter, we saw how within an agrarian system those with a claim to title in land also claimed for themselves the status of freeborn subjects. Even after the so-called revolution of the Almaamys, many groups not involved in the movement managed to retain economic control of land and even enjoyed limited political autonomy. Those who were dependent either as secondary producers, such as craftsmen and artisans, musicians and singers, or as serviles were devalued social categories within a predominantly land-based rural economy. In this chapter I want to turn away from the issue of the distribution of land and labour and consider instead the social division of knowledge and power. The question of social origins, or the tracing of what I call pedigrees or putative lines of descent, is intimately linked to issues concerning the division of knowledge and sources of power. This investigation will first entail an examination of the historical claims made about the origins of men-of-skill categories. After this initial review it will then move on to consider local conceptions of history and origins, followed by sections on the social division of knowledge and forms of charismatic power. The focus will be primarily on men-of-skill social categories in this chapter, and will then turn to the freeborn, and in particular the *toorobe*, in the next chapter.

HISTORICAL ORIGINS AND SOURCES[1]

Two tasks present themselves at the outset. The first concerns an examination of the possible historical origins of the various categories of the men-of-skill rank. This task involves assessing claims about the historicity of the development of different social groups. The second task concerns a consideration of the 'archive' of local oral genealogists who record putative lines of ancestry (*asko*, pl. *askooji*) or pedigrees of Fuuta Toro families. Men-of-skill oral historians are experts not only in the pedigrees of leading freeborn families, but some are knowledgeable about the pedigrees of craftsmen and musicians, either those lines exclusive to their own social category or those that form connections between one social category and another. *Maabuɓe* Weaver genealogists, for example, have an expertise in and knowledge of the intermarriages that link five of the six men-of-skill categories, the *awluɓe* Praise-singers being generally excluded from this reckoning.

There are at least two sets of claims about origins: first, those constructed by academic, usually European, specialists; second, those constructed by local oral genealogists. The first enterprise rests on the basis of the historical writings of early Arab and European travellers to West Africa, as well as on accounts, often written in Arabic or in Pulaar using Arabic script,[2] by indigenous historians and chroniclers – for example, Kamara (1970, 1998) and Tyam (1935) respectively.[3] This latter form of work by local scribes has increasingly gained recognition in recent years. The second enterprise involves oral traditions and performance, which is aimed at recognising, marking and celebrating past and present cultural identities of leading Fuuta Toro families and persons. These oral texts are drawn on by academic specialists who attempt to cross-check between different forms of historical source. Similarly, local indigenous scribes have frequently recorded oral histories about the origins of and the relations among different social groups in the region – for example Soh (1913).[4] Oral and written forms of history have increasingly been brought together, both in academic and indigenous enterprises, although these acts of accounting for the past may be motivated by different rationales.[5]

The problems of the historicity of oral traditions and the linkage between oral and written sources are not specific to this region of Senegal nor to Africa as a whole, for they have been confronted by many scholars who have worked in comparable cultural settings elsewhere.[6] What is striking in this particular case is that the forms of historical source and the types of cross-referencing that have occurred are skewed in favour of the dominant freeborn families.[7] That is, there are more inscriptions on the historical record, both academic and indigenous, of issues that concern the political, economic and religious dominant groups compared with those referring to men-of-skill, a more marginal rank of persons. These are the histories of what is referred to elsewhere as 'subaltern' groups,[8] those whose origins are submerged under the weight of evidence and interest relating to more conspicuous or privileged others. It might be paradoxical to refer to the histories of men-of-skill as 'muted' (Ardener's term (1989) to refer to forms of gender discourse), since in this case those oral historians who recite histories and past glories are anything but 'muted'. They speak, however, not usually of their own deeds and genealogies, but of those of the leading families and individuals; their archives are as full of the pedigrees of the freeborn as they are of the lines of ancestry of themselves. A praise-singer's recitation of the successive reigns of a line of rulers can be correlated with

ORIGINS AND PEDIGREES OF CRAFTSMEN AND MUSICIANS 59

dated historical records from other sources. However, this process of correlation is less certain for men-of-skill, simply because there are fewer external benchmarks against which to measure historical claims, and there are fewer sources anyway that record their 'submerged' pasts.[9] When craftsmen are mentioned in external written sources, furthermore, they are frequently referred to anonymously or perhaps only by extension from an account of the presence of their craft products. There are two obvious exceptions to the muteness of men-of-skill groups: the Weavers' songs (*dille*) and the Fishermen's *pekaan*s are both forms of song focused internally on the origins and lines of ancestry of their respective social categories.

Some other important issues need to be noted before we move on. First, the construction of oral histories and the notion of origins can be linked as much to processes of cultural politics as to the idea that they simply reflect past historical realities. This is certainly the case regarding the construction of putative lines of descent in Fuuta Toro, and none more so than with respect to *toorobe* Islamic clerics who appear to have concocted for themselves lines of Arab-Berber ancestry following their accession to political office in the late eighteenth century.[10] If Islamic cleric putative ancestry is closely linked to Middle Eastern origins, then men-of-skill accounts of their own historical origins merge with a mythic past in which their forebears were either the issue of spiritual beings or brought into confrontation with legendary beasts possessing fantastic powers. For instance, the Weavers' mythical ancestor was half-man, half-spirit, the offspring of a mortal man and a spirit-woman; the ancestors of the Smiths fought with a serpent who lived in a well and claimed each year the life of a sacrificial young girl in a pact with the local community to guarantee fresh water; one line of Leather-workers (*sakkeeɓe aalawɓe*) claims to trace descent from 'people of the bush', namely bush spirits or jinn. While men-of-skill histories might be inscribed in the local archive, the traces of these histories merge imperceptibly with mythic time and inscrutable spirit sources. Claims about the historicity of putative lines of ancestry have therefore to be viewed judiciously and without suspending our critical judgement.

A HISTORY OF MEN-OF-SKILL CATEGORIES

The first external written sources of evidence are the accounts of early Arab travellers who passed through West Africa around the turn of the first millennium.[11] It is evident from them that, for example, weaving must have been an activity of considerable importance in the Senegal valley given the very early reports of the use of locally produced cotton cloth. These Arab travellers were particularly sensitive to nudity and commented at length on forms of clothing worn by local populations, taking them to be an index of civility and as possible evidence of conversion to Islam. One of the earliest was al-Bakri's account which, in 1068,[12] recorded that in the town of Silla, situated on the banks of the river and thought to be part of the Takrur empire of the Senegal valley, people traded in cloth called *shaggiyyat*.[13]

This cloth was made in an area not far away from the town, and was woven from the cotton growing abundantly in fields attached to each household (Cuoq 1975: 97). Over one hundred years later, al-Idrissi noted (*c.*1185) that the local population wore clothes of broadly two types: cotton for the Muslim notables and other important inhabitants; wool for the lower social ranks (Cuoq 1975: 129). Cotton was by now becoming associated with Islam, as it had already become elsewhere in the Muslim world where the faithful wore the preferred fibre of the Prophet.[14] These references to cloth and a local weaving industry attest to the very ancient roots of at least this one industry, although we know little about who was actually producing the fabric.[15] A similar historical depth for iron working in the Senegal river valley can be constructed by means of archaeological findings, which suggest sites being worked as early as the tenth to twelfth centuries (Kyburz 1994: 383).

Much later, around the year 1400, a Fulɓe community was established at Masina far to the east of Fuuta on the Niger in present-day Mali, and it included a group of *maabuɓe* weavers (Delafosse 1912: I: 229).[16] Over a century later, there is another reference in the literature to this social category when, in 1549 or 1550, Askia Dawda, the ruler of the Songhay empire, brought with him 'mabbe' or 'mabi' singers, whom he installed in his capital city of Gao (Delafosse 1912: II: 104; Tamari 1997: 101). These singers are most certainly from the *maabuɓe* social category. Back in the Senegal valley, in 1455–56, Ca da Mosto, a seaman and merchant from Venice,[17] visited the mouth of the river where he observed 'the lords and the people of authority' dressed in cotton shirts, which they made in large quantities from locally produced cloth throughout the country (quoted in Boser-Sarivaxévanis 1972b: 53). Jannequin de Rochefort visited one of the first French trading posts set up along the banks of the river Senegal in 1638 and gave a full description of the local chief's attire, stating that the cotton cloth was woven in narrow bands of half a foot in width, because the weavers did not know how to weave fabric any wider (Cultru 1913: 74).[18] In 1668, Dapper observed that along the banks of the Senegal only weavers and blacksmiths could be found (Boser-Sarivaxévanis 1972b: 56), while some years later in 1687 Louis Moreau de Chambonneau gives us one of the first European accounts to include the titles of the Haalpulaar social categories carrying out a variety of trades (Ritchie 1968).[19] These reports are among the first to identify who was carrying out craft production. Prior to this account, early European travellers had often identified specialist occupational groups of craftsmen and musicians as 'Jews', the analogy being drawn with the position of this group within medieval and later European society

(Tamari 1997: 10). By the end of the seventeenth century, the titles of virtually all the present-day men-of-skill social categories operating in Fuuta Toro had been mentioned in dated European historical sources. Chambonneau, for example, after his voyage to the Senegal valley, recalled in 1677 the presence of weavers and smiths – the latter working gold, silver and iron – by their Wolof titles *rabb* and *tegg*, as well as the Haalpulaar titles referring to *lawɓe* ('lobez') woodcarvers and 'Cubalots' (*cuballo*) fishermen – the singular of the plural form *subalɓe*. (Ritchie 1968: 320). Jannequin, who travelled through the valley some thirty years earlier, describes the fishermen as aquatic hunters living along the river banks (Tamari 1997: 106).

Tal Tamari has conducted exhaustive research into the historical development of what are called 'caste' systems in the Western Sudan; that is, she concentrates on an institutional complex wherein craftsmen and musician groups are conceived as separate from the mainstream agricultural population (see Tamari 1991, 1995, 1997). This pattern is found particularly in the neighbouring regions of present-day Senegambia and Mali, and also to a lesser extent in adjacent areas as one moves further east and south. She proposes on the basis of linguistic and historical evidence that three centres for the development of 'caste' social organisation emerged, and these were situated among the Mande of Mali, the Soninke further north and finally the Wolof of Senegal to the west. The most ancient of these, she claims, is the Mande of the Kingdom of Mali, which established this form of social organisation as far back as the fourteenth century, whereas it developed among the Wolof further west sometime later in the 1500s (Tamari 1997: 9). Occupational specialisation, she argues, developed after this among the Haalpulaar'en of the river valley, and it was most probably the result of foreign influence (Tamari 1997: 175–6), with the Smiths, *awluɓe* Praise-singers and perhaps the Leatherworkers as the earliest to be established specialists in Fuuta Toro (Tamari 1997: 191). Added to this number of specialists were most likely those that accompanied the invading Fulɓe who founded the Deniyaŋke dynasty in the sixteenth century: included among them were *wambaaɓe* Musicians, *lawɓe* Woodcarvers and *maabuɓe* Weavers.[20] If this is the case, we are left with the question about the identity of the weavers operating in the valley as early as the eleventh century.

Much of the evidence attests to the presence of occupational specialists separated socially and culturally from the majority agricultural population well before the widespread diffusion of Islam throughout local populations. The picture is less clear in the Senegal river valley where Islam has been present for at least 1,000 years, but Tamari's research in less Islamised areas could be taken to suggest that the social institution of craft separation predates the introduction of the religion into those regions. Vaughan (1970) has suggested something similar in a review of the status of craftsmen, making a distinction between castes in the Islamised Sudan and those in the regions bordering the forest zone. Whether or not we can be sure of this fact does not deflect from the idea that the occupations of craftwork and musicianship certainly developed in contradistinction to the emergence of Islam, which saw itself as distanced from these trades in Fuuta Toro. I will return to this below.

Kyburz proposes a three-phase development of the cultural specialisation of occupations along the Senegal (1994: 413–23). The first phase involves the amalgamation of two clusters of specialists organised around specific figures of authority. The first focused on what was most likely an early Wolof-based authority, the Farba, around whom were gathered Smiths and *awluɓe* Praise-singers (Kyburz refers to this as the 'Manding' pole (1994: 418)). Mirroring this earlier development came the later settlement in the valley of the Fulɓe authorities, around whom gathered a cluster of specialists comprising *lawɓe* Woodcarvers and *wambaaɓe* Musicians. (Kyburz refers to this as the 'Peul' or Fulɓe 'pole' (ibid.).) These Fulɓe opened a new political paradigm, Kyburz argues, using a Mande hierarchical model but replacing it with a system of values specific to them alone (1994: 416). One part of the autochthonous population that was drawn into this new 'social game' (*le jeu social*, 1994: 417) was the Fishermen, now emerging as a specialised social category, he suggests. It would appear that part of this new game, if indeed it was such, was an ideological opposition between those who had mastery, knowledge and power over the water and those who had mastery, knowledge and power over the land. The extent to which this opposition was new or particular to the Senegal valley is uncertain, since there is evidence to suggest that this was a widespread distinction, and was one of the religious foundations of many different cultures throughout the Western Sudan (see Tamari 1997; Gibbal 1994). Furthermore, whether Fulɓe pastoralists can be identified with a mastery over the land rather than land-based hunters, who are renowned for their knowledge of and powers over the bush, is debatable. To be sure, Fulɓe are reputed to be experts in all manner of lore associated with the bush and with cures which are derived from it, but hunters (*waanyooɓe*) require complete mastery of the life forces of the bush which they have to kill.[21] These hunters are in some ways, therefore, a more obvious complement to the Fishermen, aquatic hunters of the river rather than of the land (recall the legendary hunter-fisherman who founded the village of Hamddi Ounare in the previous chapter).[22]

Kyburz's first phase of the development of cultural specialisms is envisaged as starting in the early part of the fourteenth century, the second phase began during the sixteenth century under the auspices of the Deniyaŋke polity, and the third phase corresponds with the loss of legitimacy

ORIGINS AND PEDIGREES OF CRAFTSMEN AND MUSICIANS 63

of the Fulɓe regime and its territorial replacement by the *tooroɓe*. It is the impact of this last phase on the position of the men-of-skill rank and the cultural processes that the Islamic regime put in train that will be the focus of the next chapter. But first I wish to consider the social origins of the men-of-skill categories as recorded in their oral archive.

LOCAL HISTORIES

A good deal of the historical reconstruction that has taken place, some of it speculative, draws upon the archive of local oral histories and of pedigrees or lines of ancestry recounted by praise-singers. Of all the men-of-skill pedigrees, *maabuɓe* lines of ancestry appear to have the greater historical depth, reaching back over eighteen generations. The master weaver who taught me the craft traced a line of fifteen exclusively male forebears back to the weavers' mythical ancestor, Juntel Jabali, whose *asko* continued for three more generations to the apical ancestor Feynar. (Kyburz (1994) has reported lines of similar depth, in which some identical strings of names occur.) Such a line of descent, if genealogically accurate, and given the dates of birth of the most immediate forefathers, would represent a historical span of around 500 years or more. This would take the origins of this social category back to the early fifteenth century, and would make the *maabuɓe*, on this reckoning, one of the oldest men-of-skill groups. Kyburz, on the basis of other pedigrees, estimates the historical origins of diverse men-of-skill groups, all of which are much more recent (Kyburz 1994: 414).[23]

It is difficult to say with precision or with any certainty at what point different men-of-skill categories emerged as distinct and separate occupational specialists. The same can also be said for when the different branches diverged within each social category. The *maabuɓe* are a social category divided into weavers (*sanyooɓe*), lute- (*hoddu*) players and praise-singers. The lute players or *maabuɓe suudu Paate*, the '*maabuɓe* of the hut of Paate the pastoralist', most likely emerged as musicians and eulogists to the Fulɓe dynasty of the *Deniyaŋkooɓe* in the sixteenth century. The branch of *maabuɓe* praise-singers (*maabuɓe jaawamɓe*) were also linked to the Fulɓe court in their role as eulogists to the *jaawamɓe* Courtiers, and perhaps developed in parallel as the Deniyaŋke dynasty established itself as a focus of patronage. *Maabuɓe* declare that, despite their divisions into various specialist branches, they are all kinsmen (*bandiraaɓe*), and will often be able to cite lines of common ancestry and links of affinity between different pedigrees. Just as the Weavers' pedigree reaches back to a spirit ancestor, so too does the praise-singer line link back to spirits of the bush. The *maabuɓe* are one of the men-of-skill groups that emphasise more than any other the equality, similarity and relatedness among category members. Other men-of-skill categories consider themselves to be made up of distinct parts, some of which claim superiority over their fellows.

The Woodcarvers, for instance, comprise branches of canoe-builders (*lawɓe laade*) and of the carvers of domestic and culinary utensils (*lawɓe worworɓe*). The latter branch is conceived as having Fulɓe origins and their ancestor is presented in myth as the brother of a cattle herder (Ly 1938), while the canoe-builders are reputed to have Wolof origins (Kyburz 1994: 342–3; Wane 1969: 57–8). Furthermore, these canoe-builders are closely linked to the fishermen – thought to be one of the oldest occupational groups in Fuuta Toro – since they are their clients supplying them with canoes for fishing and ferrying. The matrimonial strategies of the two branches are different in that the canoe-builders occasionally create alliances with Weavers, *wambaaɓe* Musicians, Leatherworkers and Smiths, leaving the utensil carvers excluded from such inter-category unions (Wane 1969: 56). The canoe-builders do from time to time contract marriages with women from the other woodcarver branch, but rarely are these exchanges reciprocated, for the former consider themselves superior to the latter. Yaya Wane suggested, however, that the general comportment of the canoe-builders betrays their self-proclaimed superiority, acting more like stereotypical craftsmen than freemen (Wane 1969: 56).

The third branch of *lawɓe* (*lawɓe gumbala*) have abandoned woodcarving altogether and have taken up singing the praises of members of the freeborn Warrior category (*sebɓe*). This development is relatively recent, occurring perhaps after the fall of the Deniyaŋke regime following the eighteenth-century *tooroɓe* uprising when the Warriors gained more autonomy from the Fulɓe court. They played an important role in defending Fuuta Toro from Moorish invasion during the second half of the eighteenth century, and were later heavily involved in the jihads of Al-Hajj Umar Taal further to the east in the nineteenth century. Both of these contexts represent occasions in which Warriors no doubt excelled, so giving impetus for the creation of a specialist subcategory of praise-singers to remember and recount their deeds (Kyburz 1994: 343–4).

The Leatherworkers are similarly divided into one branch (*sakkeeɓe wodeeɓe*) which claims Fulɓe origins and is linked to the Deniyaŋke rulers, and a second branch (*sakkeeɓe alawɓe*) that is thought to have Soninke origins, hailing from a neighbouring region and being distant from the centre of authority. Those with Fulɓe origins are labelled the 'red Leatherworkers' (*wodeeɓe* means 'those who are red') and they believe themselves to have lighter coloured skins than their fellow craftsmen, who are considered to be 'black'. The former also tend to reject marriage partners from the other 'black' Leatherworkers branch, while these rejected artisans occasionally look to Blacksmith families for partners. These 'black' Leatherworkers are, in addition, feared by the red ones for the greater occupational magic they are held to possess (Kyburz 1994: 280–2).

The Smiths constitute a complex social category, being made up of at least three branches, each of which traces different lines of descent. One is linked to the Fulɓe, another to the Moors from the north and a third to the Wolof from a region to the west of Fuuta Toro. These three branches practise, however, only two types of specialism: namely, jewellery working with gold (*kanne*) and silver (*cardi*), and blacksmithing with iron (*njamdi ɓaleeri*, literally 'black' metal), a less noble metal. It is not always clear, though, exactly how the three branches link to the two specialisms, and perhaps there is no clear structure to it. Despite the fact that Moors are renowned craftsmen in silver and gold, many of the jewellers, nonetheless, claim Fulɓe origins. They are perhaps a recent development in Fuuta Toro, as late as the nineteenth century, and they are claimed not to create matrimonial ties with other Smiths (Kyburz 1994: 405). Those who work iron are called quite literally 'black' Smiths, *waylube ɓaleeri*, and are rejected as marriage partners by the others, but they occasionally seek alliances with the 'black' Leatherworkers or other men-of-skill social categories. These Smiths certainly appear to be continuing a tradition of iron-working that has been known in the valley for a very long time, given that archaeological evidence points to the fact that sites were worked from the turn of the first millennium (Kyburz 1994: 383 *et passim*).

There is cause for concern over a number of aspects of the evidence relating to the historical origins of the men-of-skill. It revolves around the way in which all of this evidence about the lines of ancestry, about the divisions between occupational branches and sub-specialisms, and finally the discourse of racial colour coding fits within a historical frame – indeed, whether it even can be used to create a historical frame. There are various reasons for these doubts. First, locally recited pedigrees should not be mistaken for genealogies in our understanding of the word, nor is it difficult to find inconsistencies between claims for origins expressed in myth and the directions in which lines of ancestry lead. (For example, the case of the Woodcarvers and *wambaabe* Musicians being brothers to a Fulɓe herder is not borne out consistently among the sources of myth and recited pedigrees (see Kyburz 1994: 340).) Second, occupational sub-specialisms are not as exclusive to the branches of social categories as is sometimes claimed by local and foreign interpreters. Smiths, for example, seem to change from blacksmithing to jewellery with relative ease and without suffering consequent shifts in social status or category.[24] Third, the discourse on racial colour coding of different occupational branches is a complex issue. Fulɓe herders (*wodeebe*) claim they are 'red' in comparison with local agriculturalists whom they consider to be 'black'. Many of the artisans and musicians (although not the Weavers) who are linked to the Fulɓe claim similar racial colouring, namely that they are 'red' in contrast to their 'black' counterparts. With respect to the Haalpulaar'en as a whole, 'black' seems to signify people who are from the south, the Wolof and Serer, those who are supposedly autochthonous to the region. The further south one travels away from Fuuta Toro, it is thought, the 'blacker' are the populations. But black is the colour of alterity. So the supposedly foreign Soninke Leatherworkers or the Wolof Smiths are labelled 'black', even though it may be difficult today to detect any difference in skin colour, even if there were such a thing in the past. Moreover, the freeborn Warrior group (*seɓɓe*) is divided into two Pulaar-speaking branches (*worgankooɓe* and *koliyaaɓe*) and another branch of Wolof extraction who speak a different dialect of Pulaar (Wane 1969: 39; Kyburz 1994: 105). These latter are considered to be black. If the Fulɓe consider themselves to be 'red', the sedentary agriculturalist certainly *do not* think of themselves as 'black', in the way the herders think of them. Black for them is associated with autochthonous groups to the south, in contrast to the white Arab-Berber populations to the north, who are referred to by the Arabic term *baidan* or by *raneeɓe*, the Pulaar equivalent. The agriculturalists stand between these two populations of black and white, and indeed the *tooroɓe* clerics have constructed for themselves elaborate pedigrees and connections that link them not to red or black origins, but to white (*baidan*) Arab-Berber stock. It is difficult to locate historically the precise development of these ideological distinctions, but it is reasonable to think that the black–white cleavage was introduced by early Arab Muslim travellers and scribes who referred to sub-Saharan Africa as *bilad al-sudan*, 'land of the blacks', and it could therefore be a very ancient form of social demarcation. It came to ideological fruition later, I will argue below, at the hands of the *tooroɓe* clerics who, in a bid for political and cultural domination at the end of the eighteenth century, used it for hegemonic purposes. In their hands, white was associated with Islam and black with what was in their view non- or pre-Islamic beliefs and practices. I will return to investigate the question of *tooroɓe* origins and their attempts at social dominance in the next chapter. The categories of red versus black are more difficult to locate, but could well be related to an early social demarcation between transhumant herder and sedentary agriculturalist. This perhaps became symbolically developed for ideological reasons once the Deniyaŋke Fulɓe settled and established their pre-Almaamate polity.[25]

The intriguing sociological point here is that among the seemingly egalitarian men-of-skill rank, fine-grain distinctions emerge between what are conceived of as separate sub-branches that have very different origins. These different origins point to different potencies that the sub-branches are supposed to possess. Furthermore, the hierarchical structure that marks the relationship between the freeborn and the men-of-skill is imitated in parallel fashion, although in miniature as it were. However, the terms of the discourse of their construction of alterity has changed. It is not the white–black distinction, used by the dominant *tooroɓe* clerics to demarcate themselves and others, but instead is a red–black distinction, which employs the colours associated with the once dominant Fulɓe Deniyaŋke on the one hand, and the supposedly autochthonous population of the river valley on the other.

Apart from racial connotations, the terms black and white carry another significance. They are both used to refer to forms of spiritual power and potency, and 'black' is associated particularly with the wild or the bush, with spells and incantations that cause harm to others (*bolle ɓaleeje* or 'black speech') and with the idea of alterity or cultural otherness in one form or another.[26] White is linked symbolically to the spiritual powers and forces of Islam, and the two complementary terms of white and black most likely developed in contradistinction to each other. It is the connections between men-of-skill occupations and kinds of spiritual force that are thought of as 'black', that is of the wild or the bush, which I wish to pursue below. Furthermore, I wish to make a further break with the more literal or overtly historical readings of the origins and pedigrees that were considered above. I argue below that pedigrees and lines of ancestry are remembered by local genealogists and praise-singers for purposes other than those of historical veracity. They are linked crucially to local claims about the social division of knowledge, which in turn is connected closely with notions of cultural identity and the social organisation of cultural difference. These processes of constructing cultural identity and difference are not produced in a historical vacuum, for indeed they draw on elements of remembered and embodied traditions that are derived from past cultural experience. Genealogies of people are not, however, merely composed of links of descent that constitute a line of forebears, but they are also genealogies of power that point to sources and potencies of particular types.

THE SOCIAL DIVISION OF KNOWLEDGE: MEN-OF-SKILL AND THE WILD

Fishermen

Subalɓe Fishermen are thought by other freemen and women to practise an occupation more akin to those of the men-of-skill. Indeed, the weavers consider that there are many affinities between weaving and fishing, and that their founding ancestor was of a fisher family. Fishermen are also subject to an interdiction stipulating that they should not hold religious office within Islam (see also Wane 1969: 46). This religious exclusion seems to hinge on the idea that Fishermen practise an occupation that brings them into contact with the forces, both visible and invisible, of the river. Water, whether in the form of flowing currents between river banks or of large static expanses lying in a flood basin, is the dwelling place not only of powerful and dangerous animals such as hippopotamus and crocodile but also of river spirits and water demons (*munuuji maayo* and *seyɗaneeje ndiyam*). Consequently, Fishermen must be equipped spiritually to influence these powers and to have a control over the forces of the river. First among these is the *jom maayo*, literally 'river chief', a spirit figure with the form of a human body on which are four arms, a fish's tail and the head of a horse wearing a long beard. This spirit agent is responsible for accidents and misfortunes occurring on or nearby the river (upturning a boat, a drowning, etc.), and it is the responsibility of the head Fisherman (*jaaltaabe*) in each community to try to exercise control over it. The beneficence of the river as provider of sustenance and fertility is represented in another figure, that of *caamaaba*, a legendary snake and brother to the first fishermen, who according to myth was originally a Fulɓe herder by descent (see Dilley 1984: appendix 3). This snake brings good fortune to those with the ability to communicate with it.

Fishermen have at their command a body of specialist fishing knowledge, *gandal maayo* or literally 'river lore', which includes knowledge of the practical techniques of catching fish as well as magical prescriptions and spiritual procedures for dealing with the forces of the river. Fishermen, especially the head Fisherman, are able to enter into dialogue with river spirits whom they try to control, and to exercise a power over aquatic animal life. Crocodiles and hippopotamuses are thought to be not only physically the most dangerous of riverine life, but they are thought to possess their own incantations (*kince*) which they recite to themselves for protection. There are two principal sorts of fishing incantation (*cefi*): first, a form of protective magic (*cefi paddinirɓi*) that permits humans under the threat from aquatic animals and water spirits to carry out their trade; second, a form to ensure a fisherman has a good catch and to protect against the shame of returning home empty-handed due to the malicious intentions of a fellow Fisher (*cefi gawirɗi*). The incantations used by Fishers to pacify or placate river life can also be turned against their fellow specialists or indeed non-fisherfolk, who fear the knowledge they possess. These latter powers can be used to ward off non-*subalɓe*, such as a down-at-heel Warrior or destitute bondsman, who might try their luck at fishing. They are also renowned for their powers of sorcery, which can afflict someone who has crossed them, such that a mysterious fish bone will stick in a victim's throat. They are also associated with witchcraft (*sukunya*), for Tall reports that accusations of witchcraft are acknowledged locally to be more prevalent in riverine villages dominated by Fishermen than elsewhere (Tall 1984: 123–8). Such villages are also the focus of possession cult activity organised by Fisherwomen (Kyburz 1994: 30–1; Tall 1984). The head Fisherman (*jaaltaabe*) is at once the protector of the wider community of fishers and non-fishers against the forces of the river, as well as a feared and respected magician who has powers to bring misfortune or healing to others. Fishers possess expertise in curing a range of illnesses, such as bites, pricks and skin punctures, and they have remedies to protect the whole person, especially from madness caused by river spirits.

In sum, the quality of being a Fisherman is captured in the word *cubalaagu* (a Fisherman is a *cubalo*), an essence of Fisherhood, and it refers to their mastery over the realm of water, specifically the running, living water of rivers and streams. They have the knowledge and power to deal with the life of the river, both seen and unseen, are thought to have a sentimental and spiritual attachment to the water and are considered masters of that domain: they are the hunters of the water rather than of the land. The quality of the essence of the social person of the fisher is expressed and celebrated in the once regular crocodile hunt (*fiifiire*),[27] and it provides them with the foundation both for the successful practice of the craft as well as for evaluations of their social worth that are not always complementary. Their intelligence, for example, is often belittled by others who draw a parallel between it and the mental abilities of a fish (*hayyille liingu*) (Wane 1969). The essentialisation of social and cultural qualities such as these is a feature that occurs in relation to the conceptualisation of the qualities of all social categories, men-of-skill in particular. It is a feature of social thought that is also engendered by the notion of different lines of ancestry that are claimed by each set of occupational specialists, in that they are derived from different points of origin, some of them non-human. That is, castes as locally conceived are essentialist pedigrees relating to different types of humankind, to different breeds, stocks or even races among humanity (Dilley 2000).

Weavers

The *maabuɓe* Weavers, like the Fishermen, are credited with little intelligence, for there is a proverb that states 'as many Weavers die from stupidity as die by the will of Allah' (from 'natural causes'). They are, however, also attributed with fine skills and manual dexterity, for the title of the social category '*maabuɓe*' is said by indigenous etymologists to be related to a number of verbs, one of which is *mabaade*, meaning 'to arrange things with delicacy and finesse', like threads in a loom. This verb provides a substantive form *mabotoodo* for 'one who is adroit, able and cunning'. Weavers are subject, therefore, to a complex range of cultural stereotyping, such that they are associated with both stupidity and cunning, human qualities often represented in animal imagery by the hyena and hare in popular tales (*tinndi*).

Maabuɓe weavers (*sanyooɓe*) fear harmful contagion with the spirits that animate their craft, from whom their occupation was taken and with whom it is still associated. Their mythical ancestor is called Juntel Jabaali, a man born of a spirit woman, who is thought of by the *maabuɓe* as the most powerful of Weavers. Their origin myth tells how this mythical ancestor took the craft from spirits who were weaving in the bush. Present-day Weavers trace their descent from him and claim they have inherited some of his expertise, lore and power. A weaver is aware of the potential danger he is in each time he starts work, so every morning he recites various incantations to protect himself from the forces that are thought to return to the loom at night. Even before he sits at the loom he invokes beneficent spirits and banishes malevolent ones with an incantation that calls on his body to become like iron (*yo bandam laa to njamdi*), and with other verses he evokes all his strength and power at the beginning of the day. He is also fearful of the malevolent intentions of his fellow craftsmen, and possesses protective verses against such effects.

Members of this social category have a reputation for being able to cure burns and especially stomach aches, an affliction they seem to suffer from due to the cramped position in which they weave, and is one they fear most for it slows their work. They are often specialists in amulets (*pibi*) fabricated from knotted lengths of cotton thread onto which incantations (*cefi*) are muttered by the knotter (*fiboowo*) who spits out the words of his incantation as a means to transmit their power to the material of the amulet. These amulets are always made with an odd number of knots, and the finished item appears with a regular series of knots along its length. These amulets are produced in a singular act of prestidigitation from what looks like a tangled mass of intertwined threads created by the knotter. The ends of this tangled web are pulled taut to reveal the regularly knotted thread, and thus the amulet is made.

Many Weaver women are potters, and they too require protection from spiritual potencies associated with their craft. Spirits are believed to dwell in the clay deposits found along the side of the river, and the clay digger must take precautions before she collects her raw material. She possesses incantations (*cefi*) to ward off the spirits of the clay, who are allergic to impurity associated with women, such that a menstruating woman should not enter a clay pit nor work the material (Appia-Dabit 1941). Arriving at the water's edge where clay is dug, a woman pronounces a verse and sometimes throws a few grains of millet into the pit. As she digs, putting clay into her calabash, the potter sings another verse, occasionally spitting her saliva to carry the power of her words into the clay. Pottery is not an exclusive occupation to Weaver women alone, for females among the Smiths and Leatherworkers often practise the craft. Another occupation often associated with Weaver women, however, is the plaiting and braiding of hair, a skill not dissimilar in many ways to male weaving. Stories are told of how spirits in the bush plait the manes of horses that go missing from a village, and women conceive of their art as being derived from this source.

Smiths

One of the greatest trade secrets known by the Smiths, held only by the Mbow clan in the past, concerns the smelting of iron from ore using fire (Wane 1969: 52). Fire is also used in the annealing of metals (*tafde* is 'to forge') and this task, it is claimed by Smiths, was carried out by their ancestors using only their bare hands. They are supposed to have had special powers that enabled them to handle red-hot metals, and these they used until such time as one of them saw in a dream inspired by a spirit a pair of Smith's tongs which present-day forgers still use.[28] They are thought to be able to use these powers against other Smiths, such that a victim's furnace and crucibles (*kaynirde*) would be affected and he would be unable to pour his metals. Smiths also have a reputation for healing, particularly injuries associated with fire and burns to the skin, and are also called on to perform the operation of circumcision of boys, a ritual duty for which they are especially skilled through the possession of expert knowledge and incantations to help heal the young initiates.

Fire is associated in local thought with spirits, in particular jinn, a belief no doubt derived from Islamic cosmology. The Qur'an speaks of the fall of the leader of the rebellious jinn, Eblis, who proclaimed that he had been made of fire while humankind had been made of clay (Chapter of the S).[29] Elsewhere, the consequences for those who have dealings with jinn are made explicit in the Qur'an (see Chapter of the Story and Chapter of the Genii). Wane, a *toorodo* and an academic, wrote that Smiths are in permanent contact with fire, which evokes the idea of hell (Wane 1969: 54) The connection with fire is no doubt one of the reasons that smithing is a feared occupation in the eyes of those who are not men-of-skill.[30] Fellow artisans and craftsmen do not share this view, since they too frequently use fire in the course of their occupations (such as Woodcarvers) or are associated with it symbolically (Weavers).[31] The furnace used by Smiths is constructed from material taken from a termite mound and mixed with clay. Termite mounds are considered especially dangerous places and most people will avoid them, for they are the homes to powerful spirit forces. That material from them is incorporated into the structure of such a central piece of smithing equipment is yet a further association between the craft and the forces of the wild.

The title of this social category, *wayilɓe* or *waylu6e*, is said to be derived from the verb *waylude*, 'to give form to' or 'to fashion', and from a related verb *waylaade*, 'to transform or change' as in *waylaade mbaadi*, 'to change aspect, colour or form'. These verbs certainly describe processes with which the Smith is connected, and in many senses it captures the conception of the smith as transformer and fashioner of material. This is a kind of conception and connection, moreover, associated with the activities of the men-of-skill as a whole. Not only are Smiths feared but there is a belief that anything that comes from a Smith, excluding his products, will bring neither good fortune nor increase or prosperity to another person. A freeman or woman would not accept a gift from a Smith nor would consider buying anything from him apart from his products. Indeed, clothing left by a Smith in a freeman's house would never be used or worn by anyone for fear of exposure to harmful forces the garment might carry.[32] Furthermore, there is a special place (*joonde baylo*) where a Smith should sit on entering a household, for he should never be allowed onto mats used by others either for entertaining guests or for sleeping. The Smiths, however, invert the symbolic value of such an interdiction. Rather than contaminating others, a Smith avoids these mats as places of contagion that would affect his craft, especially smelting ore and annealing metals. Indeed, in the past for fear of disrupting his craft, he would abstain from sexual relations prior to smelting, a task little carried out today. What might be construed by non-smiths as a source of impurity (*soɓe*) to them is from the Smith's perspective a source of pollution and disruption to him in relation to the practice of his craft.

Smiths comprise the one men-of-skill category that attracts the most extreme forms of cultural characterisation. Despite these negative characterisations of the person of the Smith, smithing is regarded as the most powerful of crafts that can have not only negative but also positive effects. For example, if a freeman enters a smithy at the moment a new anvil (*taande*) is being forged, he will become a ruler in later life, or so it is said. Moreover, Kyburz reports (1994: 401–2) that smithing was held in high regard by some of his informants, being deemed the noblest of men-of-skill occupations. That smithing attracts both highly negative and highly positive forms of characterisation is not insignificant, for it represents perhaps the most vivid example of the transformatory powers of the men-of-skill. A story is told of how Al-Hajj Umar Taal, the nineteenth-century Muslim marabout and military campaigner, proclaimed the smith the chief of all men-of-skill occupations (Kyburz 1994: 402).[33] He asked each craftsman to bring to him an example of the fruits of their labours. The following day each one brought the products of his labours: wooden mortars, pestles and bowls, woven cloths, leather sandals, metal jewellery, a lute. Umar Taal asked each craftsman to undo the product of their labours and put it back into its original state, and it was left to the Smith, the last to be asked, to complete successfully this request. Only he could melt down his metals and recast them in a new form. This story not only highlights the powers of transformation that all men-of-skill possess, but the particular regard that Smiths are held in by religious followers of Al-Hajj Umar Taal, whose mother herself was descended from a family that bears one of the patronyms of Smiths. The important point here is that smithing is regarded as a spiritually charged occupation, and this fact might be construed in one of a number of ways. The quality of being a Smith is captured in the term *mbaylaagu*, which refers to the complex set of social and moral characteristics outlined above. Of all the men-of-skill categories Smiths are the most marked, and while Wane (1969) talks of a genuine social repulsion of Smiths, the views of other local interpreters suggest a more positive gloss on their particular social condition.

Woodcarvers

The lawɓe Woodcarvers are so called because they hollow out material to serve as recipients of various sorts, such as spoons (*kuunde*), calabashes (*lehe*), mortars (*boɓi*) dug-out canoes (*laaɗe*) and so on, and this connection is suggested by the verb *lawde* – 'to hollow out'. Other local etymologists give the derivation of the title as a deformation of the verb *lewde*, meaning 'to clear the bush' by slashing and burning in preparation for cultivation, and this gives the emphatic pronoun *lewɓe*, the 'land clearers or reclaimers' (Wane 1969). The process of felling trees, an integral part of land clearance, is a central aspect of Woodcarver activity, and is one that is fraught with danger. A home to spirits, many species of tree must be approached with caution, for if a woodcutter does not follow the correct procedures, he will fall foul of their powers. On finding a tree he wishes to fell, the Woodcarver digs a small hole at its base and places a nut there, covering it over with soil. Having left the nut buried at the root of the tree, he returns to it later, leaving time for the spirit who lives there to make it known whether it wishes him to continue or not. If the nut is uncovered when the man returns, he knows the spirit does not want him to cut the tree down. If not, he proceeds to chop. Throughout this part of his work, the Woodcarver recites incantations to protect himself from the dangers of contact with the spirit. He also communicates with the tree spirit to negotiate its departure if it is unwilling to leave. Large trees necessary for canoe-building, the specialism of the *lawɓe laaɗe*, harbour the most potent spirits which can be the most difficult to remove. The label *duuki sere* or 'rebel tree' is given to a tree felled by a woodsman but whose spirit has refused to leave. Such trees can be found lying in the bush and not brought inside the human settlement, for the wood is unable to be pacified and used by the Woodcarver and it remains the seat of invisible forces.

The *lawɓe worworɓe*, or the carvers of domestic utensils, are recalled in myth as being linked to Fulɓe cattle-herders. The myth tells of three brothers, the eldest Hamadi or Dikko became a woodcarver, the second brother Samba continued as a herdsman, and the youngest, Demba, became a *wambaaɓe* praise-singer to the pastoralists. They are remembered in song in the oft-quoted lines *labbo* Dikko, *pullo* Samba, *bambaaɗo* Demba (carver Dikko [the elder], pastoralist Samba, musician Demba). One remaining trace of this ancestry claimed in myth is that domestic Woodcarvers retain a power of curse over cattle-herds of the Fulɓe pastoralists, in whose animals they can provoke sterility, illness and loss.

Leatherworkers

The last of the manual men-of-skill occupations is leatherworking. Leatherworkers are considered to practise a debasing occupation because, in the eyes of the freeborn, they deal with skins and hides (*cawgu*) considered to be unclean through a connection with rotting meat and putrifying flesh. Their habit of gripping leather and hides in their teeth while working it is often commented upon as distasteful, hence the derogatory title for a Leatherworker, 'the biter of skin' (*natoowo cawgu*) (Wane 1969). This habit is certainly suggestive of the behaviour of a carrion-eater such as a hyena, an animal frequently associated with men-of-skill. The connection between Leatherworkers and animal skins suggests another connotation with witchcraft and witches, the 'drinkers of blood' (*yarooɓe yiiyam*) and the 'eaters of flesh'. Witches are believed to enter into a victim by means of a wind that blows into the body via an orifice. The victim is then eaten from the inside, leaving only the skin, the envelope of the person, covering a hollow form. Some Leatherworkers have a reputation for being able to enter into the body of goats or sheep – the two main species whose skins are worked – and to eat their interior substance. Following on from this association of these craftsmen with the outer shell of living forms comes their reputation for witchcraft, and they are feared by others as a result. Leatherworkers are also thought by their fellow craftsmen to be able to disrupt each other's work by transforming themselves into insects that gnaw through another worker's hides. Alternatively, by means of powerful incantations they possess, Leatherworkers are supposed to be able to make their victims' body shake so that it is impossible for them to sew leather without constantly pricking their hand.

Besides the production of everyday items such as sandals, shoes, sacks, harnesses and so on, Leatherworkers are responsible for the fabrication of amulets (*talkuru*) made from a range of substances. A person might come to a leatherworker with a carefully folded piece of paper on which is written by an Islamic cleric a Qur'anic verse, and the client will request a leather casing to be made so that he or she can wear the amulet on the body for protection or to bring about the intended effect – making oneself irresistible to the opposite sex, for example. Leatherworkers make other forms of amulet, such as those (*alaadu*) using animal horns and body parts, or those in the form of a belt (*daddorgal*) that might use a variety of animal, vegetable or mineral materials. They used to fabricate powerful protective amulets that were worn in the past by warriors to guard them from bullets and knives. Men-of-skill attribute the invulnerability of Warriors to the supply of such protective amulets made by Leatherworkers; Warriors on the other hand tend to emphasise their own essential qualities that are conceived to be derived from their pedigree from Warrior stock. They also claim that their abilities arise from the production of medicines which they, Warriors, concoct to conjure similar effects to the amulets. Like Smiths, Leatherworkers are thought to make skilled circumcisors of boys, and they too possess incantations to help them perform the operation and to protect the initiates from danger and misfortune. Leatherworker women are also sought after to carry out the operation of female excision (*ɓornaade*).

Musicians and Singers

The last two men-of-skill categories are those comprising exclusively of praise-singers and musicians. The subcategories of the Weavers and Woodcarvers who also sing rather than practise a manual occupation are considered by their members to be later developments that branched off from the original craftsman stock. What is common to all of these specialist non-manual occupations is that singers are conceived of as having the 'power of the word' over an audience in general or a patron in particular. To sing someone's praises, *askinade neddo*, is to sing the genealogy or pedigree of a person by listing their ancestors and referring to the deeds they performed. The root of the verb *askinade*, 'to praise', lends itself in substantive form to the word for pedigree or line of ancestry, *asko*. A person who has many important lines of ancestry through maternal and paternal lines is said to have 'many legs or paws' (*koyde ine keewii*), the image being the inverse of our sense of genealogical tree. Here, the person being praised is the head (*hoore*), which is supported by legs or paws (*koyde*), which represent the numerous pedigrees that might be recited in a praise-song (Kyburz 1994: 75).

The *wambaabe* are the lute or *hoddu* players and singers who often live among Fulbe herding communities, from whom they traditionally obtained their subsistence in return for their services in entertainment and eulogising. The title of this social category can be derived from the verb *wambude*, referring to a mother who carries her child on her back; thus the *wambaabe* are 'those who are carried or protected', and in a figurative sense it suggests the idea that they are carried on the backs of their Fulbe patrons. Other craftsmen and artisans claim that these Musicians are in fact Fulbe and are not really men-of-skill at all, since they have little occupational knowledge in the same sense of the manual trades. However, they do intermarry with members of other artisan categories and also possess powers analogous to them. *Wambaabe* Musicians hold a similar power over Fulbe herders as the Woodcarvers do over their cattle herds. The Musicians usually descend upon a Fulbe patron at naming ceremonies, marriages and other important family occasions, at which they are bound to eulogise the host's family and forebears. They have the power, however, through song and malediction to bring misfortune to a host if they feel that the services provided have not been properly rewarded. A disgruntled singer can, for example, strike a young groom down with impotence so compromising him on his wedding night. This power of the word is feared not just by Fulbe herders, but is shared by all members of the freeborn and servile ranks.

The *wambaabe* singers are closely associated with one of the Weaver branches of singers, the *maabube suudu Paate* (the '*maabube* of the hut of Paate the Pullo' – singular of Fulbe), who also play the lute or *hoddu*. A *maabu* myth tells of how the first weaver to sing for Paate the pastoralist was rewarded by the gift of a single-stringed instrument (*nyaanyooru* or *moolo*) played with a bow. The Weaver adapted it, adding new strings and thus produced the five-stringed lute, which was subsequently taken up by the *wambaaɓe*. Perhaps it is the association of thought between the adding of the new strings to the instrument and the laying of warp threads in the loom that makes a weaver a particularly appropriate mythic figure to produce the five-stringed *hoddu*.

The medium that a singer manipulates and transforms may not take material form, but the effects of song and word are thought to be nonetheless real. The musician's medium – word and song – is akin to what has been called an 'objet-parole' ('speech-object' – see Bacou and Biebuyck, 1986), which in itself resembles a 'power-object' (Soares 1997b). This idea is clearly illustrated in the case of the specialist *awluɓe* Praise-singers. Their title *awluɓe* can be derived from the now somewhat archaic verb *awlude*, meaning 'to stir up' or 'to mix', but it can have a figurative sense suggesting 'to affect' or 'to move emotionally', as in the phrase *jimi awluɓe ina ngawla*, 'the Praise-singers' songs are moving'. They are considered by the freeborn, and even other men-of-skill, to lack a sense of both shame and discretion (*alaa gacce, annda suturo* – Wane 1969: 61), and they will readily turn to abuse and vulgarity if they do not receive what they judge to be a reasonable recompense for their services. They have a reputation for not missing an opportunity of performing for anyone if there is a possibility of a reward. They are said to solicit everyone, but no one solicits them. They appear under the feeblest of pretexts, their patrons claim, and they are feared by those at whose expense they live. Patrons are concerned that if the obligatory gifts to a singer are not given or are deemed insufficient, then misfortune might befall the family due to the client's anger and curses. They will not stop short, either, of publicly embarrassing their patron if they feel hard done by. Patrons will point out that of all the men-of-skill, *awluɓe* Praise-singers are among the best dressed and most well fed among their clients. They are consequently thought to be avarious, greedy, grasping, that their demands know no bounds. They are, in other words, just like hyenas, to which they are assimilated metaphorically, since both move in bands and attack their victims by surprise.

Members of other men-of-skill categories regard Praise-singers as being set apart from them, for they are usually refused in marriage outside their own group. They are considered by all to be the lowest social category among the men-of-skill. Kyburz sets the two specialist musician and singer groups in complementary opposition, highlighting the ideas that the *awluɓe* play no instrument and are vociferous, vulgar and coarse, whereas the *wambaaɓe* play an instrument, and are charming, refined and noble (Kyburz 1994: 303 and 412).

While there may be a good deal of local agreement with such stereotypical characterisations of members of these social categories, the analysis should not rest here. The views embodied in these stereotypes and characterisations form a discourse about cultural difference that must be located within historical and social context. This discourse suggests the following gross characterisations at the level of social ranks.[34]

CHARACTERISATIONS OF SOCIAL RANKS

The freemen are held to possess not only economic resources and political authority, but also intelligence (*hayyille*), mental sharpness and a subtle wit (*seebre*). They believe themselves to be generous (*dokkujawdi*) with respect to their social inferiors who live off a patron's gifts. They are proud and vigorously defend their honour, a quality that is connoted by their patronym or *yettoode*. These characteristics are summed up in the word *ndimaagu*, meaning the moral quality and essence of being a freeborn person, one who also possesses the quality of *teddungal*, a more general state referring to courtesy and civility. The second rank of the men-of-skill are thought to be generously rewarded by the freemen for their services, but they are also scorned by them for the occupations they practise and by virtue of the demands for rewards for their services. They are generally held to lack self-esteem and a sense of modesty relative to their freemen superiors, and they have no sense of shame or reserve or dignity (*gacce*, *kersa*). The third rank of bondsmen and women were often talked of as though they were domestic animals, and their labour and products were used like those of the horse and donkey.[35]

If these stereotypes and caricatures form part of what might be called an indigenous discourse of difference, the views expressed immediately above embody the freemen perception of the nature and order of things. According to this dominant view, bondsmen and women stand in relation to the freemen as animals stand in relation to humanity; the serviles simply lack the defining qualities of being truly human. The men-of-skill, however, represent the inverse of the ideas of civility relating to the freemen, namely the qualities of personal dignity, manners, etiquette and decorum – all of which they are thought to lack. If the bondsmen are thought to have few if any of the qualities of human beings, then men-of-skill actually represent the perversion of, the imbalance or disproportion among, human qualities and virtues. Bondsmen and women hardly register on this moral scale, whereas men-of-skill stand at its negative pole. Within this discourse of alterity, men-of-skill are the 'other', and this sense of difference is marked by particular types of quality, usually by a negation of the qualities of the dominant group. The 'other' lacks intelligence, it knows neither grace nor wit and is charmless, shameless, without dignity and is stupid. On occasion it is represented by a marked sexuality, for having sexual relations with the other is either positively beneficial or more likely threatening and harmful, as is the case with Smith and Woodcarver women. Sexual relations of this kind, across the limits of normality, is not neutral, it is always marked symbolically.

Throughout the above account the muted voices of the 'other' can be heard. What can be made of these stereotypical characterisations? These voices suggest inversions of the dominant value impositions, such as the Smiths' attitude to sitting on other people's mats or the devaluing of the efforts of the Warriors to generate medicines to ensure their own invulnerability. If the consciousness of 'subaltern' groups is refracted through the dominant categories of the freeborn, or if at best it is more autonomous but yet fragmented and inconsistent (Gramsci 1971), it is not surprising that we should find reproduced among the men-of-skill similar kinds of distinction that are deployed against them. If it is the case that the *awluɓe* Praise-singers are to the *wambaaɓe* musicians as the men-of-skill are to the freeborn, then this perhaps is the result of the reproduction of the distinctions of the socially dominant by those who occupy a marginal position. Men-of-skill may be at one and the same time implicated in their own subjugation as well as resistant to the forms of dominance and cultural stereotyping that marginalise them. This discourse of alterity must therefore be located within the history of a political culture that has developed progressively to marginalise socially and economically men-of-skill groups. Inscribed in the discourse of 'caste' stereotyping are the traces of earlier historical experience and attempts at political domination.

This is evident if we consider again the ideological distinction between red and black branches of different men-of-skill categories – for example the Smiths or the Leatherworkers. Those branches of an occupation claiming to be 'red' by pedigree were often connected with centres of power and authority of the earlier Deniyaŋke dynasty, and they rejected their counterparts in marriage. By contrast, those who were labelled 'black' were considered to be endowed with greater spiritual powers than their 'red' fellows, were regarded as more closely related to spirits and to the bush, and were by extension more feared by all concerned. Red appears to represent that which is more noble than the black, even if in practice this distinction was not clearly borne out in the separation between social groups on the ground. While from the external freeborn perspective, the men-of-skill occupations all draw on 'black' lore and knowledge, from the internal perspective of the craftsmen's point of view, subtle distinctions are made with regard to pedigree, lore and proximity to the bush. That is, some men-of-skill categories subdivide themselves by virtue of a principle of distinction which functions to separate the men-of-skill as a whole from the freeborn rank, or more precisely the *tooroɓe* clerics. Red and black are two terms that operate as symbolic markers of separation among men-of-skill categories who find reason to make distinctions among themselves. These two terms invoke at once a history of political domination, and in particular a sense of the sources of authority and the cultural politics of difference.

GANDAL AND THE SOCIAL DIVISION OF KNOWLEDGE AND POWER

Some of the threads regarding craft occupations and the social division of knowledge can now be pulled together. Each of the men-of-skill social categories has a specific body of occupational lore, *gandal*, exclusive to it alone. This is particularly the case with respect to the manual occupations, such that *gandal maabuɓe* is the lore and knowledge of the Weavers, or *gandal wayluɓe* that of the Smiths, and so forth. These bodies of lore enable members of a social category to practise their trade (*gandal golle* or 'occupational lore'), and they encompass not only the technical aspects of the craft but also the oral traditions, myths and legends, as well as the incantations and magical procedures necessary for the successful conduct of the trade. Men-of-skill crafts and skills are conceived by them and by the freeborn to be derived from or associated with spirits and forces of the wild, and present-day practitioners view themselves as the descendents of often semi-divine ancestors from whom they have inherited their specialised talents. The powers and potencies that are considered to have been passed on to present-day craftsmen enable them not only to practise their respective crafts, but also to conduct occupational magic against their fellows or others in the community. I have argued that, by virtue of their specific bodies of lore, men-of-skill possess the powers of transformation. Their skills transform material objects into functional and stylistically pleasing objects, and their verbal and musical talents render beautiful and ornament the lives, deeds and qualities of the patrons whom they praise. These abilities are captured in the title of the men-of-skill social rank as a whole, *nyeenyɓe*, the 'beautifiers' or 'adorners', as well as in the titles of the individual social categories, such as the Smiths being glossed as 'those who transform'. Yet these transformations are not neutral or uncharged acts; they carry a valency since the sources of power and potency to effect transformations are found in or are associated with the wild, the bush (*ladde*), and not in the relatively tamed domains of the *waalo* or *jeeri* fields in which agriculture takes place, nor are they found in the village, the centre of social life.

Sets of precautions and protective devices are used by craftsmen and women in order to procure and handle the materials necessary for production. Those occupations that involve the collection of raw materials from the bush have included in their bodies of lore protective verses and incantations aimed at counteracting dangerous contacts with spirits and jinn believed to reside in them. There are other occupations and arts, not specific to the men-of-skill, that bring their practitioners into contact with spiritual and mystical forces which lie outside the compass of village life. They involve the healing arts and herbalism, the use of roots, herbs, bark, plant extracts and so forth. While these arts are open to anyone, most people regard men-of-skill as being particularly adept in these areas. Craftsmen and women are also associated with spiritual and mystical forces through the very nature of the occupations they practise, as well as through the types of material they handle. Not only do craftsmen fear contagion from the spirits that are associated with their crafts, but the craftsmen themselves are feared by both serviles and the freeborn because of the potent incantations (*cefi*) they possess, and the possibility that they can use these powers against others. The freemen have few effective specialised means to deal with the effects of the potencies of men-of-skill, and it is men-of-skill who are thought by freemen to be contaminated by the processes they undertake in the course of their occupations. They appear in the eyes of the rest of society to be in a permanent state of association with the spirit world, or at least the effects of their occasional contacts with it are immutable. Contact with spirits is usually shunned by ordinary people, for they fear the effects of associations with forces that are considered dangerous and unpredictable. Apart from men-of-skill, it is only exceptional individuals, persons of outstanding ability, those with an obvious gift, that are described in terms of having help from spiritual forces. Sufi mystics and spiritual leaders are one such group, but I will discuss them in detail in the next chapter. While the exceptional individual, the brave or the gifted might be able to approach the spirits in order to possess those forces which will turn the mind of any ordinary human, men-of-skill represent a form of social institution placed in such a position of contagion. There are two forms that power takes: first, the charismatic power of individuals who seek potency in a variety of sources; second, the institutional arrangement of power distributed among particular social ranks and categories, whose socially allotted expertise lies in specific domains. While individuals, such as mystics, may actively search out sources of knowledge and power, for the men-of-skill, this kind of connection between dangerous, contagious spirits and humans is made on a more continued and routine basis in the course of practising their crafts. These are the kinds of connections that would make ordinary people go mad, for mental illness and disturbance is conceived in terms of a person being possessed by spirits they might encounter in the bush.[36]

One occupation that is common to all men and women, no matter what rank or category, is cultivation (*dewal*). Indeed, many Muslim writers and many *hadith* express strong approval of agricultural work: 'the work of the fields is the work of the prophets' or 'God ordains us to work, as he himself worked; he who refuses to work the fields disobeys God' (see Monteil 1980: 367–8). In the village economy, members of all ranks and categories participate in cultivation and everyone cultivates food crops to some extent, even though not all may necessarily hold rights of land tenure. Whereas fishing is a primary productive activity which is associated with its own specific body of powerful black occupational lore (*gandal subalɓe* or 'fishermen's lore'), agriculture is in a comparative sense neutral as a productive activity; it carries with it no 'charge' or contagion that may affect its practitioners as fishing does. Whereas the river is considered to be a primary site of some of the most potent spiritual forces in the wild and thus has to be approached cautiously, the plant world is not so unambiguously dangerous.

The 'plant world', as we would know it, is divided into two: grass, herbs and small plants, known as *huɗo*, constitute one group; trees, shrubs and other woody plants, known as *leɗɗe*, constitute another. This division is reflected in the noun class system in Pulaar. According to this system, all nouns are placed in one of over twenty noun classes, each of which is recognised by a specific article associated with a class.[37] The nouns in any one class usually share little semantic continuity, such that the class *nde*, for example, includes words referring to small animals, predatory birds, grains and fruits, places and instruments, some parts of the body, and beings or individuals that are scorned or despised. There are only three classes that remotely suggest any semantic continuity, the first of these being the class *nge* which, apart from a few odd nouns, relates almost exclusively to cattle, the domain of the Fulɓe pastoralists. The other two classes are those into which all forms of plant life are allotted: the first is the class *ko* comprising grass, foliage and small plants (as well as human body hairs – connected through the concept of sprouting, shooting and germinating, perhaps?); the second is the class *ki* which, although broader in its content, refers to woody plants and trees as well as to manufactured wooden objects. (Contained here are also names of some body parts and some abstractions.) This latter class of plants could almost be described as the noun class of the *lawɓe* Woodcarvers, whose raw materials and finished products constitute the bulk of this class. What is peculiar about the plants and trees in this class is that they are mostly types which are considered to be the dwelling places of spirits, and special occupational *gandal* is required before they are approached. This is the domain of expertise of the *lawɓe*. By contrast, the general class of plants, grass and herbs, *ko*, is quite separate from the woody plants and is not associated inherently with any form of specific spirit life or their dwellings.

The point is that cultivable food crops require no specialised body of occupational *gandal* in order to grow, tend and harvest them. There are no protective verses (*cefi*) or other procedures that are specific to agriculturalists alone. Cultivators can of course apply forms of potency to their agriculture, but these are derived from forms of lore and knowledge that are the expertise of other specialists. It is their prescriptions that are then transferred to cultivation. For example, a *bileejo* or medicine-man can prescribe a medicine made from anteater's feet which, if buried in the ground, will ensure a good harvest. (The same medicine can also be used to kill a man.) Magical procedures and the invoking of potencies to help in agriculture are not specific to the occupation itself but are forms of expertise from other specialists that are applied to cultivation, just as one might consult such an expert over a problem in any area of one's life. In this sense, then, cultivation is neutral; it harbours in itself no particular dangers or contagions other than those one confronts in any aspect of life. For example, a person might point out that malevolent spirits have affected the plants in his field, indicating those areas where plants have died or have become diseased or discoloured. But such problems are no different from the malevolent effects that spirits can bring to numerous aspects of a person's life. What is important is that there are no specific bodies of agricultural *gandal* that are the exclusive domain of cultivators. Cultivation does not constitute the subject of a body of esoteric knowledge.

If agriculture is an act of transformation of raw plant material into socially useable subsistence foods, then it is of an altogether different order when compared with the transformative powers, dangers and creativities involved in craft occupations and dealings with the wild. Haalpulaar'en mark this latter type of activity as special, as black, as potentially threatening, and they consider its practitioners to be set apart from the rest of the population. Agriculture is an activity open to all people, it is a neutral process in that its practitioners need not protect themselves from activity-specific dangers and potencies, and hence it is not marked out as threatening and transformative in the same way craft industries are in indigenous thought.

Jackson makes the point that allegories involving alliances between individuals and bush spirits are ethically ambiguous, since they are suggestive of powers that are as potentially destructive as they are regenerative (1982: 21). The creation of community, he argues, depends not simply on people behaving well, slavishly following the rules of convention or passively adhering to routine, but upon the control of vital forces that are 'wild' or 'random', which must be fetched from outside the domain of rules and roles. Men-of-skill are cast into this mould of ethically ambiguous social characters, whose relationships with sets of spiritual forces lying outside the human community sets them apart as creators of culture and transformers of material. The derision and scorn – only one aspect of their perceived social worth – is a means by which other Haalpulaar'en come to terms with the potentially threatening and dangerous nature of the endeavours of the men-of-skill.

Men-of-skill are regarded as being different in essence or kind rather than in degree, and their lines of ancestry or pedigrees bear witness to that notion. I have argued elsewhere (Dilley 2000) that this notion is at the root of indigenous constructions of 'caste'. What to us as analysts from the outside might look like specialised occupational groups set within a division of labour is from a local perspective more like an array of separate categories of essentially different sorts of people – indeed different 'races'.[38] It is often argued by craftsmen that a person wholly unrelated to a category of occupational specialists would be driven mad by the knowledge and potency of the lore necessary to practise the trade. Exclusive occupational lore is thus intimately linked to the constitution of the social person as different in type or kind.

The lines of ancestry or pedigrees reflect less historical veracities regarding origins and a location in time, but instead point to a series of cultural criteria. I have argued that, on the one hand, they embody local conceptions of essential differences between social categories, conceived as something akin to distinct 'races', breeds or stocks. On the other, they demarcate a social division of knowledge or lore, and of powers and potencies. Hence these lines trace an indigenous theory of power and potency, delimiting the cultural conception of occupational specialisation and of metaphysical difference.

HISTORY AND HIERARCHY: A REPRISE

Occupational specialisation by 'caste'-like social groups pre-dates the Almaamate revolution of the 1770s, and it is likely that this regime changed little the terms of the general social organisation of specialisation. Gellner (1981) states that Muslim societies have a specialist-spurning ethos which, he argues, accounts for the marginalisation of specific occupational groups, but it would seem that the cultural differentiation and social separation of the men-of-skill pre-dates the widespread introduction of Islam in areas of West Africa other than Fuuta Toro. The history of Fuuta is complex in that Islam has a long history in the valley, dating back to the turn of the first millennium, and it is difficult if not impossible to talk of a pristine pre-Islamic context. It is also difficult to be certain about the forms and motivations of the cultural and ideological distinctions in earlier historical periods when an analysis is *faut de mieux* based on limited literary and oral sources. However, it would seem that the morphology of cultural difference reported in the early literature is similar to that noted more recently, and one might suspect that ideological motivations for those differences might be not that dissimilar to those investigated in more contemporary Haalpulaar society. I offer the suggestion that the forms of cultural separation analysed above that are based on the idea of different sources of knowledge-power and different social origins for the various men-of-skill categories are long-established distinctions. Trimingham (1959) suggested many years ago that such craftsmen and artisan groups represent repositories of pre-Islamic knowledge. While this might be a difficult claim to sustain in one sense, the issue leads on to the focus of invesitgation in the next chapter.

If it is difficult to excavate the ideological constructions and processes of legitimation within earlier historical periods on which there are limited sources, then the problem is magnified with respect to a subordinate rank of people whose histories have been submerged for one reason or another. The task becomes less a matter of 'archaeology' and more one of 'genealogy', in Foucault's terms, which acknowledges the processes of power in the inscription of the past. The inscriptions left to us within the local archive speak not only of a past and the historical origins of social groups, but also of the genealogies of power and the social division of knowledge among ranks and categories. That the histories of the men-of-skill are submerged points to processes of domination by various groups at different periods in history.

The literature on the sahel belt of West Africa refers to the 'scorned and despised' craftsmen, but the scorn and derision that the men-of-skill attract is only part of a complex set of social and cultural evaluations. It is part of the discourse of cultural difference that also includes ideas that craftsmen are also respected for the skills they possess and they can be admired for their masterly use of language in song and poetry. Indeed, they may be held in a sense of awe by other Haalpulaar'en, who are at once admiring, fearful, amazed, curious and scornful of what they see and of what they do not quite understand. Yet, if the negative evaluations are part of a discourse of difference whose aim it is to separate, so too can those aspects which are considered to be more positive. The exceptional qualities and skills possessed by men of skill are respected and held to be seemingly magical so that they speak of knowledge and powers which freemen do not necessarily possess.

One way in which this complex social and cultural organisation has been captured is through the concept of a 'tangled hierarchy'. The idea of a tangled hierarchy (*hiérarchie enchevêtrée*), or rather hierarchies, which comes from Wane's 1969 work, is useful here.[39] He deploys the concept as a means of talking about the complex relationships between the three social ranks (1969: 74). I adopt and adapt this term to express the concern, shared by many Haalpulaar'en alike, that there are different sets of principles that are used by local informants to order the different social ranks or categories. There is no single, neat, unambiguous system that encompasses all ranks and categories – as is claimed by some advocates of 'caste' systems – for they have developed across time. Instead, what I have examined in the last two chapters are four sets of ideas that each appear to contribute in different ways to the rank ordering of social categories. The first of these concerns the area of economic independence and dependency, for all of the freemen categories either control material resources for primary production (land-holding families) or are active primary producers of subsistence items (fishermen). The second relates to the possession of political office and authority in the villages of Fuuta Tooro, which is held almost exclusively by freemen. The third has to do with the control of religious offices within Islam (such as imam, marabout, etc.), which is almost exclusively in the hands of the *toorobe*. If it were on these three criteria alone, there would perhaps be little cause for debate or discussion – local as well as academic – about issues such as whether or not the Fishermen are of the freeborn rank. However, the fourth issue introduces a complicating element and it is also linked to the third: the exclusion of particular categories of people from religious office in Islam. It concerns different bodies of lore or knowledge and power, the sources from which they are derived, and how these sources are represented in terms of mythical and historical origins of particular social categories. The organisation of social groups and categories is then related to how these diverse sources of knowledge and power are conceived, and to the manner in which they are viewed as competing for local ascendency. The distinctions between culturally defined realms of power and knowledge provide the basis of one type of organisation, and they form the outline of another hierarchy, which is ideological and hegemonic. This is a form of social exclusion that is based on the principle of lore, and it contrasts with the principle of exclusion of those in bondage, which was governed by the rule of Islamic law.

THE FETISHISATION OF PRODUCTION

Mary Helms, in her book *Craft and the Kingly Ideal*, discusses the connection between the control of craft production and of long-distance trade with the development of political authority of elite groups. Both trade and craft industries are the means of 'creating or acquiring the tangible objects that embody intangible powers', she asserts (1993), and they confer honour and prestige upon their possessors. If this was the case in Fuuta Toro, then part of the process leading to the control of craft production also involved the devaluation of those persons who produced the embodiments of power and authority, namely craft objects. However, the situation in Fuuta does differ in some important respects from the general picture painted by Helms. In particular, the crucial element in craft products is not the powers and energies from the cosmological gods or heroes that objects embody, as Helms claims, for these are dangerous forces that many local Muslim consumers wished to distance themselves from. They laid claim instead to other forms of power and knowledge that lent support to their authority, and they did not want to be associated with those connected with craft production. It is not objects that are fetishised – to use a term coined by Marx – but it is production itself that is the object of a vivid cultural imagination and set of symbolic elaborations. This process could be called the 'fetishisation of production'.

C. Lévi-Strauss pointed out in 'The Bear and the Barber' (1963)[40] that caste groups resemble animal species in that their members conceive of themselves as different in kind and marry endogamously. However, they are related to the rest of society through the exchange of goods and services in a division of labour that offers a range of specialist products. From the last chapter it was possible to see how the division of labour is organised to produce the kind of social exchange that Lévi-Strauss indicated. However, social exchange between the freeborn and men-of-skill was conceived by the former as a form of begging, whereby patrons were solicited by clients or 'scroungers' (*nyaagotooɓe*) into parting with rewards for goods and services rendered in a patron–client system of deferred exchange (see also Dilley 1986b). This form of exchange was viewed as a social burden by the freeborn. Men-of-skill, it seems, conceived of the social totality more in terms of an equal exchange that had been morally perverted over time. However, what I want to point out here is that it is not *exchange* but *production* itself that is represented locally as the dominant metaphor of social organisation. It is the *production* of goods and services that is culturally embellished to a greater extent than economic exchange as the local image of the configuration of social ranks and categories. The freeborn are primary producers; the craftsmen and musicians are secondary producers.

Production seems to be regarded among Haalpulaar'en as the key social and cultural event, for it is subject to what Marx called 'fetishisation', a form of cultural imagination that endows processes and things with agency, or a life of their own. I have used the phrase 'mode of accountability' elsewhere (Dilley 1992) to describe the means by which human, social, material or spiritual agents are held accountable for the processes of exchange or production in particular societies. In this ethnographic case the processes of *production* appear to be held culturally accountable, that are fully elaborated symbolically; for Haalpulaar social organisation is an organisation of productive relations, a division of production and producers, each with their own form of lore and knowledge and their own domain of power and potency. However, it is not all forms of production that are fetishised. While craft production, fishing and the arts of warriorhood may be embellished symbolically, the processes of agriculture do not seem to be subject to a similar treatment. Agriculture is an activity open to everyone, and there is no social-category-specific body of lore or knowledge required to practise it. It is also highly regarded as an occupation. The processes of agriculture may in our terms transform plant life into potentially edible foodstuffs, but in local conceptions cultivation does not seem to have the same connotation of magical transformation that crafts have.

The fetishisation of craft and other forms of production can be viewed from three different aspects: raw materials, technology and relations of production. The raw materials that men-of-skill manipulate are by and large the dwelling places of dangerous forces, whether it be trees, clay, soil from termite mounds and so on. The purpose of the craft occupations is to render raw materials taken from the bush into socially useful objects that are disenchanted by the hand of the producer and subsequently introduced into the human community. Second, the processes of production and even the technology itself are 'enchanted' (Gell 1992). These are not merely technical or practical procedures but are endowed with an agency of their own, such that for example the loom itself is regarded by weavers as the nocturnal playground of spirits. The third aspect of fetishisation is the enchantment of the relations of production, and this concerns the social relations between producers. These relations, like those between craftsman and raw material or the technological process, are the subject of a wide range of incantations and 'magical' prescriptions that can be used to affect adversely fellow craftsmen. These powers to affect one's rivals in trade are extended and generalised to relations with people from the wider community.

The fetishisation of production rather than exchange, the metaphorical embellishment of the former over the latter, might be linked to the fact that a merchant class never really developed from within the Haalpulaar society of Fuuta Toro. This function was usually carried out by foreign traders called 'Julanke', although further to the east in present-day in Mali it is reported that the *jaawambe* took on this role (Schmitz 1986: 354). It was also in the interests of craft specialists who would want to protect an exclusive area of economic activity, as well as in the interests of those who wanted to distance themselves from such activities, that production of certain types be fetishised and cultural identities made essentially different, different in kind not in degree.

One final aspect of symbolic embellishment that must not go without mention relates to the Praise-singers and Musicians. Whereas the raw materials of the manual occupations are rendered neutral in the form of crafted objects through the enchanted processes of production, the objects fashioned by musicians and singers are different. Word and song become powerful and potent in the charge of these specialists. They take mundane sounds and render them into a form of enchanted objects, *objets-paroles* and 'power-objects' such that the sounds and words they produce carry a potency in themselves.[41]

Mary Helms argues (1993) that it is objects themselves which embody or carry powers and energies and potent charges, for they are a means of bestowing authority, honours and social position upon their possessors:

> ... naturally endowed or skillfully crafted things acquired from outside ... and things crafted by society's own artisans are believed to be not mere representations but actual encapsulations or embodiments of cosmological power. These encapsulations and embodiments can then be put to use either to enhance social order within or to energize the expansion of social-political order outward. (1993: 215)

In the Haalpulaar case, something different appears to have developed: apart from the example of musicians and singers, it is not the products of production that are fetishised, but instead the very processes of production. It is technologies and productive techniques that are enchanted, that are regarded with a sense of awe, the product of power-practices, and the embodiments of cosmological power. The objects of craft production are rendered neutral by productive techniques, they are left 'uncharged', without potency. Indeed, one might observe that the cosmological powers represented by craftsmen are consciously marginalised by those who are the patrons for their products, namely the freeborn. A distance is created, therefore, between those who established authority within a Muslim social-political order and those who represented threatening and dangerous forms of cosmological powers. In a plural cultural system, it would seem that it is *contestation* between those struggling to control different sources of cultural knowledge and power that is the key to the dynamics of social and historical processes.

The social reproduction of social categories and castes is supported by a number of means, one of which is the fetishisation of productive processes that each category specialises in. A consequence of this is to emphasise the exclusiveness of each category in terms of production. There are other factors too that compound this sense of exclusivity: endogamous marriages strategies of social category members, certainly at the level of the men-of-skill rank as a whole, but also evident with respect to individual social categories; the modes of training and the transmission of knowledge – public or esoteric – related to each craft and occupation; the conceptualisation of cultural difference between members of categories and of members of social ranks in essentialist terms. As we will see, the very category of *toorobe* clerics takes on the colouring of a 'caste' when viewed from the perspective of these criteria.

4

THE WHITE AND THE BLACK: IDEOLOGY AND THE RISE TO DOMINANCE OF THE ISLAMIC CLERICS

I have argued that craftsmen and musician groups are to be considered as separate from the rest of the community by virtue of their contact and association with spiritual forces that emanate from the wild. Indeed, this separation seems to pre-date the Almaamate cleric uprising in the late eighteenth century. It is difficult to say with any certainty what, in earlier historical periods, the precise ideological reasons were for this separation, but I have tentatively suggested that historical and contemporary ethnography may afford some clues. I turn now to consider the extent to which Islam, especially the Islamic revival of the late eighteenth century and then the reformist movement of the mid-nineteenth century, set in train new ideological currents. These currents are still detectable today within local debates about what should and should not constitute proper Islamic practice, and who should or should not be included within the Islamic community. The first task to be pursued here is to trace a brief history of the introduction of Islam in the Senegal river valley, and this will lead on to a discussion of the formation of the *toorobe* Islamic cleric category in the eighteenth century, culminating in the Almaamate uprising in the 1770s. I will go on to argue that this Muslim uprising involved an attempt at ideological domination by the Islamic clerics, who at the same time were claiming a good measure of political authority and economic power.[1] This discussion will subsequently form the framework in which to investigate claims made by numerous analysts that craftsmen and musicians, although nominally Muslim, 'are in fact pagans' (Trimingham 1959: 137) and that their hereditary craft lore is a repository of pre-Islamic thought and practice (Trimingham 1959: 102, fn). What I suggest below is that given the historical depth to the presence of Islam within the valley, it is difficult to talk of a 'pre-Islamic' period neatly isolated from an era of Muslim belief. Instead, there have been waves of Islamic reformers and proselytisers who have each brought different interpretations to bear on local religious practices. It is also difficult to isolate one social group that may have remained immune to the effects of the faith within the region. Craft traditions, if they do indeed draw on non-Islamic customs or 'traditional local religious practices',[2] must have been nonetheless formed with reference to Islamic notions that had taken root very early on in the river valley. The bodies of lore and occupational knowledge of the men-of-skill and those of the Islamic clerics have been mutually constituted through time, I will argue. Each one lies in a relationship of dialogue with the other, and over time they form a historically evolving cultural conversation, the voices of which are still audible today. If there is a dualism to be detected in Haalpulaar cultural thought, it is not necessarily the result of the survival of cultural forms or the processes of historical contingency. Instead, it has as much if not more to do with the politics of cultural distinction, the outcome of the activities of social actors in their bid for power and authority within a specific locality.

Rather than perceiving two stable traditions, one Islamic and the other pre-Islamic or local, that exist in a kind of dualism or parallelism, I would want to regard the waves of Islamic development as being in dialogue with craft lore and knowledge. While these latter forms of lore and knowledge are closely related to spirits of nature and of the locality, they are nonetheless accommodated within an Islamic cosmology. Although it might be analytically problematic to locate the sources and forms of a pristine pre-Islamic tradition, it does not mean to say that local Muslims do not make distinctions between forms of belief and practice they do and do not find commendable. Indeed, they often do so in terms that invoke the notions of a pre- or non-Islamic tradition and of a proper Islamic tradition.[3] In this respect, external analytical interests and internal exegetical concerns overlap, but not for the same reasons, nor do their forms necessarily coincide. What I am concerned with is the way in which local exegeses constitute part of an important dynamic in the lives that people create for themselves, and the interpretations they make of social relations over the course of the last 200 years or so. The analytical examination of Islamic thought and practice in terms of a 'pure' or 'parent type' of religion is not the focus of this investigation. Instead, the analysis pays regard to how local interpreters view their own and other's beliefs and practices, and what distinctions they make among them. Where do they draw the line between acceptable and non-acceptable belief and practice? In what terms or idioms do they represent such distinctions?

A BRIEF HISTORY OF ISLAM IN THE SENEGAL RIVER VALLEY

One of the earliest reports of Islam in the Western Sudan comes from Ibn Abi Zar', who states that one of the groups living in the neighbourhood of Adrar, to the north of Fuuta Toro, was converted to the faith by an Arab general, 'Uqba b. Nafi, who led his troops in the name of the religion into the furthest west of the Maghrib around 663 CE (Levtzion 1978). By 985 Al-Muhallabi wrote that he considered the whole of the western sahel region south of the Sahara as *Dar al-Islam*, a land over which Muslims have control (Levtzion 1978). More specific to the Senegal river valley, Al-Bakri gave the following details in 1068 about the kingdom of Takrur that was established perhaps 100 or so years earlier. Al Bakri wrote:

> The people of Takrur are black, who were previously, like all the other Sudan, idolaters and worshipped [idols] ... until War Jabi b. Rabis became their ruler. He embraced Islam, introduced among them the Muslim religious law and compelled them to observe it ... War Jabi died in 432/1040–1 and the people of Takrur are Muslims today. (Quoted in Levtzion 1979: 675)

He went on to observe that the king's treasurers, ministers and interpreters were all chosen from among the Muslims (Cuoq 1975: 99). It would appear from Al-Bakri's account, then, that Islam was well implanted at least in the Takrur court by the middle of the eleventh century.[4] Under the rule of War Jabi, the state of Takrur became a champion of Islam during the eleventh century, and it was thus assured a notoriety at the hands of Arabic scholars who carried the name forward as a symbol of the faith in West Africa.[5] The Almoravid movement of the late eleventh century brought about an Islamic renewal to the area, and after their forces had overrun the neighbouring empire of Ghana, Takrur reached its apogee as a regional power (see Levtzion 1977, 1978, 1979). Al-Idrissi in the twelfth century noted that there was not in all of Takrur one town where Islam had not penetrated (Cuoq 1975: 16). He also pointed out that the inhabitants of the kingdom raided neighbouring districts and returned with captives, adding that the 'Sultan of Takrur' had many slaves and that there was a flourishing slave trade (Cuoq 1975: 129–30).[6]

References to the inhabitants of the Senegal valley tail off in the later writings of Arab chroniclers and travellers, for their attention was attracted to the cultural and political developments further east. In particular, they attended to the rise of the empire of Mali, which grew in stature and influence from the thirteenth century onwards. Takrur came under the influence of the Mali Empire and it was not until around 1520 that it once more gained its independence, now under Koli Tengella and his Fulɓe pastoralists who installed themselves on the north bank of the river. This period is associated in the eyes of some commentators with a decline in the standing and influence of Islam in the valley for the next 250 years or so (Monteil 1980: 104), although there were notable Muslim Deniyaŋke rulers.[7] The Deniyaŋke dynasty, founded by Koli Tengella and succeeded by his sons and grandsons, developed a court tradition of Islam; however, in the eyes of eighteenth-century clerics it had not abandoned other religious observances. The local Muslim faithful claimed it had become increasingly difficult for them to practise their religion openly and their militancy was at a low ebb.

One event held to be significant for the later development of the Almaamate regime occurred around 1673, when Nasir al Din, a reformist marabout, started a jihad. He invaded Fuuta Toro and the Wolof states to the west, he sent emissaries to the Satigi, the Deniyaŋke ruler, urging him to change his way of life and observe the precepts of Islam. The invitation was refused and, according to the law of jihad, emissaries were sent a second and a third time, after which Nasir entered Fuuta and sought to rally the Muslim populations against the Satigi. Although he made great strides forward in revitalising the faith, and even managed to draw non-Muslim Fulɓe into the religion, he was ultimately unsuccessful in his attempt to replace the old regime. He died in battle in 1674, but the effect of his campaign was to give a vision for future generations of what might have been possible as a realisation of cleric political aspirations. Nasir al Din also led indigenous Berbers inhabiting the territories to the north of the Senegal river against the recently arrived Arab overlords in what became known as Shurr Bubba or the war of Bubba in 1674. Stewart reports that this event 'has taken on the importance of a foundation myth in the Moors' conception of the origins and functions of social classes in their society' (1973: 16). Al Din lost the battle and afterwards his fellow campaigners for a renewed form of Islam established *zawaaya*, clerical groupings and settlements, in opposition to the Hassani-descended Arabs. On the south bank of the river, this event was taken as a signature moment which was to be used as a model for the later uprisings elsewhere. Numerous commentators have argued that direct links from the eighteenth-century Futanke uprisings can be made back to Shurr Bubba.[8]

The political system in Fuuta Toro continued to fragment over the course of the next hundred years, to the extent that the region was divided between two competing rulers or Satigis, one at Geede supported by Moors from the north bank, and the other at Silla where the Deniyaŋke Fulɓe had first settled. In addition, the influence of French commercial traffic along the river increased and this caused tensions among local groups for control of trade. Indeed, the internal political rivalries were in part sparked by a double demand for slaves by the Moors involved in the Saharan trade to the north, and by Europeans involved in the Atlantic trade to the west. Another factor was Moorish interest in maintaining their grip on the gum arabic trade. The Haalpulaar population had also retreated to the south bank (*fergo* or 'flight' from the north bank) by the end of the eighteenth century, leaving the river as a natural barrier between themselves and the marauding Moors to the north (see Schmitz 1986, 1990, 1994). The year 1760 saw the arrival of Suleyman Baal, a Futanke cleric and Muslim reformist, who was determined to restore political unity to Fuuta Toro and to put an end to Moorish dominance and aggression. He picked up the threads of a Muslim revival started by Nasir almost one hundred years earlier and, under his direction, local Muslims turned against their Deniyaŋke rulers, overthrew the Fulɓe regime and established something close to a theocratic state. Baal was killed in battle with the Moors around 1776, and he helped establish a new politico-religious system in which he himself, however, took no part. The Muslim followers of Baal elected an imam or Almaamy as leader, the first being Abd al-Qadir b. Hammadi (Abdul Qadir Kan) in 1775 or 1776. The mood in Fuuta changed, shifting from military engagement and feats of arms initiated by Baal to a period in which mosques and Qur'anic schools were set up in most villages on the south bank. The new political system was not a strict theocracy but a religious oligarchy. Following victory, the Almaamy confiscated land from many of the former local rulers who had not converted to Islam and distributed it among the leaders of the *tooroɓe*, the social category of Islamic clerics.[9]

The conception of Islam that was spread throughout the valley in the eighteenth century was most likely highly influenced by the Sufi Qadiriyya order, and it is reasonable to assume that Abdul Qadir Kan, the first Almaamy, was affiliated to the brotherhood (Clark and Colvin Phillips 1994: 224).[10] Moorish scholars from the north, affiliated with the Qadiriyya appear to have had long-standing relations with Fuuta Toro Muslims (Stewart 1973), to the extent that even by the mid-nineteenth century 'the principal Islamic teachers and spokesmen still came from Mauritania and belonged to the Qadiri branch of Islam' (Robinson 1975a: 105). Robinson (1985) adds that the Wans of Mbumba dominated a coalition in Fuuta that was allied to a Qadiri scholar from the north bank, and that by the mid-1880s 'some Futanke belonged to Tijaniyya cells, but they were few in number' (1985: 123).

The changes that took place in the nineteenth century can be linked to a *tooroɗo* cleric and military leader, Al-Hajj Umar Taal, who introduced the Tijaniyya order into the western Sudan (Abun-Nasr 1965). The introduction of this brotherhood in the mid-nineteenth century stressed a strict and exclusive allegiance to that order alone, and so the nature of the relationship of belonging to a brotherhood changed. This was to create tensions and rivalries between the two brotherhoods. Taal's crusading mission to bring a reformed Tijani faith to local Muslims had a significant impact too on social relations between men-of-skill and the social category of Muslim clerics. For the present, I will focus on the early period of the establishment of Islam as the basis of a theocratic oligarchy and as the religion of a group that strove for social, political and cultural dominance. These issues bring us to the question of the historical formation of the *tooroɓe* as a social category.

FORMATION OF THE *TOOROBE* SOCIAL CATEGORY

The first mention of the *tooroɓe* as a socially significant group in Fuuta Toro suggests that they were something akin to a political movement seeking to establish a greater public acceptance of the faith.[11] They also sought to replace what they saw as the decadence (*fasad*) of the Fulɓe Deniyaŋke regime (Schmitz 1998: 66). It is clear that these early clerics were drawn from all levels of society, and they constituted a learned class of scholars whose main criteria of membership was mastery of Islamic learning and Arabic literacy, although the latter qualification seems to have been variable. Willis suggests that the *tooroɓe* clerisy rose from a 'mass of rootless people' (1978: 196) composed largely of 'slaves or the descendents of slaves' (1979: 2). Perhaps overstated, his general point is nonetheless important. *Tooroɓe* clerics rose from all ranks of Haalpulaar society, from the categories of the freeborn as well as from those of men-of-skill status and even from the descendants of slaves. It appears that those who acquired Islamic learning, who resided in towns and villages (rather than cattle camps) and refused to engage in occupations looked down upon as degrading came to be classified as *tooroɓe* (Willis 1979). One source of these ideas was the indigenous writer Shaykh Musa Kamara, who went on to argue that 'The turudiyya is a profession not a descent grouping' (Hilliard 1997: 184).[12] The despised occupations were primarily men-of-skill crafts and pastoralism. Kamara gives us evidence of the spirit of equality of opportunity for those who gave up these despised professions when he reports that in the mid-eighteenth century, among the cohorts of clerics from Fuuta studying at the Qur'anic centre at Pir in Kayor, along with the person who was to become the first Almaamy, Abdul Qadir Kan, were two scholars of the Weavers social category from Nioro (Kamara 1998: 314). The Muslim clerisy prior to the Almaamate uprising was, therefore, an open social group which, over the course of the establishment of the new political order, became closed to new recruitment.

That this social category did not remain open is well documented, but the reasons for its closure are not absolutely clear. Robinson observes 'in keeping with the interests of a ruling class, access to *toorodBe* [sic] status was now closed to all save a handful of noble Fulbe and foreign clerics' (Robinson 1975b: 26). Not only did the social category become closed to new members, but it increasingly came to resemble one of the men-of-skill 'castes' with a specialist metier, whose 'craft' became the practice of Islam, from which they gained a livelihood as marabouts, Islamic healers and Muslim diviners.[13] Moreover, they concocted spurious pedigrees which suggested that their origins could be traced to Arab or Berber Muslims who came from the north to marry into the local populations of the river valley. Robinson sums up this desire for new pedigrees: 'The genealogical firmament became dense with Muslim Arab stars' (1985: 85). One family I had researched during fieldwork, for example, claimed an ancestor over fourteen generations back to have originated in a town in present-day Iraq, and that their present patronym is a deformation and contraction of his name, Ali Ajhuriu.[14] He was also claimed variously as either a direct descendent of Mohammed or of one of the companions to the Prophet. The indigenous scholar Shaykh Musa Kamara set out to inspect the contradictions in *toorobe* claims about their origins. Schmitz describes Kamara's writings as having the goal of using genealogy as an instrument of deconstruction, whereby he could reveal the strategies by which the newly elevated clerics differentiated themselves socially and culturally from the rest of the population (Schmitz 1998: 56).[15] Over the course of generations, they denied their ties of kinship with and descent from their now distantly related status inferiors.

Schmitz adds to the idea of the clerics resembling a men-of-skill social category, for the movement hinged on the acquisition of a body of specialist, and at times esoteric, knowledge – namely the Islamic sciences and Qur'anic study. Moreover, religious conversion itself appeared to rest as much upon the acquisition of such knowledge as upon anything else (Schmitz 1986). To be converted to Islam was a matter of laying hold of a body of knowledge, conceived now as akin to the specialist bodies of occupational lore of the artisan groups. The *toorobe* emerged at the end of the eighteenth century as a status group unified around the idea of conversion to Islam and apprenticeship in Qur'anic studies. To become a cleric, there was a series of steps, the first of which was the adoption of Pulaar as a *lingua franca* rather than Wolof or any other neighbouring tongue, and this was followed by religious conversion. Pulaar or Fulfulde was held to be a language blessed by the Prophet and was second only in value to Arabic, the language of the Qur'an (Brenner 1983a; Brenner and Last 1985; Robinson 1985: 82). Settled Fulbe herders, warriors who had previously shown little piety, as well as Wolof and Soninke speakers, all seem to have adopted in large numbers Haalpulaar cleric status. Many of them changed their patronyms on conversion and on their adoption of the new social status. Connected to the issue of cleric knowledge is the network of pedagogical relations that sprang up around local Qur'anic schools and centres of advanced Islamic learning, such as that at the village of Pir to the south-west of Fuuta. These pedagogical networks stretched across the region, and formed circles of study which helped consolidate the sense of exclusiveness among clerics. Moreover, alliances were created between favoured, gifted pupils and a marabout, who would give a daughter in marriage to his disciple. These affinal connections came to denote lines of spiritual kinship and the inheritance of *baraka*, a form of spiritual grace, and they stood in opposition to those of blood and kin descent (see Schmitz 2000a).

A third important feature (after those of pedigree and knowledge) that characterised the shift in the nature of the new cleric status into a caste-like category was that it became increasingly endogamous. Schmitz has analysed the matrimonial strategies of the leading cleric families and argues that they created 'circles of affinity' (*cercles d'affinité*) that linked together the emerging influential households in a strategic move aimed to consolidate their grip on power and political office in Fuuta Toro (Schmitz 2000a). Complex relations of alliance were forged between those families that were eligible for the office of Almaamy and those who were the electors of the eligibles to the office. The marriage of women, the exchange of bridewealth and the redistribution of wealth and prestations associated with the election of a new Almaamy were tied together through a tightly knitted skein of relations. This resulted in the *toorobe* clerics constituting a *vaste matrimonium*, and thus the social category turned in upon itself (Schmitz 1985). The clerics consolidated their political position and their social status through endogamous marriage practices that made them resemble even more a caste-like group. What started as a social movement open to all became increasingly exclusive as it attempted to acquire more of the trappings of power and to assert its authority. No longer open simply to those versed in Qur'anic learning and Arabic literacy, membership hinged on the control over a body of knowledge linked to Islam and on supposed lines of ancestry. These putative lines of descent took on an essentialist quality, reinforced now by endogamous marriage practices. The result was that the clerics came to represent themselves, in a way comparable with the men-of-skill, as people different in type and not just degree from others.

Not only was the adoption of Islam a prerequisite to membership of the *toorobe* in the early stages of its development, but members also had to abandon disdained trades and occupations such as cattle-herding, craftwork and praise-singing. Shaykh Musa Kamara specified that aspiring *toorobe* clerics had to avoid the vocations of fishing, metal working, weaving, tannery and praise-singing, adding also that 'they not be bedouins' (Hilliard 1997: 184). The conditions attached to *toorobe* membership in the early years were, then, the acquisition of Islamic learning and sciences, and that the aspirant must not practise any 'vile occupation' as detailed above (Kamara, in Samb 1970). An expression from the *Hadith* was used against herders in a bid to initiate a change of lifestyle among them: 'Those who are made to follow the tails of cattle are lowly' (Kamara, quoted in Hilliard 1997: 181). This evaluation by the clerics of the pastoralist lifestyle comprised one part of a developing discourse of identity and cultural characterisation by both parties within an increasingly tense political context.[16]

Numerous men-of-skill managed in the early stages the transition to *toorobe* status, for it appears that many did not change their characteristic patronyms on adopting their new social status.[17] While most warriors or most herders appear to have changed their names on their adoption of *toorobe* Islam, this was not the case among 'casted' families.[18] Kyburz argues that for men-of-skill the adoption of Islam and accession to *toorobe* status took on a liberating character that was implied by Islam's conception of the egality of believers before God. For others of higher social status, by contrast, it was not simply a matter of adopting a new religion, but also of retaining a hold on power and political office. In this context, he claims, these families, especially Fulɓe ones, found it necessary to mark a break with the old order and change patronyms (Kyburz 1994: 160). Kyburz also plots the distribution of patronyms across Haalpulaar social categories and illustrates the extent to which craftsmen and others became assimilated into the cleric category in the course of the eighteenth century. While one cannot be certain that all those tooroɓe who carry men-of-skill patronyms were originally members of that rank, he concludes that there is good reason to claim that some of the present-day cleric families originated among the men-of-skill (*artisans castés*) (Kyburz 1994: 150–60). The commonality of patronyms between *tooroɓe* and men-of-skill is not an absolute seal on the argument in every case, for other factors might have come into play, but it is evidence that mobility did exist at least temporarily in the past. One distinctive men-of-skill patronym that appears among the ranks of the clerics is Caam, or alternatively Thiam or Tyam in French orthography. This name is characteristic of the Smiths, and practising metalworkers today will frequently claim these cleric brethren as part of the same line of descent.[19] Today, these clerics hold the office of village or territory chief in five villages in Fuuta Toro (Schmitz 1994). We will see in the next section below that they were significant players in Al-Hajj Umar Taal's proselytising and military mission.

The nature of the *tooroɓe* Islamic cleric social status changed radically in the course of the eighteenth century in line with the political developments of the Almaamate regime. The processes of legitimation of *tooroɓe* status shifted from learning in the Islamic sciences and the Qur'an, as well as the avoidance of the disdained trades and crafts, to a claim resting upon belonging to particular lines of putative descent that were linked by restrictive marriage practices. The result of these shifts bolstered the clerics' sense of social superiority, their caste-like exclusiveness and the conceptions of themselves as being set apart almost as a different species. Along with these developments was another strategy that was aimed at ideological domination. While the *tooroɓe* clerics attempted to gain political ascendancy, which extended to a monopoly over the centralised office of Almaamy, at the local level their political and territorial domination was only patchy. The move towards ideological hegemony was a further attempt, it might be suggested, to extend their reach and provide a legitimate basis for their authority. This was achieved by the exclusion of members of certain ranks and categories from religious office within Islam, in particular the Fishermen, men-of-skill and slaves.[20] This exclusion was not particular to the Haalpulaar'en alone, for it is reported that craftsmen and slaves were similarly excluded from Islamic office in Timbuktu, a centre of the Kunta Qadiriyya.[21]

A basic contradiction emerges between the perceived aims of the Almaamate revolution and the eventual outcome of it. For while the Islamic clerisy established a 'society open to all individuals prepared to embrace their customs and beliefs' (Willis 1978: 199), this essentially egalitarian ethos was not to be sustained throughout the progressive shift in power and authority away from the Deniyaŋke Fulɓe and towards the *tooroɓe* clerics. While adherence to the religion of Islam became the touchstone and hallmark of those who claimed superior status, the members of social categories that did not whole-heartedly subscribe to the beliefs of this new movement were denigrated and reduced further in the eyes of the faithful. Indeed, the paradox is that among the ranks of this newly-elevated social elite were members of social categories whose forebears had been practising the very occupations now being condemned with renewed vigour by the dominant religion. That a monotheistic religion which stresses equality between believers should have brought about a redefinition of a rigidly hierarchical society in terms of social, political and religious privileges might also appear somewhat paradoxical. It also supplied an ideology which contributed to the evaluation of certain groups as culturally inferior.

Gellner makes a similar point in *Muslim Society*, where he examines a contradiction or 'tension' between a 'great tradition' – egalitarian and scholarly, a 'pure' variant of Islam – and a 'folk tradition' that is hierarchical and ecstatic. Distinctions and inequalities observed in Muslim societies, he argues, come about from a translation of the egalitarian ideal into social reality with the organisation of political, religious and economic control (Gellner 1981). My point is that this process of cultural translation is a continuing one, and the outcome of it has taken different forms at various historical moments. For example, a reported incident involving Shaykhu Ahmadu, the leader of the theocratic state of Masina in the mid-nineteenth century, highlights the tension between 'caste' inequality and the ideal of equality among believers. Ahmadu's Muslim advisors, basing themselves on the Qur'anic verse which states that 'the true believers are brethren',[22] asked for the abolition of castes. The ruler responded by serving them a stew of frogs and lizards mixed with the usual fish, mutton and chicken.[23] He added that while the Holy book did not forbid it, it was repugnant to him to mix the freeborn and casted people (Monteil 1980: 381–2). The ideological justification for the continuance of the cultural separation of men-of-skill and the distinctions between 'castes' was based on the claim that although they were not advocated by Islam, neither were they forbidden by it.[24] This request for the equality of treatment among all believers, whether men-of-skill or freeborn, came at a time when the Tijani variant of Islam was in the ascendant, and this variant seems to have had a different perspective on the question of 'caste'. The Qadiriyya, a brotherhood closely associated with many of the earlier rulers, seems to have been an elite affiliation that perhaps found it difficult to entertain the acceptance of more lowly social members within the Muslim *jama'a*. I will return to this issue below. But now I want to turn to construction of the ideology by the *tooroɓe* clerics during the Almaamate regime.

THE CONSTRUCTION OF *TOOROBE* ISLAMIC IDEOLOGY

The ideological vision constructed by the *tooroɓe* clerics at one and the same time maintained 'caste' distinctions and forms of cultural separation, but yet attempted to embrace all social categories into a global conception of a social totality. This was in one sense an 'accommodationist' conception of Islam which, while it incorporated the men-of-skill in its overall cosmological purview, it also allocated them an inferior position within it. Part of that vision inhered in the definition of bodies of lore and knowledge, in particular a body of cleric lore similar to those of the men-of-skill. However, the lore and knowledge defined by the Islamic clerics was contrasted strongly with those of other groups. It was defined as *gandal diine*, 'religious lore', or as *gandal danewal*, literally 'white' lore, in contrast to *gandal ɓalewal*, the 'black' or occupational lore of the men-of-skill. Those dealing with black lore, which included the freeborn fishermen, were excluded from all consideration within the newly-prominent religious authorities: they could take no role as imam or as the leader of prayers, were ineligible to train in the Islamic sciences and could not succeed to the office of Almaamy.[25] While the *tooroɓe* conception of Islam appears to have been a force for liberation from old social statuses for many people prior to the Muslim uprising, it afterwards developed into a renewed force for the reassertion of social divisions and cultural distinctions. This accommodationist view of the position of men-of-skill within the Islamic community is the preponderant view still today, although as we will see it forms part of a dialogue with other visions of the *jama'a*. What was the foundation of this distinctive accommodationist conception of Islam?

Local Islamic cosmology includes a number of types of spirit being set within a hierarchy of spiritual powers: Allah is the all powerful omnipotent creator, followed by the angels or beings of pure light (*malaayka'en* or *rawhanaaje*).[26] Finally, there are the jinn and other spirits (*jinneeje* and *seyɗaneeje*) at the bottom of this spiritual hierarchy. Angels are the most powerful in the hierarchy of the inhabitants of the other world, although they rarely intervene in human affairs; they stand guard next to Allah and are his emissaries. Jinn comprise a large category of gendered beings more or less in accord with God. They can work as much for God's purposes as they can against them, for some jinn are converted to Islam while others are pagan.[27] This class of spirit is very influential in human affairs: they appear at certain times of the day – midday and dusk – and they are linked to natural features in the environment such as trees, water courses, termite mounds and so on. They can appear to travellers whom they meet in secluded spots and they can bring either good or bad fortune. They are thought to be the first inhabitants of the world and remain an integral part of it. A second category of spirits closely associated with the jinn is labelled *seyɗaneeje*, which corresponds to demons, deviants of the Islamic world, those who have rebelled against God; Eblis is their ancestor. The distinction between *jinneeje* and *seyɗaneeje* is not particularly clear in the minds of many Pulaar speakers, who often use the two words synonymously.[28] Rebel jinn may seek to turn people against Allah, just as demons might voluntarily oppose him. Both types of spirit are clearly devalued relative to the beings of light, and contact with them is dangerous and avoided by most people.[29] As we have seen earlier, men-of-skill are brought into close association in the course of their occupations with some of these forces, especially those associated with features of the environment, those who are thought to be unconverted. Last in this hierarchy of powers are humans who have to submit to the will of Allah and who must suffer the influences of good and bad jinn in their daily affairs.

The types of lore and knowledge (*gandal*) claimed by different social categories are thought to correspond to the different forms of spiritual being that are set within this hierarchy of powers. Knowledge is linked to spiritual agents that are believed to inspire and implant it in the minds of human beings. White lore was and still is, then, predominately the specialism of the socially superior and politically dominant Islamic clerics, whereas black lore is the specialism of the socially inferior men-of-skill, whose knowledge, sets of techniques and mystical prescriptions are considered to lay outside the mainstream, or even 'converted', religious forces of the cleric conception of Islam. It is a form of knowledge that draws on lesser spiritual sources and potencies, some of whom are unconverted and not necessarily considered to be wholly good.[30] These terms white and black bring to mind a distinction between Islamic and non-Islamic, or even pre-Islamic, forces. They are also used to denote the racial categories used by Arab writers to categorise the populations of the western Sudan into the white Moors and the black Sudanis.[31] The accommodationist conception of Islam brings these two traditions – the cleric and the men-of-skill (no matter what their actual origins) – and sets them in a hierarchy of powers. I have argued elsewhere that the relationship between the part and the whole of this set hinges on the idea of encompassment or synecdoche, whereby the superior value attached to the clerical Islam encompasses those traditions that are conceived locally as being opposed to it (Dilley 1987b).[32] Muslim men-of-skill, while part of the Islamic community, were devalued and indeed sometimes even represented as 'pre-Islamic' by the clerics.

Trimingham observed that 'Islam in its struggle to become the controlling agency in communal life condemns, not belief in, but worship of spirits' (1959: 103). Part of the struggle the *tooroɓe* clerics engaged in during the course of their rise to dominance was to create a rigid ideological distinction between white lore and black lore, between those versed in the Qur'an and Islamic sciences, on the one hand, and those involved in craft industries considered to be complicit in the worship of spirits.[33] This ideological manoeuvre was, nonetheless, Janus-faced: while it condemned those who dealt with 'black' spirits, at the same time it accommodated them within an Islamic cosmology.[34] My point is that although this distinction may be represented by clerics as absolute, it is an ideological division, a separating or dividing practice, that served a cultural and political purpose for a group aspiring to power and authority. As will become apparent below, this distinction becomes blurred when inspecting the practices of specialists in white and black lore respectively (see Chapter 7). I am not arguing that Sufi marabouts and mystics do not draw on the potencies of jinn in their practices; indeed there are examples of claims made by powerful clerics to have converted pagan spirits or to have incorporated jinn as significant 'teachers' into their chains of transmission of knowledge. To have argued this case would have been to make them unique within West African Islamic communities. While at the level of practice there is a degree of overlap in the way different specialist practitioners draw on a similar range of spirit powers, there also exists an ideological distinction propagated primarily by clerics who uphold the stark contrast between black and white forms of power and knowledge. Men-of-skill too might wish to sustain such a distinction in certain contexts as an exclusive claim to a body of specialist practice and thought.

THE MUSLIM REFORMISM OF AL-HAJJ UMAR TAAL

A development that began in the early to mid-nineteenth century, namely the Muslim reformist movement of Al-Hajj Umar Taal, has significance for the conception of these ideological divisions. Set up under the early *tooroɓe*-dominated *jama'a* that was inspired by the Qadiriyya, these ideological distinctions served the purpose of separating social categories as discrete domains of activity, each with its own specialist body of power and knowledge. While the early *tooroɓe* movement was open and accessible to all within the Muslim community, it later failed to sustain itself as a force for social elevation after the Almaamate uprising and the consolidation of an Islamic oligarchy. In a parallel manner, I will argue, the broadly-based Muslim community that crystallised around Taal's mission was ultimately no more successful than the eighteenth-century reformers.

Shaykh Umar Taal, a Muslim holy-man and warrior, is thought to have been born in Fuuta Toro between 1794 and 1797. The exact date of Taal's birth is debated in the literature, with some sources giving a date as early as 1794 or as late as 1797; but Robinson (1985) proposes 1796 as the year of his birth, arguing that this date has the most correlations across the sources. Umar's father, Eliman Saydu, 'was probably the leading Muslim in his village of Halwar' (Robinson 1985: 68), the village in which Umar was born. Eliman Saydu, born in Fuuta Toro in the mid-eighteenth century, was drawn into the *toorobe* revolution and acquired a greater prestige as a result, although the family appears to have enjoyed relatively modest economic circumstances (Willis 1970: 44). He married his eldest daughter to Lamin Sakho, a scholar and veteran of Muslim campaigns in Kayor, and gave another daughter to the Caam lineage of the nearby village of Njum (Ndioum). Saydu had only two wives: the first, Adama, was also a Taal from Halwar, indeed one of Saydu's patrilineal parallel cousins – a preferred form of marriage; the second wife was Yumma, a former slave said to have been a possession of Adama inherited from her father (Willis 1970). Adama gave him ten children, including Umar her seventh son and last child; Yumma gave him two children. There seems to be a good deal of evidence to suggest that Umar Taal was of freeborn ancestry, possibly of Fulbe origin initially and perhaps linked to Moorish Sanhaja Berbers in the opinion of some. Kamara gives a number of these multiple versions of the Taltalbe genealogy (see Samb 1970), although he complains that he has met no genealogical expert on the Taals of Halwar, adding that the family do exaggerate their claims (Samb 1970: 774).

Umar Taal grew up in Fuuta under the first Almaamy, Abdul Qadir Kan, in his natal village of Alwar or Halwar in the province of Toro – a province considered to be the cradle of the *toorobe* clerisy. His formative years as a Qur'anic scholar were spent in Fuuta Jallon in Guinée, Nigeria, Egypt and the Middle East. He was a well-travelled, learned Qur'anic scholar who was also highly trained in the Islamic sciences and esoteric arts. He struck up a marriage with the daughter of the Sokoto ruler, Muhammed Bello, and later married into a leading Muslim family in Borno. Although he started his religious life as a member of the Qadiri Sufi brotherhood, he later converted to the Tijaniyya, was declared a Khalifa of the order and regarded by his followers as a *wali*, 'a saint or friend of God' who possessed *baraka*, a blessing or beneficent force of divine origin. His mission was to proselytise the way of the Tijaniyya, which also involved a fight against religious mixing (*ikhtilât*), an ideological battle to reinstate a purified form of Islam. During the 1850s and 1860s he declared a series of jihads in the Western Sudan, one even against Masina, already a Muslim state from the beginning of the nineteenth century. He was eventually killed by troops from Masina while engaged in a campaign against this Muslim state. He died, or mysteriously disappeared according to his followers, in 1864 at the cliff of Degembere, the site of his last stand against a group of Masina Muslims who had been resisting his jihad.[35] Robinson described his movement as an 'imperial jihad', attempting to create an unbroken sweep of *toorobe* clerics from Fuuta Toro in the west to Masina in the east, a *Dar al-Islam*, a land conquered by Muslims (1985: 366–7).[36]

Within a short time, the Tijaniyya replaced the Qadiriyya order as the dominant *tariqa* in both Fuuta Toro and Fuuta Jallon (Klein 1968), and it stressed a strict exclusivism of allegiance (Cruise O'Brien 1988b). It later became an urban brotherhood characteristically, and it recruited widely among men-of-skill and those of servile status (Marone 1970). As Klein states, the 'Tijaniyya is more democratic in its conception of Islam ... though at the same time it is more puritanical' than other brotherhoods (Klein 1968: 65).³⁷ The roots of this openness and accessibility can be traced back to Umar Taal's early mission. The tensions and rivalries set up between Taal's efforts to impose a militarised Tijaniyya in areas of influence previously dominated by Qadiri Muslims, especially around Timbuktu by the Kunta clan, was to generate a particular dynamic among West African Muslims.³⁸

The status of members of 'marginal' social categories does seem to have been raised during Taal's mission, and this fact might be attributed in part to the possibility of rapid social mobility under conditions of warfare that existed during virtually all of his jihads. Certainly slaves given to Umar Taal on his return from Mecca became highly trained members of the early Tijani community and they often received important offices and assignments in Taal's new state established in the east.³⁹ The '*fergo* Umar', or the migration east of recruits from Fuuta Toro, in the mid-1800s drew people from all social ranks and categories and was staggering in its size. Estimates suggest that up to 20 per cent of the Fuuta population left to join Umar Taal's campaigns in a land untainted by European control and influence – a new 'Dar al-Islam'.⁴⁰ Until 1854, Taal recruited across the whole social spectrum and persons of humble origins might acquire positions of relative importance. As the campaigns progressed and as the reach of Taal's mission widened – for example, with the expansion of the war against Karta – Taal was forced to recruit extra men through local patronage structures, through village and regional leaders who needed reassurance that traditional social hierarchies would be respected (Robinson 1985: 344). This was an important signal, Robinson argues, in that 'the jihad would not overturn the social order', that the traditional cleavages of Fuuta Toro society should once again penetrate through the movement, through the conduct of the jihad and any successor states that might be established (Robinson 1985: 344–6). The cleric oligarchy in Fuuta resented the social elevation of persons from obscure social backgrounds such that by the late nineteenth century, the cleavages that opened up in Umar Taal's following in Segu, for example, were fuelled by issues of social status: 'the ideology of *talibe* [disciple] dedication and equality made matters worse' (Robinson 1985: 348).

Taal enlisted the services of a number of followers of modest social standing, one of whom was Mamadu Aliyu Caam (Mamadou or Mohammadou Aliou Tyam in French orthography), a man of craftsman origins bearing the patronym of a clan of smiths (Robinson 1985: 343). He joined Taal's campaign prior to the 1852 jihad, took part in all his military missions and became a militant activist in the movement. After the leader's death, Caam's fortunes were linked closely to Taal's son and successor, Ahmadu. Caam also wrote in Pulaar a hagiography, an account of Taal's mission, in which he describes himself modestly as just 'one of the bristles in the brush' with which Umar Taal swept through West Africa (Tyam 1935).[41] In Caam's view, social mobility became part of the mission of the Tijaniyya and, as Robinson notes, Caam gave the 'clearest expression of the *talibe* ideal and ideology of the jihad' (1985: 342).

Caam frequently called on people to sever ties to their mothers and fathers, ties to the society of their birth, to reject their home and attach themselves to the Shaykh and the promise of Paradise. The new Muslim community, the *jama'a*, that he envisaged took the form of a *fedde*, a term in Pulaar for age-set (Robinson 1985: 343). A *fedde* is a relatively egalitarian social form organised by boys prior to their initiation into manhood, a ritual that involves circumcision. The bonds formed among this group at this time in a young boy's life are particularly strong and supportive, and the memory of them remains vivid throughout his lifetime. In Taal's movement, Caam gained the position of *muqqadam*, a leader who authorises the recitation of prayers within a Sufi order. The Tijani *wird* or litany was bestowed upon all who showed an interest in it: 'the young and old, obedient and rebellious, man or woman, free or slave' (Willis 1989: 72, fn 80). The extent to which Caam's vision of an egalitarian *jama'a* was realised might be regarded sceptically, but he did articulate a view which one could imagine was attractive to those previously excluded from full membership of the Muslim community. Willis regards the elevation of persons of lowly social origin in Taal's movement as something resembling a strategy on Taal's part, or at least a 'social policy' of the campaign to bring a greater sense of egality to the Muslim community (see Willis 1989: ch. 3).[42] This argument about a social policy may be found not to have a great deal of support. While there is little evidence of any grand ideological or religious motivation for such a 'policy' by Taal, the fact that many marginal characters did attain positions of authority within the Tijaniyya, not seen in comparable brotherhoods in the region, is significant, I would argue. The effect of the campaign was to give the Tijaniyya under Taal a much more broadly-based and popular appeal across the lower social ranks. Whether this was the outcome of a 'social policy' or the result of the fog of war might be difficult to ascertain. The fact that social elevation did occur has social consequences for the composition of the Tijani community and for subsequent interpretations of it by local commentators in Fuuta Toro. Taal's movement appears to stand in stark contrast to the *toorobe* clerisy that was established in Fuuta Toro, for the latter closed its ranks to all but freemen, excluding from its membership craftsmen and slaves. There appears to be an echo here of what happened in the early years of the Almaamate regime, for what started as a movement in which members of all social categories could partake soon became a Muslim community where older forms of social exclusion again found expression.

If Caam saw Taal's movement as a means of liberating himself from his own lowly social position and that others might have benefited from it too, certain authorities were uneasy about such calls to throw off all previous social ties; indeed many of the faithful were also uneasy about elevating someone they took to be of blacksmith origin to a position of responsibility within Islam. This innovation was clearly distasteful to some Muslims, and it provoked disagreements with the Qadiri shaykh, Ahmad al-Bakkai al Kunti. Umar Taal and his followers clashed with the leaders of the Qadiriyya over the elevation of persons of humble origin to the status of office-holders within the Tijani community. Zebadia's work on the correspondence between Ahmad al-Bakkai, the Kunta Shaykh, and Umar Taal, and then subsequently with his followers, reveals some of the tensions and disagreements among the different parties (Zebadia 1974, 1975; see Willis 1970 which covers some of this correspondence).[43] Shaykh Ahmad's displeasure was stirred after Umar Taal had subdued the town of Segu and swept onwards towards Timbuktu. Ahmad hurried into exile, not out of fear, he proclaimed, but because the rumour had reached him that al-Hajj Umar 'had appointed low personalities from amongst his people and his slaves to administer the land' (Willis 1970: 284 and 1989: 72, fn 80).[44] He had done this, Ahmad continued, in the absence of consultation with the free men of Fuuta, and he remained unconvinced that 'the affairs of this world could be placed with confidence in the hands of low-status individuals' (Willis 1970; Zebadia 1974). He concluded with the following remark: 'If that statement is true for the affairs of the world it is all the more true for the administration of religious affairs' (Willis 1970: 284). What seems clear from these statements by Shaykh Ahmad is that there was a difference of opinion between the freeborn of Fuuta Toro and what Umar Taal was trying to achieve further east; that the elevation in status of serviles and men-of-skill within the Islamic *jama'a* was not welcomed by many. Shaykh Ahmad certainly believed he had reason to think that Fuuta clerics would not welcome this development.

There do appear to be parallels to be drawn between the social processes occurring at the beginning of the eighteenth-century *toorobe* cleric uprising in Fuuta Toro, and those that were developed in the course of Umar Taal's mission with respect to the composition of the Tijani *jama'a*: namely both were initally open and blind to caste origin. People of diverse social origins could once again look to Islam as a source of cultural identity and egality. But this impetus was not sustained, for after Taal's death and during the time of his successors, the restrictions on the aspirations of men-of-skill and slaves were repeated again: the movement closed in upon itself and excluded men-of-skill from its highest ranks.[45] I now want to turn to the bases of Umar Taal's charismatic powers and the foundation of his legitimacy in the eyes of some of his followers.

UMAR TAAL, THE 'MYSTICAL WARRIOR'[46]

Umar Taal's life is surrounded by mystery and it has been the subject of much local elaboration (see Tyam 1935 and Robinson 1985). His early life, as well as much of his later career, 'is more that of a legendary than historical figure' (Willis 1970: 45). Little is known about the history of his early childhood or about the background of his family. But one series of connections that has been little commented on in scholarly works, although it has been the subject of much local discussion and debate, is his own ancestry or at least the glosses put on it by local commentators.[47] The argument here is that given the openness and accessibility of the Tijani *jama'a* to those of caste origin, a debate about the nature of Taal's own ancestry was set in train, a debate in part stimulated by men-of-skill reading into the reformist movement a set of issues close to their hearts and to their own experience. Taal's mission was focused on stamping out paganism, religious syncretism and mixing (*ikhtilât*), on suppressing certain forms of Islamic magic (*sihr*) and elements of polytheism (*shirk*) (Willis 1970; Robinson 1985). The men-of-skill reading of Taal's powers and of the knowledge that he drew on was not an attempt to reinstate illicit or pagan forms of practice necessarily, but derived from a perspective through which they sought to see in him a way of reconciling competing domains of power and knowledge, of which they controlled one. It was a reading that related directly to issues connected with men-of-skill social identity. The investigation that follows does not aim to analyse Taal's Tijaniyya in terms of theology and doctrine, but instead focuses on some of the cultural readings of his movement from a popular perspective.

Like many aspects of his life, much is surrounded by mystery and legend, and Taal's origins are no exception to that rule. For some, it is possible to trace connections within his family background that point to a past rooted within the ranks of the men-of-skill. These putative connections have been seized upon by those eager to make cultural capital out of them. A family with the patronym Caam has held the office of village chief in Taal's natal village of Halwar for as long as anyone can remember. These Caams vigorously deny any artisan origin, in the face of local rumours to the contrary, despite the fact that their patronym belongs distinctively to the social category of Smiths. It seems very likely that if they had been Smiths at some point then they must have joined *toorobe* clerics at very early stages of the category's development. Umar Taal's mother, Sokhna Adama, was a Caam through her mother's side from this village (Kyburz 1994: 73 and 151).[48] Her father was a Taal from a colateral line linked to her husband, Saydu, the father of Umar. It is conventional to trace inherited caste status through the female line in cases of mixed marriages of a freeman and a woman of the men-of-skill rank. This connection that links Umar to the Caams is deemed highly significant by some within the rigidly hierarchical society of Fuuta Toro. So too is a putative link made by local commentators between the Taal family and a group of Woodcarvers. These Woodcarvers also claim Umar Taal as one of theirs through his father's side, the idea being that perhaps one of Umar's earlier ancestors switched social status to that of the emerging *toorobe* at some point in the early eighteenth century. In the village of Njum, close to Taal's natal village, there is a long-established family of *lawbe* Woodcarvers with the patronym Tal. Much to the evident displeasure of the cleric Taals, the Woodcarvers claim common lines of descent with Umar's line. Indeed, Gaden reported in 1913 that the elders of the area believed the Woodcarvers to have good reason for this claim, and they suggested also that this fact explains something of the success Umar enjoyed in his military campaigns after his return from Mecca (see Gaden, in Soh 1913: 278). Gaden added an interesting footnote to the processes of social differentiation, suggesting that in the case of both the Cams and the Tals, the patronym that is in use among the clerics is pronounced with a long vowel sound, to distinguish it from the men-of-skill who bear the same name but who pronounce it with a shortened vowel (ibid.). Thus Tal becomes Taal, and Cam Caam. This is perhaps a Haalpulaar parallel to the elongation of vowel sounds in English pronunciation as a linguistic symbol of social status.

The suggestion of traces of craft origins claimed by some local commentators did and does not seem to detract from the legitimacy of Umar Taal as a Muslim leader; indeed it might be seen as consistent with the opportunities of access offered by his Tijani movement to all ranks of society. Far from detracting from his legitimacy, it seems to have added to it in the eyes of some of his followers. While the Woodcarver Tals suggest that part of the success of his campaigns can be attributed to his craft ancestry, praise-singers from the town of Kayes presented Umar as a 'magician' who had the power to make the jinn obey him (Monteil 1980: 114). They tell a story about Umar, in the period just prior to one of his campaigns, spending the rainy season in a town in Fuuta Toro.[49] He was trying to recruit an army, but according to the story, not an army of men but one of jinn or spirits. He would leave the town at night, slipping away under the cover of darkness, to a tree on top of a small hill. There he would summon the chief jinni, passing the night with him in conversation and in prayer to Allah.[50] Thus he asked if the spirit chief could procure for him an army of jinn, which was eventually recruited from non-Muslim areas of Senegal and surrounding regions. One hundred thousand jinn were called up and Umar Taal was seen marching away from the town with them at the end of the rainy season, moving east for the next campaign. Onlookers saw only an army of men carrying guns, failing to recognise them as the jinn (*neddo jinneeje*, lit. 'person jinn') that they were. Here Umar is cast in the role, not of a warrior or a saint, but of one who seeks power, a power associated with jinn who live in trees (Kane and Robinson 1984). Fused in the figure of this charismatic leader of authority are images of the worlds of Islam and other competing forces that are associated with *lawɓe* Woodcarvers. In the figure of Taal, Islam is harnessed to other forms of knowledge and expertise – black forms – usually conceived to stand in opposition to cleric-dominated forms of power and knowledge. All of these spiritual agents are summoned for Taal's cause and submit to his authority. The figure of Umar Taal is represented as uniting them all and drawing them into a hierarchy of powers that is put to the service of his reformist Islamic mission. His actions are characteristic not only of a great Muslim mystic but they also resonate with the echoes of the powers of a Woodcarver whose lore and knowledge allow him to communicate with tree-dwelling spirits. The image of Taal manages to bring together, in this story, forces and forms of knowledge that were kept separate under the accommodationist construction of Islam. The idea of a great Sufi mystic summoning the power of jinn and other spirits is by no means unique in West Africa, but what makes it significant in this case are the highly charged signs of 'caste' with which his image is imbued. It becomes significant, in short, in the context of an organisation of castes which are defined in relation to their exclusive control of different bodies of knowledge and power.

The gloss derived from this story by some local commentators, particularly men-of-skill ones, is that the individual charismatic powers of this religious leader were based upon the breaking of the ideological rules of separation between bodies of power and knowledge that had been established under an earlier elitist *tooroɓe* conception of Islam.[51] In the eighteenth century, among the conditions of claiming *tooroɓe* status were learning in Qur'anic studies and distancing oneself from the despised and scorned occupations of the men-of-skill. While the elitist *tooroɓe* conception of the local Muslim community was accommodationist, in that it allocated men-of-skill a subordinate place as Muslims, the new gloss on Taal's Tijani community was that it had become 'integrationist'. This new integrationist version acknowledged as a source of power and authority black lore and knowledge alongside that of the white knowledge and lore of Islam. The former was seen to be given an equal and undifferentiated status to the latter. The two were fused, moreover, in the single figure of a charismatic religious leader in the eyes of many – his *tooroɓe* detractors and critics, as well as his men-of-skill adherents. The former might use it to condemn the movement, the latter as a reason to adhere themselves to it. This integrationist view of Taal's mission seems to have been successful as a means of construing the legitimacy of the powers of a charismatic leader for those of lowly social status, who could see their interests written into this account. This is not to say that Taal's mission itself was defined, nor would he necessarily have defined it, in such terms. Many of the stories that cast Taal in the role of mystic and man-of-skill 'magician' are the property of the men-of-skill themselves, who recognised in his actions the potencies and powers of which they are the inheritors. This representation of Taal is an example of a form of cultural translation of the relationship between the black and the white, part of a dialogue between local social categories and their varying conceptions of the composition of the Muslim community. The view of Taal as 'magician', as an able-man possessing knowledge and power, is part of a muted or submerged history of the men-of-skill.

Another variant on this theme involves one of Umar Taal's descendants: Ceerno Bokar Taal, who died in 1940 in Mali. He was Shaykh Umar's great grandchild, and as such inherited *baraka* or charisma from him.[52] He was at once the inheritor of Umar's version of the Tijaniyya and later a disciple of Shaykh Hamallah, a Muslim reformist. Ceerno Bokar also seems to have taken a vision of the integration of the black and the white to a conclusion, although an unsatisfactory one in the eyes of some. He developed a populist Islam aimed at local animists, women and those who wanted to deepen their involvement in Islam without relying on a knowledge of Arabic. He spent most of his life at Bandiagara, Mali, in Dogon country. There he worked with a traditional 'pagan' Dogon healer and translated his knowledge of plants and cures into Islamic analogies, thus integrating this knowledge within a Muslim framework. Brenner reports (1983a) that Ceerno Bokar and the Dogon, Ancamba Nandigi, began to practise their healing arts together, and a close relationship developed between the two. The Dogon's traditional knowledge of plants, animals and the life of the bush would no doubt have been classified as 'black' by the local Muslim Haalpulaar community. What Ceerno did, therefore, was in effect to convert 'black' 'pre-Islamic' Dogon knowledge into Muslim terms and integrate it into a new composite body of knowledge and practice. Brenner states 'His approach to knowledge was not based on concepts of the exclusivity of Islam ... but on a desire to understand the lessons to be found in the diversity of God's creation' (1983a: 90). This seems to have been a conscious strategy in the development of his mission, one which we cannot be sure was in the forefront of Shaykh Umar's mind when he appeared to breach, in the eyes of some, cultural and religious categories. It was, however, an element in the construction of the legitimacy of Umar's authority in the eyes of some of his followers.[53]

Whereas Umar Taal gained a measure of legitimacy, at least in some quarters, from his putative men-of-skill ancestry and connections with powers of the bush, Ceerno Bokar appears to have suffered because of it. He lost legitimacy in the eyes of the Muslim community, which appears to have reverted to an earlier accommodationist view of Islam: the black was subordinate to the white, not to be elevated to a complementary status with it. Ceerno Bokar had perhaps gone one step too far in trying to integrate the 'black' with the 'white'. He had attempted to integrate that which should have been kept apart.[54]

The argument that in the figure of Taal can be seen the merging of two ideologically distinct bodies of knowledge and power does not detract from the idea that each body is discrete at the level of thought. Nor does the possibility that in practice specialist practitioners – either marabouts or expert men-of-skill – might blur the boundaries of this ideological distinction in their activities. What the argument does suggest is that for those of men-of-skill status, what is acknowledged is the complementarity of the powers behind their own specialisms. The 'integration' of the *gandal* of men-of-skill might be read as a metaphor of the integration of members of this social rank into Taal's Tijani *jama'a*.

CONCLUDING REMARKS – ISLAM AND THE OTHER

The relationship between Islamic belief and practice and local religious traditions has long been considered by scholars. Few social anthropologists would today wish to compare Muslim religious thought and practice of, say, West Africa with those of the Middle East in terms of trying to define deviations or transformations of a pure or parent-type of religious system.[55] That tendency toward comparison with a pure or parent-type arose from the efforts of an earlier generation of scholars who regarded the relationship between Islam and forms of local religious tradition as either involving a duality or a parallelism or involving syncretism.[56] Theories of parallelism suggested a dualistic nature of religious thought and practice, that two religious traditions, located in separate social domains, remained relatively intact – for example, pre-Islamic and Islamic systems – each operating in parallel with the other. Such a theory helps identify those aspects of religious life that are held to be part of an Islamic heritage and those which derive from indigenous religious traditions. For example, there might be a courtly tradition of Islam versus a popular paganism or, as Trimingham argued, craftsmen and artisans were the repositories of pre-Islamic survivals (1959: 102, fn).[57] Craftsmen were, according to this view, Muslims in name but pagans in practice.

Theories of syncretism, by contrast, suggested that Islam and local religious beliefs worked out a *modus operandi* in which both traditions were positively assimilated into a unitary system of religious thought. According to this view, people did not live out their lives in a state of spiritual ambiguity or ambivalence, but instead experienced a more or less seamless continuity of religious thought and practice. One product of this latter perspective was the concept of *Islam noir*, black Islam, a syncretic form of a religious system of an Africanised Muslim faith proposed famously by Vincent Monteil (1980).[58] According to theorists influenced by Edward Said, the concept of *Islam noir* can be seen as part of a political policy towards Islam in Francophone West Africa.[59] But such a viewpoint denies the possibility that indigenous groups were involved in the localisation of religious thought and practice, that it was simply a result of colonial policy.

One critique of dualist theories is that there is little understanding of social context, and that lines between one tradition and another are too inflexibly drawn. While syncretic theories trace the forms that religious thought and practice take in specific cultural contexts, the problem with them is that they often involve an overzealous search for unity, integration and coherence. The idea of a plurality of religious views is lost; the idea of contestation between competing claims for religious ascendancy is overlooked. What is certain is that the issue of Islamic thought and practice can longer be viewed from a static viewpoint, but an analysis needs to follow the changes, developments and indeed the plurality of views among the collectivity of the faithful. Some years ago, Peter Lienhardt, with regard to Islamic practices in East Africa, defined an enduring anthropological perspective which is concerned with where distinctions between forms of religious thought and practice are consciously drawn by members of particular communities (1968: 38). This opens up the possibility of a sensitive anthropological investigation of how and where the line is drawn, and what social processes are involved in such cultural and political acts. However, Asad (1986) critiques this purely interpretativist view: namely that what indigenous interpreters call Islam must therefore be taken as being Islamic. Instead, his discursive approach recommends in addition that attention be paid to political structures and relationships of powers, a recommendation that is embraced by this present examination. One can distinguish, therefore, between an 'external' analytical perspective that would wish to compare religious systems with reference to a pure or parent type (an Islamic orthodoxy of Mecca), and an 'internal' interpretative anthropological perspective which seeks to understand local categories and cultural distinctions within a setting of political relations and struggles for power. The interpretative perspective is complicated, furthermore, by the fact that indigenous interpreters of thought and practice will often draw on ideas that overlap with the analytical categories of the comparative religionists; namely, whether a practice or custom is pre- or non-Islamic or not. It must also be extended to consider the power relations between such religious-political categories.

I have tried to take such a nuanced view, drawing on local interpretations of religious practice, but having regard for the fact that they too are involved in the cultural politics of making distinctions. I have throughout this chapter argued that one cannot talk simply of two separate static traditions – one pre- or non-Islamic and the other Islamic.[60] Indeed, the co-presence of the Muslim and local traditions in the Senegal valley over a period of over a thousand years must have meant that both developed in conversation with each other. Fairclough (1992) suggests the term 'interdiscursivity' to describe the way in which two or more discourses may be mutually linked, one feeding off and responding to the other. The cleric uprising of the eighteenth century was a significant moment in this cultural conversation for it established a new level or intensity of dialogue. The acquisition of bodies of lore and knowledge became politicised in such a way that it was now important to make radical distinctions between one sort of lore and knowledge and another. Knowledge became politicised to the extent that ideological distinctions were, I would suggest, overlaid on a mutually informed dialogue that fostered a variety of specialist practices.

I am reminded too of Humphrey Fisher's approach to Islam in West Africa which defines a framework for capturing the dynamic of historical shifts in religious thought and practice in terms of the stages of quarantine, mixing and reform (Fisher 1973, 1985). This is a dialectic movement from the introduction of Islam in quarantined enclaves of believers, through the stage in which Islam mixes with local religions, to an ideological reaction of reform against syncretic forms of practice. While this framework admits a dynamic historical approach,[61] the inadequacy of the term 'mixing' or 'syncretism' is apparent, for it says nothing about how elements are mixed and in what manner they are mixed. What I have defined as 'accommodationist' or as 'integrationist' conceptions of the Islamic community were attempts at mixing or localisation; but these strategies of localisation were relative to particular social groups. In one, the clerics attempted to accommodate but yet dominate the expertise of the men-of-skill; in the other, integration was a counter-version, a submerged re-casting of terms, which was a 'localising strategy' for the men-of-skill in their attempt to re-read social relationships.[62] In this version, Umar Taal was cast as a fellow 'magician', a manipulator of dangerous forces and spiritual agents, just like the men-of-skill themselves.

It has been argued that the Almaamate regime did little to change the overall social hierarchy of Haalpulaar society.[63] This is true to the extent that the three main social ranks existed prior to and continued after the cleric uprising and the position of the subordinate ranks remained somewhat similar. The outcome of the eighteenth-century cleric uprising was an ideological reconfiguration of social groups and categories in comparison with the earlier regime. First, the overthrow of Deniyaŋke rule replaced a system based upon the inheritance of office and authority within dynastic lineages. It substituted instead a class of people of diverse social origins who, adhering to Islam, claimed a place at the top of the social pyramid. They quickly closed ranks to become an exclusive social category, and established the non-dynastic elective office of Almaamy that continued into the late nineteenth century. The evaluation of other social categories by the clerics emerged as an important feature of the Almaamate regime, in which the touchstone of superiority for them became the adherence of its members to the now exclusive religion of Islam. While Willis claims that there is 'Little doubt that *Torodbe* [*sic*] Islam ... shook the social foundation of the societies in which it burst forth' (1978: 208), perhaps the tremors did less to destroy the social fabric than to produce a cloud of ideological reevaluations of social groups.

One of the most enduring results of this ideological rather than social earthquake was that the hierarchical relationship between freeborn master and slave was cast in terms of the principles of Islamic law (see Chapter 3 above). In addition, the clerics on acceding to power re-emphasised the distinction between themselves as the purveyors of the Muslim faith in terms of a contrast between 'Islamic' and 'non-Islamic' lore – the white and the black. This was a form of hegemonic dominance effected through the *rule of lore*, rather than the *rule of law* which governed relationships of slavery. The fundamental change was not in the overall classification of social groups and categories, but it was in the relations between these categories, especially in their ideological configuration. The *toorobe* clerics' attempt at ideological dominance accentuated the distinction between the clerisy and men-of-skill in stark terms, and it set in motion a debate about the position of Islam regarding the social inclusion and exclusion of specific social groups. This cultural dialogue concerned where the line should be drawn between acceptable and unacceptable religious thought and practice, at least according to local lights. The integrationist view of Umar Taal's nineteenth-century mission did not last, but it represents one part of an emerging cultural dialogue about how caste and Islam might be married.

Another enduring result of the cultural earthquake of the *toorobe* uprising was a sense, instilled by the Islamic clerics, of ambiguity and ambivalence which men-of-skill experienced regarding the perceived nature of their activities and the place these activities were allotted with respect to Islam. While many practising craftsmen regarded themselves as good Muslims, there existed a tension about how they should regard certain aspects of their crafts, since these had become an obstacle to full participation in the Islamic community. There was not, and there is not, a seamless syncretic unity to religious thought and practice but a plurality of forms. Lewis pointed out some years ago the question of whether Muslims in Africa experience a difficulty in reconciling the various imperatives that direct the conduct of their lives (1980). Attempts at ideological dominance are one thing, the nature of local human social experience is another.

5

ACCOMMODATIONIST SUFI ISLAM AND RITES OF PASSAGE: TENSIONS AND AMBIGUITIES

In the last chapter, I proposed the concept of an accommodationist Islam which sought, from the time of the Almaamate regime, to accommodate but yet subordinate forms of lore and knowledge derived from spirit agents devalued within a local Islamic cosmology. Without wishing to fall into the trap of reifying this vision of Islam held by *tooroɓe* clerics, I seek to tease out the ideological configuration that is its foundation, and then analyse the role that men-of-skill play in certain rites of passage, in particular male and female circumcision. This will lead on to an investigation into the ways in which an accommodationist Islam is contested, and into the forms of ambiguity and ambivalence generated by opposing social and cultural imperatives which are experienced by some of the Muslim faithful. This process will be illustrated through the acts of reinterpretation of men-of-skill occupational origin myths that craftsmen and musicians have entered into with self-conscious reference to overt Islamic themes and motifs. This theme of ambiguity and ambivalence is one that will be carried forward into future chapters as a feature of social practice and indigenous cultural interpretation.

THE IDEOLOGICAL CONFIGURATION OF ACCOMMODATIONIST ISLAM

The idea of higher and lower spiritual forces associated with the white and the black forms of lore and knowledge respectively forms the basis of the ideological distinction at the heart of accommodationist Islam. Artisan practices were assimilated into local Haalpulaar Islamic conceptions with reference to jinn, lower spiritual beings but nonetheless part of Muslim cosmology. The black is subordinate to the white, according to this view, just as the jinn and spirits of nature are thought to be subordinate to higher spiritual forces. Association with these jinn and nature spirits is condemned, just as the men-of-skill are scorned for their craft activities that bring practitioners into contact with them. This represents the contrary of good Muslim practice to the clerics, and indeed it was members of this cleric social category who urged those newly elevated to this new social status to abandon these trades in the eighteenth century.

According to certain analytical perspectives, it could be possible to regard the categories of the black and the white as complementary, being linked in an equally weighted binarism or dualism. My argument is, however, that while these two categories are complementary, there is a significant degree of asymmetry in the relationship between them. The black and the white, in the accommodationist view, are differentially valued. 'To adopt value is to introduce hierarchy', claimed Dumont (quoted in Barnes et al. 1985: 8).[1] This hierarchical relationship inheres in the encompassment of the subordinate value by the superordinate or dominant value; that is 'hierarchy is the encompassing of the contrary' (Dumont 1979: 809). In this case one can conceive of a form of hierarchical relationship in terms of the encompassment by Islam of its contrary – that which stands as the antithesis to good Muslim practice in the clerics' eyes, that is craft activity and black lore and knowledge. It is nonetheless brought within an Islamic cosmology via the notion of jinn, and subsequently the black is encompassed by the white. This hierarchical relationship is no doubt linked to a vision of an Islamic Sufi cosmology organised around the concept of the great chain of being. In an explanation of the doctrines which underlie Sufi religious practice, the idea of hierarchy has been expressed in the following way:

> The chain of being essentially means that all beings in the Universe exist according to a continuous hierarchy which is ontological as well as cosmological. A particular entity has a position in the great chain of being depending upon the degree to which it participates in Being and Intelligence; or one might say, upon the degree to which it possesses the perfections and virtues which in the absolute sense belong only to Pure Being, or God, who is transcendent with respect to this chain. (Seyyed Nasr quoted in Brenner 1983a: 92)

This chain of being is not dissimilar to the one that was current in medieval Europe – namely Universitas – a topic discussed by Dumont as an exemplar of a hierarchy of value that was formed at a particular moment in our own history (Dumont 1986).[2]

The hierarchical relationship of value can be further illustrated by reference to an ethnographic example concerning ideas about the efficacy of different types of cure and remedy that are derived from different bodies of lore and knowledge. Among Haalpulaar'en, misfortune and illness are often thought to be caused by invisible spirit forces that can be treated by specialist techniques. Marabouts versed in the Qur'an set themselves up as healers based on their knowledge of Islamic texts and Muslim esoteric sciences. For instance, a victim or injured party might consult a marabout and be prescribed an amulet (*binndi*) incorporating a piece of paper on which is written a Qur'anic verse, or the person may be asked to drink or wash with a preparation (*aaye*) made from erasing with water the ink of Qur'anic script from a wooden writing tablet (*alluwal*). Such knowledge is classified as white. Alternatively, a victim or injured party may consult other forms of specialist such as a *bileejo*, a witch-hunter and curer. The cures these specialists dispense are based on the use of incantations (*cefi*), herbal and plant remedies considered to harbour spiritual potencies, or procedures close to those used by sorcerers who cast spells (*bolle baleeje*). These realms of knowledge are classified as black.

A distinction is made by many Haalpulaar'en between the modes of action of these two types of magical efficacy or power practice. They maintain that a victim struck by black lore, or one who is treated by it, will feel the effects of the treatment almost immediately, while the treatment based upon white lore is much slower in showing its effects and is less dramatic in appearance. The change, however, which results from white lore is thought to be immutable compared with the results of black lore. The action of white lore then is thought to be permanent and eternal, in the sense that the ministrations of clerical marabouts might not even be apparent in this life, for Allah, in his wisdom, might choose to alleviate the problem only in the afterlife. The efficacy of white lore, from this perspective, operates in a timeframe that stretches to the afterlife and eternity; it is timeless and concerns relations with the other world as much as relations with this world. While more immediately effective, black lore, by contrast, is perceived as being ultimately subservient to the will of Allah and the longer view of Islamic religious lore. White or Islamic lore is, therefore, seen to be superior in its general healing properties, even though in the short term the black may be more immediately effective. The white has a timeless, more permanent quality about it, for indeed it is this which defines the way to eternity and is concerned with judgement in the next life. White lore is in this sense not only superior to black lore, but it could be said to encompass it by a different timeframe and by its mode of efficacy. Within the accommodationist vision of Islam, these two bodies of lore and knowledge stand in a hierarchical relationship to each other with reference to efficacy and time. White lore encompasses the black just as eternity encompasses the past, present and future.[3]

The theme of Islam and the dimension of time have been commented on by other scholars writing on the faith in Africa. Islam cannot convey a sense of immediate relief compared with the concerns for the 'here-and-now' of local religious cults. Its concerns, it is argued, are with eternity, divine judgement, reward and retribution in the afterlife rather than in this life. Indeed, J. D. Y. Peel and R. Horton have discussed at length the otherworldly aspects of world religions, especially the version of Christianity introduced by western missionaries, in comparison with the this-worldly quality of 'traditional African religious thought'.[4] This theme emerges too from the present analysis of accommodationist Islam among Haalpulaar'en. There is, however, another arena of social life in which this relationship between diverse forms of knowledge and dimensions of time is expressed. This arena comprises the rituals associated with life changes, the rites of passage of death, initiation into adulthood, birth and the naming of infants. I noted in an earlier chapter how European observers in the seventeenth and eighteenth centuries had remarked upon Muslim practices related to life-cycle rituals. The role of marabouts was noted with regard to the preparation of the corpse and burial of the dead in particular. It is to the varying degrees of the participation of Muslim clerics or other religious practitioners in rites of passage which I now turn.

RITUAL SPECIALISTS AND RITES OF PASSAGE

The extent to which marabouts participate in the range of rites of passage is variable. For example, in relation to marriage (*dewgal*), a marabout's role is relatively simple and straightforward. First, a long series of prestations is made by the groom to his bride and her family, and the groom's age-mates assist with the nuptial arrangements. After most of these prestations have occurred, the groom and certain members of his family visit the mosque where the local imam will formally bless the union. The bride does not attend this ceremony of benediction, and it is not strictly necessary for the groom to do so either. Other rites of passage involve more complex forms of participation.

Naming an infant

A ceremony is held seven days after the birth of a child, who hitherto has been sheltered in the mother's hut or room for fear of witchcraft attack. The baby is formally presented to the father for the first time, and the mother receives presents from him and from her close family and friends. The newborn is officially named by a marabout who recites the Qur'anic verse *Al-Fatihah* and gives a Qur'anic name or 'book name' (*inde deftere*) to the infant. He simply states: 'we will call him or her so-and-so', and expresses the wish that the infant follow in the footsteps of the mother or the father, depending on the sex of the child. Afterwards, the infant's close relatives, especially the father's sister (*gorgol*) and the mother's brother (*kaaw*), propose names, often one that has been agreed by all concerned and sometimes given in remembrance of an ancestor. The official book name is seldom used by family and friends, and often it is the one chosen by the mother's brother that is preferred.[5] The newborn's head is washed and shaved by the marabout, and he will attach amulets containing Qur'anic verse to the wrists, ankles and around the waist at the level of the kidneys to guard the infant against predatory witches and evil spells. The rite is called *loocital*, the 'first washing' after the head is shaved (Gaden 1912b), and it will be attended by the family praise-singers who will perform and demand recompense for their services.

The burial of corpses

The rituals surrounding the burial of the dead are influenced by Islamic practices, and have long been associated with the social role of marabouts.[6] His role in the preparation of the body for burial has been reported as far back as the seventeenth century, and it would appear that this was one of the first rites of passage to have been dominated by Muslim practitioners. A marabout washes a corpse to the accompaniment of prayer, and treats the body with incense before it is wrapped in a burial cloth (*kasanke*; *hasnude maydo* is 'to shroud a body'). It is carried on a bier to the grave, which is oriented towards Mecca, and the body is placed on its right side with its head in the direction of the *qibla*. There are periodic observations of remembrance of the dead, some of which are conducted by young Qur'anic scholars who, for a small recompense, will recite prayers over a tomb, especially to commemorate the period forty days following death.

Circumcision

While ceremonies involving the naming of infants and the burial of the dead have a clear and defined role for practising Muslim clerics, the rites surrounding circumcision are more ambiguous. Indeed, there is a high-profile role for men-of-skill and for ritual functionaries who are considered to draw on black rather than white power and knowledge. This might seem paradoxical, for the circumcision of boys is considered to be a fundamental rite of passage for those who want to embrace the Muslim religion (see Ba 1985–86, ch. 2). Although not mentioned in the Qur'an, it has come to be regarded as one of the indispensable marks of adherence to the religion. Circumcision is one of the two crucial steps for the development of a boy within the religion, the second being apprenticeship in the Qur'an. Ethnographic detail on female excision is much more patchy compared with that available for the male operation, and there is little work carried out generally on the development of women within Islam.[7] Nonetheless, Botte has pointed out that Qur'anic education of girls in Fuuta Jallon often finished at the time of their excision, after which they have little role to play within the religion. It was not unknown, however, for a woman to follow a cycle of Qur'anic education and even receive the title 'Ceerno' (Botte 1990: 47–8).

The vocabulary referring to circumcision is rich and varied in Pulaar; however, a semantic connection can be made between the adoption of the faith and circumcision.[8] *Juulnude* means 'to convert, to circumcise and to excise', and from the same root comes *juulde*, 'to perform Muslim prayers', and the substantive *juuldo*, a Muslim or 'one who prays'. Linked to this is the word for 'one who has been circumcised', *njuuli*. Besides the sense of purification of the person prior to adulthood and full participation in the Muslim community, there is another cultural sense to circumcision. Female excision of the clitoris is regarded as removing a male attribute from girls in order for them to develop fully into womanhood. It is a kind of 'devirilisation' (Monteil 1980: 189). Likewise, for the boys, there is a shedding of femininity during the rites of circumcision and initiation, which involves moments of the boys' cross-dressing prior to their emergence as fully fledged males entitled to wear adult male clothing. While male circumcision and initiation is the focus of much communal activity, female excision, involving clitoridectomy and sometimes infibulation, is done much more privately behind closed doors and with little public ceremony (see also Gaden 1931: 22). In both cases, however, those who carry out the operation are drawn from the ranks of the men-of-skill, frequently either Smith or Leatherworker men and women for their respective initiates. The process of initiation, however, is culturally distinct, being referred to by the verb *hasde* (to initiate into adult knowledge), and the rituals associated with this involve people with special spiritual powers, powers that lie outside the purview of white lore.

In order to appreciate the complex social interrelationships involved in the circumcision and initiation of boys, I will present a description of the ritual. Boys should be circumcised between twelve and fifteen years of age, and this operation is linked conventionally to the initiation of a group of boys who undergo a series of rituals collectively. Prior to the operation and initiation proper, from the age of ten, children of the same village or neighbourhood within an age range of around three years or thereabouts form a recreational group. The boys eventually form a *fedde worde*, a male age-set, and the girls, a *fedde rewre*, the female equivalent. The children's mothers often push for the formation of an age-set out of the informal ties and associations children create through play. They do this by encouraging the youngsters to meet at one of their houses and by providing meals for them. The young boys often secure the use of a house of a child of the men-of-skill rank, a *nyeenyo*, and there they pass the night eating, sleeping and in recreation. A leader is nominated within the group, usually the son of a cleric or of the local dominant group, such as Fishermen or Warriors in riverine villages. Using one of the titles *lamɗo*, *mawɗo* or even *almaamy*, the leader presides over group meetings, intervenes in differences between members, organises receptions and entertainment, and is expected to contribute more food and resources to festivities than the others. He also assembles the group for carrying out agricultural or other tasks for households in the community. Although the distinctions of the larger society are reflected in the make-up of the *fedde*, it is claimed to be more democratic and less hierarchical than adult social relations.[9] The term for 'age-mates', those circumcised and initiated together, is *giyiraaɓe*, which shares the same root as the word for placenta (*giyiraado*). Moreover, the relations among members of an age-set are often referred to as the same as those of kinship (*giyiraagal ko bandiraagal*, 'age-matehood is kinship'). Nonetheless, certain tasks are allocated specific to social category and rank, such that, for example, a craftsman's son might be asked to act as a delivery boy or messenger, and his house would be the focus of age-set activity; a boy from the local dominant social group is usually chosen as a leader.

The initiation of boys (*jarle*) is conventionally organised around the circumcision operation. The members of an age-set are circumcised together and this marks a change in status for the initiates: they are on the cusp of manhood and social responsibility. Five or six days before the ceremony, feasts are organised and praise-singers are invited to provide entertainment and to bolster the courage of the initiates. Boys spend the eve of the operation dancing with young girls of the corresponding age-set in a dance called *rippo*, 'the dance of the uncircumcised'. In the morning they take a bath prepared by a *bileejo*, a witch-hunter and curer, after which they dress for the ceremony as initiates (*solimaaɓe*, singular *solima*). The operation is carried out by the circumcisor in front of the age-set, and to this ritual are invited members of the boys' families and girls from the corresponding female age-set, in front of whom the initiates should show an unflinching courage in silence and dignity. The circumcisor himself, usually a Smith or Leatherworker, is supposed to earn clemency from Allah once he has performed 100 operations.

The newly circumcised boys now enter a period of seclusion or separation (*suukere*) and live together in an especially prepared enclosure (*wuurngo*) and shelter (*mbara*), which are sometimes located beyond the village towards the bush. Here they pass much of their time over the next one to two months until their wounds have healed and for the duration of their education and initiation. This ceremony takes place during the dry season, for it is feared that the songs the circumcised boys learn at camp would prevent the rains from falling. They are watched over by two sorts of initiators. The first is the *baawo*, an able man with special powers, who has a spiritual and protective role to guard the boys, now in a vulnerable state, from attack by witches and other evil-doers. He sits up all night with the boys and will also instruct them in songs, incantations and secret languages (*kasol* is the knowledge given during initiation). The second functionary is a *selbe*, often a circumcised young adult, who is responsible for helping to educate and discipline the boys. He is accountable to the *baawo* and other ritual specialists, and enforces the strict regime and punishing series of challenges and tasks, such as wrestling, rabbit and gazelle hunting, long walks and combat exercises, night vigils and so on. The boys are also subject to a range of specific prohibtions, for instance, against digging holes, making designs on wood, or walking near the village public latrines. The boys, now referred to as *burlol* (pl. *burli*) – 'one who is circumcised but yet to wear men's clothing' – are integrated back into the community with a series of carnivalesque events and indulgences, such as dressing up in old, or in women's clothing or raiding households to steal property and livestock. This initiation ritual follows the classic tripartite structure of a rite of passage as described by van Gennep (1960).

Marabouts and specialist Muslim practitioners are conspicuous by their absence from this and other accounts of male circumcision rituals. Moreover, the prominent roles are afforded to men-of-skill circumcisors and to ritual specialists whose powers and knowledge are not necessarily those of the Islamic clerics. The *bileejo* witch-hunter/curer practices arts that are categorised as black, but yet they participate in a ritual that is fundamental to the development and formation of future practising Muslims. Furthermore, not only are they instrumental in reproducing the future generation of Muslims through male circumcision, they are also key participants in the social transformation of boys into men and, in the parallel female ritual, girls into women. The roles of the men-of-skill in circumcision, and of the specialists in other black arts in initiation, highlight the capacities of these practitioners as transformers. Just as the men-of-skill are transformers of raw materials into socially useful objects, here they are part of a process, along with others too, of transforming social persons from one social status to another. Circumcision and initiation are, then, two social processes fundamental to cultural reproduction, two key events in the transformations necessary for the maintenance and reproduction of life in this world. They are involved with time-bound social and cultural reproduction. If this interpretation is correct, it may go some way towards explaining the dominant role of marabouts in infant-naming and burial rituals too, for each concerns the passage of a soul from one world to another: the incarnation of new souls into this world with the naming of infants; the departure of the souls of the dead through the preparation of the body for burial. It is perhaps no coincidence that marabouts appear to have exerted greater control over these two rites of passage, and indeed seem to have done so from an early point in the history of Fuuta Toro. It is only in the rituals of circumcision and initiation, processes fundamental to the maintenance and transformation of life already incarnated, that practitioners of black arts have a role as specialists in the affairs of this world.[10] Again, we see the motif of hierarchical values correlating with different dimensions of time and different forms of lore and spiritual power. These ideas chime well with the earlier arguments about the ideological configuration of an accommodationist Islam. However, this ideological configuration does not go uncontested.

There are two distinct parts to the ritual process of initiation: first the circumcision of boys, which is required as a religious rite of purification demanded by Muslims; second, the process of initiation and education, within which circumcision is conventionally placed. Increasingly in recent years, the actual operation of circumcision takes place in clinics or hospitals where available, although age-sets are still formed and the processes of initiation nonetheless continue. There are, however, dissenting voices that express disquiet over participating in a ritual that involves specialists regarded as standing outside a local Muslim dominant orthodoxy. This issue focuses particularly on the role of the *bileejo* witch-hunter/curer and the *baawo*, the specialist initiator. As early as 1930s, *toorobe* clerics expressed a concern about these matters and tried to restrict the participation of their sons in parts of the initiation rituals. Moreover, they devised a separate circumcision ritual that was exclusively Muslim and presided over by a marabout, and it took boys from cleric families as early as five years old for the operation (Kane 1935). Kane also reported at the same time that initiation (*jarle*) was reserved only for the other castes, cleric children avoiding it wherever possible. Similarly, Ly noted (1938) that clerics took no part in the festivities prior to the operation of collective circumcision, especially in the dance of the uncircumcised boys, the *rippo*, on the eve of the ritual. The many accounts of these rituals that we have are not always consistent over the issue of whether cleric boys participated or not. It seems to be related to local circumstance and the predilections of particular imams who might take against certain practices. Although I did not witness circumcision and initiation rituals myself during fieldwork, my interviews with people who had been through them suggested that cleric as well as men-of-skill boys went through the procedure together. Indeed, many long-lasting and deeply felt relations were developed through common suffering experienced by boys of very different social statuses. Whatever the precise extent to which the cleric revisionist discourse has had an effect, the point remains: the example of circumcision and initiation serves to illustrate a sense of ambivalence felt by the clerics over participation in rites of passage dominated by men-of-skill and the practitioners of black arts. They have sought either to absent themselves from aspects of the ritual cycle they find most offensive, or they have attempted to substitute Islamic specialists in the roles of ritual functionary.[11] If accommodationist Islam had previously worked out a *modus operandi* with spiritual powers and forces subordinate within an Islamic hierarchy, the fault line revealed by *toorobe* cleric revisionism is a manifestation of the experience of a sense of ambiguity and ambivalence in thought and practice.

This sense of ambivalence in religious thought and practice can be illustrated by reference to two examples, and they are relevant to any Haalpulaar Muslim, no matter what their social rank.

AMBIVALENCE IN RELIGIOUS THOUGHT

A household shrine

I only ever encountered one family that maintained a household shrine (*feere*) at which libations were poured for specific ancestors. These ancestors were also referred to as jinn, or spirits. The only other example I came across was of an old *bileejo*, a witch-hunter/curer who maintained a shrine as part of his professional practice. This whole area of discussion about ancestral spirits was always fraught with tension, and there was a good deal of reticence about such matters. For instance, when I first broached the subject of libation ceremonies at his shrine, the householder seemed offended that I knew anything about the matter. I had been told by one of his sons that the family held regular ceremonies and it was only some time after the meeting with the father that I was invited to witness the ceremony and to talk more about the religious imperatives and intentions behind the practice. Libations of milk and millet, sometimes sweetened with honey or sugar, were offered by pouring the white mixture over upturned pestles sticking out of the ground by twelve inches or so. The householder considered himself a good Muslim and had been on the pilgrimage to Mecca. He entertained hopes for Paradise for his own soul, yet the ancestral spirits he identified as being associated with the shrine were ghosts who haunted the earth. It was necessary to placate them and help them on their way to the afterlife. The householder, since his return from Mecca, had felt uneasy about conducting the libations, and he now left the role of ritual officiant to his younger brother. The household head obviously experienced a difficulty in reconciling the religious imperatives that had been newly impressed upon him by his trip to Mecca and sense of obligation towards his dead ancestors who required his assistance. Only recently had a child in the household been seized by the spirit of a dead grandfather, and it was necessary to construct another pestle in the shrine over which libations would be dedicated to his soul.

Abdou Sow and *shirk*

Abdou and I were discussing the practices of a number of different types of expert in esoteric arts such as witch-hunters and curers (*wileeɓe*), magicians (*nyeŋgotooɓe*), diviners (*tiimooɓe*) and even some marabouts who make amulets using Qur'anic verses. Abdou is a *toroodo* whose sister is married to a teacher of Arabic, who is also the imam at the local mosque and has leanings towards Islamist radicalism. The brother-in-law is steeped in the writings of Islam, and around his room are stacked handsomely bound copies of the Qur'an, the Hadith and various commentaries and law books in Arabic. Sitting in the brother-in-law's room, Abdou's first reaction to the topic of our conversation was to condemn outright all practices of 'magic' (*sihr*) as animistic. All these practitioners, including those marabouts who prescribed the wearing of Qur'anic verses as a form of protective magic, were committing the sin of *shirk*, an offence within Islam of attributing partners to Allah, thus undermining His position as the one and only God. These were some of the worst sins (*akbarru kabba iri*) that could be committed by man, he added.[12] Islam says, he continued, that man should not profit himself from the use of such 'animistic' (he used the French term) powers, and that it was for Allah to judge and bring retribution to sinners. It was not for man to intervene in the course of events for his own ends and purposes. These sentiments were obviously felt strongly and his case was put over passionately.

The conversation moved on to the subject of sports, in particular the summer football season and the upcoming wrestling match that was on everyone's lips, for these were examples of events that involve illicit maraboutic practice. The wrestling match was to be held between the top two wrestlers in the country. It had been trailed in the newspapers, it was discussed on the radio and was to be televised, and those lucky enough to have a television would be particularly popular neighbours on the evening of the fight. Both wrestlers employed marabouts who administered a whole range of medicines, amulets and potions to their prized fighters. On the night of the fight, the wrestlers emerged into the ring adorned with strings of talismans, and one was covered in a slimy, milky substance that had been poured over him as part of a libation to the spirits. One fighter was a Lebu, a coastal dweller and sea fisherman from the Cap Vert region; the other was a Serer, a much darker giant of a man, from the central southern region. Everyone I spoke to said the Serer was bound to win since the Serer have more 'magic' (*gandal* or *xamxam* in Wolof) than the Lebu, and this 'magic' was blacker (as was the wrestler) and more potent than anything the Lebu could conjure. In fact, the match was becoming billed as a spiritual contest of battle-magic between the two respective marabouts who would use any means, any powers or potencies to ensure that their man would win. At one stage in the fight the smaller Lebu lost one of his amulets from around his forehead, and the assembled audience groaned in disbelief since he was now bound to lose for his most potent weapon had gone. In fact the match, which dragged on for forty-five uneventful minutes, ended in an unsatisfying draw.

The point of this digression is to highlight the switch that can occur in people's attitudes towards local practices once they are no longer talked of in the abstract but are related to as part of people's lives. The use of marabouts to lend magical support to sportsmen and sporting activities in general is a common practice that is integral to the conduct of games. It is a practice that is condemned by Islamists as a sin. Indeed, Abdou, having first condemned the use of maraboutic medicines in general, then related how he, as the trainer of the local youth football team, relied upon an extremely effective marabout who helped the team prior to every game. Medicines could be produced to affect the opposition's star players such that they might be injured, and magic could be used to secure the right result and protect one's own team. I was struck by the obvious change of attitude towards marabouts once discussed in the context of football, and Abdou's condoning of, if not his sense of pride in, the exploits of his team's marabout. Here condemnation had turned to jocular boasts about his team's performance aided by magical means; no longer were these practices outlawed simply as *shirk*, but they were a coherent part of a social practice in which he was engaged.

One frequently encounters such seemingly contradictory stances. Indeed, many Senegalese of no matter what ethnic origin often joke about whether a statement about Islam reflects local practice or according to the book. Local Muslims are involved in their own debates about what is and what is not good Islamic practice; they are aware of the distinction between theoretical statements on an issue, no doubt echoed in an imam's sermon, on the one hand, and reflections of actual social practice on the other. There is an inherent ambiguity about the status of certain activities, and the concerns of everyday life seem to demand that forms of action be taken to secure particular kinds of outcome.

The accommodations and condemnations of particular kinds of practice are responses or stances that inform part of a local debate about where the lines of demarcation should be drawn around forms of religious conduct. They are attempts to define what should or should not be accepted by Muslims, what should and should not be included as good Islamic practice. Perhaps it is not for analysts to say where this line should be drawn by comparing local forms of Islam to some pure or parent type of the religion, but it is for them to highlight the contours of local debate and discourse, as well as the kinds of issue that come under scrutiny.

This general sense of ambivalence is reflected in the words of Cheikh Hamidou Kane, author of the semi-autobiographical novel *L'Adventure ambigue*: 'If Islam should appear to me, by whatever trait, to be in contradiction with the African personality, I would prefer "to forget" for the present, this discord' (quoted by Monteil 1980: 420, my translation).

ISLAM AND THE REINTERPRETATION OF MYTH

If the above examples are illustrations of ambivalence that is felt by many Haalpulaar'en over a range of religious practices, there is a domain in which men-of-skill experience a particularly poignant sense of ambivalence, and this concerns their own conceptions of the origins of their crafts. Their myths of origin tell predominantly the story of a series of connections between their mythical ancestor and spiritual forces associated with the bush, the domain of the wild, whence their crafts are taken.[13] This section of the chapter develops the theme of ambivalence that is evident within such myths, and it also reprises a motif from the last chapter, namely the extent of the influence of the elevation of *toorobe* Islam on the ideological position of the men-of-skill social categories.

Kyburz has recently argued that the social category of *toorobe* clerics does not form a point of reference for the definition of the hierarchical organisation of Haalpulaar'en social relations. This is true to the extent that the clerics substituted, *mutatis mutandis*, for the earlier dominant group, and they did not radically affect the threefold structure of social divisions. This argument is well taken, and is a counterweight to the over-emphasis placed on the rise of the *tooroɓe* by an earlier generation of writers (see for example Wane 1969). However, Kyburz goes on to suggest that no myth of origin of a metier or of the foundation of a men-of-skill social category makes reference to the *tooroɓe* clerics (Kyburz 1994: 158–60). While this argument is not wrong, it misses an essential point. For virtually all the men-of-skill categories have produced versions of myths that cast the origins of crafts, no longer simply in the domain of jinn and spirits of the wild, but with respect to Islam, that is to the inspiration that motivated the revived Muslim *tooroɓe* clerisy.[14] My point is that the ideological impact of *tooroɓe* Islam in the eighteenth century set in train a cultural debate about the relative positions and cultural status of the men-of-skill groups. This influence has extended to the development of reinterpreted versions of craft origins in an attempt to resolve an ambivalence or tension felt between the imperatives of *tooroɓe* Islam, on the one hand, and the practice of their own crafts and trades on the other.

In an article published some years ago, I described the process of Islamic reinterpretation of the origins of weaving (Dilley 1987c). It focused on a debate that ensued between a cleric who argued that it was the spider that brought weaving to mankind, and a Weaver who protested that it was the *maabuɓe*'s mythical ancestor, Juntel Jabaali, and he had taken the craft from jinn weaving in the bush. Moreover, it concentrated on a version of weaving origins recited by an old *mabu* Weaver who claimed a different source for the craft. According to his version, the first man, Adam, at the beginning of time, was conceived as the first weaver and the *maabuɓe* took over the craft from him. Indeed, the craft received the seal of the Prophet, who blessed those who wove cotton cloth, the fabric of the faithful. Juntel, the weavers' ancestor, became in this version a *waliyu*, a saint or 'friend of God' in the Sufi tradition, and Juntel's mother, conventionally conceived of as a spirit woman, did not feature at all in the myth. There is also an interesting passage which describes how weavers were mocked for constructing their looms over a hole in which they sat while weaving. This I had interpreted earlier as a reference to Serer weavers who indeed hollow out a space beneath the loom where the weaver's feet operate the poles attached to the heddles. Perhaps this was a reference to an earlier common cultural origin, I had ventured, with this episode symbolically marking a separation of the two weaving traditions. I now realise that this might be a figurative reference to the primitive or uncivilised state the weavers found themselves in. It finds an echo in the reports about Malik Sy, a Fuutanke cleric and founder of the seventeenth-century polity of Bundu in the upper Senegal valley – a forerunner of the later Almaamate revolution in the middle valley. Sy made a reference to the primitive existence of the people who lived in the upper valley on his arrival there having fled Fuuta Toro as a Muslim activist. The inhabitants are described as 'living in holes' or 'subterranean hollows', and according to tradition Malik Sy became their Shaykh only on condition that they turn away from this primitive practice and live in fixed dwellings constructed above the ground (see Willis 1979: 36, fn 155). In the myth, the Weavers too abandon their practice of sitting in holes, and the old Weaver narrator could well have been drawing on this idiom from a 'Maliki' Muslim tradition. Certainly, this Islamic version was in strict contrast to the usual origin myths I had heard; indeed, it was met with a sense of disbelief by other Weavers to whom I recounted it. The old man was clearly losing his senses, they ventured, for it was completely wrong in their view. This new version denied all the fundamental aspects that were at the heart of *maabuɓe* cultural identity and of their conception of their craft. The denial of the very attributes that make up *maabuɓe* identity is related to the problem of ambiguity and ambivalence of belief and practice, over what constitutes good Muslim practice and what does not. The impulse that brought about the generation of Islamic reinterpretations of the origin myth is an attempt to marry the contradictions posed by the Weaver's fear of being condemned by *toorobe* clerics for what they would consider as 'non-Islamic' belief.

Besides these myths referring to the origins of weaving, there are other reports of similar kinds of reinterpretation of the origins of other crafts into Islamic idiom and imagery (see Kante 1993; Kyburz 1994; Morice 1982). For example, the canoe-building sub-branch of the Woodcarvers category have set the origins of their occupation in a time of flood, rather than of drought and famine as is the case with many other crafts. Moreover, they claim to be descendants of Noah (*annabi Nuhu*, the Prophet Noah) and it is from him that they have inherited the knowledge of boat-building. This myth takes its reference from the Qur'anic scripture Sura XI, Chapter of the Hûd. Smiths too claim descent from a Qur'anic and Biblical figure, *annabi Dawda*, or the Prophet David, from whom knowledge of how to handle hot metals is derived. The angel Gabriel appeared to David in the night and indicated to him a form in the shape of a cross lying on the ground next to his forge. The following morning David realised the significance of the vision and made a pair of smith's tongs (Morice 1982: 101). Prior to this David had miraculous powers to enable him to handle red-hot metal with his bare hands.

A final example is the *awluɓe* Praise-singers. A very widespread origin myth of the praise-singing profession in general speaks of a relationship between two brothers during a time of drought and famine. On the point of starvation, the two brothers can find no game or fruits or nuts to nourish themselves. The elder brother, noticing that his younger sibling is close to death, disappears into the bush one last time in a desperate bid to save his brother. He returns with some meat which he cooks and feeds to his companion. Having eaten the meat and having been revived, the younger brother realises that he has consumed flesh his elder brother took from his own thigh. Recognising this heroic deed, the younger brother pledges to sing his elder sibling's praises from then on in honour of his sacrifice and in return for his own life. Thus was born the social category of Praise-singers. This relationship between eulogist and recipient of the praise is called *hoo serre*, the 'piece of meat or flesh', and it is a motif that recurs in virtually all of the praise-singer social categories (on the *maabuɓe jaawamɓe*, for example, see Dilley 1984). This relationship was described by the Arabic term *shirk* by numerous strict *tooroɓe* clerics, that is it is the sin of association, of ascribing partners to God, in the veneration of one brother by his sibling. Furthermore, the cannibalistic act portrayed in the myth suggests connotations of witchcraft, which also involves the consumption of human victims. By contrast, reinterpretations of Praise-singer origins have cast the emergence of the group back to the time of the Prophet Mohammed. The first *awluɓe* Praise-singer, it recalls, was a companion of the Prophet, a brilliant orator, singer and public crier who was part of Mohammed's early mission to spread the faith. He would stand at the gates of the city to announce in a loud voice the Prophet's arrival. The inhabitants would be enchanted by his words and would leave their houses to welcome Mohammed, the messenger of God (see Kyburz 1994: 406–12).

DISCUSSION

Each of the examples of the reinterpretation of the origins of occupations presented above, I would argue, evinces a sense of ambivalence on the part of men-of-skill about the conception of their crafts and musical arts in relation to the religion of Islam. While on the one hand they have been accommodated ideologically into a version of Sufi Islam, at the level of experience, on the other, these craftsmen and musicians are ambivalent about their position. Freeman clerics are also ambivalent about their perception of the value to be placed upon 'black arts'. Men-of-skill have been allocated a subordinate position within an encompassing Islamic cosmology, in which they play specialist roles that complement those of the clerics. These differing roles refer to the 'this-worldly' versus the 'other-worldly' aspects of religion. Ideological formations, however, cannot account for the nature of human experience.

Craftsmen and musicians also attempt to redress the sense of disdain and scorn that *tooroɓe* Islam has poured upon their occupations since the formation of the clerics as a social category. This ambivalence was set in train by a revitalised *tooroɓe* Islam that asserted a form of ideological hegemony that was based on religious criteria.[15] In particular, it highlighted the connection between craft occupations and the type of source of knowledge and power they draw on. Moreover, it set these connections within a rigidly dualistic and hierarchical model. Although an accommodationist Islam granted a place to men-of-skill within a cosmological framework, it was a subordinate position they occupied and barriers were set up against their full participation in the community of the faithful. The cleric-inspired disdain of craftsmen is captured in the profanity recorded by Gaden (1931): *Allaa bonnii nyeenyo*, 'God damn the *nyeenyo* or craftsman', and used in the sense of the exclamation 'God damn it'. The Islamic reinterpretations of myth, then, reflect an experience of ambiguity that men-of-skill must have felt in the past and still do feel today about their position relative to Islam: on the one hand they proclaim themselves to be good Muslims; yet by virtue of the occupations they practise they are marginalised in the *jama'a* and reduced in the estimation of the faithful. What better way to address this experience of ambiguity and ambivalence than to redefine the nature of the occupations they practise? The price for this, however, is that such a strategy strikes at the heart of the cultural identity of the men-of-skill, of who and what they are as occupational specialists. The exclusivity of their status is thus undermined, and this represents too a potential threat to their monopoly over their occupations. That these versions do not have such a wide currency as origin myths speaks of the price that has to be paid. To redress the balance regarding the negative evaluations of *toorobe* Islam is at the same time to betray their self-perception as experts in forms of power and knowledge over which the clerics have very little control. Men-of-skill are caught in a double-bind only partly of their own making. But as Gramsci (1971) has indicated, the consciousness of the subaltern groups is often contradictory and confused.

While *toorobe* clerics and others may hold men-of-skill occupations in disdain, there is another side to their perception of them. Craftsmen and musicians may at times scoff at the negative evaluations attached to them, and they present an oppositional cultural identity. But there is a richer tableau of cultural value beneath this veneer. Despite the scorn and derision, the men-of-skill are also held in awe for the powers they control and are respected for the skills they possess. They are even feared for the effects they can bring about and the spiritual associations and company they are thought to keep.[16] It is by virtue of this aspect of their social character that they are allocated specialist duties with respect to certain rites of passage. They are at once key social actors, but yet despised and feared for the very roles they carry out.

These issues lead us onto another area of consideration, one that has been noted by a number of commentators on 'Muslim societies'. Lewis, for example, points out that 'Muslim theology is equally tolerant in attitude towards divination, magic, witchcraft and sorcery' (1980: 60). Although it might condemn the use of the last two, it does not question their efficacy. As we learnt earlier, men-of-skill are often linked with witchcraft and sorcery, and I will turn to consider these issues in the next chapter. The discussion of witchcraft in particular will lead us into areas that are not necessarily neatly accommodated or even encompassed by Muslim cleric ideology; indeed, they are seen by some people to stand outside it, to be opposed to it, and even to represent a threat to it. In this respect, the social differentiation of specialist practitioners, each with their own expertise in a particular domain of power and knowledge, sets up competing claims to ascendancy in spiritual matters.[17] This is another aspect, therefore, of the idea of multiple sources of power and knowledge. The opposition between the mosque and the termite mound is figured again in the images of the marabout and the witch-hunter/curer, the topic of the next chapter.

6

THE WITCH-HUNTER AND THE MARABOUT: COMPETING DOMAINS OF KNOWLEDGE AND POWER

The opposition between white lore and knowledge and black lore and knowledge connotes the separation between locally conceived Islamic specialists, the *tooroɓe* clerics in particular, and men-of-skill, along with other specialists whose occupations or arts are considered to be 'non-' or 'pre-Islamic' by the Muslim faithful. These latter specialisms are thought to lie outside exclusive Muslim expertise, and each of them has its own specific body of lore and knowledge classified under the rubric 'black'. That is, they represent competing realms of power and knowledge that stand in opposition to that of the *tooroɓe* clerics.

In some Islamised societies in Africa, such as the Berti of Sudan, formal, orthodox Muslim practice is defined in relation to the ritual concerns of men, whereas those practices which are considered local, unorthodox and customary are considered to be the domain of women. A distinction between two classes of ritual expresses a distinction between genders, each of which constitutes a part of a Berti religious system (Holy 1991). Berti men, therefore, place into the category of the other the popular, supposedly pre-Islamic, practices of their womenfolk. Among Haalpulaar'en, I argue that a parallel process occurs, whereby all those forms of lore, knowledge and power that lie outside a culturally defined Muslim sphere and that compete with the expertise of the *tooroɓe* clerics is placed in the category of the 'other' and labelled 'black'. Whereas Berti men have devalued the religious activities of women, among Haalpulaar'en it is the freeborn and the *tooroɓe* clerics in particular who have devalued the activities and knowledge associated with men-of-skill specialists in much the same way. Indeed, the position of Haalpulaar women suggests a comparison with that of the craftsmen and musicians with respect to Islam. Both categories were, and still are in many respects, marginalised and excluded from complete participation in the Muslim faith. Not only this, but as we will see below, it is women and children rather than men who are reported to be more reliant on the services of the practitioners of black arts (see Tall 1984).

This chapter describes at the outset some aspects of the range of lore and knowledge considered to be outside the remit of specialist Muslim clerics. It then moves on to examine in particular the witch-hunter, whom I contrast with the marabout, an Islamic healer and ritual specialist. But first, I turn to consider the indigenous conception of knowledge.

THE BLACK ARTS AND FIELDS OF KNOWLEDGE

The 'black' is a kind of residual category for that which is not controlled by or associated with *toorobe* clerics, and is composed of all those practices, forms of knowledge and areas of expertise that draw on powers and potencies that lie outside the spiritual forces respected and valued by Muslim clerics. Moreover, it is apparent that practitioners of these arts and occupations seem willing to accept the ascription 'black', an ideological coding that delimits a domain in which they can excel, beyond the control and authority of the clerics. There is also a popular demand for these bodies of expertise in the face of illness, misfortune and the immediate concerns of this world.

The key vernacular term that denotes what I have been translating thus far as lore and knowledge is *gandal*. *Gandal* can be translated as 'knowledge' or 'science', and it is directly linked to the verb *andude*, meaning 'to know' or 'to have a knowledge of' a particular subject. The related term *gandudo* (plural, *anduɓe*) can be glossed as *savant*, whether in the form of a 'magician' or a literate cleric scribe (Gaden 1914: 4). *Gandal* refers to all forms of specialist knowledge that are required in order to carry out particular tasks, and it embraces both Qur'anic or religious learning (*gandal diine*) or 'white' lore and knowledge (*gandal danewal*), as well as craft and occupational lore which is classed as 'black' (*gandal ɓalewal*). The term *gandal* invokes both the sense of lore and knowledge as well as of a general mystical power that can be used to bring about effects in the world. I have also translated it elsewhere (Dilley 2000) by the rather cumbersome compound 'knowledge-power', for it is both a body of learning and a form of agency that results in effects being brought about by means of that learning.[1] The word 'lore' in English refers to 'a body of traditions and knowledge *on a subject*' (as the *Oxford English Dictionary* puts it, emphasis added) and to 'that which is taught' as part of 'a doctrine or teaching', and is applied chiefly to religious doctrine, as in 'God's lore' or 'holy lore'. The English term 'lore' then retains some of the sense suggested by the Pulaar word *gandal*, namely its connection to specialist knowledge, often held by a specific group, and it has religious and spiritual connotations. While the word 'lore' does then capture a good deal about the concept of *gandal*, it misses one of the essential aspects for Pulaar speakers. That is, it can be used synonymously for the idea of power, something that brings about effects in the world. To say that someone has *gandal* is to say that the person is capable as well as knowledgeable, that is he or she can use that knowledge to bring about effects, that knowledge is power. Knowledge and power are ultimately linked in the figure of Allah, one of whose ninety-nine names is

Ganndo, 'The-All-Knowing', and another is *Dundari*, 'The-All-Powerful'. Knowledge can bring about effects, and one of those effects is to bring further knowledge by means of the power it entrains, especially through dreams or encounters with spirits (see Dilley 1992). In the last chapter, I glossed a whole range of activities which are considered to entrain often invisible, non-human, spiritual agents as 'magic' or, better, 'power-practices'. Here and in the next chapter I will turn to analysing the foundations of these purportedly 'magical' acts in terms of the knowledge-power (*gandal*), or lore, by means of an archaeology of specialist thought and practice.

The origin of *gandal* is the spiritual world. Since there are different sorts of spirit being, different sorts of knowledge can be derived from them, such as 'black' lore in relation to the spirits that animate craft occupations, and 'white' lore from those associated with the 'higher' arts of Islamic learning and knowledge. The world of spirits is the *fons et origo* of many of the men-of-skill crafts, their knowledge and their expertise, and superior ability in the craft is discussed in terms of one person possessing more or greater *gandal* than another. Despite the rather cumbersome nature of this Foucauldian sounding translation, the compound 'knowledge-power' does have valuable resonances. It suggests the ability to act, to bring about effects on the basis of knowledge, and this extends the sense of the translation to a culturally defined conception of human agency. A person possessing *gandal* can bring about effects, not necessarily through the physical strength (*sembe*) or force or energy (*doole*), nor necessarily through the power and authority of political office (*laamu*); instead they are brought about through the potency inherent in lore or *gandal* itself. Someone who is capable of performing a range of tasks is called a *baawo*, a term linked to the verb *waawde*, 'to be able'. *Baawo* is also the title of the ritual initiator of boys, and is one who possesses knowledge (*gandal*) of and powers linked to spiritual matters. In the figure of the *baawo*, the able-man, is represented the combination of knowledge and ability to act, that is a form of human agency stemming from the possession of lore. Another of the ninety-nine names of Allah is *Bawdo*, 'The-Able-One'. I have, therefore, coined the translation 'knowledge-power' rather than 'lore' for the Pulaar word *gandal* in those contexts specifically where it is this aspect of mystical causation that is to be highlighted. Elsewhere I have resorted to the simple gloss 'lore'.

Gandal is likened to a vast field (*ngesa gandal ine yaaje*, literally 'the field of *gandal* is vast') which is divided into specific plots or areas of expertise. Moreover, this metaphor is extended, for there is a maxim that states: '*Gandal* is a field, but if it is neither worked on or looked after, it will yield no harvest' (*Gandal ko ngesa, soko noon, so remaaka reenaa, sonyetaake*) (Gaden 1931). The possession of lore in itself does not yield benefits or produce effects, but has to be linked to human effort in mobilising that knowledge for particular effects. The choice of the metaphor of the field for *gandal* is perhaps apt for, as I described in an earlier chapter, land is rigidly divided for cultivation on the basis of membership of social categories. Just as the cultivable plots of land in the flood basins are allocated according to social criteria, so the field of knowledge and power is divided according to social specialism. This link to specialised forms of practice marks *gandal* out as a particular kind of knowledge-power that is manifested only in some kinds of action and in some types of agency. *Gandal* is the domain of the specialist that requires effort to acquire it and perseverance and dedication to maintain its efficacy. Those who are thought to possess *gandal*, of whatever sort – black or white – or who are believed to have a special aptitude for learning it, are referred to as having 'large heads' or 'old heads' (*hoore mawnde* – the root '*maw*' can refer to size or age).

The field of *gandal* is, however, divided in a number of ways such that access to particular areas of knowledge varies according to its social location: some domains are exclusive to particular social categories while others are open for all to learn; some of these domains are by their nature in the public realm while others are private, esoteric and secret, and access to them is through initiatory procedures. The relationship between occupation or activity on the one hand, and the bodies of lore that may or may not be connected to them on the other, may be defined in one of four ways. First, there are category-specific bodies of occupational and craft lore and knowledge (*gandal golle* or 'occupational lore') that are exclusive to members of these social categories alone. The lore of these occupations is closely linked to ideas of ancestry and descent, for it is held that an outsider to a group who learns exclusive craft knowledge could be sent mad by it. Second, there are some occupations that are exclusive to a social category but they have no specific body of lore or knowledge-power attached to them. This is claimed by men-of-skill for the social category of Warriors, or by the craftsmen of the Musicians and Praise-singers who, they argue, possess only genealogies and the power of words. Members of these social categories may, however, dispute these claims. Third, there are occupational specialisms open to all Haalpulaar'en but which have no *gandal* attached to them, such as cultivation. Finally, there are bodies of lore and knowledge that are specific to particular occupations, which are nonetheless open to anyone who might choose to take them up.

The fourth type of relation is characteristic of a range of arts of healing and curing. Some specialisms in this area are confined to specific lineages – often inherited through women – and can include the gift to cure, for example, animal and insect bites. In addition, some Fulɓe cattle-herding lineages are gifted with the ability to make charms (*ɓayre* is a charm) to attract riches (*ɓayre jawdi*), power and office (*ɓayre laamu*) or for the purposes of seduction (*ɓayre rewɓe*). Some lineages are held to possess specialist knowledge of plants or the arts of interpreting the language of animals. Many of the most important arts are, however, open for anyone to learn if the person is able to be apprenticed to an expert willing to teach them. Although open to all in theory, because of the initiatory procedures involved in apprenticeship, these arts are in practice limited, but not limited according to membership of specific social categories. An example of an open profession with a specific body of lore was that of marabout, particularly during the eighteenth century prior to the Almaamate uprising and the closing of *toorobe* cleric ranks to new membership. They attempted after that to make Muslim cleric expertise an area exclusive to them alone in the form of 'caste' lore akin to craftsmen's lore. Other specialisms that remain open to all, although they involve esoteric forms of knowledge, are the arts of the *wileebe* (*bileejo*, in the singular), witch-hunters, curers and magicians, or the arts of diviners (*timoobe*) who use a variety of techniques of divination such as the use of cowrie shells or plant stalks, small animal horns or sand scattered across a flat surface. There are also the healing arts of the *safroobe*, practitioners who use herbs and plant extracts to cure, or those of the *mocoowo*, who apply herbs and massage to the body. Specialisms in the production of protective amulets, although considered open to all, are often the expertise of specific men-of-skill. For instance, amulets (*pibi*) made from twisted and knotted cotton thread are usually produced by Weavers (a knotter is a *fiboowo*) or those made from tree bark (made by a *fibirbaaji*) are often fabricated by Fishermen and Woodcarvers. Similarly, the 'diggers of roots' (*asoobe dadi*) collect the roots of certain plants, shrubs and trees, while the *ledde baleebe*, literally the 'tree-black-ones', are those who gather up leaves or branches and tear off bark (*sirde baayi lekki*) from various kinds of tree. Both of these occupations bring their practitioners into contact with spirits who live in most species of native tree and some larger woody plants, and they are closely associated with the practices of the Woodcarvers who possess the lore of trees of the bush (*gandal lekki*). Indeed, any body of lore associated with the bush (*gandal ladde*) is assimilated in popular thought with the activities of men-of-skill.

Despite the fact that many of these occupations and arts are open to all, there is a sense that they are by association close to the expertise of the men-of-skill. There is an elective affinity between these two domains of lore. Kante, discussing blacksmiths in Mali, suggests a similar affinity. His understanding of the connection between smithing and healing and magic is through the friendships craftsmen forge with spirits. These powers assist them to become diviners, seers, healers and indeed feared 'magicians' (Kante 1993: 29). Likewise, the connections with the spirit forces of the wild suggest that Haalpulaar men-of-skill can make particularly good witch-hunters, diviners and so on, or that Leatherworkers are associated with the nefarious activities of witches. All of these arts are classed not only as 'black lore', *gandal balewal*, but are also referred to as *gandal aada*, lore of local customs and traditions, from the Islamic conception of *adat* (local customary practice).

The emergence of *gandal maabuɓe*

For the Weavers, the origins of *maabuɓe* lore and knowledge are shrouded in mystery, and only those with a depth of understanding can supply anything more than the basic details of it. These details are contained in *taarik*s, stories or myths relating to the past and defining the origins of things. The oldest, most ancient of these *taarik*s (*taarik burɗo ɗum duubi*) are thought to contain the most important and most secret details.[2] The stories that constitute an important part of weaving *gandal* speak of the beginning of time and the emergence of social groups within a division of labour. In terms of a general scheme of development, they tell of how at the beginning of time man was like an animal, roaming around the bush, lacking a proper language and communicating only by grunts and groans. People later became herders (*aynaaɓe*), for this was the first occupation among humans. They then divided themselves, some becoming fishermen[3] and some remaining cattle-herders, and through this division black *gandal*, lore and knowledge, emerged (*gandal ɓalewal yalti*). People began to understand and acquire knowledge; they became knowledgeable (*yimɓe ɓe ganndi*). It was Allah who brought this about, it was he who divided people into two, and it was he who brought forth knowledge; indeed, black lore and knowledge was brought forth through him. The purpose of this division was to enable people to become friends (*sehilaaɓe*); in other words people were encouraged by means of this division to exchange and have social intercourse that would be mutually beneficial to all.

The birth of Juntel, the Weavers' mythical ancestor, is one of the most important events for the *maabuɓe*. Feeynar is the first in the line of men after humans had acquired language, and he is the apical ancestor of not only the *maabuɓe* but also of the *lawɓe laana* (woodcutters and boat-makers) some of whom trace a line to a mythical ancestor, Dawda Mbawa Feeynar. Feynaar begat Naango, and Naango begat Jabaali, Juntel's father. Not every *maabu* weaver has a line of ancestry or pedigree (*asko*) that can be traced back to Juntel, but many will go back to Naango Feeynar. Although Juntel's actions were the defining moment in weaving coming into the possession of the *maabuɓe*, not all 'true' *maabuɓe* (especially those bearing one of the ten or eleven exclusive patronyms) can claim him as a forefather.[4] My master weaver who bore the patronym Gisse (Guisse) claimed Juntel was also Gisse, and that he himself had a direct and 'pure' pedigree (*asko ranewo*) back to the ancestor who actually took weaving from the bush spirits.[5] Juntel's father Jabaali was a man of great powers and possessed much knowledge-power (*gandal*), for he was able to marry a female bush spirit (*debbo ladde* or 'woman of the bush'), and together they had a child, Juntel, who was half-man half-spirit. At this time, according to local narrators, the *subalɓe* Fishermen, the *lawɓe laana* Woodcarvers and the *maabuɓe* had not yet fully divided off, but constituted a much larger general category. *Maabuɓe* lore is closely associated with the lore and knowledge of the *subalɓe* Fishermen; it is said that there is a close resemblance between the two. The two occupations are linked in the origin myth of weaving; furthermore, of the two brothers who feature in the myth, the elder becomes the first *cubbalo* (singular of *subalɓe*) Fisherman and the younger is the mythical ancestor of the Weavers. Weavers sometimes even possess some fishing incantations and river magic, such as those dealing with the hunting of hippopotamuses.

People in those days were more open than they are today, they did not have to hide their knowledge and be secretive about the powers and potencies they possessed. Indeed, it is because of this openness, and the fact that deception (*naafigaagu*) and greed (*ndeereeru*) did not exist, that the mythical ancestor Juntel Jabaali was able to listen to and learn the spells and incantations shouted out by spirits as they wove at the loom in the bush. Juntel was able, therefore, to learn a good deal of weaving *gandal* very quickly, for the spirits and people alike were not secretive or afraid of losing their knowledge. When Juntel returned home with parts of the loom tangled up in the bottom of a dugout canoe with fishing nets etc., his mother, a spirit, recognised the equipment and knew where it had come from. She also decided to teach her son many things about weaving, as well as about the powers and potencies that lay behind it. Thus, Juntel came to possess the *gandal* of his mother's people (*omo jogii e gandal yummiraaɓe*), namely of the jinn or spirits. Moreover, he knew his mother's given name (*inde*), and with this name he could perform magical tasks. He had only to pronounce it and he could make cloth appear, often by burning threads and pulling cloth strips from the ashes or by stretching threads across the river and calling them to him in the form of cloth by using his mother's name.[6] They would arrive on the opposite bank in the form of cloth. Many such methods were used to create cloth, but it was his mother's name that gave him the potency to weave without a loom. It was possible to do almost anything simply by pronouncing this name, and today this name is the most secret and powerful part of *gandal maabuɓe*. Such was the potency of this name, however, that the weavers became fearful of it, for it could be used to destroy (*saa haali inde ko heewi ine bona* or 'if you said the name many things were spoilt'). Because of the damage that could be done with this name it became a secret (*sirru* or *suunde*)[7] among the Weavers, and few people today know the name let alone dare pronounce it. Furthermore, out of respect for Juntel, no *maabu* today would name his child after the mythical ancestor.

These events mark a change in the golden age of humanity. The narrators of these stories suggest how a fall from a golden age occurred and how greed, deceitfulness and dishonesty became the hallmark of relations between humans. Before all of this, people were 'friends' and open in their dealings one with another. Narrators are not always clear as to why man became greedy, deceitful and dishonest, but a change was certainly marked by the realisation among the Weavers of the potency of Juntel's mother's name. Perhaps it was the will to power that arose between people who found themselves in competition as craftsmen that was the cause of this fall from grace. One other particularly significant event retold in mythical history is the eating of hyena by the early weavers during a period of famine and drought – during 'a time of great hunger'.[8] Hyena meat would normally be considered impure and thus not eaten by humans. This act set them apart as an exclusive social category or *lenyol* in the form of the *maabuɓe* with their own patronyms (*jettoode*). A sense of identity as well as a source, an origin or point of departure for lines of ancestry and pedigree were thus established.

The moral dilemma of the story is thus highlighted, and the story becomes a vehicle to invite reflection upon questions of ethics and the social bonds of fraternity. This episode not only marks another point in the fall from grace of humanity in general, and of the Weavers in particular, but it also points to an aspect of *gandal maabuɓe*. Hyenas are thought to possess *gandal* as do many other bush animals, and their fur alongside that of the jackal (*boyi*) and other creatures is often found on sale on market stalls for manufacture into amulets and talismans. By eating hyena flesh, the Weavers' forefathers took in as part of themselves the animal's *gandal* or lore, knowledge and potency. This act is more than a metaphor of identity, for it involves an act of consubstantiation, of the *maabuɓe* taking in part of the substance of the hyena. The myth is, therefore, also an image of a covert and indirect means of acquiring lore and knowledge, compared with the open and direct means characteristic of earlier times.

From this point onwards, other *nyeenyɓe* occupations emerged, such that each social category or stock (*lenyol*) gained their own métier (*golle*) in order to create relations between groups. Each and every one had his own métier (*gooto heen fof jogii ko gollal mum*), so that people could exchange one with the other. A weaver would search for a freeman (*dimo*) patron and would enter into a relationship with him. This conception of the initial division of labour appears to be rather Durkheimian in function, since it expresses the notions of complementarity, functionality and sentiments of solidarity. The division as it developed, however, generated tensions that have remained a reality for present-day Weavers. The *nyeenyɓe* were forced into competition with each other (*nyeenyɓe mbatti gattude*) for the patronage of freemen, and moreover came into competition (*gattondiral*) with their own fellow craftsmen for superiority in economic and spiritual matters. The introduction of power into the division of labour seems to upset the harmony of the original state of grace, and this produced something similar to what Durkheim (1984) considered to be aberrant, dysfunctional forms of the division of labour.[9] Lore and knowledge-power (*gandal*) became exclusive, hidden and secret in the context of competition among weavers for patronage. Moreover, one weaver could now gain a march over a rival by possessing some aspect of lore which the other lacked; he could produce perhaps more or better cloth than his rival, and would be able to dispose of it more quickly and under better terms.

These *taarik*s relating to the beginnings of time and the origins of *gandal* as lore, knowledge and potency might be construed in terms of articulating an indigenous theory about the sources of *gandal*, about the division of labour in society and about the generation of conflict, domination and power politics in the affairs of craftsmen in competition for outlets, increased production and superiority in all aspects of the craft. This gave rise also to *gandal bonnude neddo*, that is lore and knowledge-power that can harm another person, particularly those against whom one has a grudge – namely one's competitors.

This account of the origins of weaving lore, based on discussions with two master weavers in particular, makes little or no reference to explicitly Muslim themes. It has been presented here as an example that should be read as an indigenous interpretation of the origin of one aspect of black lore and knowledge, *gandal balewal*. The ability to do the things that Weavers do is linked in these accounts to the acquisition and continued possession of *gandal maabuɓe*, Weavers' lore, or knowledge-power. Yet, accommodationist Islam has been able to find an ideological place for such bodies of knowledge within its cosmology. Clerics do not necessarily become consumed by the issue of opposing this alternative reading of the origins of things. They simply think it wrong and muddle-headed of Weavers to regard such matters in this way. What has been more problematic for cleric Islam are other aspects of black lore which are not so easily accommodated, or in relation to which they so easily suspend moral judgement. Some of these aspects of black lore inform arts that can bring to mind among local inhabitants the activities of men-of-skill. Witchcraft, witch-curing and associated arts of healing and magic represent such practices.

It has been frequently pointed out by commentators on West African Islam that while local Muslims may condemn witchcraft, sorcery, possession and some forms of divination and 'magic', they often are at the same time equally tolerant towards them (Lewis 1980: 60; Sanneh 1989). The existence of such domains external to the areas of expertise of Muslim clerics brings into question the extent to which accommodationist Islam has managed to bring into its encompassing vision all forms of spiritual force. It is said by some practitioners of 'black arts' that witches and certain 'pre-Islamic' jinn from the south of Senegal are among the most malign and difficult forces to control; indeed, they recognise no master or God who can subdue them. Witchcraft in particular represents another problematic area for Muslim specialists. Clerics have few if any means of dealing with it, and so specialists lying outside the domain annexed by Muslims are 'a necessity for Muslim society' (Trimingham 1959: 73).[10] It is to witchcraft that I now turn, in order to understand the nature of the ideas and practices that lie at its heart. Indeed, a comparison with the ideas and practices of maraboutic magic which follows is intended to shed light on areas of similarity and difference between the two ideologically distinct domains.

THE WITCH-HUNTER AND THE MARABOUT

Omar Ba, in a discussion of the relationship between 'Islamic' and 'non-Islamic' practice in Fuuta Toro (Ba 1985–86: 36–7), relates the following story which he collected during the course of his research:

> A marabout was leading a group of his pupils and disciples (*taalibes*) across a dangerous stretch of land inhabited by lions. In crossing the territory, the group came across a magician, who joined them, and he demanded that the marabout use his theological knowledge to preserve the caravan from attack by wild animals. The recitation of Qur'anic verses and other techniques at the cleric's command, however, failed to prevent lions from devouring a number of his student followers. The magician asked permission of the marabout to use his own magical knowledge to bring about the desired aim. He was granted permission and the caravan continued safely across the dangerous territory. (My translation)

Ba introduces this story as part of a discussion about how 'non-Islamic' practice is on the retreat. The latter, in the form of witchcraft, sorcery and other forms of healing, are under attack from marabouts, who have declared a war against 'mystification and mockery'. It is a culture on the road to perdition. While arguing that the culture of the marabout is replacing that of the 'sorcerer', little has dented the latter's prestige and social standing, he points out. Such stories, he declares, offer a testament to the important position that 'sorcerers' occupy and bear witness to the degree of popular credulity in magical practices. Not only that, but they bear witness to a plurality of competing forms of religious thought and practice, which I discussed in Chapter 5. I now wish to turn to these to investigate two competing bodies of magical thought and practice, in the figures of the witch-hunter/curer (*bileejo*) and of the marabout.

The witch-hunter

Witch-hunters (*wileeɓe* or *bileejo* in the singular) are the counter-agents to witches (*sukunyaaɓe*) whose practice of witchcraft (*cukunyaagu*) is associated with the eating of human flesh and the drinking of blood. Hence, witches are also called 'those who eat others' (*nyamneeɓe*) or 'the drinkers of blood' (*yarooɓe yiiyam*).[11] Trimingham reported that the witch-hunter (*bileejo*) is a 'general medicine-man who continues to flourish, even in these deeply Islamised regions [in Fuuta Toro and Fuuta Jallon]' (1959: 119). He correctly identifies him as a religious functionary, operating in parallel with Muslim cleric specialists. He dispenses a range of magical cures and healing techniques that involve medicinal potions (*safaara*), herbal and plant remedies, or incantations (*cefi*) and spells (*bolle ɓaleeje*). Some people fear that witch-hunters are themselves reformed witches – indeed, the one I worked with claimed to have eaten twenty souls – and that they may also be involved in offensive magic and sorcery (*dabare*).

As Evans-Pritchard pointed out for the Azande many years ago (1937), witchcraft is an involuntary act arising from the possession of witch-substance that is passed down through women. Among Haalpulaar'en, the potential for witchcraft is also believed to be inherited through the female line, although it can affect both men and women alike. A son or daughter of a female witch is likely to be a witch him or herself, although if treated sufficiently well, the person may no longer feel the urge to eat other people but instead becomes a witch-hunter. He or she has the same spiritual power as witches but can use it to oppose them. The child of a male witch is neither necessarily a witch nor a witch-hunter, but a witch-seer (*nyookooro*, pl. *nyookorɓe*), and this involves the gift of being able to see through clothes and human skin into the body of a person and to the internal organs. In this way they can see if a person is disposed towards witchcraft or has been attacked by witches. Male descendents of male witches may not have this ability but may suffer from an illness that is difficult to cure. The difference between a witch and those who are variously related to witches is that the latter are not possessed by the force of witchcraft (*cukunyaagu*) that makes people want to eat human prey – a force transmitted along the female line.

The victims of witchcraft (*cukunyaado* or *cukunyaaɓe* in the plural) might suffer a range of afflictions. A woman who repeatedly miscarries or who loses infants at birth or in the early months of life is described as being in a state of *yeret*, that is provoked by witch attack. A person who becomes increasingly listless and lethargic or who slips into a trance-like state is also thought to be a victim of witchcraft. Such a person is said 'to be with' or 'taken by witches' (*o wondi e ɓaleeɓe*), who are sometimes referred to figuratively as *ɓaleeɓe*, 'those who are black'. Someone enquiring as to whether an individual has been the victim of a witch attack might ask if the person is 'pure' or 'impure' (*laaɓi* or *laaɓaani*).

Witches are thought to be in league with spirits or jinn from the bush, who are often summoned from tamarind trees to help them. These spirits assist in securing the shadow-self (*mbeelu*) of the witch's victim, which is held in safe keeping until the witch demands its return. To capture a victim, witches operate at night and transform themselves into animals, or more precisely their souls (*fittandu* or *wonki*) can take different forms, often that of a vulture (*dutal*) that can fly far from their home into order to search for a victim to eat. They can also strike closer to home, in the heart of the family or within their own settlement. Bondsmen and women are thought to be able to attack in the form of witches the households of their masters. Alternatively they might transform themselves into a serpent that bites or a fly that can enter the victim's body via the nostril. The witch removes its human skin (*nguru*, pl. *guri*), which it folds carefully and hides until its return, then takes off in search of its victims. After trapping a victim, the witch regains human form by retrieving and clothing itself again with its human skin.

Witches attack a person in the region of the *bernde*, a word often translated as 'heart' but which is also a euphemism for 'stomach' (Gaden 1914: 24). The word also indicates a region of the body at the level of the solar plexus that is the seat of emotions, for the *bernde* is associated with sensations such as anger and it is used figuratively to refer to a person's disposition. In English idiom, this would be located in the heart, for instance 'being kind hearted' or 'having no heart' (Niang 1997). The witch then enters the victim's body in a number of ways to attack the heart or stomach region, and it often does so by becoming a wind or a breath of air, *hendu*, that enters the victim via any bodily orifice: an ear, nostril, mouth, anus, vagina. The victim may lose consciousness (*jiilol*), fainting at the moment when the witch has blown into his or her body. A witch attack may be presaged in a dream in which the victim feels him or herself to be chased by a hideously ugly person. Once inside, the witch will eat the body of the victim, leaving only the skin intact. A child can be made a witch by giving it human flesh to eat or by rubbing its lips with human blood or fat. Social relations among witches are organised around the model of human society, a double or parallel world in which they meet at night for feasts and banquets, to which each witch in turn must contribute human flesh. To be in debt to the witch community threatens the existence of a witch, whose fellows will seek retribution if he or she does not make a contribution of human flesh.

The *bileejo* or witch-hunter, the counter-agent in dealing with the consequences of witchcraft, does not often choose such a role but is in a sense chosen for it. Being born to a known witch is one way of qualifying to be a witch-hunter. Another is by an 'election' that is indicated by a set of signs, the most important of which is being born with teeth (*jibinaa nyiiye*). This state predisposes the person towards witchcraft, for he or she is thought to be especially vulnerable to attack. Children born with teeth have white shadow-selves (*mbeelu ndaneewu*) which grant them the gift of second sight. Their white soul, however, also attracts the attention of evil creatures and witches, and their gift of second sight means they can see witches, who appear to them as persons with two wings growing from the shoulder blades and with four eyes, two of which are located in the nape of the neck in order to see their victims. A child particularly affected by nightmares can be interpreted as coming under the gaze of witches at night. Tall points out that an 'illness-event' is often the stimulus for a mother, concerned about witchcraft, to take her suffering child to see a *bileejo* (Tall 1984).[12] This consultation may spur the child to develop this specialism later in life. One of the foci of Tall's study was a *bileejo* who descended from a *toorobe* cleric family, and whose father was a *ceerno* or master of the Qur'an. She reports that the witch-hunter did not preach or even read the Qur'an, except to extract passages for use in the healing branches of his art. The *bileejo* with whom I conducted a number of interviews was a *maabu* of the social category of Weavers. He had inherited his powers (*mbilewaagu*) from his mother and practised his art in a neighbourhood of *maabube* weavers on the outskirts of the town of Diourbel, situated in Senegal's peanut basin far to the south of Fuuta Toro. An integral part of his art was that he maintained a spirit shrine, comprising two or three upturned pestles buried in the ground, at which he supplicated spirits by pouring libations of millet, milk and sugar twice a week. This shrine was related to other aspects of his healing methods, but was also central to him acquiring further knowledge of witch-hunting (*mbileewu*) that was given him by spirits. This method of acquiring knowledge is in addition to formal apprenticeship. Tall's *bileejo* spent a period of seven years studying under a master witch-hunter, a woman named Buudi Jamel from Mauritania, and another renowned female *bileejo*, Buudi Faay, is claimed to have taught many of those practising the art today (Tall 1984).

A *bileejo*'s methods involve the use of herbs and tree bark, both of which are burnt as part of a treatment of fumigation of a victim of witch attack. If the patient is a witch, the smoke will cause vomiting, which is thought to represent the regurgitation of the shadow-selves of the victims he or she has eaten. What is passed up may be cooked and given to potential victims of witchcraft as a cure. The treatment for a witch will also include two incisions made on the nape of the neck, corresponding to where the second pair of witch eyes are located. This operation will make the second set of eyes disappear. Incantations (*cefi*) are also used, being whispered into the ear of a patient or spread by the medium of saliva (*tuute*) spat while the words are being uttered.

Patients tend to consult a witch-hunter either at night or very early in the morning, for they fear being spotted entering his or her compound. Most people will attempt to visit the *bileejo* on the sly, at times when few people will be about or when it would be difficult to be detected. A *bileejo* is a feared and despised member of a community, and most will shun him in public. Tall reports the case of the famous *bileejo*, Buudi Faay, whose death on a

Friday was marked by few in her village. Her neighbours chose to visit the mosque and on their way home avoided passing by her compound in order to express the conventional condolences (1984: 249–50). The *bileejo* with whom I worked was the only person to keep a spirit shrine in the neighbourhood, a practice scorned upon by his neighbours, his fellow weavers and even his kinsfolk, who claimed it was *shirk* and contrary to Muslim law. He was, nevertheless continually called upon, especially by women who sought his service for their young children suffering from some malady or another. The large number of clients he had bore witness to the fact that the treatments he was offering were in demand by the community, which at the same time condemned him for his persistence in what they considered to be non-Muslim or even pre-Islamic practices.

Although peripheral to the community in many ways – for they often live on the edge of settlements where people can take themselves discretely – *bileejo*s are also involved in mediation between disputing parties. Indeed, while they may be condemned by the devout within a community, they offer services that many, mostly adolescents or women with young children, find important. They frequently consult the *bileejo* when all else has failed, including treatment by a marabout, or when the specific symptoms associated with witchcraft arise. In many ways the *bileejo* is the inverse of the image of the marabout, who frequently lives at the centre of the village close to the mosque, is associated with public life and is a positively valued figure in the community. The life of a *bileejo* is solitary, private and his or her business is conducted surreptitiously under the cover of darkness. There is no community that arises from the network of apprentice relations that exist between witch-hunters (*wileeɓe*) in quite the same way that marabout-disciple (*taalibe*) relations create enduring social bonds and long-remembered pedagogic connections.[13] In addition, witch-hunters labour under the knowledge that they will not die in tranquillity but, being caught off guard at one moment or another by an adversary, they will eventually be trapped by those who chase them, sent mad and suffer a painful death. They therefore require a range of incantations to protect themselves from their old adveraries and accomplices who are a constant threat.

*Bileejo*s (*wileeɓe*) have also developed other healing arts. Tall reports her *bileejo* using Qur'anic script-potions or erasures, especially from the writing of the names of Allah, for a range of cures to wash a patient's body or for ingestion. The *bileejo* is reported to favour incantations rather than written Arabic verses in the treatment of witches. They also employ forms of magic (*dabare*) that involve the use of animal parts (skins, horns, teeth, etc.) or plant materials (*ledɗe*) and it can be used with the aim of causing harm or injury to others (see Figure 6.1). In this sense they fill the role of more general curers and magicians and not just that of witch-hunter. Their magic can be deployed to render a man impotent in relation to his wife or to one

6.1 Two vendors selling the raw materials for amulet-makers, namely animal fur and skins, horns and skulls, birds' feet, quills and so forth.

particular wife, to make a wife feel repugnance towards her husband, to make an enemy or thief go mad, or to force someone into exile without the hope of returning. A practitioner will collect the plant materials – roots, bark, leaves, twigs and so on – he requires from the bush. In collecting these materials, he recites special incantations to protect himself, and he places them in an earthenware pot to prepare his concoction, a *hawde loonde*, over which more incantations are spat (*tuutde*). The pot and its contents are taken back out into the bush, where twigs are collected, placed in the pot and the whole lot set alight. When it has all been reduced to ashes, he might bury the pot with its contents in a cemetery, by a termite mound, or at a mosque or behind the *mihrab* in a mosque (the niche or slab of stone indicating the direction of Mecca). He might also go out at night, when no one is abroad, and smash the pot and spread its contents at the fork in a road. Whichever of these procedures is chosen, each one is accompanied by the recitation of incantations into which the personal name (*inde*) of the victim is integrated in order for the force of the act to reach the intended target, no matter where or how far away he or she may be.

The use of animal parts to effect *dabare* can take the form of an *allaadu jopteendu*, 'a horn that one points' like a finger. These can be obtained from a *bileejo* and can be deployed against an enemy, for whom one must wait at dusk to ambush. The attacker crouches down, closes his right eye and aims his horn, held between the thumb and index finger of the left hand, pointing it in the direction of his enemy, and thus imitating the manner of someone firing a gun. While he does this, the assailant recites the incantation the *bileejo* has taught him, a formula that includes the victim's personal name. Should the victim spot his assailant in the process of 'firing' his spell, it is thought that the force of the incantation will return upon the aggresssor. An alternative mode to deploy the horn is to have it wrapped in a pouch as an amulet either to be carried by the owner or left at some strategic place to affect the intended target.

This kind of spiritual agency is aimed specifically at affecting other people (*dabrude neddo*), and its effect is to produce incurable illnesses that no doctor or modern medicine can cure. These illness are not simply bodily afflictions but they affect the 'soul' (*fittaandu* or *wonki*), so that the cause of the malady or the cause of death is spiritual, not material and physical. To the *bileejo* is attributed, therefore, the power of putting into movement forces that are held to exist everywhere, and these forces can be made to act either to cure the effects of witchcraft or in the form of malevolent *dabare* practices to cause harm and injury to others in the community.[14] The use of this power as a malevolent force is condemned by most people as evil (*bonde*), although a good number might use the services of a *bileejo*, justifying their actions with reference to the desire to protect themselves as much as to do harm to others. As Lienhardt once pointed out, the problem of attributing the moral evaluations of good and evil to specific acts of 'magic' is akin to viewing shot silk: its colour depends on the angle from which it is seen (1968: 51). Particularly pious Muslims condemn these practices as *shirk*, the attribution of powers to entities other than God. However, a good number of Muslim marabouts, also condemned by their pious brethren, practise a parallel form of 'magic' (*sihr*), and likewise most ordinary people fear its use, no matter in whose hands the expertise lies. It is to these specialist practitioners that I now turn.

The art of maraboutic magic

The Muslim marabout offers little protection against witchcraft attack, for the hunting and curing of witches is a specialism particular to the *bileejo*. Moreover, the attribution of specific causes to particular sets of symptoms may vary according to the social position of the interlocutor. Aetiology is a function of social perspective. For example, Fisher villages appear to have a greater incidence of witchcraft accusations, as well as a broad occurrence of spirit possession cults, compared with those settlements dominated by *tooroɓe* clerics. Fisherfolk will also more readily than Muslim clerics attribute an illness, which is marked by a sudden crisis or a rapid descent into apathy and even coma, to the actions of witches rather than to other possible causes (Tall 1984). Members of cleric families will more frequently consult first, not a *bileejo*, but a practising marabout to ascertain whether the cause of the malady lies within his specialised remit. His concerns are with the protection, care and well-being of the *fittandu* or 'soul', which is at risk from a range of spiritual forces such as evil jinn, as well as from the effects of interpersonal magic. Jinn act through the medium of wind, and they can be detected by a cool breeze that passes over the skin, which then becomes swollen or inert. The wind, creating a feeling of numbness or a tingling sensation on the body, can also leave limbs or one side of the body paralysed. The mode of action of jinn is upon the exterior of the person, and they will escape with the intellect, thereby causing the loss of mental functions and intelligence (*rafi hoore* and *rafi hakkille*). While witches, like jinn, also take the form of a wind to attack a victim, they act upon the interior of the person by entering the body by one of the orifices and eating the victim from the inside.

The education of a marabout

The title 'marabout' is a French invention for cleric religious practitioners;[15] however, in Pulaar they are referred to as *seernaaɓe* (*ceerno* in the singular), a title that is derived from the verb *seernude*, meaning 'to make separate' (that is, the truth from falsehood). A *ceerno*, then, is someone who can distinguish truth from falsehood, one who has mastered a body of Islamic learning, and is equivalent to the Arabic *âlim*, a scholar in the religious sciences. He might be compared with master marabouts (*sirruyaŋkooɓe*, or singular, *sirruyaŋke*) who have a specialised knowledge of Islamic secrets or mysteries (*sirru*), or finally with saints or 'friends of God' (*waliyaaɓe*, or singular, *waliyu*), who have attained a measure of divine grace and have achieved direct communion with Allah, a state that is referred to as *wusuli*, a union or rebirth in God in the Sufi tradition. Some marabouts too practise a form of maraboutic magic (*dabare*), a kind of power-practice sometimes known in the French literature as *maraboutage*.

Access to these statuses within local Islam is achieved through a series of stages of learning in Qur'anic studies and initiatory apprenticeship in Islamic arts and sciences. Virtually all children from the age of seven years onwards will attend a local Qur'anic school (*ɗuɗal*)[16] located in their village or neighbourhood of a town in order to attain a basic knowledge of the Muslim religion (see Figure 6.2). The early stages of Qur'anic study are dominated by rote learning, the memorisation of texts without translation or comment. Emphasis is placed on precise and correct recitation, first of the Arabic alphabet (*abajadu*, recital of Arabic alphabet) followed by simple texts, and little attempt is made on the part of instructors (*jaŋginooɓe*) to convey the meaning of the words.[17] Few pupils will continue onto the higher stages of learning, and most of those who do are males.[18] It is only then that an understanding of the Arabic language and a sense of the meaning of the texts begins to develop through the now more formalised study of language

6.2 The old house of the local imam and site of the Qur'anic school in the village of Dumga, Fuuta Toro.

and linguistics (*lugha*), grammar (*nawhu*) and mellifluous recitation (*tagwid*). By the time a youth reaches his early to mid twenties, he might expect to have finished the first part of his training that is sufficient for him to set up as a preliminary Qur'anic teacher in his own right. Ba reports (1985–86) the use of the title *al-muudo* for someone who has reached this stage, although *ceerno* is also used as an honorific form. By this point, the student will have covered a range of subjects classed under the rubric *fannuuji*,[19] including the scientific and language disciplines of logic (*mandiq*), poetry (*shorao*) and rhetoric (*bayana*) as well as the study of the *Hadith* and moral tales (*magama*). Elements of the second stage of Qur'anic exegesis (*tafsir koran*) might well have been introduced already, but this discipline is the focus of advanced study and is often referred to as *gandal koran* or Qur'anic knowledge. Apart from Qur'anic exegesis, advanced learning, mastered only by a selected group of students, also entails the study of jurisprudence (*fiqh*), the *Hadith* and the biography of the Prophet (*sira*). The passive and rote learning of earlier stages is replaced by the detailed interpretation of texts, which the student will have to grasp and then repeat back to his teacher until it is fully understood. For a pupil to follow this advanced level, he will need to attend one of the many specialist centres of learning dotted throughout Fuuta Toro, or one of the two 'universities' of Islamic sciences and literature at Nguijilon or Cilon in the middle valley (Ba 1985–86), or even one further afield such as at Pir in Kayor or at those in the Casamance in the south of the country or in Fuuta Jallon in Guinée. At the successful completion of these studies the student graduates with the title of *tafsir*, an honorific acquired when the student has learnt to recite by heart large parts, if not all, of the Qur'an and to give historical interpretation and religious exegesis of the holy book chapter by chapter, verse by verse. Supplementary to this form of learning are yet further steps in the development of Qur'anic study, in particular the interpretation of hidden or esoteric meanings of the Qur'an (*ta'wâl*) (Brenner 2000c).

The study of the Qur'an at introductory and advanced levels is open to most students who desire knowledge or who have the ability to pursue more complex higher disciplines. The realm of secrets and mysteries, by contrast, is only accessible to those who can find a suitable master willing to accept a pupil as a *taalibe*, a disciple; consequently this individualised, initiatory form of transmission (*talqin*) of Qur'anic knowledge and mystical sciences is much more restricted and involves only a very select few. Someone considered capable of continuing on to this level is talked of as having a 'large' or 'old head' (*hoore mawnde*), which refers to a special predisposition for learning, whether this learning be advanced study of the Islamic knowledge or the learning of incantations (*cefi*), herbal medicine and divination that comprise the arts of the witch-hunter and magician (*bileejo*). In both cases, the characteristic of having a 'large head' distinguishes a person from his fellows in that it is thought to allow him or her access to knowledge not given for all to acquire. Secret Islamic knowledge (*gandal sirru*), knowledge of mysteries, involves, as Brenner puts it, 'a level of understanding beyond that communicated by the intellect and is reserved for the very few who have achieved direct knowledge of the Divine through gnosis' (2000c: 341). Qur'anic apprenticeship is thus transformed into an initiatory process, in which the disciple forms a very particular relationship with his master. Not only does he seek to absorb the substance of the master's teaching, but he is also drawn into a personal relationship with him as a spiritual guide (*murshid*). Spiritual chains of transmission of knowledge, *silsila*, are set up between disciple (*murîd*) and master, and these chains may connect back to the founding Shaykhs of a Sufi order. The links in these chains are not necessarily those of blood or lineage, but can be of 'breath' or 'saliva' (*tuute*), the media through which blessings and *baraka* or spiritual grace are passed from master to disciple (Schmitz 2000a). Furthermore, this bond may be expressed through the gift by the marabout of his daughter to a favoured disciple as a seal of a line of spiritual inheritance. This line of descent stands in juxtaposition to that of the master's own blood line, and this is known to cause tensions among those – particularly his sons – seeking to claim succession to a marabout's position (Schmitz 2000a).

Gandal sirru, or 'knowledge of secrets', has a number of applications in the range of arts practised, as well as offered as services by marabouts. This knowledge takes the form of a range of practices often referred to as 'esoteric sciences', but might just as well be considered as techniques to tap into a variety of sources of spiritual power; they are another sort of power-practice. Maraboutic arts involve the capacity of human beings to attempt to contact and manipulate dangerous, hidden, spiritual forces. Personal communication with Allah is the highest form of knowledge that can be acquired, and this is part of a spiritual quest (*tarbiyu* or *tarbiyya*) to achieve a union with or rebirth through God.[20] This mystical aim lies at the heart of Sufism (*tasawwuf*). One technique to achieve communication is to conduct periods of retreat, *khalwa*, often for up to seven days or more, during which time the marabout will pray and recite Qur'anic verses in a bid to open the doors of human perception to divine inspiration.[21] This may come in the form of visions, dreams and prophetic revelation, and may be engendered by a range of spiritual forces from Muslim jinn to the angels and higher beings of light. To communicate with Allah and his host in this way is to guarantee redemption after death. This technique can be used as much to acquire knowledge either for the marabout himself or for clients who might seek advice, healing and so forth from him. Before taking decisions of crucial importance, a *khalwa* retreat may be organised, such as is reported to have been the case with Al-Hajj Umar Taal prior to setting off on his jihads of the mid-nineteenth century (Robinson 1985).

Another similar technique is known as *listikaar*, a form of dream divination which is supported by a series of north African dream interpretation manuals. Usually lasting only one night, a marabout will enter a session of *listikaar* divination at the request of a client who has posed a question concerning perhaps undertaking a voyage, meeting an important political leader or dignitary, or prior to making a commitment in marriage (see Gaden 1931 and also Dilley 1992 on dream interpretation). The retreat involves entrusting to Allah a choice between a number of possible options or outcomes and, by submission to his will and by virtue of the marabout's piety, a decision will be made known to the diviner. The dream is often the medium for such divination, but equally the will of Allah might be made known through the use of a rosary or by signs in the sand, a form of geomancy.[22] While the gifts of visions and prophecy associated with sainthood are by and large accepted as the respectable face of esoteric Muslim sciences, those involving the manipulation of the existing state of affairs and of the predictive sciences are less respectable (Brenner 1985b).

The most contentious areas of what French-speakers label 'maraboutage' include those sciences involving the manipulation of the power of letters, words and numbers, in particular the knowledge and use of the names of God, numerology and the tracing of magic squares and talismans (*haatumeere*). Maraboutic practices known as *lasrari* extend the language-based discipline of Qur'anic study from the mundane arts of exegesis and interpretation to a practical science that taps into spiritual forces and powers inherent in, or evoked by, writing, script and text. *Binndi* is the general category of written Qur'anic verses used in talismans (*haatumeere*) and amulets (*talki*), and *aaya* are therapeutic Qur'anic verses used as 'script-potions' or 'erasures' to treat the body of a client or to be ingested. *Binndi* and *aaya* are to the marabout what incantations (*cefi*) and herbal potions are to the witch-hunters and magicians (*wileeɓe*, or *bileejo*), to Fishermen, Weavers and other men-of-skill. It is said by some people who find these arts unacceptable that the specialist literature on Islamic magic and mysticism used by master marabouts (*sirruyaŋkooɓe*) was in fact written by jinn and that they pre-date the introduction of Islam, and are thus considered non-Islamic.

There would seem to be an obvious opposition here between different forms of power-practice: the written and the oral. This opposition might be taken to describe a distinction between Islamic and 'non-Islamic' healing arts. Indeed, this distinction is captured in the two Pulaar terms *windooɓe* or 'writers' for marabouts practising 'literary' Islamic magic and *haalooɓe* or 'speakers', those versed in the oral magic of the witch-hunters and men-of-skill. A number of commentators have suggested that the importance of this distinction lies in delimiting a division between a pre-Islamic domain that is oral and an Islamic one that is written, the marabout having substituted the magic of the written word for that of the spoken word.[23] While there is a salient cultural distinction between the power of the written word and the power of the spoken word – both of which have an ability to work directly on living beings and things – it is misleading to regard this as describing a division of labour between Islamic marabouts and non-Islamic religious practitioners. I will develop an analysis of the power of the oral and the written in Chapter 7 which follows, but here I want merely to question the analytical and descriptive usefulness of such a distinction.

Numerous points can be made that undermine this distinction between writers and speakers as representing two separate and diverse traditions. First is that one of the pillars of West African Sufi Islam, the predominant form of the religion in the region, is the power of prayer and recitation. A Sufi order (*tariqa*) prescribes a set of prayers or litanies (*wird*) specific to it alone, and new initiates receive the *wird* from a spiritual leader, a *muqaddam*, as a sign authorising entry into the order. The focused chanting of the litany and of sets of devotional prayers which recall the name of God (*dhikr*) are thought to initiate a process of inner spiritual development which will cleanse the soul of its impurities and will render God's presence throughout one's being. Second, the emphasis on oral recitation and harmonious performance of Qur'anic text has already been highlighted above in the context of Muslim education; indeed, as Brenner points out, 'Muslim education was in effect the oral transmission of the written word' (1983a: 76).[24] Third, imams and marabouts provide for members of their community blessings and benedictions (*duwaawuuji*) that take the form of utterances that are spat out in the same way as a *bileejo* or a man-of-skill recites his incantations (*cefi*). Moreover, a group waiting to receive the blessing from a marabout will repeat the cleric's words and spit them into their cupped hands, which are held out in front of their faces. The hands are then rubbed onto the face to transmit the blessing to the whole person. These few points suggest, therefore, that the distinction between the written and the oral does not neatly describe a simple dichotomy of clerical Islam and local, non-Islamic practice. At the heart of West African Sufi Islam is the power of the spoken word to at least the same extent as among those practitioners of 'black arts', which tend to be much more orally based. There could well be merit in perceiving the relationship between the written and the oral as one of hierarchical encompassment, whereby the predominantly literate religious tradition of Islam has assimilated verbal and performative aspects of other specialisms.

DISCUSSION: A SOCIAL DIVISION OF HEALING

In the course of this analysis a generalised social division of labour has emerged among specialists whose expertise comprises the arts of healing, divination and the averting of misfortune through a range of practices aimed at sourcing different forms and realms of power. This social division mirrors one considered earlier with respect to economic production and political control, although it is neither quite so neat nor exclusive. The two figures of the *bileejo* and the *marabout* are images that represent mastery of two contrasting domains of power: the *bileejo*, the master witch-hunter and magician whose arts are considered 'black'; and the marabout, the learned cleric whose studies in white lore link to domains of Sufi mysticism. The images of the termite mound and the mosque resurface as metaphors of two competing sources of knowledge and power. The juxtaposition of these two religious functionaries highlights as well differing social roles that each one plays. While the *bileejo* is shunned within the community and consultations are done on the sly or take place under the cover of darkness, the marabout is a public figure of religious and political importance. There is less fear of public reprimand in consulting a marabout (*sirruyaŋke*) versed in Islamic magic and mysteries – despite the fact that some of his practices might be condemned by the pious – than there is in being seen patronising a *bileejo*, even if this latter performs a useful social and spiritual function. Tall has pointed out that the role of the marabout is as ambiguous as that of the *bileejo* (1984: 157); to this one might add that while the *bileejo* deals in nefarious forces whose actions may bring benefit and healing to the patient, the marabout is projected as dealing with forces of light whose actions will bring blessing, grace and enlightenment. However, an ambiguity inheres in the latter's practice too, for ordinary folk can never be certain exactly what forces a marabout might be dealing in, since the practices associated with secret Islamic lore are hidden from view.

An area of common ground between the arts of the *bileejo* and that of the marabout can be illustrated with reference to the operation and performance of their two forms of power-practice. I described how a *bileejo* effects his magical powers through the utterance of incantations and the disposal of material charged with the powers of contagion with the target victim. The operation and performance of one area of maraboutic magic (*gandal lasrari*) involves the writing of talismans on paper using Qur'anic text, the names of God and the numerical value of the letters of the patient's or victim's name which is placed in the centre of the design. These talismans are called *haatumeere*, a potent design written on paper in the form of a rectangle. The name written at the centre of these designs must be the personal name (*inde*) given to someone at their naming ceremony, rather than a pet-name (*inde wacoore*) or double-name (*soowoore*). In the case of an untutored marabout ignorant of numerology, the victim's name is simply written in Arabic script, whereas an expert *sirruyaŋke* will translate it into its numerical equivalent, which is considered a more powerful procedure. This number is considered to represent the whole person at whom the talisman is aimed, and its value is inscribed into the very structure of the design.

Talismans produced by master marabouts (*haatumeere sirru*) are considered distinct from those produced mechanically by marabouts lacking proper instruction (*haatumeere maŋkataba*, copied talismans), for these latter are limited copies of more powerful prescriptions. When the aim is to disrupt or to intervene in interpersonal relations, that is to cause injury or harm to someone or to protect him or her from aggression or malevolence, the person's name is inscribed at the centre of the design of the talisman, just as it is interlaced into the recitation of the *bileejo*'s incantations. The name and its intercalation into the structure of the power medium are important to both operations.

Once a talisman is written, the marabout disposes of it in much the same way as the *bileejo* treats his specialist preparations. He might burn it in the bush and scatter the ashes, or bury it at the fork in a road, next to a termite mound, in a cemetery, or at a mosque especially behind the *mihrab*. To make a person die, the talisman is wrapped in a piece of burial shroud dug up from a grave and is subsequently buried again, or to send the victim mad it is burnt. Qur'anic script-potions (*aaye* or *safara*)[25] involve similar designs and inscriptions that are written onto wooden writing tablets, and the script is removed with water that is subsequently carefully collected. These are the medicinal counterparts to talismans and they can carry the same potent charge but in liquid form. They can now be purchased in small medicine bottles, in appearance very similar to those western prescriptions obtained from chemists.

At the level of practice there are lines of comparison to be drawn between the operations and performance of black and white magical techniques. There are, however, other points of similarity. Brenner has alerted us to relations between different religious practices in Africa, suggesting that they share many epistemological and practical features in common. He defines an 'esoteric paradigm' (2000c) or an 'esoteric episteme' (2000d) of knowledge, which he argues underlies a variety of religious practice throughout West Africa. The esoteric paradigm is founded on 'the idea that a secret and powerful knowledge exists which is available to those who can gain access to it' (2000c: 341), although not everyone has the means or capacities to attain the appropriate levels of intellectual or spiritual achievement.[26] The intersections of power relations and access to and control of knowledge constitute an important part of this esoteric episteme, and Brenner has described these features at length with respect to West African Sufi Islam. What is striking are the commonalities between the Sufi formation of knowledge and that which I have described among *maabuɓe* weavers and other men-of-skill in a range of publications (Dilley 1989b, 1999, 2000).

Each of the culturally defined domains of knowledge-power (*gandal*) I have been discussing above, and those of the men-of-skill as well, share a common epistemology based upon the restricted availability of bodies of secret lore. Moreover, the stages of learning I have described above for the Qur'anic student reflect those undergone by apprentices in weaving, for example, that I have detailed elsewhere (Dilley 1987b and 1999). In both, learning moves from imitation of a teacher and repetition of mundane tasks required by him to an informed social practice, which is followed by the possibility of gaining access to hidden knowledge by means of a personal relationship with a particular master. The acquisition of this knowledge is acknowledged in both Qur'anic studies and craft apprenticeship by the donation of a gift from the trainee to the master, often in the form of a head of cattle. This was the form of gift described to me by my master weaver who had received instruction in weaving lore (*gandal maabuɓe*) from his father; it is also reported as the form of gift given by a newly-qualified Islamic scholar anything up to two to three years after the end of his education (Ba 1985–86).[27] Training takes the form of an initiatory process that progressively reveals hidden domains, and proximity to the spiritual entities connected with the specialisms entail dangers for the ordinary person. Experts have specialised roles in relation to these secret bodies of lore, whether they be 'caste'-specific practitioners – as in the case of the men-of-skill – or whether they be practitioners who have selected a specialism on grounds other than caste membership.

NYENGO AND SPIRITUAL TUTELAGE

I now turn to another specialism that is not 'caste' specific, training in the methods of which takes the form of an initiatory process that entails contact with powers otherwise hidden and condemned as dangerous and malevolent by ordinary people. This specialism is a particular form of power-practice known as *nyeŋgo* or *nyeŋgi* which is performed by a *nyeŋgotoodo*, a specialist magician or sorcerer. While a marabout deals with afflictions of the soul and illnesses of the body often caused by jinn, the *nyeŋgotoodo* seeks out the patronage of such spirits in order to effect the art of *nyeŋgo*. While a person may come to *nyeŋgo* through the teaching of a specialist, the art itself is only fully developed by means of a tutelary spirit helper. A person enters into a pact with a jinni, and the two are joined in a mutually beneficial relationship. The spirit will ask the person for a sacrifice, perhaps his little finger or even his child. If he agrees, the finger will be accidentally cut off or badly damaged and have to be amputated for medical reasons; alternatively, the child will die of a mysterious illness or be killed in an accident. It is said that some *nyeŋgotoodo* opt for a slow, painful and lingering death in exchange for the absolute powers a spirit can bring. Once a seal has been set upon this gruesome Faustian pact, the practitioner can ask the spirit to carry out his instructions. It will steal things for its patron, it will set fire to the crops or possessions of his enemies, or it will change the shape of things, such that a sandal becomes a snake, in order to bring about some effect –

such as death through snakebite. (One observer noted that spirits do not actually change the shape of things so that a sandal becomes a snake; rather the spirit removes the sandal and replaces it with a snake.) Whatever the mechanism involved, the intended effect on the victim of the practice is the same. *Nyeŋgo* involves, therefore, an initiatory process in the creation of a relationship with a tutelary spirit, whose knowledge and powers are subsequently put into the hands of the magician for his own personal benefit. *Nyeŋgo* nonetheless differs from other forms of power-practice for it rarely involves the manipulation of material objects to bring about its intended effects. In this case a specific agent, a spirit, is the power that brings about effects, and the potency of *nyeŋgo* is thus represented as an abstract, discrete and separate force that does not inhere in material things or technical manipulations. These features can be contrasted with those forms of magical efficacy reviewed above, that is the respective arts of the *bileejo* and of the marabout which rely upon the manipulation of things – herbs, potions, paper and so forth. While *dabare*, the making of charms (*nyawndude*) and the confection of talismans and Qur'anic script-potions may be considered to embody forms of potency, it is a potency that is effected through operations applied to material things. Embodied in the very material procedures of certain arts – both 'black' and 'white' – are the potencies that have an effect on the world. This can be contrasted with *nyeŋgo* practices whose operations lie essentially in the ability to 'call up' or 'invoke' a tutelary spirit (*noddude jinne*), and these procedures find an echo in the techniques of master marabouts (*sirruyaŋkooɓe*) whose advanced methods (*khalwa* and *listikaar*) of consultation entail entering into the revered presence of divine forces.[28]

Nyeŋgo is almost universally condemned by ardent Muslims and by those less self-conscious about their religious practice as a reprehensible form of 'magic'. It is considered by them as evil and self-serving. Although it is open to all to learn, few people would openly and publicly admit to practising the art. One of the master weavers with whom I learnt the craft used to practise *nyeŋgo* magic, but gave it up a long time ago because it was 'not good'. He confessed to using it primarily to steal other people's property and possessions. There is, however, an obvious affinity between the art of the *nyeŋgotoodo* and the activities of the *nyeenyɓe* or men-of-skill in general. Craft occupations bring their practitioners into a relationship with the jinn that animate the craft or that are associated with aspects of production. Craftsmen by virtue of practising a craft are required to forge relationships with jinn, and it is by virtue of this relationship, I argue, that the lore and knowledge of their trades is classified as 'black'. The *nyeŋgotoodo* similarly creates a connection with a jinni, although the nature of that relationship might be different from that in the case of craftsmen.[29] There is, therefore, an elective affinity between the two activities regarding their connections to the spirit world, and although it is by no means true to say that only craftsmen practice the art of magic, they are thought by others to have a proclivity towards the art and a propensity to do well in it.[30]

This idea of a pact, however, gives a clue to the relationship between a weaver and their craft's mythical ancestor, a half-man, half-spirit named Juntel Jabaali. Compared with the *nyeŋgo* pact between practitioner and spirit, often sealed after the man has offered a large personal sacrifice to the spirit, the Weaver–ancestor relationship is much more substantial in the sense that Juntel is a forefather in many lines of weaving ancestry, and as kinsmen common substance is shared (blood, *yiiyam*, and bone, *yiyal*). The master weaver, Seydou Gisse (Guisse), claimed direct ancestry from Juntel Jabaali, some sixteen generations back. Although admittedly a historical person in the sense of being separated by time, the mythical ancestor was nonetheless a contemporary presence for the master weaver, with whom he would commune.[31] Juntel appeared in the weaver's dreams at night to give him spells, incantations, words for his songs (*dillere*) and other forms of knowledge related to the range of specialisms he pursues. Here we find echoes of the relationship between a practitioner and his tutelary spirit in *nyeŋgo*, the difference being that no price is paid for the knowledge and power (*gandal*) gained through the relationship with a weaving ancestor – it is a matter of social being. The Weaver gains access to what is part of his spiritual patrimony by virtue of his membership of a particular social category. There is a price to be paid, however, in a relationship with a tutelary spirit; the *nyeŋgotoodo* sells his soul.

SUMMARY

Accommodationist Islam allocated a place to a variety of spiritual forces and a range of forms of power and knowledge by drawing them into a hierarchy of Muslim-defined potencies. One element that was left at the limits of this hierarchy, and over which Islamic clerics had little control, was witchcraft, the area of expertise of the *bileejo* rather than the marabout. These two figures in one perspective stand in opposition to each other as experts in two distinct domains of knowledge-power. They also stand in opposition to each other with respect to the social position they occupy and the kind of cultural value and public prominence each attracts. From other perspectives these two figures stand as complementary specialists whose arts are founded upon similar kinds of conception: first, with respect to the operations and procedures of the power-practices they conduct; second, in view of the forms of training and initiatory process undergone by students of the respective arts; third, with reference to the epistemological foundations of the bodies of knowledge and power upon which they draw. There are also affinities between these features and those characteristic of the bodies of lore of men-of-skill craftsmen.

The distinction between the forms of knowledge-power is not only expressed in terms of white versus black domains, but it has been discussed in terms of another vernacular distinction between 'writers' and 'speakers'. This distinction has been taken by some commentators as describing a dichotomy of Islamic and non- or pre-Islamic religious systems. While the power of the written word and the power of the spoken word are two crucial media in the operation of power-practices, they are not exclusive to either specialism. Although practitioners of 'black' arts rely predominantly upon oral techniques of spells, incantations and so on, Muslim marabouts employ both modes of efficacy in their procedures. The spoken word is as important for them as it is for other non-literate practitioners. There is a revealing proverbial saying in Pulaar: 'The writers of magic are like witch-hunter/ magicians' (*windooɓe ko wileeɓe*). No doubt having been coined by sceptical Fulɓe quizzically regarding the historical emergence of the *tooroɓe* clerics and the development of their maraboutic practices, and concluding that it is little different from that of the witch-hunter, there is good reason to think that this saying holds another truth. On the basis of the perspective constructed here, there is a common ground between the two at the level of epistemology, practice and operation of knowledge-power.

From a historical perspective it is indisputable that Islam brought Arabic literacy to the region, hence in one sense it is no doubt correct to talk of the oral and written representing two separate religious traditions at some point in time. But what has developed over the intervening years – possibly a thousand years or more – is a system of religious thought and practice that is complex and evolving, and which is made up of a number of different domains of knowledge-power (*gandal*). Each domain has developed in dialogue or more broadly in conversation with the others, and so it becomes analytically difficult to tease out the pure and parent branches emerging from the original rootstock. Both have become intertwined, and the presence of one shades the development of the other. It is at this point that an anthropological imperative is emphasised, wherein the dialogical, systematic and interrelated quality of institutions and practices is evident. Such systems are neither static nor necessarily coherent, and are instead informed by local debate, discussion and contestation about what is and is not 'good' Muslim practice.

It would seem, therefore, that given the centrality of Arabic literacy within the religion of Islam introduced into West Africa, an obvious marker of religious difference was available to be symbolically elaborated. This occurred in contrast to local religions based upon orality and verbal performance of different kinds of speech act. As Hamès points out recently, echoing the ideas of Paul Marty some sixty years earlier, 'the Islamisation of West Africa [was] by way of magic', and that an essential part of those Muslim 'magical' techniques involved writing.[32] Indeed, to paraphrase

Marty, it was through the written word that the Muslim talisman gained the admiration of local populations.[33] Given that the configurations of social relations among Haalpulaar'en have so often been formed with regard to competition for control over diverse realms of power and knowledge – a kind of contestation that has arisen through a will to power and domination – it is not surprising then that the symbols of the written word and of the spoken word have become the ideological expression of that competition. It should be equally unsurprising that analytically these two domains are not as distinct or separate as the ideological constructions would lead us to believe. I turn to this issue in the next chapter.

7

THE POWER OF THE WORD: THE ORAL AND THE WRITTEN

It is often reported in the West African literature that the spoken word has a power or potency; that it would appear to be endowed with an agency to bring about effects in the world (see, for example, Dieterlen 1965; Griaule 1965; Johnson 1986; Sanneh 1979, 1989; Trimingham 1959). Other commentators, by contrast, have argued that language and speech should not be considered as a form of agency that can replace actions or physical doings. Labutut (1987), for instance, argues that Fulfulde speakers have a realist conception of language that embodies the view that 'saying cannot replace doing'. This conclusion is based upon the examination of 'Peul' or Fulɓe proverbs and maxims, many of which certainly express these particular ideas. However, there are ambivalent sentiments suggested in such proverbial sayings, and what needs further investigation, it seems to me, is what forms of speech and what modes of language are considered to possess agency, and which forms do not have such a direct effect on the world. All speech and verbal performance can be considered as a species of social action, as Barber argues (1989). But which forms are marked indigenously as being effective and efficacious, either having an inherent agency in itself or acting as a vehicle for agency? These questions need careful ethnographic consideration.

It is also a feature of West African ethnography that the written word in certain forms is similarly endowed with potent efficacy. According to Goody (1968a), this power derives from the extent to which the techniques of writing are developed within a context of 'restricted literacy', that is where one class or group of people hold a monopoly, at the exclusion of the majority population, over the knowledge of writing procedures and the interpretation of texts. In such contexts the 'magic' or power of the book emerges as an important social institution. While this may largely be the case in Fuuta Toro, there is another more general point to make about the word in Islam. As Gilsenan explains, the Qur'an is held to be the direct Revelation in Arabic from God, and its recitation and reading 'is the miraculous source of the *umma*, the Islamic community'. Furthermore, he talks of: 'The directness of the relationship with Allah through the word ...', such that words and letters from Qur'anic verses 'are felt as intrinsically full of divine energy and grace' (1982: 16). It is not only then socially restricted literacy practices that provide the aura of 'book magic', but the divinity of the Word is inscribed within Islamic mysticism itself.

One of the aims of this chapter is to investigate individually two domains of the agency of the word: that is the word in its spoken and its written forms. This is followed by a comparative analysis of the two forms, and it attempts to highlight commonalities between them. The extent to which there is common ground might be construed as evidence that sheds light upon the local ideological distinction between 'writers' and 'speakers' as experts in two mutually exclusive forms of power practice.

PROVERBIAL SAYINGS AND THE DENIAL OF AGENCY

Labutut discusses (1987) a series of Peul proverbs that deny the agency of language and speech. Similar sentiments are found in the Futanke corpus of *malli*, or 'allusions'.[1] These are pithy proverbs and maxims that are often taken by commentators to embody a general truth, or to define the lineaments of a cultural, perhaps even a universal, wisdom. They are collectively recognised by such analysts as the door to these truths and to this wisdom. This kind of conception reflects no doubt our own western concerns about Biblical truths contained within the didactic poetic Old Testament book of maxims, the Book of Proverbs. The search for a cultural or a general truth behind what we call proverbs, and what they call 'allusions', must not detract from an examination of the place of such a genre in Haalpulaar discourse and cultural exchange. For it is apparent that there are often ambiguous and contradictory messages set up within this form of discourse; they constitute a kind of social commentary, a debate and dialogue over contested issues.

The idea that speech has no value and that it is only actions that count is expressed in a range of sayings such as 'a person who speaks does nothing' (*neddo ina haala ko wadataa*), or 'speech pleases little, but acts please [more]' (*ina famdi ko haala welata, balle mbela*). Yet local social practice and cultural understandings suggest that certain words and some forms and modes of language are particularly potent. How can one account for such discrepancies between what is acted out in everyday life and the content of 'proverbial' sayings? I would suggest that Haalpulaar allusions (*malli*) embody what might be called a form of cultural 'common-sense', the sense and discourse of the non-specialist, the *miskineeɓe* or peasant farmers who possess no particular expertise themselves but who nonetheless consult experts from time to time in the course of their daily lives. Rather than proverbs alluding to a form of general truth, they represent perhaps parts of a social commentary of the non-specialist, of those who are expert in no particular aspect of local culture, whether it be maraboutic practice, craft activity, praise-singing or whatever. These specialised activities demand specialised forms of knowing, often esoteric, and they are frequently based on the idea of agency arising from particular forms of potency. The contrariety evident in proverbial sayings reflects the views of those not included in these specialisms, and they are part of a sceptical commentary that devalues the role and expertise of the specialist.[2] This could be thought of as part of what Gellner (1981) has called the 'specialist-spurning ethos' of Muslim societies. Moreover, the contrariety expressed in many maxims relates to a deeply felt sense of ambivalence about the practices of experts: while perhaps fearful and condemnatory of them, ordinary folk nonetheless rely on specialists in times of need and misfortune, or when faced by difficult choices and circumstances.

Views opposed to those given above on language and speech are also represented in the corpus of allusions. The idea that language itself is a vehicle of potency can be seen in the following two sayings: 'vexed speech is more painful than a bullet' (*haala mettuka ɓuri muusde kural*); and 'a wound heals, but malicious words do not' (*nyawannde na sella, konngol bonngol sellataa*). Here language carries the negative intentions of the speaker and can do harm to the recipient. These allusions suggest that there is a range of issues about agency and language that need further investigation. Furthermore, the idea that human personhood is defined through language is seen in the following maxims: 'the person is speech' (*neɗɗo ko haala*), or 'the person is language' (*neɗɗo ko ɗemngal*). Without speech the human being is simply an animal, or equally a slave; without language he or she is all that is brute, coarse, uncultivated, ill-mannered, lacking in shame and discretion, and is dominated by emotions and desires and not by the intellect (Labutut 1987). This idea of full social personhood being represented through the possession of language is expressed as follows: 'the freeborn person is the word (language); the bondsman is the rope' (*dimo ko konngol; maccuɗo ko ɓoggol*). This is a saying that vividly captures the differences in the conception of those occupying different social stations, and suggests that speech constitutes part of the dignity of full social personhood.

The possession of language is linked intimately to the cultural conception of persons and of the idea of humankind as distinct from the rest of the animal kingdom. I explained earlier that the Weaver narrator with whom I worked closely held the view that at the dawn of time, before knowledge had been acquired and the division of labour had been established, humans could only utter inarticulate grunts and noises like animals. The use of language was then a key moment in the formation of human culture. This absence of language among animals is denoted in the figurative expression referring to all animals other than humans: they are 'Allah's mutes' (*muumantel Allah* in the singular; the Haalpulaar word *muumantel* derives from the verb 'to be mute or dumb' (*muumɗude*)).[3] Not only was language, then, a key moment in this Haalpulaar interpretation of human evolution, but language – or more particularly its absence – is also a feature that defines a sharp distinction between humans and animals. Furthermore, within the category of animals, there are those which might be considered to be endowed with a 'voice', most frequently those animals that emit roars and cries. These animal 'voices' are specified in Pulaar and a rich vocabulary describes the sounds of large predators.[4] They are seen to be endowed with the faculty to make sounds that are in some way akin to the human voice, but they lack language as such. The sounds they make are merely grumblings, growls and grunts, for they are not structured in the forms that human language take.[5]

THE VOCABULARY OF SPEECH AND LANGUAGE

There are various words current in Pulaar that are used to denote aspects of speech and language. The most prominent words stem from the root *haal* (of Arabic origin) which provides the verb 'to speak' (*haalde*), as well as the substantives 'speech, narration, account' (*haala*, plural *haalaaji*). *Konngol* is another term which, although it has no verb form, refers to a speech act, a proposition or an affirmation, and especially to words, phrases and sentences as the material constituents of language (see Niang 1997; Seydou 1987). The act of talking (*wiide* means 'to talk') is part of a process of having and revealing intentions, and it is therefore a type of purposive behaviour that expresses inner motivations. This conception is expressed in the saying: 'a word, if it matures in the stomach and if it comes out, will be found to be fat/meat' (*konngol, so benndi nder reedu, so yalti, tawat ina fayi*). In other words, what is said has to be considered and moulded by intentions and purposes, the seat of which is the belly, in order for it to be substantial. This manner of expression can be contrasted with ill-considered title-tattle (*leɓa*, from the verb *lebde*, meaning 'to speak without stopping'), a term which suggests the lack of purposiveness and rumination before speaking.

Another purely substantive term is *demngal* which refers to 'tongue' in both senses of the English translation, that is as the anatomical feature used in the act of speaking and as that which is spoken, a language. Allusions referring to 'tongue' play on both its anatomical and its linguistic senses, and it is seen in the same ambivalent light as language itself: for it is often portrayed as the organ of error, of lies and calumny, and as the way to perdition; alternatively, it is also imagined as the organ of truth and intelligence, whose praises can earn its master a fortune. Finally, there is the term *bolle* which means 'speech', 'talk' or 'conversation' (as in *bolle worɓe ɗiɗo*, or 'a conversation between two men'), but it can also be used in the sense of 'language' as in *bolle Fulɓe*, 'the Fulɓe language'. This term is derived from the verb *wolwude* or *wowlude*, meaning 'to speak', but it now appears to be supplanted in Fuuta Toro by the verb *haalde* from the Arabic root (Seydou 1987). This substitution seems virtually complete, except in the case of the derived substantive *bolle*. One of the main uses of this word is in the phrase *bolle ɓaleeje*, literally 'black speech' or 'magic' formulae, verses or incantations that are thought to possess a power in and of themselves. It is worth noting that it is the obsolete and supplanted root *wol* that provides the term *bolle* to refer to speech as potency rather than the Arabic-derived root *haal*. Black speech is connected with the activities of the witch-hunter/magician (*wileeɓe*) and the men-of-skill (*nyeenyɓe*), and is not primarily associated with the freeborn Islam clerics, the *tooroɓe*, who are accorded the historical role of revitalising and spreading Islam throughout the region from the mid-eighteenth century onwards. This linguistic distinction has, I would suggest, numerous social and cultural implications. This particular form of speech, *bolle*, is not considered part of the mainstream Muslim practice and is distanced from it by the use of the term 'black', denoting otherness and marginality.

Both *haala* as 'speech' and *konngol* as 'word' can be employed to suggest a potency in language, but the agency implicated is of a different order from that of 'black speech'. For instance, *haala mettuka* means 'vexed speech' and *konngol bonngol* is 'the malicious word', and it would seem that it is the intention of the speaker (vexation, anger, maliciousness) that is carried via the medium of the utterance rather than the words themselves which are imbued with power or potency, as it is in the case of 'black speech', *bolle ɓaleeje*. Language, therefore, as an everyday medium of communication is a neutral medium in that it carries no agency beyond the effects of its meanings on the listener, nor beyond the responses its statements invoke within particular social settings. In those instances where speech is thought to have an effect beyond the transparent meaning of the words as spoken, or beyond any functions relating to the phatic communion of linguistic exchange, then language itself is conceived to carry particular kinds of malicious intentionality and malevolent purposiveness. This agency of words, if it can be rightly called such, is transmitted via the meanings and intentions of the speaker behind the words, rather than as an inherent quality of the words themselves.

THE POTENCY AND DANGER OF NAMES

There is a power and a danger in the possession and use of names. We have seen how the use of personal names is central to the operation of forms of power practice, particularly if it is to reach its intended target: the victim's or client's name is inserted into the magical formulae employed. Moreover, to utter a name is also to summon the presence of the thing named – whether an object, person or spiritual agent. This is also true of animals as it is of humans and other beings. People in rural areas sometimes fear to name large predatory animals or those that are dangerous to humans. For instance, lions, certain species of snake and crocodiles are often referred to by epithets that include the label 'killer' (*mbaroodi*), such that a lion is 'killer of the bush' (*mbaroodi ladde*) or even the 'clawed killer' (*mbaroodi taktakri*); 'killer of the land' is the snake (*mbaroodi leydi*), and 'killer of the water' (*mbaroodi maayo*) is the crocodile. These animals are also referred to by other epithets: the lion is 'master or chief of the bush' (*jom ladde*), or 'older sibling of the bush' (*dikko ladde*); the snake is known as 'rope of the land' (*ɓoggol leydi*), 'strip of bark of the land' (*baaɗol leydi*), the 'creeper' (*ladoori*), or the 'one that trails along the ground' (*ndaasoori*). The leopard is simply called 'the svelt or slender one' (*cewngu*), a term derived from the verb *sewde*, 'to be slender or svelt'. These ways of alluding to animals are means of avoiding invoking their presence through a single 'name', a practice reflected along the Niger river, where fishermen fear to pronounce the name of the hippopotamus so as not to provoke an attack by the animal on their boats (Gaden 1931). This power to name is the same in the case of jinn and other spirits, whose presence can be invoked by the use of their names. Frequently, incantations, spells or Muslim talismans and amulets evoke the help of spiritual forces by employing their names in magical formulae: Islamic formulae call upon specific angels, Gibrael, Israel and so on, or other forms of incantation summon named jinn, such as 'the most powerful' or the 'cause' jinni (*saabu jinne*), the 'patron' jinni (*njaartige jinne*), the 'bull' or chief jinni (*ngaari jinne*), or the 'cow' jinni (*naage jinne*). Alternatively, spirits might have personal names such as 'Kumba Ciɓoyi'. Likewise, the personal name (*inde*) of the mother of the weavers' mythical ancestor, herself a jinni, is thought by the *maabuɓe* to be their most powerful utterance, and it is a secret (*sirru*) that is almost impossible to get anyone to reveal. It is this name that the mythical ancestor, Juntel Jabaali, uttered to make cloth simply through the power of speech and without the aid of a loom. The Weavers fear this name greatly, for it can 'spoil' (*bonde*) many things they say. This is a power whose name dared not be spoken.

Juntel's mother's name

It was only during the last few months of my field-trip that anything of substance concerning weaving *gandal* was told to me. By this time, over one year later, I had become jointly apprenticed to my original teacher and his younger brother. Both men were highly respected *maabu*s, and I had been spending a good deal of time with the younger brother discussing praise-singing (another specialised occupational role of the *maabuɓe*) and aspects of their oral literature. My original master had by now related to me a number of interesting items of their lore, concerned mostly with detailed aspects of weaving origin myths and how they related to present-day practice. However, it fell to the younger brother to teach me some of the secrets of the trade. During the course of a number of days we sat together in the courtyard of his house while I took down numerous verses, incantations and spells. Throughout these sessions he was very serious, talking in a low, almost conspiratorial, whisper out of earshot of the rest of the household, and I wrote down his words (a mixture of Pulaar, Arabic and 'spirit' language) in my notebook. This method was a compromise means of recording his utterances verbatim – a tape-recorder had been ruled out. Since I had to memorise these verses correctly, it was the only way of impressing them on my mind, for I was told that if one used such verses it was imperative to have the correct formulation, lest the power of the verse return to those who pronounce it incorrectly.

The brother taught me numerous verses that could be used at various times and for different purposes. Some verses were for weaving at incredible speeds, some were for weaving cloth magically at the loom in one's absence, and others were for affecting other weavers in competition with oneself. Verses not specific to weaving were also taught, such as how to influence people in high places and protective magic to hunt a hippopotamus. One of the most powerful utterances in the possession of the *maabuɓe* is the name of Juntel Jabaali's mother, herself a spirit who begat the mythical ancestor. I had been told that her name is greatly feared by all *maabuɓe*, but only a few knew it. It was said that to pronounce the name caused things to burst into flames, and numerous accounts had been given about its use. One particular story was told of a weaver in Fuuta Toro who could weave without a loom, much like the mythical ancestor. It was also said that if you crossed him in some way or other he would use the spirit name to burn the warp threads on your loom. I asked the younger brother at the end of my lessons in *gandal maabuɓe* what this name was. During this, our last session together, his wife was preparing the midday meal and the cooking pot containing oil was heating over an open fire. The brother was musing for a few moments after I had asked my question when suddenly, to his and my surprise, the cooking pot and oil burst into flames. This was something I had never seen before. After quickly dealing with the fire, he sat down, composed himself, ruefully smiled at me and said that he had only been thinking of the name and I could see for myself what had happened.

The ninety-nine names of Allah in the Sufi tradition of Islam is another feature that has been adopted by the local specialists who place an importance on the potency of names. Some of these names were mentioned in the last chapter, but others include: the 'Creator of All Things' (*Tagoowo*), the 'Writer of the World' (*Bindoowo*), the 'Unique' (*Gooto*), the 'Defender' (*Kadoowo*), the 'Comforter' (*Newnoowo*), the 'Generous' (*Dokkoowo*) and so on. Allah represents form of power and agency in the world, and his qualities are captured in his names. Allah alone has the ability to judge both the living and the dead, and as a consequence can have an effect as a force that can intervene in the course of world and human events. Afflictions that strike people down may be seen as the actions of God in bringing recompense or in calling someone to account; an example is the recurring droughts of the 1970s and 1980s that were seen by many Muslims to be Allah's judgement on the decadent lifestyle Senegalese youth in particular had fallen into – discotheques were closed as a result.

Other words and phrases are regarded as potent. The construction *bisimillaay*, 'In the name of Allah' (derived from the Arabic), is used in a way that suggests it has a potency in and of itself.[6] Simply to utter the word affords a protection to the speaker from malevolence and evil-doers. Indeed, two letters abstracted from the phrase *bisimillaay* also possess a similar potency, and can be used to invoke the power of the whole phrase. These two essential elements are the 's' (*sin*: س), and the 'm' (*mim*: م), although these letters are often pronounced 'siinykon' and 'miimerak' in verses. They are used, for example, as part of a protective verse used by a master weaver in order to protect the hands and the legs of a weaver, without the use of which weaving would be impossible. He utters the formula: 'the letter "s" that is their hands; the letter "m" that is their feet/legs' (*siinykon ko juuɗe maɓɓe, miimerak e koyde maɓɓe*). Similarly, a version of the first letter in the Arabic alphabet (*alif*) pronounced *alifun* or *aliif* is sometimes used in incantations and verses, again in order to afford protection.

The power and potency of individual words and sounds are a feature of the analysis of incantations, spells and Islamic talismans that follows below. But I turn briefly, by way of a digression, to the idea of the power inherent in different genres of language and social discourse. There would appear to be numerous genres of oral expression, ranging from ordinary speech, through poetry and song to types of verse that are powerful incantations and spells. I have touched on the issue of ordinary language, and I now consider praise-songs, poetry and prayer.

PRAISE-SONGS, POETRY AND PRAYER

The language of songs and poetry is another form of orality that produces different sorts of effect. Semantic and metaphorical creativity, and the use of images and allusions summoned by the richness of the language employed can induce particular kinds of effect in the listener. Powerful mental images are created on the basis of a number of relatively simple words, associated and juxtaposed in particular ways.[7] The style of articulation of such songs marks them out as distinct from other forms of verbal expression. A *dillere* or weaver's song, for instance, is sung in a particularly stylised manner similar to a chant or plain-song and is delivered in a louder and slightly higher pitched voice than is normal. There is no strict metrical structure or constant rhythm that dictates the tempo of the recitation, since different parts of a song develop their own pace. This can be seen in different sections such as the languid and more melodic sections often repeating a refrain, or as in the staccato, highly punctuated and rhythmical recital of *asko*s or pedigrees.[8] By contrast, one form of poem adopted by clerics to teach subjects associated with Islam is a *qacida*, often written in Pulaar but using the form of Arabic composition. These have a strict metrical structure.[9] The sonority of recital, the stylistic embellishment of performance and the use of allusion, image and metaphor in such songs and poetry mark them out as distinct genres of expression that have particular means to move listeners. The praise-songs of a *gawlo* praise-singer are said in particular to affect people, particularly a patron who listens with pride at the deeds of his illustrious ancestors. He is said to feel a heightened sense of pride to a feeling of elation in response to the praises being bestowed upon him. Some people say that after hearing their praises sung by a skilled praise-singer, they feel as though they could take on almost any challenge, such is the effect of the words on them. The language in poetic or verse form has a power that is effective through its aesthetic quality, through its poetic intensity and the use of allusion, and through its effect on the imagination and sense of social pride of the listener. Language has, in the form of praise-songs, a power that inheres in the speaker's ability to use words to convey messages about the social standing and prestige of a patron; a praise-singer, however, has the ability not only to praise but to defame and slander.

Prayer is another form of verbal expression that is linked to a form of agency, particularly the power of Allah or his host in answering the demands, requests and implorings of the faithful.[10] There are numerous terms that denote different types of, or contexts for, prayer. *Juulde* means 'to perform Muslim prayers' in a general sense, and related forms also mean 'to be a Muslim' or 'to convert to Islam' while a substantive form means 'a Muslim religious festival'. Various terms are derived from Arabic roots, such that *duwaade* means 'to implore God' and *duwaawu* is such a type of petitionary prayer; *juraade* is 'to pray and sacrifice for the dead over a tomb', and *jikrude* is 'to say the rosary'. All these various forms of religious expression and communication can have a power to effect changes in the world, and they constitute a particular mode of verbal utterance. They are often marked by a repetitive chanting beat, by a rhythm that develops in the course of uttering the same phrase again and again.[11] The mode of articulation varies from the low muttering under one's breath of rosary prayers to the loud chanting of prayers on a Friday afternoon in the Mosque. For example, the *wird* or litany of a particular Sufi sect is chanted with mantra-like repetitiveness during Friday afternoon prayers, and the number of times the sections of the *wird* is repeated varies according to the sect. A Tijani, for instance, would chant in the mosque on a Friday some verses and formulas 1,000 times, in addition to repeating the first chapter of the Qur'an (*al-Fatiha*) three times, and ending with each of the following formulae thirty-three times: *subhana ilaha* (Glory to God); *alhamdulilahi* (Praise be to God); *Allahu akbar* (God is great). Similarly, at one prayer time during each day, either in the morning or in the evening, a second version of the *wird* (*wazifa*) is chanted quietly to oneself, and is made up of various verses and formulas chanted in any order at the end of the series of *raka*s or bowings. This, together with the *lazima* or first part of the Tijani *wird*, constitute the main body of prayers recited by a member of the brotherhood each day.

Prayers form a mode of language that is imbued with agency, for the repeated pronouncing of certain words, phrases and verses are thought to effect a spiritual change within the person; they are part of a set of spiritual exercises in Sufi tradition to 'render God's presence throughout one's being'. It would appear that the mantra-like repetition of words, verses and formulas sets up rhythms and patterns of sound, and that this feature is characteristic of other modes of speech which are imbued with power. This power or potency of words, I go on to argue below, inheres in the very patterns and rhythms of spoken language, and it is to this subject I now turn.

THE PATTERNS OF LANGUAGE

Pulaar as an everyday tongue has its own particular rhythms, intonations and tempi; it has a mellifluous and melodious quality that is important to many of its speakers. Pulaar, or more generally Fulfulde, is considered by certain clerics to be second only to Arabic as a sacred language.[12] The emphasis put upon polished spoken performance of Pulaar perhaps reflects this conception of the language, and it mirrors the emphasis put upon the harmonious recitation of Arabic in Qur'anic schools. The oral performance of both languages, one associated historically with literacy and the other not, is important, and stress is placed upon correct and proper recitation. There are areas, however, where the 'natural' rhythms and prosodic structure of spoken language are disrupted, either recast or repatterned in particular ways that reflect different functions and modes of speech.

In contrast to both praise-songs and certain forms of prayer that are publicly recited and performed, there are forms of verbal expression that are esoteric, covert and secretive. These forms include secret languages and magical verses, protective incantations and spells. Secret or special languages are referred to as *gane*, a word meaning literally 'pieces or chunks', as in the sense of a fish that has been cut up. Indeed, just as *ande liingu* means 'to cut up a fish into pieces', so the phrase *ande haalamum* signifies 'to cut up our language' or to render it incomprehensible to those who are excluded or uninitiated in a special code (see Gaden 1914). Such special languages are developed particularly during the initiation of boys and girls in traditional bush encampments when members of the local age-set (*fedde*) would devise their own codes and ways of speaking among themselves.[13] Language is quite literally cut up to form secret codes, and there are often a number of principles at work in this repatterning of sound.[14] For example, one of the most common formulae is to insert one or more consonants into a lexical root, which usually takes the form of consonant-vowel-consonant. After inserting the new consonants, the vowel stem in the original root is repeated. This can be illustrated by the term *suudu* (hut), which becomes *suulfuudu* ('hut' in code form) after inserting the consonants 'lf' and repeating the vowel stem 'uu'. Similarly, *hokkam ndiyam* ('give me water') becomes *holfokkam ndilfiyam* ('give me water' in code form). One other principle, among many others, by which language is cut up and restructured is to swap the syllable order and to prefix the word with an 'i' sound. So the phrase *a windi suukama leeter* (s/he has written a letter to her/his friend) is transformed into *a indiwi ikamasuu iterlee* (Delafosse 1922). These are two simple examples that involve modifying the maternal tongue in order to talk of things that others should not be party to, but other principles for the creation of secret languages include the integration of alien terms or the introduction of artificial vocabulary. In cases where consonants are introduced into existing words, the number or type of consonants introduced can vary greatly from one area to another, or from one generation to another. The point about these transformations is that they repattern and reorder the rhythmical structure or prosodic composition of spoken language to create novel forms that are not instantly recognisable. The examples above can be written out in terms of their feet or prosodic components:[15]

suudu	– ^	(trochee)
becomes		
suulfuudu	– ^ ^	(dactyl)
hokkam ndiyam	– ^ / – ^	(2 trochees)
becomes		
holfokkam ndilfiyam	– ^ ^ / – ^ ^	(2 dactyls)

The effect of introducing the new elements not only disrupts the metre of the original but it also slows the tempo of the stretch of speech.

a wiindi suukama leeter	^ / – ^ / – ^ ^ / – ^
becomes	
a indiiwi ikamasuu iterlee	^ / ^ – ^ / ^ ^ ^ ^ / ^ – ^

Key: – is a stressed or long unit of speech;
^ is an unstressed or short unit of speech.

It becomes obvious from this representation how the prosodic structures have been radically altered, how the rhythm, the pulse and metre of the stretch of speech have been transformed. Those who are particularly skilled at creating these special languages are the *nyeenyɓe*, men-of-skill, for they allow craftsmen to talk of craft secrets; moreover, it is members of these social categories who are thought of primarily as masters of language and as transformers of various media. Here, they transform the basic rhythms of sound to produce new secret codes. The mystery that surrounds these secret codes derives from the repatterning of language, the fact that it now has new rhythms and prosodic structures. These principles of repatterning are developed in the next section, where the formation of such structures is associated directly with the potency of language.

SPELLS, PROTECTIVE VERSES AND INCANTATIONS

Finally, I wish to consider another mode of verbal expression, namely protective verses (*cefi*) and incantations and spells (*bolle ɓaleeje*) that are claimed to have an effect on persons and things. These stretches of potent speech can incorporate powerful and divine names and even the decompositions of individual letters rather than whole words. But the question posed here is whether these stretches of speech in themselves hold particular properties that might suggest why they are regarded as having efficacy. The two types of utterance to be dealt with here – *cefi* and *bolle ɓaleeje* – are conceptually distinct, although in practice the distinction between the two is often blurred. The word *cefi*, incantation, shares the same root as the verb *sefaade*,[16] meaning 'to separate' as in carefully teasing out seeds of cotton from the cotton fibres. *Cefi*, in this light, is associated semantically with spoken verses that 'separate' or protect the speaker from danger. *Bolle ɓaleeje* or 'black speech' at one level embraces all incantations and spoken verses, and their colour coding is related to the classification of types of knowledge between forms considered to be white or black. The phrase does, however, carry a pejorative connotation for some people, suggesting a sinister sense of the evil word that intends to do harm to someone or something. In practice, this distinction is sometimes hard to sustain, particularly if a protective verse, under the guise of protection, causes harm to another person. Like shot silk whose colour varies according to the point from which it is viewed, so the moral evaluation of and conceptual distinctions between special forms of speech depend on the viewpoint of the observer (Lienhardt 1968).

Verses and incantations are made up of a mixture of everyday Pulaar – sometimes archaic forms – as well as what practitioners call 'spirit language' (*haala jinne*). This language sounds very much like Pulaar but it has no apparent sense, much like what Malinowski reported about untranslatable passages of magical speech among the Trobrianders.[17] In fact, some of these words may be borrowed items from neighbouring languages, particularly from Mande or Soninke, but they are not recognised locally as such. What is particularly striking about these verses is the pronounced metrical structure and pattern that is developed within a verse, especially within those sections thought to be recited in the language of the spirits. There appear, then, to be three styles of language each with their own prosody running through incantations or verses.[18] First, there are the rhythms of everyday speech that compose those passages of a verse that can often have a transparent meaning and can thus be translated. These passages do not necessarily scan, and have neither a regular metre nor rhythm. Second, ordinary language can be structured so as to have rhyme and rhythm and the regular metres of these passages of verse often complement those passages in 'spirit language' which may follow similar patterns. One way in which ordinary language can be patterned is by means of the linguistic rules governing the agreement of noun and adjective. These require that the appropriate suffix be attached to each, and the result is rhyming, rhythmical couplets that appear in ordinary speech, such as in *konngol bonngol* ('evil' word) (^ ^ / ^ ^) and *larki bonki* ('evil' eye) (^ ^ / ^ ^). Where spirit language occurs in a verse it is virtually always structured in highly rhythmical patterns with a regular metre, although these patterns are sometimes punctuated or broken to mark the end of a section, perhaps with non-scanning prose. To summarise, the three styles of verse language are: (1) non-scanning ordinary speech; (2) scanning ordinary speech ('poetry'); and (3) scanning, highly rhythmical spirit language.

One could perhaps define a fourth style, namely the local pronunciations of Arabic words and phrases which, although they are not spirit language, are thought to have an inherent potency and are held to have a translatable meaning. One example has already been discussed in earlier sections (e.g. the compound *bisimillaay*) but others are frequently used as opening phrases in incantations. The most common phrase that has been adapted from the Arabic (*salaah ['ala] Muhammad wa Ali Muhammad*, meaning 'may Muhammad and his family be blessed') becomes in local parlance a potent, rhythmical utterance pronounced *salaali Mohammed walaali Mohammed*.[19] The prosody of the phrase can be represented:

salaali Mohammed   ^ _ ^ / ^ _ ^
walaali Mohammed   ^ _ ^ / ^ _ ^

^ = short or unstressed   _ = long or stressed

This opening passage to most incantations gives it a strongly rhythmical introduction, and indeed it could be regarded as a kind of highly patterned language akin to spirit language for many people. These incantations are sometimes referred to familiarly as *salaali walaali*s, a slightly disrespectful and jocular reference to the introductory passage. Such a comment was once made by the wife of a cleric about verses her client weaver used in his healing practices.

I will now give some examples of the styles of language introduced above, choosing a series of illustrations that highlight aspects of potent language.[20] The first example is a weaver's verse used to protect the craftsman's hands before weaving, and it illustrates how the rhythms of 'spirit language' are developed, then punctuated and broken by non-scanning prose:

1. *salaali Mohammed*   ^ _ ^ / ^ _ ^
2. *walaali Mohammed*   ^ _ ^ / ^ _ ^
3. *suukusa, muukusa*   _ ^ ^ / _ ^ ^
4. *suuku ali saa*   _ ^ / ^ ^ / _
5. *Allaa e nyaamo*   ^ _ / ^ / _ ^
6. *Anabe e nano*   ^ ^ ^ / ^ / ^ ^

Lines 1 and 2 open the incantation with the usual blessing, and lines 3 and 4 are 'spirit language'. Lines 5 and 6, which mean 'Allah on the right', 'the Prophet on the left', break the rhythm developed in lines 1 and 2 and then modified in lines 3 and 4. Prosody is not, however, the only principle, for it is apparent that the repetition of the vowel stem 'uu' alternating with consonants 's' and 'm' (two significant sounds, see above), and the repetition of the stem *kusa* are important ingredients in the verse. Indeed, line 4, the last line with a regular metre, incorporates the element 'ali' into the original word *suukusa*, thus altering the prosody of the word and bringing the rhythm to a satisfying resolution with an elongated vowel sound. This rhythm is then broken by the non-scanning prose of lines 5 and 6.

The second example is also a weaver's incantation uttered at the moment when the warp threads in the loom are attached to a drag-weight and weaving is set to begin. It illustrates how everyday Pulaar takes on a rhythm of its own, and how these rhythms are then repeated in spirit language.

1. *salaahi Mohammed*   ^ _ ^ / ^ _ ^
2. *walaahi Mohammed*   ^ _ ^ / ^ _ ^
3. *dutal pural*   _ ^ / _ ^
4. *limbi lamba*   _ ^ / _ ^
5. *Anabe liifi laafa*   ^ ^ ^ / _ ^ / _ ^
6. *finendam doolam*   ^ ^ ^ / _ ^
7. *ndas ndam dow*   ^ ^ ^ / _

Following the blessing in lines 1 and 2, line 3 means 'fawn-coloured vulture'. This phrase not only sets up a rhythmical pattern repeated in the alliteration of line 4 (perhaps an allusion to the movement of a bird in flight?), but itself gains its rhythm and rhyme from the agreement between the noun and the adjective by use of the appropriate suffixes. Line 5 introduces a new rhythm of three short beats with the word 'Anabe' (the Prophet), and this is followed by an altered alliteration that picks up on the sounds and metre of the original one in line 4. Lines 6 and 7 repeat the triplet of short beats, and the rhythmical pattern is resolved in line 7 with a single long, stressed beat that fades away on the last foot. The last two lines can be translated as follows:

6. *finendam doolam*   my awakening [in the morning] my strength
7. *ndas ndam dow*   my drag weight [on a loom] [come] up

A third example, a protective verse inserted into a weaver's song, is composed of a mixture of derived Arabic terms and probably borrowed Mande words. In addition, sounds are included that develop a strong rhythmical beat through the repetition of stems to which are added either suffixes or prefixes:

1. *Aliifyo Allaahu naŋgube*   ^ _ ^ / ^ _ ^ / ^ _ ^
2. *tuŋkala, taŋkala, fatanyaaŋ*   _ ^ ^ / _ ^ ^ / ^ ^ _
3. *seekum, beekum*   _ ^ / _ ^
4. *kamkum kamakum*   _ ^ / ^ ^ ^
5. *kamdullaay*   ^ ^ _

Line 1 starts with the first letter of Arabic alphabet, *alif*, and is followed by a reference to Allah. The rest of the verse is in the language of the spirits and, according to the reciter, has no literal meaning. The sounds are structured in such a way as to create a rhythmical pattern based on triplets composed of short-long-short beats, and these triplets are repatterned in line 2, with the final anapaest drawing that pattern to a close. Also, the stem *kala* is repeated with the same prefix apart from a modified vowel sound. This kind of repetition is seen again in lines 3 and 4 in which the stem *kum* is prefixed by sounds in which either the vowels remain the same but the initial consonant changes (*see* and *bee*), or in which the prefix is added to it. By repeating these stems at the end of the line, not only is a rhythm created but also a rhyme is produced. In addition, the tempo of the verse increases at line 4 with the introduction of an extra vowel sound in *kamkum*, and the verse then slows to a halt in line 5 with two rapid beats and a long faded third beat of the final anapaest.

There are many other verses or parts of verses that could illustrate these and other points in order to indicate a wider range of prosody and the patterning of sound. These might include others from a collection assembled during fieldwork, such as a fisherman's verse used in hippopotamus hunting, or a *bileejo*'s spells. Alternatively, Appia-Dabit (1941) provides us with a range of protective verses used by craftsmen, and Gaden (1931) translated, for instance, a verse for protection against hyenas. These and the examples given here suggest the centrality of rhythm, metre and pattern in the composition of incantations and magical verses.[21] Verses seem to exaggerate the prosody of ordinary language, although they do not always follow a uniform metrical structure, nor do all the lines necessarily scan. I would suggest that the juxtaposition of non-scanning lines and lines with a strong and powerful beat emphasises the contrast between the two, and this feature constitutes part of the verse's effectiveness. The verse or incantation impresses rhythms of language upon the world. The literal meaning or semantic content of these verses does not seem to be their most important feature, and this is certainly the case for those who recite them. Where it is possible to decipher the semantics of the verse, the literal meaning is often trivial, banal or of little significance. These verses are, as it were, a form of expression that is under-determined at the level of surface semantic content; yet they appear almost over-determined at the level of prosody and metre. These are forms of expression in which the prosody of everyday speech is exaggerated and emphasised to such an extent that the linguistic meaning of the verse becomes virtually irrelevant. The 'meaning' of these verses lies not in the area of the semantics of the lexical and linguistic items either individually or as a whole, but it seems to inhere in their composition with respect to rhythm, metre and tempo generated in the articulation of the sounds.[22] It is in prosody that the significance of the verses is to be found. Perhaps 'meaning' is the wrong word to use, since the 'meaning' of these verses is their power and potency; what is important is their power to protect, their efficacy and their instrumentality to bring about effects. This power and potency lies not in the descriptive or referential functions of language, but instead in the *correct performance* of them; indeed, it rests on their 'illocutionary' and 'perlocutionary' force. These verses must be recited without a mistake, and to make a mistake is to interrupt the rhythm and tempo of the verse, and so disrupt the ability of the incantation to be a potent agent in the world. If a mistake were to be made – and here a warning to the reader! – then the power of the verse returns upon the speaker and causes him or her misfortune.

DISCUSSION OF SPOKEN 'MAGIC'

First a note on the use of the word 'magic': I have avoided this term as an analytical category in the ethnography above since it has connotations that detract from my argument. The phrase 'power-practices' has often been used in its place to describe those activities that are conceived to be potent in some way or other. Their potency derives from the idea that invisible, human and non-human forces are put in motion through these practices, such that aspects of the practices themselves are considered to be endowed with agency, the ability to bring about effects. The term 'magic', as Tambiah (1990) recalls, developed in Europe as part of a discourse that contrasted religion with magic; it is also the case that many Islamic scholars make a similar contrast, such that 'magic' (*sihr*) is a category into which activities that are regarded as condemnable are placed and thus made distinct from orthodox religious practice. The argument here is that maraboutic power-practices and those of craftsmen and other specialists should be considered within the same category of analysis, even if they may be regarded by local commentators as two separate specialisms. To introduce the concept of 'magic' would be to give credence to a distinction between orthodox religious practice and heretical or condemnable practice that is part of local cultural politics between competing social groups. This admission would also move the analysis away from a consideration of the commonalities between the two sets of practices. I employ the term 'magic' in the heading above, not as a calculated snub to my own argument, but as a means of linking this discussion to a body of comparable literature describing practices labelled 'magic' elsewhere.

Different forms of verbal expression among Pulaar speakers have been reviewed with a view to highlighting a continuity between the structure, rhythm and prosody of language on the one hand, and conceptions of power and potency on the other. In the realm of human speech and orality it would seem that types of agency and forms of potency are linked to an increasing stress on prosody and rhythmical patterns in the articulation of sound. Animals, particularly large ones, may possess the ability to make sounds – and are indeed attributed with 'voices' of a kind – but these sounds are by and large unpunctuated noises and grunts that lack harmoniousness, rhythm and structure. One noted exception to this is birdsong, references to which focus on its melodic and rhythmic nature; moreover, it is employed, for instance, as a metaphor for a type of group weavers' song, *daaɗe gelloode*, an allusion to the 'voices' of songbirds (*gelloogal*) that sit and sing in the *gellooki* tree (sp. *Guiera senegalensis*). There is something of a continuum then extending from animals that lack language proper – but some of whom seem to possess voices closer than others to humans – through to humans who possess a range of speech genres, from ordinary speech, through poetry and song, to powerful words and verses with an agency of their own. Along this continuum, there is a progressive development of prosodic structure and rhythmical pattern that is evident most strongly in magical verse. In parallel with this increase in metre and rhythm is the sense that the power and potency of the spoken medium becomes greater.

Malinowski suggested that there were two 'crystallisations' of language in all societies: the ordinary language of technology and science, and the language of magic and persuasion (Tambiah 1990: 80). In the case of Haalpulaar utterances, I would propose that there are at least four 'crystallisations' of language: (1) ordinary language which carries with it no potency or power; (2) poetic and intentional speech, that is speech that can move people or which is the vehicle for a range of human intentions and wishes; (3) 'magical' language which involves the power of individual words and letters; (4) the power of stretches of speech that are structured in particular ways. Tambiah points out (1990: 80) one unsettled issue in Malinowski's work: is 'magical language' a different genre of language from ordinary speech or is it an intensification of ordinary forms like poetic diction, for example? Certainly at the level of prosody and the patterning of the spoken word, it would seem that in this case there is a continuum rather than a discontinuous array of genres. This issue, however, raises further areas for investigation.

The ordinary language of everyday exchange is a neutral mode of communication, it is founded upon a distance separating the signifier from the signified, such that the signs of language become 'wrested free from things', as Foucault describes it (1989). Language that possesses a form of potency to effect the state of persons in the world does so by virtue of it being a vehicle for the transmission of intentions, motivations and feelings of the speaker. This is the case in praise-singing and poetry, where people are moved and affected by words; it also applies to the case of intentional speech – the evil word (*konngol bonngol*) or 'vexed' speech (*haala mettuka*) – in which the desires and motivations of the speaker can affect the recipient via the medium of language. Here language might be seen as a mode of communication that is inalienable from the person of the speaker. It remains part and parcel of the speaker's self; it transmits an aspect of the person in the form of words; its message embraces, as it were, the 'spirit' of the language. A comparison might be drawn here between this form of language and the concept of the 'gift', the spirit of which can be seen to represent an aspect of the person or self of the giver transmitted to the possession of the receiver (Mauss 1990). Because both forms carry with them an aspect of the self of the giver/speaker, they also carry with them a potency that can have an effect upon those who receive the gift or the word. If 'evil words' can be likened to the gift, then the ordinary speech of everyday human exchange could be likened to market exchange in which the self or person of the giver is not transmitted across the gulf of the transaction; there is a separation of people and things in the case of commodity exchange, as there is a separation of words and things in ordinary language. Such words in themselves have neither an inherent potency nor are they the potent vehicles of intentions, motivations and feelings of the speaker.

The potency of particular, individual words poses a different kind of relationship between words and things. In this case, there is a close identity between word and thing. The signs of language and the signatures that are conceived to be found in the world are linked by resemblances and similitudes, to echo Foucault's formulation of the Renaissance worldview (1989). Language seems to take on a perfectly transparent form in which the word and the thing are almost identical. The 'magic of the word' is possible because of the way humans have deciphered the world, by conceiving and revealing the resemblances beneath its signs (Foucault 1989: 47–8). There is, thus, a similitude between certain words and certain things, such that to pronounce the word is to invoke the thing itself, to articulate a name is to summon into existence that which is named.[23] 'Magical language', however, at the level of individual words and names is a restricted referential code, for it denotes only a limited range of things and beings, most usually persons, mystics or saints, caliphs, the Prophet, or spirits, jinn and angels. The language of 'magic' in the form of stretches of speech, as has been analysed above, suggests another dimension to power-practice. The re-patterning of the prosodic structures of language poses yet further questions about the nature of the relationship between language and the world. But before this analysis can be developed, it is necessary to investigate another area of potent language – the 'magic of writing'.

WRITING AND THE ORDER OF THINGS

The potency of the spoken word appears to inhere in the rhythm and the prosodic patterns of sound. Potent sounds are particularly structured through the rhythms developed through repetition and the elaboration of repetitions, and these metrical forms are punctuated and broken by introducing elements that disrupt patterns of sound. They are thus emphasised. Patterns occur within lines or phrases of sound as well as within verses as a whole. Prosody, however, is not the only significant dimension, for alliteration and repetition of sound are also important elements. Talents in these spoken areas of language are the specialisms of men-of-skill (*nyeenyɓe*), who in this regard are also referred to as the *haaloobe*, literally 'speakers'; that is, they are wordsmiths, praise-singers and poets who have the ability to transform language from the medium of mundane expression into a potent one.[24] In this form, language itself has the power to transform the human, social world. Men-of-skill, then, are recognised as experts in language, along with the *wileeɓe*, or witch-hunters, magicians and curers. Witch-hunters have at their command not only powerful substances that can cure or afflict people with illness, but they also possess incantations and spells which they use to bring about effects through the power of the word. Like men-of-skill who are masters of raw materials that are manipulated in the course of their manual crafts as well as masters of oral arts and performance, witch-hunters are masters of potent objects and potions as well as of the potency of words. A broad association can be drawn, therefore, between the modes of transformation of witch-hunters, on the one hand, and of men-of-skill on the other: both share an expertise in language and the potency of the spoken word; both deal with the word-as-object, regarded now as a kind of potent 'power-object'.[25] What I wish to turn to in this section is the idea of the written-word-as-object, and together the two modes of efficacy relate to the main two forms of mystical agency recognised by Haalpulaar'en: the written and the spoken, the literate and the oral. This subject also takes us into the domain predominantly of the *tooroɓe* clerics.

The respective power-practices of witch-hunters and of Muslim marabouts was the subject of discussion in Chapter 6. It was concluded that there are areas of similarity between the two: parallels could be drawn, for instance, between the use of names and the disposal of materials manipulated in the course of either set of procedures. Despite the local cultural distinction, therefore, between *haaloobe* and *windooɓe*, the speakers and the writers of 'magic', the connections at the level of 'magical' operations suggested the separation was less apparent in practice. The distinction, however, is linked to an important social cleavage between *tooroɓe* cleric marabouts, the writers of Arabic script, and witch-hunter/magicians and men-of-skill, the speakers of incantations, spells and spoken verses. Again, however, this distinction of speakers-versus-writers does not adequately delimit the specialisms of each social category: while the speakers rarely rely upon the written word in the practice of their arts, marabouts do depend on both the spoken and written form, as indeed do West African traditions of Islam as a whole. I now turn to an analysis of the structure of maraboutic written talismans as a counterpoint to the analysis of speakers' verbal incantations.

Binndi is a general term in Pulaar that refers to a variety of forms of potent writing, and it includes *aaye*, 'script'-potions or 'erasures'.[26] These are made by carefully washing Arabic script of selected Qur'anic verses off a writing tablet (*alluwal*) on which a marabout has written prescribed texts. The patient who has consulted the marabout with an ailment or problem will be required to drink the potion or to wash in it at various times of day. Usually used for therapeutic and protective purposes, the script-potions can be made more palatable by the addition of scent. Alternatively, Qur'anic script is written on paper (called a *talki* or *talkuru*), which might be carried on the person in a leather pouch or put in a pocket. Another practice offered by some marabouts is the writing of *haatumeere*, potent designs or talismans, the patterns of which are based on geometrical designs which incorporate Qur'anic script and number. A very basic form of talisman involves marabouts (*seerenaaɓe*) copying designs from magical treatises and manuals (*defte lasaar* – 'books of magic'), a rather limited art that demands little instruction.

A more complex form of prescribing written talismans is *haatumeere sirru* or 'secret magic patterns' made exclusively by master marabouts (*sirruyankooɓe*) trained in Muslim occult sciences.[27] They involve the use of numerology to ascertain the numerical value of the letters of a person's name (*inde* or given name), and this number is used in the design to represent the person, who is either the client or the intended victim. Both the copied designs and the secret designs can be used for protection as well as for causing harm to others. These designs can be used to cause a man to become impotent towards his wife or one of his wives, to cause a woman to take offence at her husband, to cause a thief or enemy to become mad, or to cause a person to leave home and become stranded in a foreign place. To kill a person, the graphic design is either written on or wrapped in a piece of burial shroud dug up from a grave. These techniques were described above in Chapter 6. In these cases, for the design to have an effect on a specific individual, the name of the intended victim has to be written or represented in the pattern, either spelt out in Arabic script or included as a number integrated into the design. Thus names are written rather than spoken, and the medium by which the effects of this power-practice are produced is text-based and scriptural rather than the oral arts of the 'speakers'.

Hamès (1997), in his study of a dozen or more Senegalese written talismans, defines a range of elements that contribute to the potency of these designs. They include: first, the materials used in their fabrication – the paper, the ink, etc.; second, the impress of the person who has made the talisman; third, the form and structure of the design itself, a combination of Arabic script and number, a geometrical format and an overall graphic 'architecture' of the composition. The potency or charge instilled in the talisman by the individual marabout who produces it is a function of his social and religious status, of his charisma and *baraka* or grace. Thus a bespoke talisman from a renowned *sirruyanke* is considered more powerful than a copied version peddled by a minor marabout from a market stall. The *baraka* or spiritual grace of the master marabout is transmitted by his hand through the pen onto the paper. Many talismans, however, issued by master marabouts are in fact written by their *taalibe*s or pupils. In this case, the final touch is added by the master who impregnates the paper with his *baraka*, a quality transmitted by his breath and saliva as he utters a blessing over it.[28]

The third and most important element is the structure and content of the graphic design and text. Hamès links the production of written talismans to a broader 'graphic' field which includes patterns and designs made at the hands of craftsmen, such as leatherworkers, woodcarvers and smiths and jewellers. He talks of a secular tradition which associates 'graphism' without writing with 'magical' efficacy. Written talismans and other graphic designs, Hamès argues, both employ geometrical form (Hamès 1997: 28–35). By contrast, I am concerned here to compare and contrast two modes of power-practice: written graphic designs in the form of *haatumeere* and the spoken word. Indeed, my task is to investigate the form and mode of language in both media. I will return to discuss other aspects of Hamès's work below, but first I will present three simple talismans I collected in Senegal. I will then turn to some of Hamès's examples and conclusions.

Examples

The first example is a copied talisman that was on sale on a market stall, and which had been written out by the trader who 'mass-produced' them.

On his stall the trader had a collection of parts of animals (horns, skin, bones, etc. for use in amulet production), plants, tree bark, leaves and so forth (see Figure 7.1). I suspected him of being a *bileejo* or witch-hunter and magician, which he did not deny when asked. Moreover, he had on offer a whole range of products and services. He conducted cowrie shell divination

7.1 A Haalpulaar healer/marabout's market stall in Rufisque, showing cowrie shells (*right*) laid out for divination, medicine bottles (*left*) containing liquid remedies, and his writing materials and writing-board or *alluwal* (*back left*).

(*tiimgal*) for clients who would stop at his stall for a consultation. He also had displayed in a prominent place at the front of his stall a curious eye-catching device made from a horn with feather and fur attached to it (see Figure 7.2). This contraption was supported at a seemingly impossible angle by the end of the horn that balanced on the tip of a needle that protruded from the top of a cork stuffed into the neck of a bottle. Balanced in this way, it appeared to defy the laws of gravity and the principles of moment around a pivotal point. It swung hypnotically like a mesmerised weathervane, catching the slightest breeze to suggest it had a life of its own. This device was, however, a divinatory technique whose movement during a consultation could be discerned and read by the diviner (*timoowo*). In the bottle that supported the horn and the feather-vaned oracle was a cluster of sticks bound tightly together. This cluster was obviously too large to be inserted into the bottle and gave the impression of a Senegalese equivalent to a ship in a bottle. The contents, however, referred to another form of divination offered by the stall-holder, a method that involves throwing sticks onto the ground or the surface of a bowl of water for their pattern to be interpreted by the diviner.

Amid all these diverse magical and divinatory devices was a pile of *binndi*, including written talismans, one of which is the focus of an analysis here. The trader's expertise in these matters went only as far as copying out a limited

7.2 The Rufisque healer/marabout with his 'magical' 'weathervane'. The bottle at the base of this device contains a tightly packed bundle of sticks larger than the aperture of the bottle itself.

number of designs again and again, without much knowledge as to what the significance of the scriptural forms and graphic designs might be. The talismans were not bespoke prescriptions produced on an individual basis for specific ailments, as master marabouts do, but were 'off-the-peg' medicines, each with its own specified function: to cure headaches and fevers, or menstrual problems, aching limbs, etc. He would himself prescribe the most appropriate of all the designs he had on offer in relation to specific illnesses or complaints brought to him by clients. I suspect this trader to be someone who only moved into the area of written talismans without formal training; indeed if he were a *bileejo* or witch-hunter/magician, his case provides evidence of the limited up-take of written 'magic' by the stereotypical 'speakers' of 'magic'.

The particular talisman shown in Figure 7.3 is to cure headaches and fevers. The form of the talisman is in two parts: an introductory text and a rectangle or schema. The introductory text usually comprises indications about the object sought, the mode of operation, the result to be obtained and so on. The writer of this particular one shows little expertise in Arabic, as many of the inscriptions are unformed and diacritical marks indicating emphases and vowel sounds as they would appear in the Qur'an have been omitted from the opening text; thus it becomes virtually meaningless. The main

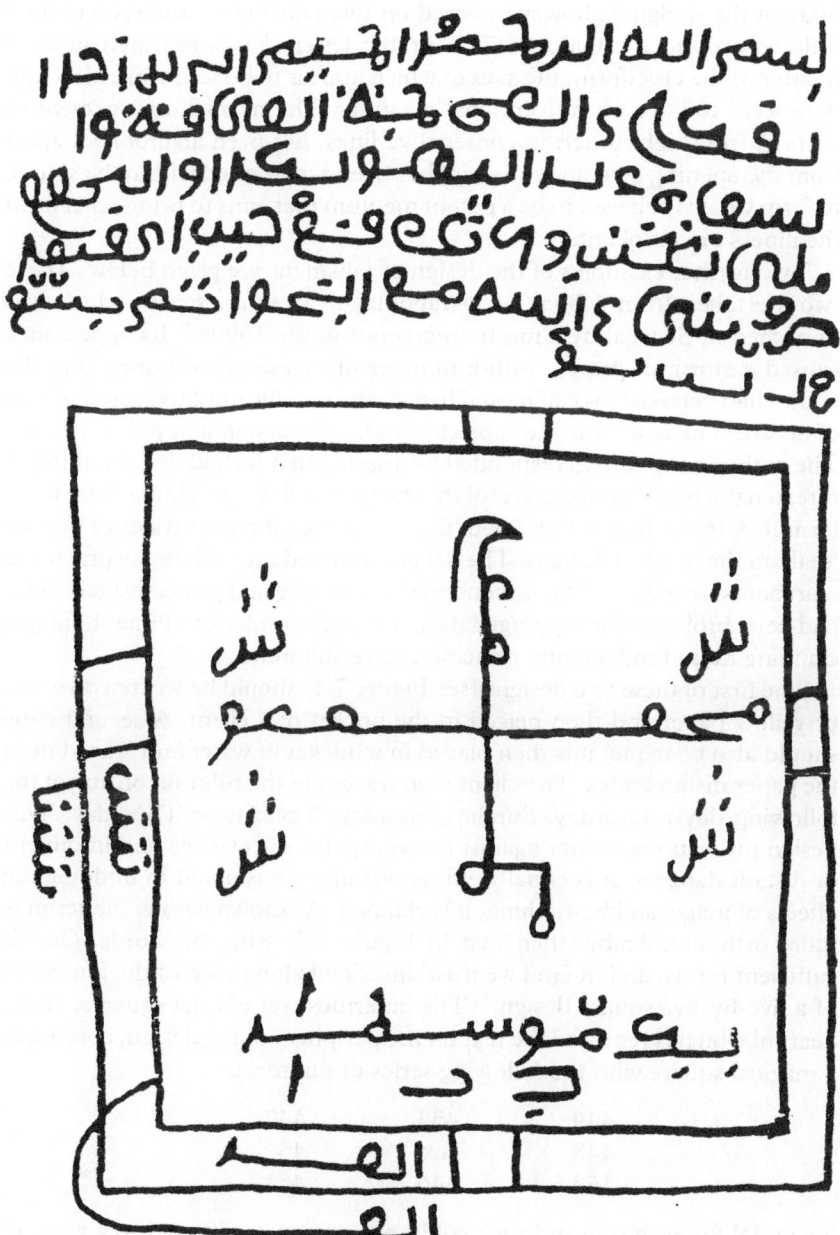

7.3 A *haatumeere* or 'magical' design written by a healer/marabout.

body of the design is, however, based on two concentric squares with text ordered around a cruciform. The Arabic letter *shin* is repeated in each quarter of the cruciform, the axes of which appear to be script-like although they seem to have no conventional meaning. The normal arrangement of writing, from right to left in consecutive lines, has been abandoned, apart from the opening text, and the script has been repatterned within the square to form what is believed to be a potent medium that aims to bring relief from the illness or complaint.

Two further examples of the design of talismans are given below. These two are taken from a book of maraboutage, *Niche des secrets*, which was published in Senegal by a master marabout in the 1990s.[29] Its appearance caused a storm of protest with a number of marabouts claiming that the author had betrayed his calling and had given away the most treasured secrets of his art. The issue was the subject of radio discussion and public debate. The author's supporters responded by arguing that he had done nothing to threaten the integrity of the arts of the *sirruyaŋkooɓe* by providing these mere formulae, for he had not revealed 'the key' to maraboutic mysteries nor the 'seal' on the magical designs. The debate rumbled on, with many practising marabouts worried that their monopoly on curative and protective talismans had been broken; others plunged deeper into the esoterica of maraboutage, claiming more fundamental principles were still intact.

The first of these two designs (see Figure 7.4) should be written on white or yellow paper and then placed in the pocket of a client. A second copy should also be made; it is then placed in a bucket of water and stirred until the paper disintegrates. The client then washes in the solution on any of the following days: Saturday, Sunday, Monday, Tuesday or Thursday. This design protects the bearer against curses, spells, the evil eye and imminent or distant dangers. It is equally efficacious in exorcism and in undoing the effects of magic and bewitching, it is claimed. As shown below, the script is more orthodox Arabic than that in Figure 7.3, with the words 'God is sufficient for us, and in God we trust' inscribed along each of the four sides of a five-by-five square design.[30] The innermost set of nine squares, at the heart of which is repeated the text on the periphery of the design, comprises a magical square with the following series of numbers:

449	454	447
448	Text	452
453	446	451

The total for each row and each column comes to 1,350, and so a value of 450 can be assigned to the central-most square in order to complete the magical square and to give the same total across all directions, including the diagonals.

The second of these two examples (see Figure 7.5) is claimed to be an

THE POWER OF THE WORD

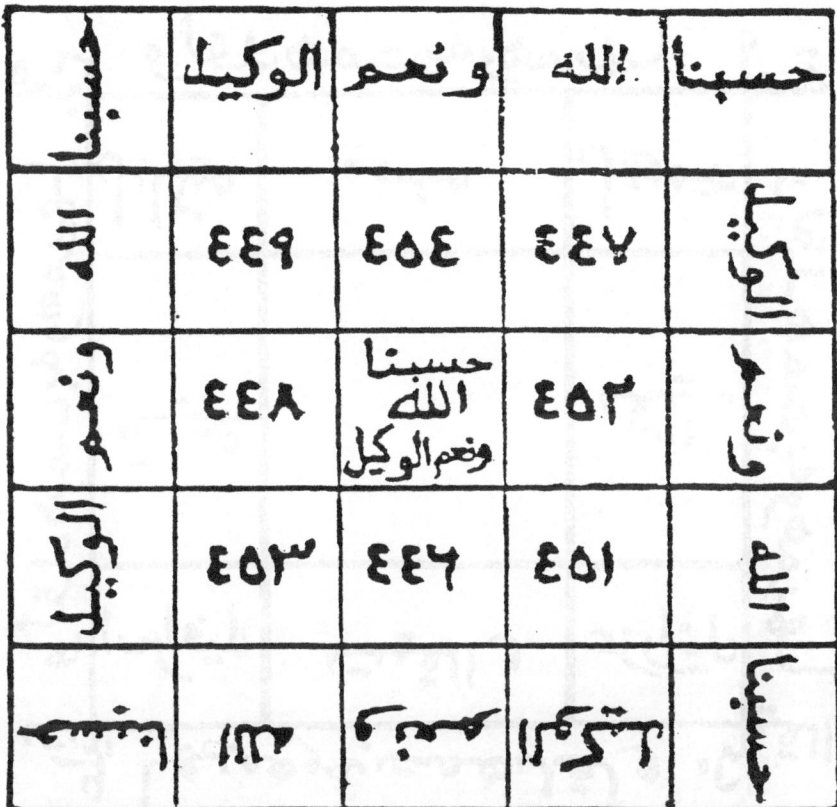

7.4 An example of a *haatumeere* or 'magical' design written by Cheikh Tall. (*Source*: Tall 1994: 41.)

extremely efficacious design for retrieving a lost person or thing, and is particularly powerful in charming one person to fall in love with another. The client washes in a solution made from the disintegrated paper on which the design was written. Again, around the outside of a three-by-three square is text repeated four times, once on each side: 'She did with passion desire him, and he would have desired her'. In each of the corners of the three-by-three square are the names of each of the four angels: Israfil, Israel, Mechail and Jibriel or Gibrael. In the middle four squares on each of the sides are the words: 'love', 'on you', 'from me', 'shed on you'. The innermost square of the nine is reserved for the name or names of those whose love the person seeks or of the personal possessions lost.

In all three of these examples of written talismans, Arabic script has been reordered, repatterned on the page so that it no longer appears in its conventional order or form as ordinary text. These are 'super-scripts', as it were, that denote not only conventional meanings signified through the

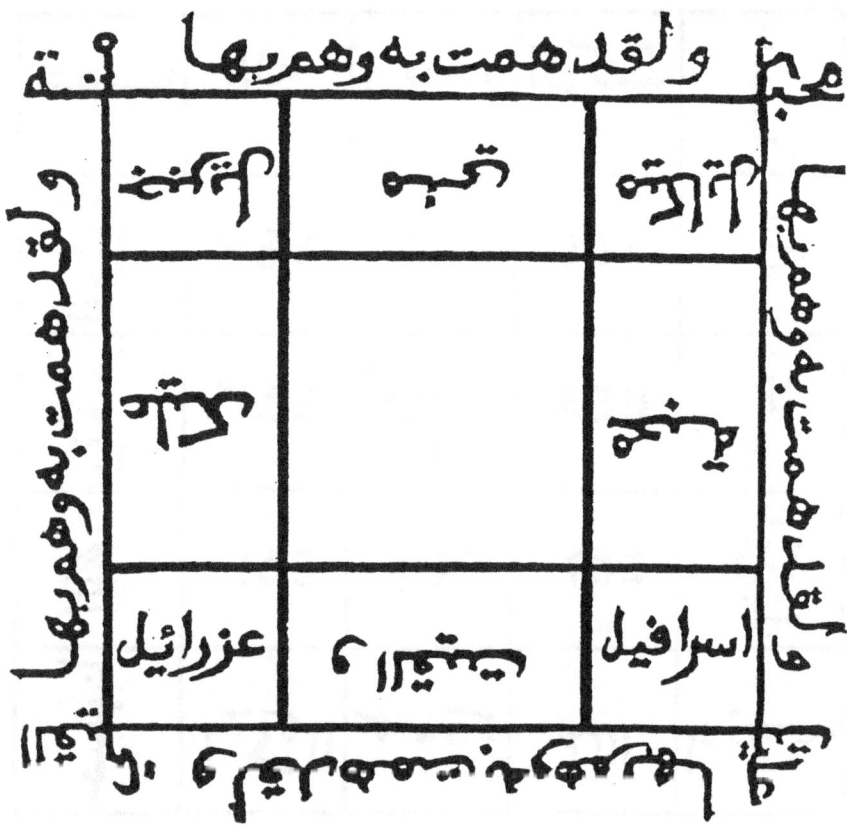

7.5 A further example of a *haatumeere* or 'magical' design written by Cheikh Tall. (*Source*: Tall 1994: 100.)

Arabic text, but they also carry with them the potency of words rearranged in designs especially established to bring about effects in the world. Does the selection of Qur'anic text for use in talismans suggest any connection between the purpose or target of the practice and the conventional meaning of the text? In the first example of the market trader's copied talisman given in Figure 7.3), the writer seems to be unaware of the literal meaning of the inscriptions he made on the paper, and it is difficult to decipher any. This example fits well with Goody's ideas of the 'magic of writing' in the context of restricted literacy (Goody 1968a). The writer of this particular talisman, not an educated Muslim *tooroɓe* cleric, evinces the idea of not only the secrecy and potency that gathers around the Qur'an itself, but also of the status and prestige that surrounds the custodians and purveyors of these secrets (Goody 1968b). A little like Lévi-Strauss's Amazonian scribe, who copies the ethnographer in filling sheets of paper with inscriptions in an attempt to increase his social standing among his fellows (1976), so the copier of this talisman mimics the art of the powerful *toorobe* cleric marabouts.

The last two examples included above point to there being a connection of sorts between the meaning of the texts chosen and the intended purpose of the talisman. Only in the second of these, though, is there a direct reference to one specific function of the talisman – inducing another into love. The scope of my sample is, however, too limited to sustain many general conclusions. A much broader survey of Senegalese talismans has been made by Hamès. He suggests that only a limited selection of texts, of single words and of decompositions into individual letters is used in his corpus. One of the most often-used texts is *al-Fatihah*, the introduction to, and Chapter 1 of, the Qur'an. Also well used are Chapter 112, 'The Declaration of God's Unity', Chapter 113, 'The Daybreak', and Chapter 114, entitled 'Men'.[31] Chapter 1 of the Qur'an is highly venerated and esteemed as the quintessence of the whole of the Qur'an; it is itself a prayer that is repeated in public and private devotions. Chapter 112 is also a venerated text and is declared to be equal to a third part of the whole Qur'an. Chapters 113 and 114 both deal with undoing or banishing evil. The former alludes to a story in which Mohammed is bewitched by a man and his daughters, who tie him up in eleven knots. This and the latter Chapter were revealed to Mohammed, and on repeating the eleven verses that comprise them, he was entirely freed from the spell. Chapter 114 talks of the 'whisperers' of evil, and refers to demons who withdraw from the presence of humans when the name of God is mentioned. The choice of these texts, therefore, suggests a broad connection with the general purpose of many talismans, although not necessarily with the specific aims of individual ones.

Hamès's conclusion (1997: 147–9) on the use of Qur'anic verses suggests that what takes place is a transformation of a liturgical text that is subsequently set within a new context – that is, within the design of a talisman. This echoes the idea cited above from Malinowski (1935) about the recontextualisation of stretches of speech in spoken magical verse. Hamès goes on to argue that the process of pruning a liturgical text for use in its new context establishes a language that has now become in a sense trivial and banal, but in another sense potent and effective. For instance, he cites the example of the text from one verse running into that of another without separation, such that the last word of one becomes the first word of the second. On this basis, Hamès points out, the potency of the talisman arises not simply from the addition of separate individual texts, but from a unity of the design that hinges on 'language play' or a 'linguistic game' as he calls it (1997: 151). The whole design is greater, then, than the sum of its parts. The talisman creates a new graphic context in which text and figure are arranged in space, creating a kind of elaborate unified 'architecture'.[32] Indeed, one of the designs Hamès analyses is formed from a complex pattern of nested squares and triangles, from which radiates a set of eight rectangles that resemble the vanes of a windmill.

THE PROSE OF THE WORLD

As in the case of the oral arts of incantations and spells, the prime consideration in the selection and presentation of words or text does not seem to hinge necessarily on the literal semantic content. The language of magical writing signifies meanings of a different order, and these do not inhere in the linguistic properties of the medium as it is used in mundane social settings. Goody points to the reasons for the enchantment of the written word in social contexts of restricted literacy, and argues that written language gains its 'magical function' from its proven role as a mode of communication between humans. Its function becomes extended beyond the natural to the supernatural (1968c). This latter role, according to Goody, arises from writing's initial 'rational' function, that is the 'objectification of speech' (1968b: 1). Granted that the potency of language appears to be in part linked to the role it plays as a medium of communication with unseen forces in the universe, there is, nonetheless, another aspect. The role played by language in Islamic talismans is informed by a particular metaphysics. Part of the 'language play' in talismans is the creation of 'super-scripts' that signify visual as well as verbal meanings. At the heart of the sophisticated organisation and layout on paper in two dimensions of number and text, in which alphabetic, numerical and graphic inscription are intricately intercalated, is a metaphysical connection between writing and a conception of being and creation.[33] Writing in the form of letters, words and text is linked to spiritual powers which are summoned by their inscribed 'signatures' and thereby activated to move on and to have an effect in the world. Hamès states: '... letters, just like divine names and chapters of the Qur'an, do not only correspond with the remainder of the world but put into motion and bring into action "beings" called "servants" ... whose powers are put at the disposition of these letters, names, chapters when they are written under very precise conditions' (1997: 223, my translation).[34] There is certainly a communication function here, but this function does not exhaust the set of associations suggested in Pulaar semantics.

The conception of the written word as a form of communication that can have an effect upon the world is found throughout the peripheries of the Muslim world. Yet a series of much more localised associations between the power of the word and the constitution of the world can also be made: the written word does not merely have an effect upon the world, but it also constitutes the image by means of which the world itself is conceived. In Pulaar, the world can be referred to as 'the writing of Allah' (*windere Allaa*), and Allah as the creator is referred to as 'The Writer', *Bindoowo*, one of the names of God. The world is a text that has been created by God. The conception of the patterning of script in talismans is linked to the creation and existence of the world and of the order of things in it. There is, furthermore, a parallel here to be drawn with the analysis of spoken incantations: in that case, the order of things is linked with prosody and the metrical structure of the spoken word.[35] The patterns in language, and especially the repatterning of sound in spoken verse, have an effect on the patterns and orders of things in the world. In a similar manner, the patterns and designs incorporating the written word are the literate analogue to the oral. There is a parallel between the metaphysics behind the written patterns of talismans and the oral patterns of rhythm and prosody in spoken verse. There are, perhaps, two forms of conception of the link between the potency of language and the ordering of things, and these two share a common ground: the first is articulated through the patterning of sound and the spoken word; the second is articulated through the patterning of script and the inscription of designs on paper. Activities and affairs in this world are capable of being ordered and of being disrupted by the patterning that occurs in certain forms of language. This order can be continually recreated and readjusted through the procedures of specialists who reorder either sound in verbal utterances or the written word by means of inscriptions on paper. Particular categories of specialist claim these processes of creation and transformation as their own: the *windoobe*, the 'writers', are characteristically *toorobe* cleric marabouts versed in the visual arts of patterning script and text; the *haaloobe* or 'speakers' are the masters of speech and the patterning of sound. As men-of-skill and witch-hunter/magicians (*wileebe*), these speakers-practitioners also manipulate and transform material objects. It is these two types of specialist who try to impose order and organisation on the world, on beings and things in it and on human affairs. They do so by their restrictive hold on the mysteries of their arts and by laying claim to domains of power exclusive to them alone. While the ideological distinction separating these two sets of specialists might suggest a rigid dichotomy of the literate versus the oral, it would seem that these two modes of potency within language share much in common.[36]

There is an intriguing set of semantic associations in Pulaar that point to a further set of connections between the oral and the literate, the ordering of language and the world, and the idea of order and disorder, of pattern and disrupting patterns. These associations cluster around the lexical root *wil*. The verb *wiltude* carries the sense 'to order pages in a manuscript or book', while the verb *wilde* is used with respect to a manuscript or book whose pages are out of order (see Gaden 1914).[37] The latter can also mean 'to perform sorcery' (Niang 1997), although Gaden gives the verb *wildude* the sense of 'to perform the operations of the *bileejo*'s magic' (1914). The root *wil* also provides the substantive *wileebe*, the plural of *bileejo*, or witch-hunter/magician. This lexical item is the root for a set of terms associated with a range of magical operations or power-practices. Also, if the metaphor of the order of the world and the order of text is highlighted, then this root is associated with a process of ordering and indeed disordering things in the world. Also closely associated with order is disorder and 'magic'. An image is created through this nexus of associations of the world as text, or better the 'prose of the world' – both oral and written – as ordered and reordered through the operations of specialist power-practices. Gaden provides a final note for this discussion when he remarked that the verb *windude*, 'to write' is actually a contraction or elided form of *wilndude*, which comes from the same root *wil* as the other verbs. This is suggestive of a conception, perhaps made long ago and now of little conscious salience, of writing as a form of 'magic' akin to the operations of the arts of the *wileeɓe*. Here, then, is another indication of the possible connection of the oral and the written as forms of potency. One is reminded once again of the Pulaar adage *windooɓe ko wileeɓe*, 'those who write are witch-hunter/magicians'. There are numerous ways of interpreting this statement. First, it could be construed in a derogatory sense as a devaluation of the activities of marabouts by those who are suspicious about their intentions, believing them to have dubious motives like the *wileeɓe*. Second, it could be seen to mean that both written talismans and spoken verses can be used for harmful, offensive purposes (*dabare*), and that there is little to choose between the two in terms of the ability of each to bring misfortune and suffering to a victim. Third, it could be construed as suggesting that both the *windooɓe* or 'writers' and the *wileeɓe* as 'speakers' share similar abilities to reorder, rewrite, redesign, rephrase or restructure the world. Both possess the key to the order of things that inheres in the patterning of sound and ordering of inscriptions, and both have the ability to transform the world conceived as prose.[38] Both may be similarly classified as power-practices, perhaps a closer translation than 'magic', for they create and recreate the world. The two types of specialist who carry them out can act as agents through the potency of their media, and so both practitioners are seen as potentially dangerous and possibly morally dubious. Nonetheless, while the writers are thought to draw on lore and knowledge that is considered to be white, Islamic and inspired by higher potencies, the speakers and the *wileeɓe* in particular draw on lore and knowledge that is black and inspired by lower potencies. This ideological distinction, however, belies a series of mutual connections.

Hayden White regards Foucault as being ironic in his reference to the order of things and the prose of the world, for it is merely a representation of the order of things by means of an order of words and discourse (1973). What seems to have emerged from this analysis is that both maraboutic written talismans and other forms of spoken verse and incantation are founded on, in a non-ironic way, the identity between the order of things and persons on the one hand, and the prose of the world on the other. The order of things is also an order of language both as script and as spoken word. The sign of written and spoken language is certainly not arbitrary in this case. The connection between the domain of language and the ordering of things is direct, transparent and causal for the order of things can be disrupted or repatterned by the reordering of words in script or in verse. These ideas seem to hold only in relation to 'magical' language – namely language as power-practice – that is endowed with agency, with a power and potency to effect changes in the world. The language of everyday speech, by contrast, is a two-dimensional language of signifiers and signifieds, and it breaks the connections of similitude, resemblance and the transparent identity of language and things. There appears to be, therefore, two different modes of representation and identity that are embodied in genres of language: the mode of ordinary language on the one hand and the mode of 'magical language' on the other. Rather than these two modes constituting two different 'epistemes' that are characteristic of different historical epochs (such as the Renaissance or the Classical for Foucault), they are contemporaneous and simultaneous; they exist side by side as alternative forms of expression, of representation of the world, and even of acting upon the world. Thus the continuum established earlier with respect to the progressive patterning of language as sound and inscription seems to be dislodged by a sense of discontinuity in view of the modes of representation and identity inherent in the different social uses of language. The specialist language of experts is a language that is claimed to be three-dimensional: the notion of power mediates between the signifier and the signified. The mundane language of the everyday might disregard that connection, and has the independence to formulate critical commentary about it.

8

ISLAMIC REFORMERS, ISLAMISTS AND THE MUSLIM COMMUNITY

I argued in the last chapter that a series of power-practices in the form of both oral and written 'magic' exhibit a range of connections between the two technologies of power. One central area of maraboutic expertise is the control of Arabic literacy, for 'book magic' (Goody 1968b) is one of the most significant technologies that they control. A certain form of literacy goes to the heart of both their exploitation of power-objects such as talismans and their esoteric paradigm of knowledge. But this esoteric construction of knowledge and the role of literacy within it are under attack. The main protagonists in this contest are Islamic reformers and Islamists who are leading an assault on contemporary forms of Sufi mystical practice in West Africa. This chapter examines the role of Arabic literacy in local Muslim education, and investigates the changes this has brought about within the Islamic community. Reformers and Islamists have traced anew where the limits to this community should be drawn. And their new definitions of this community have entailed the inclusion and the exclusion of specific categories of people. The chapter then returns to consider the question of the position of the men-of-skill and of those dealing with 'black' lore and knowledge within the Islamic community. This is a question that was raised at the outset of this book. What seems to be happening today is a bifurcation in the Muslim community: Islamists and reformers propose radically new visions of the *jama'a*, the Muslim community; at the same time, accommodationists and others reinvent and recast conventional forms of West African Sufism. There is then a diversification in conceptions of Islam in Senegal.

This diversification is connected with the generation of new forms of authority within the Islamic community, and in particular to a new set of geographical locations for those forms of authority. *Tooroɓe* clerics in the late eighteenth and early nineteenth centuries looked towards the Middle East as a source of 'originary authority' (Launay 1992, 2000) that took the form of the concoction of pedigrees that linked them 'genealogically' with distant Arab origins. Muslim status eventually became a kind of hereditary category and the transmission of knowledge via chains of learning and initiation (*isnad* and *silsila*) lent an exclusiveness and moral authority to cleric status. Under Umar Taal's reformist Tijaniyya, the locations of authority may have varied to some extent, but they were still distant. The Tijani focus on Fez as the established centre of the brotherhood is one such example. Whatever Wahhabi influences were present in Taal's vision of his mission (Willis 1967), Taal would have absorbed them during his time spent in the Hijaz, and they have been put forward as the reason to account for the renewed sense of dedication to Shari'a law he proselytised. While Taal's Muslim community may initially have loosened the hold of exclusiveness attached to being a full participating Muslim for caste practitioners within the community, conservative *toorobe* clerics eventually reinstated the importance of differential social status within the order. Again being a Muslim cleric was restricted to a hereditary status bolstered by the processes of Islamic learning and initiation.

The interwar and postwar years in Senegal witnessed a period in which more direct and unmediated links to external sources of Islamic authority could be effected. No longer having to appeal to Muslim leaders among the *toorobe* clerics as the mediating conduit between the faithful and the Hijaz, new generations of Muslims, some of whom were educated in Egypt and the Middle East, could look beyond localised marabout conceptions of Islam to other variants that bypassed local constructions of authority. Study in other Muslim countries offered the opportunity for students to seek out alternative and seemingly superior sources of knowledge and forms of authority, which called into question the local scholarly traditions and constructions of knowledge practices. Launay describes similar processes among the Dyula of Côte d'Ivoire, among whom this new generation of students denied the salience of ethnic, local and other cultural identities in favour of a distinction between what was conceived as a truly Islamic community and the mass of believers who remained in ignorance, mingling in their eyes Islamic and extra-Islamic practices (Launay 1992: 100 and 2000: 196). They provided a 'model for a different kind of Muslim community that in principle ignores all hereditary distinctions and focuses exclusively on religious practice as the criterion for inclusion in the Muslim community' (Launay 2000: 197). This younger generation looked beyond the obstacles that validated traditional social distinctions and categories inherent in the local community of the faithful, and emphasised instead the idea of Islam as a universalist doctrine.

'BOOK MAGIC'

Goody makes the point that what he calls 'book magic' flourishes in situations of restricted literacy, and its efficacy rests upon the concrete achievements of the written word as a newly-introduced medium of cultural communication (1968b: 17–19). The 'magical function' of the book is underpinned, he argues, by the rational social function of writing, namely communication. Yet 'book magic' continues to thrive in social contexts in which literacy is expanding and is no longer restricted to a cleric class. The closed contexts of restricted literacy have been opened up, and talismans and maraboutic techniques are found among a diversity of new contexts. Contemporary West African communities in Paris, for example, continue to practise forms of Qur'anic 'magic', and agents on the streets of the eighteenth *arrondissement* hand out flyers advertising the services of a range of religious experts living in the vicinity. Furthermore, the small advertisements at the back of many Asian-focused magazines in Britain proclaim the expertise of many a West African or Asian-named spiritual healer employing methods akin to maraboutic techniques. In Senegal itself, reading and writing have been encouraged through a range of educational initiatives and literacy programmes established in the country from the 1920s onwards. This period in particular saw the growth of new forms of Arabic schooling, and these developed in parallel with the institutional frameworks of education laid down by the French colonial authorities. These two sets of initiatives pushed back restricted practices that surrounded literacy. Doubt has been cast by other commentators on the role of restricted literacy alone in the conjuring of 'book magic'. Cruise O'Brien, for instance, remarks that '... Arabic literacy was by the 19th century no longer enough for the individual in pursuit of the extraordinary', that is, personal charismatic power. Rather, 'As Arabic literacy spread, so did the special disciplines of Islamic mysticism come to the fore in the preparation of charisma' (Cruise O'Brien 1988a: 16). While Sufism may have offered new opportunities for those seeking personal power, particularly in the form of religious retreats (*khalwa*), revelation and 'supernatural perception' (Ibn Khaldun, in Brenner, 2000c), the practice of writing maraboutic talismans continued. But, as we shall see below, this practice does not remain uncontested as new sources of knowledge and authority situated in different social locations are drawn upon.

Hamès notes that it is with regard to their aims and methods that one of the changes to Islamic talismans has occurred. While nineteenth-century talismans were often concerned with the military demands of protection and victory in acts of war, today's objectives are more pacific and may be aimed at people seeking assistance in the battle for paid employment, for instance. He also notes that techniques have changed too, such that those marabouts operating in France or in the elite urban contexts of Senegal tend to prescribe washes or baths in preference to drinking script-potions, for this method is more attuned to European standards of hygiene. It also translates the notion of Muslim ablutions into a new idiom (Hamès 1997: 15). Alternatively, paper amulets are carried in the pockets of clothing or in a bag rather than being wrapped inside leather belts or collars and worn on the person.

Issues surrounding the changing nature of literacy practices, the status of 'book magic' and the development of new forms of education throw up a series of concerns about Sufi brotherhoods and maraboutic practices. In particular, what were and are the sources of knowledge and forms of authority? How have these been challenged by new processes of legitimacy? What forms do knowledge and power now take? Despite the continuance of a variety of forms of West African mysticism underpinned by what Brenner calls the 'esoteric episteme' (2000d), new forms of knowledge and conceptions of power have been developed by means of novel systems of educational practice. These new forms of knowledge and conceptions of power have been used to challenge accommodationist Sufism. This challenge comes not only in the form of a secular Western education, but it is also derived from within Islam itself, especially from radical reformist movements bent on confronting what they regard in Sufi religious practice as wrongful innovation (*bid'a*), condemnable magical and religious acts (*sihr*), religious mixing (*ikhtilât*), and the sin of association (*shirk*) in the near deification of marabouts. Sufism for them is a degenerate form of worship that has lost sight of the Islamic law and custom (*shari'a* and *sunna*) and has moved away from the message of the Qur'an and the motivations of the early Muslim community.

DEVELOPMENTS IN THE FIELD OF EDUCATION

In the early nineteenth century, French administrators established a European-oriented educational system in Senegal, but it was not until the late 1850s that solid foundations were laid by Governor Louis Faidherbe, who implemented a policy aimed at educating Senegalese for administrative positions in the expanding colonial government. There is debate about the extent to which it was adapted to local conditions (Bouche 1968), but this system did establish literacy in French as a key skill for the emerging local urban elites. What developed was something akin to a dual educational system which has persisted to this day, in which Muslims had their own system of Qur'anic study – as described earlier – and the French attempted to modify progressively their own European system to accommodate Muslim needs. These attempts, however, met with little success (Bouche 1974). The traditional Qur'anic school (*dudal*) constituted an element within the system of literacy restricted by and large to the children of cleric families, although by the 1960s, one-third of all children in Senegal attended Muslim schools, especially in those rural areas where there was little or no state provision of education (Diallo 1972). The gulf between education in rural and urban areas became apparent too in wider divisions over the direction of educational policy in the country as a whole. One view advocated a universal education system based upon the European tradition and another on the realities of Senegalese social life in the countryside (Colin 1980). In the more recent period of structural adjustment, characterised by the withdrawal of the arm of the state from rural areas such as Fuuta Toro, there has been a mobilisation of self-help schemes (*bamtaare*, mutual-aid groups) of which most have been based upon remittances from emigrant workers in France and elsewhere. These schemes have provided health and educational facilities as well as provision for the construction of new mosques (Knight 1994), a development encouraged by Muslim radicals and reformers.

The installation of new European-based schooling did much to encourage a secular rationalist discourse (Brenner 2000d) in which knowledge and power are differently construed in comparison to West African Sufism. Access to knowledge was no longer effected through an initiatory process linked to a single spiritual and divinely gifted individual, but, instead, learning became a topic of public acquisition and enquiry. Personalised methods of Sufi Islamic apprenticeship were replaced by impersonalised techniques of learning. Brenner states – in relation to Mali – 'The grip of the esoteric episteme would begin to erode [with the arrival of European colonial powers], challenged by the imposition of new power structures that ignored and denigrated esoteric claims to knowledge and power' (2000d: 38). The emerging system of education was not simply dualistic, however, with European secular rationalism opposing Muslim Sufi mysticism, for within the Islamic community a series of fundamental shifts were taking place.

Muslim reformers, often operating outside the system of Sufi brotherhoods, began a two-pronged attack on education provision from the 1930s onwards in Senegal. Critical of what they considered to be the neglect of Islam in the French system, reformers attempted to establish a broadly-based education in which the use of Arabic was central, sometimes alongside French, as the language of instruction, and a broader curriculum was developed beyond strict Qur'anic studies. Subjects such as mathematics, geography and history were introduced into these new Arabic schools, which were called *medersas* (Schmitz 2000b). In Fuuta Toro, Al-Hajj Mahmud Ba, for example, on his return from the Hijaz set up a new school during this period in the village of Jowol. Another individual, Ahmad Al-Azhari, university-trained in Egypt, sought to achieve the same status for Arabic that French had attained as a language of study (Ba 1985–6: 250 *et passim*). He encouraged the development of modern Arabic culture in the valley, and belonged to that category of young people who, often educated abroad in the Maghreb, the Middle East or Arabia, fluent in Arabic language and culture, and well versed in Islamic theology, were labelled 'arabisers' (*arabisants* in French).

Developments such as these were part of a wider Islamic revivalist movement in West Africa. Often mistakenly labelled 'Wahhabist' (Monteil 1980: 274) – a movement drawn from central Arabia and associated with the house of Saud[1] – a host of reformers from across a spectrum of Islamic viewpoints launched campaigns for the renewal of Muslim religious beliefs. Not only were they concerned about the imposition of western education and European-centred models of social, economic and cultural development, they also railed against what they regarded as religious and moral laxity, condemned the veneration of marabouts, and labelled maraboutic magic a 'superstition'. Book magic, so central to West African Sufism, was disenchanted and its aura of mystique stripped away by them. While Wahhabis in the strict sense have been few on the ground in Senegal, their presence does indicate the radical impact of 'arabisation' and the severity of the attack on Sufi Islam.[2] Along with French education, reformed Islamic schooling encouraged a rationalist paradigm of thought and spread a functional literacy in Arabic to a much wider section of the population. It propagated literacy in the general population to an extent never seen before.[3] This form of schooling also undermined, like its European counterpart, the relationship of apprenticeship and devotion of a disciple to his marabout, and encouraged more impersonal forms of learning. Schmitz (2000b), for example, reports the use of cassette tapes, which are circulated among Muslim students eager to hear lectures of Middle Eastern Arabic teachers and Islamic scholars.

The new *medersas* contrasted therefore with schools offering a traditional Qur'anic education. These latter contributed to the development of a narrow literate clerical elite who possessed a competence, albeit often uneven, in Arabic. They also provided the foundation upon which gifted scholars could progress into esoteric sciences and Islamic arts. At the heart of this system of education was what has been called the oral transmission of the written word, and this mode of transmission continued throughout the highly personalised relationship of disciple (*taalibe* or *murîd*) and marabout that characterised the higher stages of learning and initiation. The reformed *medersas* developed a broader curriculum comprising a range of subjects and taught a competence in Arabic based less on rote memorisation of texts and more focused on the language as a medium of study and communication. As Brenner and Last point out: 'competent literacy in Arabic is the major factor in West Africa which separates establishment from popular Islam' (1985: 443). But the effect of the development of reformist Muslim schools was to offer new routes to Arabic literacy and to challenge the nature of the literate Islamic establishment.[4]

ISLAMIC REFORM MOVEMENTS

Within the plural educational context, a challenge was mounted to the institutions that were part of restricted literacy practices of an earlier period in Fuuta Toro. The result was that the scope and level of access to an expanded literacy programme increased. Alongside this change was a two-pronged attack on the previous 'establishment' Sufi marabouts: French-based education encouraged secularism that charged maraboutism with religious archaism, superstition and unwarranted privilege; the campaigners for Islamic reform charged maraboutism with the corruption of their religion, moral laxity and degeneracy. Reformers embraced a vision of a revived Muslim faith which was particularly attractive to young urban dwellers in that it was seen as a force for an international and universalist conception of the religion that transcended local boundaries and was identified with a wider Muslim world (Brenner 1983b; Evers Rosander and Westerlund 1997; Soares 1999). This vision also sought to re-establish the sovereignty and uniqueness of God and offered the prospect of a state run according to Shari'a principles.

Muslim militants who have held to this latter position have frequently been referred to as 'fundamentalists', although this term is rejected in much of the literature. Instead, the preferred term for those movements calling for a link to be made between the structure of the state and the Muslim religion is 'Islamist', since their members often regard themselves not simply as returning to a fundamental tradition but as representing a contemporary alternative to western modernity.[5] The Islamist movement took hold in Senegal in 1970s and 1980s, adding another dimension to, or even replacing, earlier Muslim reformists that had begun their activities in the 1930s.[6] Reformism had placed a different emphasis upon Muslim sources such as the Qur'an, the Sunna and *ijma* or consensus, none of which was to be renounced but which could be accommodated within a modern world. Indeed, Islam had to be integrated into this new context, but it would accept aspects of western thought and culture in a modified form.

One of the earliest Senegalese reform groups was *La Fraternité Musulmane*, established in the town of Saint Louis in 1935 (Gomez-Perez 1991). This group, for example, intervened over escalating bridewealth payments in Fuuta Toro in the 1930s, and attempted to cap prestations at affordable levels (Robin 1947). It also complained about the excessive demands of praise-singers at ceremonies, a complaint heard often from a range of more contemporary Muslim leaders. Another influential reformist group, the *Union Culturelle Musulman* (UCM), was founded by Cheikh Touré in 1953.[7] It engaged in a struggle against the effects of French colonialism and opposed the stance of the leading Sufi marabouts who had collaborated with the colonial powers. It criticised the French authorities for interfering with the practice of Islam and railed against the archaism of maraboutism – its mysticism, its talismans and amulets as well as the complete submission of a disciple to a spiritual guide. The tone of the Union's attack on maraboutism can be gleaned from the following rallying call to fight against:

religious fetishism and exploitation, under the sway of which is the mass population that is the victim of a prefabricated Islam ... It is in part a devalued religion with which our populations have been intoxicated and it will be by a renewed faith that detoxification will be brought about.[8]

The Union also forbade the young to go to cinemas and night-clubs or to attend French schools, and encouraged cultural 'arabisation', a secular state and a universal fraternity among all Muslims.

While voices of the Muslim reformers became muted after independence, a decade or so later the cries of Islamist militants could be clearly heard.[9] However, as early as 1956 a movement called 'Harakat al-Fallah' ('Movement of Salvation'), as it was later known, influenced by Wahhabism, called for the establishment of an Islamic republic in Senegal. During the 1970s and 1980s, similar kinds of group flourished: the 'Society of the Servants of the Merciful', the Jama'at Ibad ar-Rahman or Jamaatou Ibadou Arraham[10] began as an offshoot of the UCM following a breakaway by a group of young dissenters, who struck up associations with the al-Fallah movement. Much more politically engaged than either the UCM or al-Fallah, the majority of its members were young urban intellectuals. Another Islamist group was created in 1985 by Cheikh Touré, founder of the moderate UCM, which he deserted due to its pro-government and politically uncritical stance. This group, *L'Organisation pour l'Action Islamique* (OAI), adopted a more virulent and critical anti-European discourse and took as a model of political organisation the theocratic state of Iran. These reform movements are part of the second generation of Islamist groups, some of which gained especial social influence in the sphere of education. They developed a critique of maraboutic Sufism, but also adopted a critical stance towards the secular Senegalese state. In this respect they found common cause with the marabouts, and it appears that their public discourse in the 1990s concentrated less on the confrontation with Sufi brotherhoods and more on creating a broad-based Muslim alliance against secular politics (Loimeier 2000).

A wide variety of Muslim reformist and Islamist groups in the post-Second World War period formulated a critique not only of the French-bequeathed political structure and western modernity, but also attacked Sufi maraboutism, its mysticism and forms of 'magic'.[11] Traditional forms of charisma came under attack. The esoteric episteme of Sufi maraboutic knowledge and power was criticised, and with it by implication the esoteric construction of knowledge and power of the men-of-skill. Another area that became contested was the position and status of members of hereditary, occupationally specialised craftsmen and musician categories, the so-called 'castes',[12] which had by and large been excluded from the central religious offices within Sufi Islam. Reformist and Islamist groups, such as those mentioned above, offered new opportunities for previously marginalised members of the Muslim *jama'a* to enter into a more active engagement with the religious community.

THE RENEGOTIATION OF ISLAM AND SOCIAL EXCLUSION

As already discussed in Chapter 4, in the mid-nineteenth century the newly-introduced Tijaniyya order under Al-Hajj Umar Taal was more open to individuals of lower social rank than the existing orders. Those members of men-of-skill categories or of slave descent who rose through the ranks of the Sufi brotherhood did so during the militaristic and expansionist phase of Taal's Muslim campaigns. The order appears subsequently to have reverted to an earlier model of social organisation in which 'caste' prejudices surfaced again and craftsmen and musicians were once more marginalised and excluded from religious office. By contrast, the Qadiriyya, a much older order in West Africa,[13] appears to have been much less flexible in assimilating and promoting those of artisan origin, while the uniquely Senegalese Murid order is generally held to be more open as regards the caste status of its members.[14] The family of the founder of the Murids, Amadu Bamba (1850–1927), is linked through his mother to an important Fuuta Toro family, the Busso clerics who hold village political office in a river valley (Morice 1982: 282). Amadu Bamba's father's patronym, Mbacké, is also thought to be connected to Haalpulaar roots. Bamba promoted Praise-singers and Smiths to the summit of the Murid hierarchy (Monteil 1980: 362) and in the 1950s a singer called Ali Samba Guêye officially represented the brotherhood at Kaolack, making a collection of one million CFA for the *Grand Serigne* (ibid.: 365). Smiths, Woodcarvers and other artisans were particularly sought out by the brotherhood for their practical skills, especially during its formative period when it was settling new lands (*Terres Neuves*) of Salum and Senegal Oriental to establish their characteristic village organisation based around ground-nut cultivation.[15] Indeed, the late Khalif Général of the Murids, El-Hajj Falilu Mbacké (d. 1968), second son of Amadu Bamba, once declared that 'castes' derive in the most part from 'pre-Islamic beliefs', but yet he cited a number of instances of marriage contracted by members of his own freeborn family with persons considered to belong to inferior social ranks (Diouf 1983: 230). Muslim leaders, such as he, are caught on the horns of a dilemma when they proclaim equality among all Muslims regardless of 'caste' and rank; for in trying to gain the sympathy and support of those of inferior status whom they seek to protect, at the same time they run the risk of alienating significant numbers of their freeborn members. Indeed, despite the words of the late Khalif Général about caste equality, Murid marabouts continued to seek marriage partners predominantly among freeborn families or within the ancient Wolof ruling families (Diouf 1983).

This example of the Murids throws into relief the complex issue of renegotiation and indeed contestation that has gone and is still going on within Sufi brotherhoods over the status of believers of 'caste' origin. To assert that 'the notion of a hierarchical caste system is anathema to the tenets of Islam' does little justice to the complex processes that are being played out.[16] A number of concerns can be raised in this respect. First, such statements elide the distinction between the rhetoric of equality and the social practice of a religion; second, they neglect local debate about the issue; third, they treat West African Islam as a single undifferentiated whole, a single system of belief and practice. As I have argued earlier, accommodationist Sufi Islam allowed craftsmen and musicians a marginal but inferior position within it, but it also encompassed 'caste' groups within a complex ideological framework. The proclaimed ideology of Sufi brotherhood ignored the question of caste and was rarely used to oppose the social exclusion resting at the heart of these orders. Taal's mid-nineteenth century reform movement attempted to renegotitate the limits of inclusion, but this eventually met with little success. The orthodox Sufi view on the matter was that while the Holy Book did not sanction caste distinction, it did not forbid it either. The issue was often left to benign neglect. As indicated in the Murid example, one major field of social life, and a key area of social reproduction in which 'caste' considerations remained an important determinant, was and still is marriage.[17] The exclusive matrimonial strategies of leading marabout families, who often sought alliances with high-ranking freeborn families rather than other social categories, evinces the gulf between rhetoric and social action. This exclusivity in marriage, however, was prized as much by members of 'caste' groups as by those of higher social status. Islam in itself did not provide an ideological justification of caste differentiation, and did not play the same role as the Hindu religion in relation to Indian caste. Moreover, its muted voice in relation to the question of brotherhood allowed for the possibility of accommodating a broad range of practices in different domains of social life.

Post-independence, a good deal of debate in Senegal has centred on whether 'castes' would disappear. One obvious factor it would have to confront was changing employment opportunities offered in urban settings, in expanding markets and so forth. Modernisation would see an end to such an archaic social structure, so many commentators thought. The rupture of the connection between caste status and occupation in urban areas did contribute to the loosening of the organisation of social groups compared with that in the rural economy. Indeed, economic possibilities for members of lower-caste groups offering manual skills might be greater than those for higher status clerics, who had few practical talents to offer (see Diop 1965). However, it must be remembered that social status of men-of-skill categories has never been linked tightly to a unique connection with one occupation. The practice of a trade never constituted the only criterion of 'caste' membership, since notions of descent and inheritance contributed as much if not more to the recognition of status.[18] 'Caste' occupations have not been stable over time (see Tamari 1997).

Another dimension to this debate about the continuance of 'caste' concerns the ideological and discursive nature of the relation between social differentiation and the presumed equality of the community of the faithful. Some authors have argued that Islam would come to 'whiten' or bleach the stain of low social status deriving from membership of a 'caste'.[19] This idiom of 'whitening' gains a significance if it is placed in the context of the opposition between white and black bodies of lore and knowledge that is used to distinguish Islamic from craft expertise respectively. From this perspective of the relationship between Islam and caste, the black is not accommodated within nor encompassed by Muslim lore and knowledge but is in fact stripped of colour and transformed by it. Diop, in 1981, concluded pessimistically about the outcome of this proposed transformation:

> It is to be admitted that Islam has not brought about in a society of castes the revolution that might have been expected of it. Marabouts have shown themselves to be conservative in the face of the force of traditions that they have not dared or wanted to dismantle, being themselves the offspring, in the majority of cases, of the superior caste.[20]

He went on to argue that Islam had adapted itself more to the caste system than the latter had adapted itself to the religion, above all in the area of the equality and fraternity of believers. If certain marabouts made pronouncements condemning the institution of caste difference as contrary to the fraternal spirit of Islam, and if some attempted to abolish it, then even fewer succeeded in making many gains in rolling it back.

Ambiguity and ambivalence surround the issue of caste at various levels of debate: it is in turns denied and subsequently claimed by those inhabitants of the country who live within it; different voices within Islam contest it; and the Senegalese state has contributed in no small way to the contradictory tensions surrounding it. As Morice states: 'the attitude of public powers with regard to castes is marked with a large measure of ambiguity' (1982: 99, my translation). Since independence, it has been against the law to make reference to an individual's caste origins or to discriminate against a person in employment on these grounds. It is also illegal to organise an official political party around the issue of caste or on the basis of religion. A complex and ambiguous situation has arisen which has its roots in colonial times, when a system of European-based law ran in parallel with customary tribunals (*tribunaux indigènes*). In the latter context it was possible to claim divorce on the grounds of one partner withholding or hiding his or her true caste origins. Changes brought about in the legal system, shifting the emphasis away from customary law and towards European-based law, involved the introduction of new codes, especially the Family Code (*Code de la Famille*) of 1972, revised in 1990 (Callaway and Creevy 1994). These codes attempted to establish changes to procedures in marriage, divorce, inheritance and the economic independence of women, but were opposed on many fronts by marabouts and Islamists as an attack on the principles of Islamic law. While part of customary practice had been to allow a recognition of caste, changes brought in to 'modernise' and simplify the plurality of legal codes were condemned. Moreover, the implementation of the Family Code was much more effective in urban areas than in rural towns and villages, where issues of caste are more deeply rooted.[21] The issue of the Family Code illustrates a case in which Islamists and Sufi marabouts have buried their theological differences and have worked towards a common cause to protect an Islamic domain.

The Islamic reformist groups that developed between the two world wars, and then after independence, have frequently sought to abolish caste distinctions that were a feature of many Sufi brotherhoods. The educational reformer Al-Hajj Mahmud Ba, who set up *medersa* schools in Fuuta Toro, called for the abandonment of 'tribal and professional considerations' in the provision of schooling; that is a coded reference to caste (Ba 1985–86: 250 *et passim*). Many reformist groups appealed to nouveaux riches traders, to craftsmen, artisans and praise-singers (Schmitz 2000b), for they found in them the opportunity for social elevation and religious advancement previously denied to them. Similarly, Islamist movements attracted individuals of low 'caste' origin. But there were contradictory forces of inclusion and exclusion working within them upon different marginal groups. Generally within Sufi brotherhoods, women were placed in a subordinate position: it was harder for them to receive the same level of Qur'anic education as boys; there were barriers to them becoming disciples to a male marabout; and women seldom held formal religious office or positions of responsibility within Sufi orders. There were, however, instances of women creating 'shadow' or parallel organisations that ran alongside those of the men, but they rarely attained the same public profile as their male counterparts.[22] Despite slight differences among the Sufi brotherhoods regarding this issue, the marginalised position of women was nonetheless never as extreme as that advocated by certain Islamist groups. Members of these radical reform groups called for the seclusion of women, the wearing of the veil and their withdrawal from public life.[23] These demands placed on women by Islamists mark a significant disjuncture with the older Sufi orders, and their exclusionary force suggests an intriguing paradoxical movement within radical reformist groups. While they advocate the differential treatment of followers on the basis of gender, they have attracted followers previously marked out as different on the basis of caste. Earlier, I argued that within Sufi Islam, the position of women and the position of craftsmen and musician groups were in some ways comparable: both were marginalised, muted and treated with mistrust regarding the full and proper functioning of the Muslim community. In relation to reformist and especially Islamist groups, the integration or 'whitening' of one category of persons is accompanied by the extreme differential marking or exclusion of the other. Moreover, while a European-educated urban elite militate for western-style equality of opportunity between genders and among castes, an Arab-educated urban sector of the population militate for one but not the other.

THE CHANGING NATURE OF CASTE AND ISLAM

I now turn to two examples of the renegotiation of the connection between caste and Islam to illustrate something of the dynamism of their relation. The first example concerns the role of members of praise-singer and musician social categories; the second provides an echo of an earlier theme – namely, the way in which exceptional individuals who became powerful Muslim reformers have emerged from time to time in West African history; they combine the mystery of Sufism with the potency of traditional artisan status. They have harnessed the institutional division of power and knowledge among 'castes' to the driving force of individual charismatic power.

Example 1: Singers, popular song and Islam

Praise-singers, musicians and entertainers (in Pulaar, *naalankooɓe*) have frequently been the target of complaints made by marabouts concerned about the excessive demands of these low caste members who claimed large donations in return for their services at collective ceremonies, rituals and family gatherings. The members of the Muslim Fraternity made such complaints in the 1930s and Monteil reports similar protests made by marabouts against abuse of guests at reunions held at night (*khaware*), at which praise-singers and others attempted to 'exploit' those donating gifts to them. In addition, the imam of the mosque in the town of Matam in Fuuta Toro complained about their role in extorting money from guests at marriages and naming ceremonies (Monteil 1980: 364–5). The relationship, therefore, between such praise-singers and musicians, on the one hand, and Muslim authorities, on the other, has often been tense.

Moreover, the traditional songs of praise-singer and musician groups – for instance, the *dillere* of the Weavers, Fishermen's *pekaan* and so forth – have often been condemned and interpreted by Islamic clerics as anti-Islamic. Popular among the young and sung by members of low caste groups, songs were often banned by local religious authorities. Such proscriptions were a feature of stricter Islamic communities, and were reported in a number of cases.²⁴ Young people, in an attempt to circumvent these restrictions, would seek an isolated place outside the town or village where they could amuse themselves away from the prying eye of the local Muslim authorities. These activities, thought by marabouts and imams to be linked to magic (*sihr*) and possession, were seen as a menace to morality and Shari'a law. Ba reports (1985-86), for instance, that a form of song popular (*leele*) at the turn of the twentieth century sung by Haalpulaar *wambaaɓe* singers mocked the town of Cilon, an important centre of Islamic learning and Muslim authority in Fuuta Toro. He adds that other forms of song (e.g. *cooloo*) were even more offensive to Muslim morals, for they employed vile language and obscene gestures. These different types of song are interpreted by Ba as a form of expression of popular resistance to Islamic authorities in Fuuta Toro (1985-86: 39-44). Like the condemnations by marabouts of the demands of praise-singers and entertainers, so we find members of these same social categories at odds with local Muslim leaders who disapprove not only of their begging but also of the moral content of their activities and songs.

Recent work suggests that these very same praise-singers who were not long ago condemned for their activities have adapted themselves to the strictures of the Muslim authorities and have developed roles more in keeping with the concerns of the religion. Praise-singers are thought to be particularly appropriate to the role of muezzin, the caller of prayer from the mosque (see, for example, Villalón 1995), and they act as spokesmen for marabouts whose words are transmitted to collective masses of the faithful at public meetings by spokesmen of praise-singer origin, who broadcast the leader's message with customary style and elaboration. Furthermore, what appears to have emerged over recent years is that members of praise-singer and musician castes have transferred the focus of their attention away from honouring ruling families from earlier historical periods to singing the praises of religious leaders within Islam.²⁵ Singers such as Moustapha Seck, a Murid *griot* or Ndiga Ndiaye, a Tijani musician, have found new roles in singing the praises of Allah, the Prophet and leading marabouts, rather than traditional patrons, in the hope of receiving gifts and rewards in the form of alms. Panzacchi notes too that Wolof *griots* have found a lucrative avenue of employment by linking themselves to political parties, whose praises they sing – a Senegalese version of spin-doctoring perhaps. They also have developed a role in larger and more anonymous urban settings of acting as private detectives for freeborn families who wish to investigate the social backgrounds of potential marriage partners for relatives seeking a spouse.

The example of praise-singers and musicians suggests a radical form of redefinition of their role and activities in relation to Sufi authorities and their place in the Islamic community (*jama'a*). If Ba (1985-86) is correct in his interpretation of low caste songs of an earlier generation being construed as anti-Islamic by the Muslim faithful, then the shift in the activities of these singers to embrace eulogising Muslim leaders and praise-songs to Allah is significant.[26] Islam may not have 'whitened' or bleached the cultural salience from the institution of 'caste', but it has in this form redefined the lines of allegiance of members of caste groups. It has harnessed caste to the carriage of Islam such that it is seen to pull in the right direction. The social organisation of the religion, in this example, has not abolished 'caste', but it has given its members a new and more valued role within its structure. This example of praise-singers and Islam shows, in addition, the nature of the dynamic and evolving relationship between members of low caste social categories and mainstream Islamic groups.

Example 2: The Islamic brotherhood of the Nyasiyya

This second example requires a more sustained treatment, for it is necessary to describe something of the background to this Senegalese Muslim brotherhood and the significance that is read into its development by members of different social categories. This is an example not so much of how Islam might be considered to 'whiten' low status castes, but how, from the perspective of some followers of the Nyasiyya, caste status has as it were 'blackened' Islam. In this example will be heard an echo of the earlier analysis of the Sufi reform movement started in the mid-nineteenth century by Al-Hajj Umar Taal. It evokes too echoes of the example of Ceerno Bokar Taal, Umar's grandson and an ascetic, who developed a programme of Muslim study in Mali in the first part of the twentieth century (see Chapter 4 above).

Members of the Nyas family now based in the town of Kaolack are part of a relatively new offshoot of the Tijaniyya Sufi order.[27] The establishment of the order goes back to a late nineteenth-century forefather of the Nyas line, one Abdoulaye Nyas who died in 1922. The main contemporary branches of the family stem from two of Abdoulaye's sons, the elder son Khalifa who was supposed to succeed his father and his younger brother Ibrahima 'Baye' who developed the Nyasiyya order into the important movement it is today. Two of Khalifa's sons, Ahmed Khalifa and Sidi Lamine, disseminated Islamist ideas, the latter especially through a newspaper *Wal Fadjri* established in 1983, of which he was editor. Various calls were made by them for the creation of an Islamic state in Senegal, and Ahmed Khalifa gained the reputation as the 'ayatollah of Kaolack' following pronouncements that drew on ideas used in the Iranian revolution (Gomez-Perez 1991). It is, however, the Nyas line from Abdoulaye through to Ibrahima 'Baye' that represents the focus of interest here.

Abdoulaye Nyas, a Wolof speaker born in the country's northern region around the town of Louga in 1844 or 1845,[28] was descended from a line of blacksmiths. His father, Mamadou, was nonetheless a marabout who had migrated to the central regions of Senegal around 1865. There he founded the village of Niassene, and later his son Abdoulaye established the settlement of Taiba Niassene. Abdoulaye too became a marabout, having studied in Mauritania, and under Matar Fal Ndiaye is said to have received the Tijani *wird* from a companion of Shaykh Umar Taal, the mid-nineteenth century militant and mystic. In the Tijani tradition, tracing a chain of transmission of knowledge (*silsila*) back to Umar Taal is an important ingredient in establishing authority as a religious leader. Abdoulaye had also fought alongside the Islamic leader Ma Ba in the jihads conducted in Senegal's central regions in the 1860s. The Nyas family thus gained a reputation for leadership in religious affairs: they possessed as well an erudition in Islamic sciences, advanced expertise in Qur'anic study and Muslim theology, and they were also renowned for their mastery of Arabic.

On Abdoulaye's death in 1922, his eldest son Muhammad, also known as Khalifa, succeeded his father and took over as religious leader within the family. However, it would be Ibrahima, his younger brother (born 1902), who was to become the more influential of the two sons. Ibrahima, who died in 1975, was a charismatic religious leader who developed a massive international following among Muslims in West Africa,[29] and set up his headquarters (*zawiya*)[30] on the outskirts of the town of Kaolack, the centre of ground-nut production in the middle belt of the country. Here in 'Medina' he built a mosque and a school, and it is to this religious centre that up to a reported 30,000 pilgrims flock each year for the annual *ziyara* ceremony in celebration of the Prophet's birthday (*mawlud*).[31] Some Islamist groups are especially critical of the Nyas order for what they see as excessive veneration of the Prophet's birthday and naming-day.

Ibrahima was hailed by some members of the Muslim Sufi community as the 'saviour of the age' (*ghawth al-zaman*) and as the 'pole' or 'axis' (*qutb*) of the saints, one who has reached the summit of spiritual discipline. He was made Khalifa of the Tijaniyya order by a shaykh in Fez in 1937 at the age of around thirty-five years. He also created important religious alliances with the Emir of Kano in Nigeria, where there is a huge following, and he emerged as a man of remarkable stature throughout West Africa, being consulted by political leaders such as Nkrumah and Egypt's Nasser. On his death in the mid-1970s, Ibrahima was succeeded by his son Abdoulaye, although the position of Khalifa of the order was left to Ibrahima's son-in-law, disciple and imam of the Kaolack Medina mosque, a man named El-Hajj Alioune Cissé.[32] This has created tension in the movement between blood relatives and their direct descendents and a line of 'spiritual kinship' and the inheritance of *baraka* established through ties of 'breath or saliva' (Schmitz 2000a). The religious following that has developed around Ibrahima Nyas is drawn from virtually all countries within the region of West Africa, and most notably in

Nigeria and now the USA too. Indeed the movement is perhaps better recognised outside of Senegal than within its borders.[33] There are reasons for this large disparity in the numbers of followers at home and abroad. Schmitz accounts in part for the success of the Nyas religious movement as a consequence of the ability of its leaders to slide into the space vacated in the course of rivalry and competition between the Tijaniyya and the Qadiriyya (2000b: 128). There are, I suggest, other reasons for this skewed popularity.

The Nyas family background is intriguing given the historical depth to, and the widespread nature of, the claims that the nineteenth-century marabout Mamadou Nyas and his son Abdoulaye Nyas were of blacksmith stock.[34] It is taken as evidence of the social mobility made possible by the Tijaniyya, in particular, that someone of caste origins could have been elevated to the position of religious leader (Gray 1988). This openness among the Tijaniyya was noted above during the mid-nineteenth century under the leadership of Umar Taal. The elevation in status of Nyas, if indeed it was such, must have occurred in the late eighteenth or at least the early nineteenth century, and he would probably have been dead or if not very old by the time Umar Taal's militant Tijani movement got under way. Nyas may have been caught up in a reorganisation of members of various social categories that mirrored what was happening in Fuuta Toro in the mid to late eighteenth century under Abdul Qadir Kan, a member of the Qadiri order. The period just prior to the Almaamate uprising in Fuuta Toro (1790s) was characterised by the possibility of social promotion for those of caste origin who affliliated themselves to the cause of the then radical reformist Islam of the tooroɓe clerics. Perhaps a similar situation prevailed around Louga, the area just south of Fuuta Toro from where the Nyas family hailed prior to their migration south towards Kaolack. Like the Caams (Tyams or Thiams) of Fuuta Toro who are reputed to have blacksmith origins but yet became important in Umar Taal's movement, so too perhaps Nyas achieved the same degree of elevation under a liberating and open form of a Sufism that was later to close ranks after its initial impetus was lost.

Morice (1982) reports that the evocation of this artisan past is altogether prohibited by the Nyas family. It is likewise the case that it would be seen as a huge insult to accuse the descendants of Taal or Caam lines of having a similar ancestry. The Nyas family today observes a strict form of endogamy among only those of freeborn descent (Morice 1982: 99). Again, there are parallels here with the situation of the newly elevated families in Fuuta Toro, which, having assimilated themselves among the ranks of the *tooroɓe* clerics, began progressively to marry within that social category to the exclusion of their own cognate kinsmen.[35] The Nyas family have married many times into the old nobility of the Siin and Saloum (Diouf 1983: 229), although these unions were not uncontested by members of those high-ranking families. Silla (1966) reports the following anecdote (also repeated in

Diouf 1983) that tells of how a proposed marriage between Nyas and a woman of freeborn stock stirred up discontentment in the region. Those opposed to the marriage decided to boycott the ceremonies and moreover planned to abscond with the bride, so preventing the union. They were not able, however, to carry out their plan, for a serious car accident involving a number of the conspirators put an end to the proposed abduction. The accident was seen by many sympathetic to the Nyas cause as a punishment from God and his Prophet on those who wanted to obstruct the desire of one of His representatives on earth.

The hugely successful Muslim proselytiser Ibrahima Nyas, who presided over the enormous expansion of the order into territories beyond the boundaries of Senegal, is an ambiguous and ambivalent figure in the eyes of many Senegalese. A charismatic figure, Ibrahima was reported to have possessed marvellous esoteric abilities and controlled an array of supernatural powers. He is attributed by educated Senegalese with the power of magically crippling one of the country's politicians who opposed him. Furthermore, he was said to able to talk to trees and summon the spirits who lived there in order to attack his enemies (Gray 1988). These are the powers associated with craftsmen, and Woodcarvers (lawbe) in particular, and bring an image to mind of Umar Taal, who was likewise attributed with such powers, an idea that stemmed in the minds of some of his followers from a putative line of common ancestry with both blacksmiths and tree-fellers. Ibrahima Nyas was also the target of pejorative remarks, defamatory characterisations and attacks upon his moral integrity, not only in official reports but more generally in popular circulation (O. Kane 1997). He was described as being a 'dubious' or 'unwholesome Sufi', a person of 'questionable morality' and person of 'detestable filiation' or ancestry. These reports again echo the kinds of moral evaluation attached to members of craftsman and praise-singer castes which we have encountered earlier.

The 'taint of caste' on the Nyas family history seems to have been an important factor in restricting the spread of the movement within Senegal among freeborn sectors of the population.[36] The fact that these matters of social origin carry very little significance beyond the geographical boundaries of Senegambia might contribute to our understanding of Ibrahima's success in places such as northern Nigeria. There, it is Nyas's high reputation for Islamic erudition, his abilities in esoteric sciences and Arabic language, and his depth of Qur'anic exegesis that are indexes of his popularity and authority among his following. O. Kane attributes the attraction of the movement in large measure to the fact that it advocated a much greater 'democratisation of the sacred' than other Sufi orders,[37] but with this democratisation of the sacred comes the possibility of involvement of members of lower castes in positions of authority within the brotherhood. Those Senegalese who have become attached to the Nyasiyya are attracted by its openness and its lack of restriction on religious promotion to those of low caste origin. Not only have craftsmen and musicians been attracted to and prospered within the order, but women too have been drawn by its spirit of openness. Women have been encouraged to pursue Qur'anic study and Islamic learning, and some have even become *muqaddam*s or religious leaders appointed to transmit the *wird* or litany of the brotherhood; a number of Ibrahima's sisters and daughters have achieved renowned scholarly and spiritual reputations (see Callaway and Creevy 1994; Schmitz 2000b). This Sufi order – in many ways not different from other Tijani movements, but in contrast to Sunna militants and Islamists – has embraced and promoted the interests of persons of low caste origin and of women, both of whom were previously marginalised by cleric-dominated brotherhoods.

The last issue to be developed in this discussion is the idea of legitimacy of the Nyas movement in the eyes of those who have joined, especially from the point of view of previously marginalised craftsmen and musicians. While a sense of the conventional cleric freemen perception of the low caste status of Nyas's Islamic brotherhood has already been suggested – namely, it is morally repugnant, 'unwholesome Sufisim' led by an individual of 'detestable' ancestry – those who are persuaded of the Nyas family's spiritual mission evaluate it differently. A *dahira* linked to the Nyas order operated in a location on the outskirts of Dakar where I conducted fieldwork during periods in the early 1980s and mid-1990s among re-settled Haalpulaar'en from Fuuta Toro. A *dahira* (or *daaira*) is a cell or 'circle' (from the Arabic) or local unit of a Senegalese Sufi order based in urban areas. Located near Tiaroye a few miles from the capital city, a Haalpulaar community established itself in a *quartier* centred around the household of a *tooroɓo* cleric, El-Hajj Demba Ngaydo. He had been the patron (*njartigi*) to a number of men-of-skill or low caste families, one of whom was the weaver family Gisse that I had worked closely with. In the mid-1960s, during the early stages of settlement of the *quartier*, nineteen families had formed a mutual aid and support group called the *Fedde Sahabaaɓe*, or literally the 'Age-set of the Companions of the Prophet'. It organised savings for members, each of whom paid a weekly subscription, and it was the focus of rituals and celebrations on the occasion of the births, marriages or deaths of its family's members. It also met each Thursday for entertainment and a meal, and these weekly *soirées* were held in turn in members' households. In this context, the specialised roles of each of the social categories represented by its members were played out, such that, for instance, the *maabu* weaver sang songs accompanied by the young *bambaaɗo* hoddu-player, or those of servile origin made the preparations and served food during the collective festive or ceremonial gatherings (see Dilley 1984).

By the mid-1990s, the patron cleric Ngaydo was dead, and although the mutual aid group (*Fedde*) continued, a new organisation had established itself. This was a Nyas *dahira* or cell of the brotherhood linked to Ceerno Alhusseni Nyas. The local cell was led by an imam who was of Haalpulaar Fisherman origin, a 'caste' that like craftsmen and musicians was previously excluded from holding religious office within Islam. For those of men-of-skill origin, the Nyas *dahira* represented a synthesis of the white lore and knowledge of Islam (*gandal danewal*) and the black lore and knowledge (*gandal ɓalewal*) of the 'caste' specialist that is derived from the bush or the wild. This union was evinced, various members pointed out, by the nature of the origins of the Nyas family – namely it was of blacksmithing stock – and by the fact that the imam was a Fisherman (*cubbalo*), which is a social category associated with the powerful black lore of the river. Moreover, my weaver friend had become the *imam as-salat*, the leader of the group prayers, who chanted the litany and performed the *raka*s which the congregation would follow. This role contrasted with the one he occupied in the *Fedde*, which would also conduct communal prayers for the last two scheduled daily prayer times at dusk and at dark on a Thursday evening. In this context, he would defer to the religious authority of a group member of *jawaanɗo* or Courtier origin. Since joining the Nyas prayer group, the weaver had felt it necessary to give up cowrie divination, for on the advice of his new imam his prayers would not be heard for forty days after each divinatory consultation. The weaver had much earlier been persuaded to cease practising *nyeŋgi* magic since it led to eternal damnation, he had been told. He continued, however, with the practice of herbal medicine and curing with incantations and protective verses. It would seem that what informants meant by the idea that this brotherhood represented a synthesis of white and black lore was not that it entertained a series of ritual practices that might be condemned by other branches of Islam. It did not amalgamate in a novel combination Islamic with non- or pre-Islamic beliefs and practices. Instead, what appears to have been meant by this claim was that the close association between men-of-skill and spiritual powers that derived from the wild did not deflect from the possibility of divine blessing offered by the Muslim religion. It is as though the spiritual expertise that men-of-skill possessed by virtue of their ancestry could be an important ingredient in building a foundation of legitimacy for religious authority in this branch of Islam. The legitimacy of Umar Taal and of Ibrahima Nyas had been built around precisely this combination in the eyes of certain sectors of their followings.

Discussion

This case study illustrates how, at the grassroots organisation of the Nyas brotherhood, the issue of 'caste', forbidden as a topic of discussion by the family, appears to be a key element in the construction of a religious following among members of particular social categories. While this feature works to attract a following from the ranks of lower caste or marginalised sections of the population, it also acts as an obstacle to the members of those social categories previously associated with religious leadership in longer established Sufi brotherhoods. The pattern in these conventional cleric-dominated brotherhoods has been to accommodate the faithful from low caste ancestry, albeit in an inferior position of dependence and not of spiritual leadership. This is a pattern of accommodation and not of integration. The Nyasiyya at grassroots level has, in the eyes of some of its followers, integrated and embraced the powers of caste groups, such that these powers become an essential element in its ideological scheme and in the process of legitimising its authority. Al-Hajj Umar Taal's Tijani mission in the mid-nineteenth century appealed to similar sectors of society for similar reasons and was successful in establishing a more egalitarian Muslim community, at least in the early stages of its development. The other example we have examined in the course of this investigation has been the case of Ceerno Bokar Taal, a pacific mystic and ascetic, and a descendant of Umar Taal from whom he is recognised as inheriting spiritual charisma. Ceerno Bokar too attempted an integration of two kinds of lore and knowledge: he developed a series of links between his own Islamic understanding and a Dogon knowledge of the bush. This ideological integration appears to have failed to achieve legitimacy within a Haalpulaar community in Mali still dominated at that time by *toorodo* clerics. The grassroots organisation of the Nyas order, by contrast, seems to have succeeded where others have failed, although the extent of that success is tempered by the *toorodo* resistance to membership of the Nyas religious community.

We have come full circle then, back to the sources of power and potency that form part of the contested field of culturally defined realms of mystical force that constitutes one of the key dynamics in the social relations of Haalpulaar'en and other neighbouring language groups. As Villalón points out, we must recognise the 'very real centrality of the metaphysical' that is 'all too often ignored in secular discussions of Senegalese Islamic organisations' (1995: 122). While the critiques of West African Sufism, stemming from western educated elites versed in secular rationalism and from *arabisants* and Islamists versed in ideas of Middle Eastern origin, have attacked this metaphysical core of brotherhood practice, the popular view of legitimate religious authority holds fast to such spiritual considerations. A bifurcation of the Muslim community has occurred around the opposition to Sufi mysticism. Western-educated Senegalese intellectuals and Arabic-educated Islamists make odd bedfellows in their stance against Sufi brotherhoods. These attacks on Sufi mysticism and its particular esoteric construction of knowledge and power is also by implication an attack upon the similar construction of knowledge and power among men-of-skill groups. However, these two parties are joined in a common voice of criticism by the conventional freeborn Muslim clerics. These latter denounce brotherhoods such as the Nyasiyya for proposing a form of integration of cultural knowledge and power that should normally, from their point of view, be kept apart. Freeborn clerics, while recognising the legitimacy of Sufi constructions of knowledge and power, are critical of its assimilation with those forms associated with men-of-skill. The Islamists hold that Sufi mysticism represents a retrograde step in the standing of the Muslim religion. They reject outright the esoteric paradigm of conventional forms of knowledge and power. The cultural dialogue instigated by the cleric-inspired Islamic revolution in the mid-eighteenth century has broadened to become today a conversation involving numerous parties, each with its own view of the composition of the Muslim community.

The Islamic community is perhaps more fractured than at any time in recent history: Islamists are blind to caste, but eagle-eyed with regard to gender; clerics and the followers of the Nyas brotherhood both recognise it, although with very different consequences. The two symbols of competing forms of knowledge-power – the mosque and the termite-mound – have a continued salience today. The termite mound might be dismissed as a symbol of irrelevance and superstition by Islamists, in much the same way as they dismiss Sufi mysticism. But the image of the termite mound resurfaces with renewed significance within the Nyas Tijani brotherhood.

Sources of Muslim authority and processes of legitimacy have multiplied to the extent that those critical of localised conceptions of Islam, which draw upon notions of hereditary status, initiatory forms of knowledge and power, the charismatic power of individual marabouts and so on, have a range of more direct and unmediated connections to distant centres of knowledge and power. Changing forms of education, and of modes of communication in the shape of cassettes and television, have been some of the factors that have made accessible different knowledges and sources of authority. Also important has been the increased opportunity for travel, particularly to the Hijaz – once the destination of only a very small minority but now a place of pilgrimage open to many more. The Nyas brotherhood stands at an intriguing juncture in this discussion; it is Janus-faced. From one perspective it is part of a broadening internationalist version of Islam, drawing in followers from Nigeria and elsewhere in West Africa as well as spreading to North America. From another perspective it represents a counter-movement to cleric-dominated Muslim communities, a localising strategy for certain Senegalese Muslims who see in it echoes of their own interests and experiences as members of caste social categories. They read into the movement forms of authority and they legitimate it in terms that resonate with the images of competing sources of knowledge and power: the mosque and the termite mound.

AFTERWORD

This study began by considering two opposed and competing forms of spiritual power – the mosque and the termite mound. Last refers to a similar opposition, to two opposing symbols or 'poles' of charismatic power that are represented in the Kano chronicles of Muslim northern Nigeria (1988: 183). The aim here has been to show that while these two 'poles' are represented as competing and opposing at the level of ideology, they do at the level of practice and of epistemology share much common ground. Indeed, the ambivalences and ambiguities that surround them, and the practitioners associated with them, are key signatures in forming the social experience of many Haalpulaar'en. Moreover, this sense of ambivalence and of ambiguity is the motor of a historical dynamic that generates reinterpretations of conceptions of the Muslim community that have been reviewed above.

The two contesting forms of mystical power have been connected by means of very different kinds of relationship over the course of the historical changes that have taken place within a Haalpulaar 'Islamic religious culture' (Brenner 2000c). That relationship varies between accommodation and integration on the one hand, and rejection and exclusion on the other, with respect to members of social groups historically pushed out beyond the pale of the Almaamate Muslim reform. Conceptions of Islam and of the Muslim community are indissolubly aspects of the dynamics of social life. Indeed, 'Islamic reform and opposition movements are often manifestations of conflicts of authority and conflicts of generations' within a specific social group (Loimeier 2000: 169), rather than a struggle of religious ideas over doctrine and supposed non-Islamic innovations and so forth. The question 'What is it to be a Muslim?' is as much a sociological one as a religious or doctrinal issue. And this issue has a 'genealogy', the outlines of which have been traced during the course of this study. Answers to this question from local commentators have shown a remarkable consistency over time with respect to what it is to be a 'casted' Muslim. What accounts for this consistency is, I argue, connected with how knowledge and power have been conceived and how relationships between socially differentiated specialisms have been construed.

Do the two images of the mosque and the termite mound, resonant in an earlier period as symbols of competing forms of knowledge and power, still today connote similar ideas and conceptions for members of Muslim communities? The view that 'Muslim communities, like all religious communities, are imagined' (Eickelman and Piscatori 2000a: 4) gives rise to the question of the extent to which these two images are redolent within the imagination of members of present-day Muslim communities.

The mosque remains the central image and practical focus of Muslim religious practice, but the perception of it may have undergone change. In some cases it has shifted from a place (along with the lodge or *zawiya*) of Sufi ritual practice based on the ecstatic recitation of prayer to the more austere setting of ritual observance. Furthermore, many mosques built recently in the towns and villages of Senegal have been funded by sources of finance external to the region. Monies from Saudi Arabian and other Middle Eastern financiers or from migrant communities living in France have been channelled into local building projects for mosques, health centres, schools and so on. These mosques and other institutions have taken on, therefore, a new meaning by virtue of their originary locations and of the contexts of their establishment, becoming symbols of new sources of ideas and forms of Muslim authority.

The termite mound, my chosen symbol of the forces of the wild and of the possibility of knowledge and power from sources situated within the bush, takes on a changed aspect too in recent times. Over 40 per cent of the Senegalese population are urban dwellers (Loimeier 2000), and a high proportion of that population is under twenty years of age. A consequence of this is that many young urban dwellers will not have had an immediate experience of the bush as previous generations did. The termite mound might well, therefore, for generations of young urbanites become a more distant symbol of a competing form of knowledge-power that stands in opposition to that of Islam. The greater distance between the human community on the one hand, and the domain of the wild and the bush on the other, may serve to alienate the symbol of the termite mound as a crystallisation of the experience of the forms of knowledge and power in the imagination of urban Muslims. In rural towns and villages the bush is much more proximate: the presence of the river, of wild animals, of features of natural environment impress themselves as images that represent the powers of the bush (Dilley 1988). These are constant reminders of the potencies of the wild, of what exists beyond the human community. In the absence of the experience of the bush and of the retelling of oral traditions that might reinforce those images,[1] the question is raised: what forms of image could take the place of the termite mound as an imagined embodiment of the forces of the wild?

Within the urban setting another set of processes might be seen to be taking place. The images of the jinn and other spirits can be regarded as becoming narrowed to the extent that such imagined figures are identified progressively less and less with features of the bush. With the alienation from the conventional images of the wild, the forms of expression and representation of these aspects of human experience are bound to change. In the place of a polythetic category of jinn and spirits of the wild, there develops a concept of spirit powers that is detached from place, species and natural phenomena. This development suggests a means by which a distinction between different forms of jinn, some of which are identified with men-of-skill and with forces of the wild, might be overcome. The result could be that experts in lower spirit powers, now divorced from concrete markers of the wild, could be integrated within urban Islam less problematically: they could be summoned to the cause of Islam without taint. If this proves to be so, it seems possible that the integration of men-of-skill powers in urban Muslim organisations might be effected. The prospect is of an emergence of a new charismatic movement which could, in due course, become the basis for an alternative reading of the constitution of the Muslim community.[2]

Lewis points out (1980) that different conceptions of Islam may be more or less relevant to different kinds of political context. Sufism, he suggests, was an attractive avenue for Islamisation in less centralised polities, whereas more centralised polities might favour the more formal and legalistic elements of Shari'a law as the dynamic for Islamisation (1980: 34). The centralisation of political processes by means of the modern nation-state has, in this respect, been accompanied by calls from Islamic reformers and Islamists for the establishment of a Muslim state in Senegal. Robinson, however, describes the post-colony as 'a secular time and space' (1997: 568), and this secular frame also poses challenges to both Sufism in West Africa and contemporary forms of Islamism.

What is the future of Sufi brotherhoods in Senegal? Cruise O'Brien (1988a) plots a periodisation in the evolution of Sufi orders in West Africa: the first, prior to the mid-eighteenth century, in which brotherhoods were a kind of 'secret society' reserved for the learned elite – they were esoteric and 'aristocratic'; the second period, in which brotherhoods constituted a revivalist movement in the mid-nineteenth century; the third, in which marabouts entered the public domain in the organisation of worldly and spiritual affairs. More recently Robinson and Triaud have focused on the 'time of the marabouts' (1997), a period they demarcate as occurring between 1880 and 1960, since when 'les saints de la grande époque ont disparu de la scène principale' (Triaud 1997: 11). The time of the marabouts refers to a period of cooperation between Muslim elites and the colonial authorities, during which the marabouts themselves, as charismatic religious personalities, mediated between those elites and the European power. Conditions of social disruption and crisis may provide part of the answer as to why charismatic religious leaders emerge in certain contexts (Cruise O'Brien 1988a). Their charisma is formed through the pursuit of holy learning, literacy in Arabic and knowledge gained through initiation; it is thus formed by way of an inner quest for a range of mystical experience. Threats to Sufi orders, in Cruise O'Brien's view, are to be found in the internal splitting within brotherhoods that 'saps the power of the *tariqa*', the spread of popular literacy giving people access to alternative translations and interpretations of texts, and the crisis in rural agriculture that is undermining the traditional power base of orders such as the Muridiyya. Indeed, Magassouba (1985) has questioned whether the chronic economic and social crisis in Senegal, seen as the backdrop to the resurgence of Islamist conceptions of the religion in the 1980s, might lead to some form of Islamic republic. If it is to be *Demain les Mollahs*, then the form of religious authority and charisma upon which their position might be based would be radically different from that of the marabouts.

While political scientists and other commentators have often emphasised the secular role of Muslim brotherhoods,[3] I have attempted to focus on the 'actor's idiom of the sacred'. Indeed, I would argue that to lose sight of that idiom is to close off a perspective on the cultural politics of being a Muslim and belonging to a brotherhood and an imagined Muslim community. Furthermore, the 'manifestations of universalism' (Launay 1992) that might be seen to be occurring in terms of Islamist critiques of marabout modes of learning and disciplehood, mysticism and maraboutage are not all that they might appear. As Launay points out, the choices people make in regard of their religious affiliation are not between a 'particularistic Islam' and a 'universalist' one, but involve people locating themselves within different communities of interest, and how they situate themselves regarding relations outside their immediate social networks (1992: 223).

If the concept of *Islam noir* (Monteil 1980) is tainted by the role it purportedly played in a colonial policy toward what administrators saw as the rising threat to the maintenance of social order of militant nineteenth-century Islam, then the idea of 'localisation' of religious thought and practice should not be dismissed with it.[4] It should not be dismissed because religious thought and practice always occur within networks of social relations and are formed with reference specific to the localising strategies of human agents; that is people are continually trying to make sense to themselves of the histories of their own practices with which they are engaged, as well as the streams of exogenous notions and activities which they seek out or which others bring to them. As has been argued throught this work, religious identities are always defined and negotiated with reference to other social and cultural identities. The central ones that have been emphasised here are that of being Muslim and that of being of 'caste' status.

In the eyes of popular believers, Sufi marabouts continue to represent an important source of mystical authority and legitimate religious leadership. They also act as significant political brokers between the state and their predominately rural followings (Villalón 1995). Brotherhoods are at the focal point of what Last (1988) has called a 'prayer-economy', and they have established a pivotal position at the centre of the political, religious and economic organisation of the country.[5] Young urban dwellers are much more critical of Sufi brotherhoods, and it is this burgeoning sector of the population that has been the vanguard of an Islamist and reformist faith (Loimeier 2000; van Hoven 2000). Recent elections have ousted the once dominant Socialist party (*Parti Socialiste*) of Abdou Diouf and Léopold Senghor, which held power for forty years since independence. The skilful balance it maintained between the demands of a secular state and the representation and recognition of Sufi brotherhoods has now been shaken. Abdoulaye Wade's *Parti Démocratique Sénégalai*s courted Murid patronage prior to its success in the 2000 elections, and the extent to which the new government can maintain such connections with the leading Sufi marabouts remains a question to be answered. The future role of the brotherhoods as political brokers and as channels for the distribution of state resources must also be thrown into question. If this role is undermined, the extent to which the marabouts' mystical authority and religious leadership might too be eroded in the eyes of popular followers is a factor that must also hang in the balance.

The state, Sufi marabouts and Islamic reformers represent three competing parties, each of which has created temporary and shifting alliances with the others in relation to specific issues and matters of policy. Marabouts and Islamists may find common cause in opposing the encroachment of the secular state into matters they consider to be the rightful territory of the Islamic community. One example reviewed above is the *Code de la Famille*, which both parties wanted to revise in favour of statutes more in line with Shari'a law. Another area is the extent to which the secular state could be held responsible for the social and economic problems of the 1990s. If reformist critiques of Sufi brotherhoods and maraboutic practice have been suspended, it was in order to gain a broad-based Muslim coalition against state secularism.

The state has relied upon marabouts and their followings to achieve a measure of legitimacy in the eyes of the general population, and the consequences of alienating these religious leaders might be difficult to predict. Senegalese government policy in the 1990s was to integrate Islamic reformers and Islamist groups into the political system in order to provide a public impression of accommodation of their radical religious agenda (Loimeier 2000). The success of the state in containing Islamic reform has led to a questioning of the nature of the Muslim platform of reforms and of the Islamist critique of establishment politics. A debate about the present and future contribution of Islam within nation-state politics is taking place, and Loimeier reports (2000) that 'Islam no longer sells', for the reformers have become integrated into state politics, to a point where they resemble any other opposition political grouping. Popular opinion has thus increasingly ignored the Islamist critique of the secular state, and the 1980s revival of Muslim reformism has been replaced by a general indifference to religious topics. Moreover, reformers now participate increasingly in the Sufi rituals and celebrations they once criticised. By contrast, van Hoven (2000) argues that Senegal is entering a new phase of nationalism based on new religious forms in which a religious, Muslim nationalism will emerge. It is proposed that Muridism might provide the vehicle for that new phase.

It would seem that reports of the death of maraboutism are premature. To predict what future forms charismatic power might take would require a divinatory technique more powerful than those once condemned vehemently by Islamic reformers.

NOTES

CHAPTER 1

1. See, for example, Conrad and Frank (1995), Richter (1980), Rivière (1969), Tamari (1997), Todd (1977), Vaughan (1970).
2. Among Wolof speakers these categories are known as *nyeenyo* and Mande speakers refer to them as *nyamakalaw*.
3. The use of the term 'genealogy' is derived in a general sense from Foucault to mean a mode of historical enquiry that involves a concern with origins, but not necessarily in terms of actual causes; instead it has regard for the combination of knowledge and power (here regarded in an indigenous sense) that generates particular categories or objects to be known (Foucault 1984). See also Asad (1993).
4. I use this term 'cleric' to denote a particular social category of Haalpulaar'en. They dominate religious functions within Islam and have historically come to form an exclusive social category holding political office. The use of the term should not be confused with the Christian sense of 'clergy', in whose hands are the keys to paradise or hell, who operate a system of confession and penitences and are God's substitute on earth. See Gilsenan (1982: 30), and cf. Gilsenan (1987).
5. I use the term 'archaeology' again in a broad sense derived from Foucault to suggest a mode of historical and epistemological enquiry that is concerned with emphasising the conditions that make a certain form of thought possible (Foucault 1989), conceived of as an 'episteme' whose scope here is extended to encompass the relationship between knowledge and power in Islam and craft-based specialisms.
6. Coulon states: *La dynamique de l'islam, c'est d'abord dans sa capacité de resistance au pouvoir qu'il convient de la rechercher* (1983: 12); and again: *L'islam doit une grande partie de son succès à sa capacité de se demarquer du centre, du pouvoir* (1983: 13).
7. See, for example, Copans (1980), Cruise O'Brien (1971), Sy (1969) on the Murids, and Marone (1970) on the Tijaniyya.
8. See, for example, Behrman (1970, 1977), Coulon (1981, 1983), Cruise O'Brien (1975), Klein (1968), Villalon (1993, 1994, 1995).
9. See Robinson (1975a, 1985) on two prominent historical figures from Fuuta Toro.
10. See also Schmitz (1983a, 1985a and b, 2000a).
11. See, however, Cruise O'Brien and Coulon (1988), whose work on charisma within West African Sufi brotherhoods moves in this direction.
12. See, for example, Dilley (1987a, 1987b, 1987c, 1989b, 1992).
13. Two recent exceptions are McLaughlin (1997, 2000) and Panzacchi (1994).
14. El-Zein (1977) proposed the idea of 'multiple Islams' in an argument intended

to displace 'essentialist' views of Islam as a set of universalist and transcendental principles. This view is criticised by Asad (1986) and others, who point out that this 'underplays the adherent's view of Islam as unified and closed' (Eickelman and Piscatori 2000: 18).

Monteil's conception of an *Islam noir* as a characterisation of West African Islam has been criticised for suggesting such a multiple of Islam, and for reproducing categories of thought drawn from French colonial administrators who sought to give order to the problem of addressing Muslim communities in the territories over which they had influence (see, among others, Amselle 1998; Robinson and Triaud 1997). While such criticism is forceful and persuasive, it must not detract from local understandings of the differences that adherents to the faith recognise between their own local practices and those they encounter on pilgrimage to other centres of the religion, especially on the Haj. To anticipate a point made in later chapters, ambivalence and ambiguity are often aspects of religious thought and practice.

15. Cf. Gilsenan on the increasing emphasis placed on genealogy among Lebanese Sheikhs and Sayyeds (1982: 67–70).
16. See Ka (n.d.) for further details on the history of this Qur'anic school.
17. Gilsenan also discusses how Sufism has historically followed two separate streams: an individual discipline for those who felt a call to the mystical and devotional life; a corporate pursuit of the way (*tariqa*) by groups of Muslims coming together in a Sufi brotherhood to follow a great saint or spiritual leader (1973: 1–2).
18. More fanciful derivations have been suggested, such that the term comes from the English phrase 'two colours' or the French one for 'all colours', a reference to their supposed origins as a mix of Arab and African blood.
19. In earlier publications I followed this convention in order to link the work to an extant body of literature which employs this label, while at the same time pointing out its misconception (see, for example, Dilley 1984: 70–1; 1999: 159). I have reverted in this work to the designation 'Haalpulaar'en' as a global term of reference since this present analysis is much more concerned with the overall social configuration of social groups than previous ones, where I focused more exclusively on *maabuɓe* Weavers alone.
20. While these cattle-herders found throughout West Africa are known as 'Fulani' in English (being a Hausa derivation of the Arabic 'Fulania' in use in Nigeria), they are also known in the French literature as 'Fulɓe' or more commonly 'Peul', a Wolof deformation adopted by the French, of the singular *pullo* (plural Fulɓe), a term by which they refer to themselves individually. In the literature, 'Peul' and 'Fulɓe' have taken on the sense of ethnic labels for Fulfulde-speaking cattle-herders. But in addition, like the English equivalent 'Fulani', these ethnic labels are used to denote not only transhumant pastoralists, but also those of cattle-herder origin who have chosen a sedentary lifestyle.
21. For a critique of the translation of the term *lenyol* as 'caste' see Dilley (2000). Also note that the term 'racism' in Pulaar is glossed by a neologism *lenyamlenyaagu* (see Niang 1997).
22. See Ingold (1996) on the debate about the idea that society is theoretically obsolete. The problem is also one of 'context' as to where to and how to delimit that network and set of expanding relations (see Dilley 1999).
23. 'Culture of power' is Murray Last's phrase (1988) to describe the historical situation in Muslim northern Nigeria regarding competing claims to legitimacy and to the formulation of concepts of power.
24. See Arens and Karp's edited collection (1989) *The Creativity of Power in Africa*,

which draws on Foucault's idea of the enabling as much as the constraining effects of power.

CHAPTER 2

1. See A. B. Diop (1981, 1985), for example.
2. L. Dumont (1980) has argued against the export of the concept of caste from the Indian subcontinent, and Goody has revealed the inadequacy of concepts derived from European feudalism in relation to the centralised polities of West Africa (1980). Schmitz has proposed, moreover, that the notion of a caste organisation over-systematises what has developed as a much more historically contingent cluster of social groups and categories. He avoids the term 'caste' in his work, preferring instead the Weberian concept of 'status group' (see Schmitz 1986 and 1994).
3. See both Gaden (1914) and Niang (1997) for further details on linguistic derivations.
4. Wane (1969) reported that pottery used to be a male occupation of the *burnaaɓe* social category, but on abandoning it women from other groups took up the trade.
5. The past tense rather than the 'ethnographic present' is used in many sections of this work. One reason is that this analysis is explicitly historical, another that the damming of the River Senegal in the 1980s makes some of these observations no longer strictly pertinent in the contemporary period.
6. From an evolutionary perspective, Thurnwald theorised about specialisation and differentiation of craft groups and their associated skills within sedentary agricultural communities. Given the prime importance of food production, it consequently gains pre-eminence in the system of values of that community. 'Hence', he stated, 'there arises a tendency to depreciate those who are under the necessity of buying their food, so that ... the craftsmen find themselves in a despised and dependent position' (1965: 85).
7. See also Anonymous (1960), Boutillier et al. (1962), Curtin (1975) for comparable figures.
8. This cleric evaluation of the Deniyanke regime no doubt involved elements of propaganda; see Johnson (1974) who highlights the importance of Islam for some of the Deniyanke rulers
9. There are numerous derivations given for this label *tooroɓe*, one of which includes the idea that the original members of this category came from Toro, one of the provinces of Fuuta, the cradle of eighteenth-century Islamic reformism; another suggests it is derived from the verb *tooraade*, 'to ask' or 'to implore' with the connotation here of 'in the name of Allah'.
10. The word marabout is a deformation of the Portuguese pronunciation *marbuto* of the Arabic *murâbit*, a soldier-monk; see Evans-Pritchard (1949), Monteil (1980). See also Triaud (1997) on the multiple connotations of this word, some pejorative, in current usage in West Africa.
11. See El-Tom (1985) on the practice of 'erasure' in the Sudan.
12. See Stewart (1973) on the Mauritanian connections with Fuuta Toro.
13. Two important centres of learning outside Fuuta were at Pir and Coki to the south of the region, the former being especially important in the formation of many of the early clerics to take a prominent role in the Almaamate regime.
14. See Robinson (1975a) for a view of the situation in Fuuta Toro towards the end of the Almaamiat, and see Robinson et al. (1972) for a potted chronology of the region.

15. The phrase village republics was coined as 'republiques villageoises' by Schmitz (1994).
16. I have adopted Quigley's convention (1995) with reference to the Indian caste system of using an initial capital letter when denoting the translation of a name of an occupational category (e.g. Weavers for the *maabuɓe*). Thus, the members of the category of Weavers may not all be practising weavers.
17. In Wolof a 'griot' is *gewel* and in Pulaar *gawlo*, two words which might be the basis for the European derivation of *griot* (see Monteil 1980: 25).
18. There are well-documented examples of smiths of Haalpulaar origin shifting between working iron and working gold, this change often being triggered by the securing of patronage to a noble family. See, for example, Morice (1982) and Diouf (1983).
19. The issue of the symbolic colour coding of the various sub-branches of men-of-skill specialisms as either 'black' or 'red' will be considered again in Chapter 3.
20. *Jeyde* is the verb 'to own' or 'to possess', and *jeyal* means 'ownership'.
21. See Botte (1990), Wane (1969), Schmitz (1983a, 1986), Meillassoux (1975, 1986), Gaden (1931), Curtin (1975), for example.
22. Weaving was a specific skill developed by *maccuɓe*, one of the few examples of bondsmen encroaching on the trades of men-of-skill. This created competition between the two groups for commissions and patronage within the village economy, and also for a share of market trade in the urban economy (see Dilley 1986b). Bondsmen were not able to integrate into the ranks of the *maabuɓe*, who rejected them as imposters and who intimidated them through their supposed superior abilities in weaving lore and 'magic' (*gandal maabuɓe*).
23. The original French is: *les esclaves ne sont pas tant ces humains, dont ils offrent l'apparence, que des bêtes de somme*. It is my translation in the main text.
24. See Trimingham (1959: 133–5) for a discussion of slavery as a legal status, defined in relation to freeman status. Islamic law states that slaves born in the house of a master were chattels that could be inherited and that Muslims were prohibited from marrying their own slaves by contract, but could take them as slave-wives or concubines whose children by the master would then be free. Allowed to buy their own freedom, slaves received on emancipation a written statement generally from a court, a malam shaved his head and he received a Muslim name by means of a ritual much like an infant's naming ceremony. An attitude of paternalism between master and slave was allowed by the Malikite code, a school of law which also gave a slave certain rights enjoyed by freemen (other schools give him only half rights). Trimingham added that he can hold property and even act as *imam-as-salat*, a 'leader of prayers', although in practice in Fuuta Toro this was often disputed. Sanneh (1989: 231) also notes that as a general law among Jakhanke communities a slave cannot assume the position of imam, although this evidently varies in some schools of thought. Again, it is possible to allow a slave to lead public prayers provided that this function carries with it no judicial or similar responsibilities. Sanneh includes in this work a lengthy discussion of slavery and Islam among the Jakhanke.

    Lewis (1980: 46) introduces the idea of an 'index of status' in relation to the treatment of delicts and torts in Islamic jurisprudence. The establishment of a sliding scale of tariffs of indemnifications, such as full bloodwealth for the death of a freeborn person, half that amount for a woman and lower rates still for non-Muslims, evinces the idea of an index of status in the application of Islamic law.
25. In 1815 the French government banned traders from exporting slaves from their territories, and in 1848 slavery was legally abolished on the isle of Gorée and in the town of Saint Louis, which were part of the French colony. Slavery, however,

within the French protectorate, which covered areas such as the Senegal river valley, was not immediately banned but would eventually be eliminated. Slave trading continued in these areas until the early twentieth century.
26. See Kyburz (1994: 146–51) for an analysis of the distribution of patronyms across social categories and of the implications that can be drawn for a theory of social mobility at specific moments in history.
27. Another sense in which the rural hierarchy has become tangled occurs today in urban areas. Here, for example, men-of-skill could find more ready-available markets for their skills and products than freeborn clerics or simple agriculturalists, thereby earning greater incomes than their proclaimed social superiors (Diop 1965; Dilley 1986b). Praise-singers or *griots* also have a long-established reputation for prospering better than other members of their social rank. They command gifts for their services that impoverish their patrons and make them more wealthy than many freeborn as well as many craftsmen and artisans. On the present-day condition of praise-singer groups, see Panzacchi (1994) and McLaughlin (1997).
28. This combination of occupations is suggestive, for such people are thought to have knowledge and mastery over both the life of the river and that of the land – especially large animals such as hippotamuses, crocodiles, gazelles, antelopes, etc. This joint specialism is reminiscent of that reported for the 'Jaawɓe Dalli' or the 'Jawdalli', powerful masters of land and water (see Tall 1984; Kyburz 1994). Indeed, my Weaver informants talked of some of his *mabu* ancestors being descended from Jaawɓe Dalli. Moreover, Hamadi Ounare is a place to which many Weavers trace their origins. See the second case study.
29. The accounts given by Kamara (1998) and LeBlanc (1964) on the settlement of the village by these two families seem to diverge on the question of which *tooroɓe* clan was the first to arrive. LeBlanc suggests that the Dems, who do have the largest landholding in the lowest flood basins, were followed by the Tallas, who control higher ground. Kamara seems to suggest that the Tallas were the first to arrive, indeed were the first to inhabit the village after Hamadi Hunaare. LeBlanc notes that there were muted tensions between the Tallas and the other *tooroɓe* clans. This rivalry is perhaps reflected in these different versions about the origins of the village, and stem from competing claims for authority that rest upon the grounds of first settlement.
30. The village is in a province of Fuuta Toro that was the focus of the Deniyaŋke polity, the capital being situated not far away. Perhaps it was an especially organised village of weavers to provide fabric for the Fulɓe court. Cloth was moreover an important trade item throughout the networks of West African commerce, and this village may have been a centre through which the Deniyaŋke elite might control production of the trade commodity.
31. The details of this case study are taken from Dilley (1984).
32. Abdul Qadir, having been imprisoned by the Jolof leader after failing in a campaign against him, found his position weakened when he returned to Fuuta Toro some years later. He was ousted from Cilon in a move that was to anticipate the establishment of at least five important families as electors (*jaagorde*) of future Almaamys, the Acc family being one such elector. See Robinson (1975).
33. See Dilley (1987b). Kyburz notes (1994) the favourable position of Weavers relative to other men-of-skill groups with regard to landholdings elsewhere in Fuuta Toro. This may perhaps be connected to the premium placed on woven cotton fabric by Muslims, and the importance of the cloth in regional trading networks. To lure weavers to a newly established village may therefore have been a prime concern of clerics and inducements may have been necessary.

34. This version of cultural development was recorded during conversations with Seydou Guisse in 1981.
35. See, by contrast, Durkheim's view of *The Division of Labour in Society*, whereby he holds that power only enters to produce aberrant forms of the division of labour, distorting an otherwise functional complementarity (1984).

CHAPTER 3

1. These sections are not based upon original historical research of primary sources but rather rely in the main on published works by social and political historians, scholars of Islam, historical ethnographers and colonial writers.
2. A form of writing known as *ajami*.
3. Robinson et al. (1972) note that Fuuta Toro never developed a strong indigenous tradition of Arabic composition as occurred in Timbuktu, at least not one that stressed historical writing.
4. Siré Abbâs Soh, a local genealogist of high repute and celebrated for his knowledge of local traditions and literacy in Arabic, wrote *Chroniques de Foûta sénégalais*, a manuscript acquired by H. Gaden in 1911 and translated and published by him and M. Delafosse in 1913. Soh was a *wodaabe* or Fulɓe from Dyaaba near Hoore Foonde, and his father was of noble birth and his mother a descendant of the dynasty of Koli Tengella.
5. See Robinson (1985) for an account of many of these sources, their authors and their agendas.
6. Thomas has recently highlighted the means by which 'the lives and the perceptions of those beneath or at the margins of the historical record were to be ... partially recovered' (1996: 273). Moreover, there is something of a convergence between anthropologists and oral historians with regard to a 'shared realization that an oral source is never a neutral and a social datum' (Finnegan 1996: 891), for it is inevitably linked to its social, cultural and performative contexts. Indeed, oral histories can be motivated by different concerns: the recovery of a group's perceptions of the past; the collection of information concerning past events, giving on to a method that treats oral accounts as a 'kind of quarry for shreds of evidence' (Thomas 1996: 276). There are, moreover, tensions that arise between the two concerns: the first suggests the possibility of different apprehensions of the past and of 'different genres of historical knowledge'; the second the archaeological recovery of an 'objective history' (ibid.).
7. Robinson et al. (1972) point out that the presence of the clerics with Arabic writing skills strongly influenced hereditary oral historians, the *awluɓe* and *maabuɓe* in particular. They frequently incorporated material from Arabic manuscripts in their performances, as was noted by Gaden (in Tyam 1935) with respect to Tyam's (Caam's) popular Arabic *qacida* poem written in Pulaar on the life of Al Hajj Umar Taal.

    Henri Gaden, born in 1867 and died in 1939, encouraged the writing and had published the work of many indigenous scholars and scribes, in particular Shaykh Musa Kamara (see Samb 1970 and Kamara 1998) and Mohammadu Aliou Tyam (Caam) (1935). He was *Gouveneur de la Mauritanie* from 1920 to 1927, took an interest in Haalpulaar social life and published a collection of annotated proverbs and maxims in 1931, a rich source of ethnographic observations. He translated works across three languages – Arabic, French and Pulaar – and was responsible for publishing a number of Pulaar dictionaries.
8. My use of the term 'subaltern' derives from Gramsci's usage, especially with

respect to the ability such groups have to put forward claims about their own understandings of their social position and to assert in perhaps partial and limited ways their own autonomy. Moreover, the threefold relation implied by the term 'subaltern' (an officer who is situated between superiors and the rank and file) finds an echo in the position of the men-of-skill with respect to the freeborn and those in bondage (see Macey 2000: 282 and 367).

9. See Hayden White (1973) who uses this term to describe aspects of Foucault's historical archaeology.
10. See Robinson (1985), Schmitz (1983a, 1998), among others on this topic.
11. Cuoq compiled and translated into French numerous Arab travellers' and scholars' accounts of West Africa (1975).
12. Al-Bakri, one of the main sources on the region in the eleventh century, was by origin and education of Andalusia in southern Spain. He left an account entitled in French translation *Le livre des itinéraires et des royaumes*. Monteil (1968) also gives a translation of his work in his *Routier de l'Afrique blanche et noire du nord-ouest*. He died in October or November 1094.

Another major source some 100 years later is al-Idrissi, born in Ceuta, north Africa, in 1100 and died around 1166. He drew up his account of the region for his patron, Roger II of Sicily.
13. See V. Monteil (1968). Note also that the word *shaggiyyat* is Arabic and is derived from the verb 'to tear' (P. Lienhardt, personal communication), indicating perhaps narrow-strip cloth that is still today woven by local weavers.
14. See Gibb (1980: 89) regarding the use of cotton versus wool elsewhere in the Muslim world.
15. Mauny (1961) pointed out that many Arab writers noted the effects of the religion of Islam upon the clothing habits of 'pagan' peoples: in the pre-Islamic period, numerous West African peoples went naked while others wore bouquets of leaves, bark-cloth or animal skins. He then went on to argue that since Islam obliges converts to dress, and since we know that local Muslims were highly active in the cloth trade, then it is not inconceivable that the religion brought with it the means by which these demands could be realised – namely weaving (1961: 3 43–5). Trimingham too made the point: 'The stress Islam places upon clothing encourages the art of weaving ...' (1959: 117). Mauny concluded that, after having started timidly towards the beginning of the eleventh century in the Senegal valley most probably, the fabrication of cotton stuffs had reached by the fifteenth and above all by the sixteenth centuries an important stage of prosperity. Cotton strips were certainly in use as an important form of currency by the eleventh century, as recorded by al-Bakri in 1068 (Cuoq 1975: 97), and Johnson has documented the history and geographical spread of strip-cloth currencies (see Johnson 1977, 1980).

The wearing of cotton garments by early Muslim converts could be interpreted as a symbolic statement about their adherence to the faith, expressing a wish on the part of the faithful to mark themselves off from the surrounding pagan and scantily dressed neighbours and fellow townspeople. C. Monteil observed that: *L'Islam et le coton sont toujours côte à côte au Soudan, sans doute parce que la morale islamique comporte une décence extérieure que le coton aide à réaliser* (1926: 596); and also: *La culture et le tissage du coton sont un signe indiscutable d'islamisation* (C. Monteil, 1926: 100, also quoted in V. Monteil 1968).
16. C. Monteil claimed that the *maabuɓe* go back to an ancient Fulɓe settlement which used to exist in the region of Hodh and Assaba to the north-east of Fuuta Toro, from where they migrated south in sixteenth century (1926: 637). However, Gaden, on the basis of linguistic evidence, suggested Manding origins,

stating that they most likely hived off from the Mali Empire in the fourteenth or fifteenth century (1931: 322).
17. Alvise Ca da Mosto (c.1429–88) left Venice to voyage to the West African coast in 1455 and 1456 under the patronage of Henry the Navigator. His descriptions of his meetings with peoples along the Senegal and Gambia rivers have a 'modern' ethnographic feel to them, portraying a detailed understanding of the daily lives of Berber and Sudanese alike.
18. Jannequin de Rochefort voyaged through Libya, Senegal and along the length of the Niger. His account was published under the title *Voyage de Libye au Royaume de Sénéga, le long du Niger, avec la description des habitants* in 1643.

The prominence of cloth in many of the descriptions of Senegambia written by early European travellers is perhaps due to the fact that strip-fabric was still used as a currency throughout the area, and indeed throughout much of West Africa until the height of the colonial period (Johnson 1977, 1980).
19. L. Moreau de Chambonneau published his account of his voyages under the title *La decouverte de la chute de Fétou*.
20. Kyburz (1994) argues for the non-Fulɓe origins of the *maabuɓe*, while Tamari suggests (1997) possible Mande origins ultimately for this social category.
21. Animals are thought to possess 'knowledge-power' (*gandal*) similar to some humans. In order to kill an animal, the hunter must have greater spiritual strength and protection than the prey itself, otherwise he might himself be killed or sent mad. Among the land animals particularly endowed with *gandal* are: a species of large antelope (*kooba*), gazelle (*lella*), guinea fowl (*jaawngal*), as well as other species that are not sought after: for instance, hyena (*fowru*), jackal (*boyi*), scorpion (*yaare*). The hippopotamus (*ngabu*) and crocodile (*nooro*) are the most powerful aquatic animals, and the owl (*pupuɓal*) is so among the birds.
22. Wane reported that hunters were feared and significant social persons by virtue of their nocturnal activities with animals and perhaps also by implication with spirits. The mighty hunter was a kind of magician (Wane 1969: 25). If I were to venture a speculation about complementarities of occupation and symbolic domains, then it would be between fishermen and hunters, the first of whom were *seɓɓe* Warriors, according to Wane (1969). The opposition would be between *subalɓe* Fishers and *seɓɓe* Warriors, not between *subalɓe* and Fulɓe. Moreover, in a Weavers' song (*dillere*), the hunter is one of the prime images of the 'able-man' (*baawo*), along with those who have mastered the river and can swim (Dilley 1987b). Here are two images of the master of the land and the master of the river, I would suggest.

On a related point, there is a clan of Fulɓe called the *Jaawɓe dalli* or *Jawooɓe dalli*, which is considered one of the most ancient social groups in Fuuta Toro dating back to the empire of Takrur, and is found spread across all seven provinces of the region (Wane 1969: 18). They have a reputation for a mastery, knowledge and power over the life of the river superior to that of the *subalɓe* Fishermen, as well as being all-powerful and masterful in the domain of the land and the bush. They possess *gandal dow* or 'lore of the above', that is of the land, as well as *gandal maayo*, 'lore of the waters' below; and because of this double mastery they are feared by ordinary valley dwellers. Moreover, the name of their clan situates them symbolically in a liminal zone between the waters and the land. Where else better to stand as masters of both domains? The *Jaawɓe dalli* are the members of the clan from the *dalli* or wet marsh areas. (See also Tall (1984) who mentions them as a group possessing special healing powers.)
23. Davis (1991 and 1992) refers to the use of genealogies elsewhere as constituting a form of 'precedental history' conceived in terms of genealogical connections. I

draw broadly on this idea in what follows.
24. See Morice on Smith flexibility between the two specialisms (1982: 274–6).
25. The term *bastu* was sometimes used to refer to indigenous people who have no hint of Fulɓe blood (see, for example, Kamara's usage 1998).
26. The lexical root *bal* for 'black' is used as the symbol of alterity, of difference, of distance and separation. Black can connote that which is base in contrast to that which is pure, noble or untainted, as in the distinction between iron (*njamdi ɓaleeri*, 'black metal') and 'noble' metal (*njamdi ndimri – ndimri* comes from the root *rim* as in *rimɓe*, the 'freeborn'). *Baleeɓe* are also 'witches', and to suggest that someone is very very dark in colour (*ɓaleejo, wi kurum*) is also to suggest he or she might also be a witch; or to say *o wondi e ɓaleeɓe* means 'he is with or has been taken by blacks/witches'. Black as an adjective can suggest malevolence and maliciousness in something or someone. For instance, to say that 'someone has a black stomach' (*o ɓawli reedu*) means that the person has malicious intentions. Black is, therefore, always the Other, that which is different, the non-self compared with the marked self: it is local infidels in relation to the pious *tooroɓe*; it is men-of-skill in opposition to freemen; it is the more threatening of the *nyeenyɓe* compared with the rest of the craftsmen; it is witches rather than ordinary people; it is those who harbour malicious intentions rather than those that are good and the true.
27. See Ly (1938) for a brief description of the hunt.
28. See Kante (1993: 85–6) for a similar myth among Mande smiths.
29. References to the Qur'an relate to Sale's translation.
30. Kante (1993: 25 and 28) claims that Mande smiths, who are regarded as having expertise in fire, are also deprecated by Islam.
31. For Weavers fire is used in a figurative sense in many myths and in their magic. Their mythical ancestor is said to have had the power to draw cloth from the ashes of a dying fire he had kindled under a bundle of loose threads. It is also conceived by Weavers that the name of the mother of their mythical ancestor – itself the most highly guarded secret – is a powerful magic which when pronounced causes things to burst into flame.
32. It might be referred to as *soɓe*, meaning 'polluted, stained or impure', and contrasts with the state *laabal*, 'clean and untainted'.
33. This positive gloss put on smiths could no doubt be linked to the importance of these craftsmen for Taal's war efforts during his jihads in the east. He recruited followers from Fuuta Toro prior to his campaigns.
34. See Wane's account (1969) of social ranks and categories from which this draws quite heavily.
35. Cf. Leach 1970: 62, where he states that the Kachin classify slaves and domestic animals in the same category.
36. The expression is used: *hoore ndee na artee*, literally 'the head is visited (by spirits)'.
37. On the Pulaar noun-class system see, for example, Labouret (1952), Sylla (1982), Niang (1997).
38. Niang (1997) gives the Pulaar term for 'racism' as *lenyamlenyaagu*, a neologism no doubt, but one that is derived from the indigenous term *lenyol* often translated as 'caste'.
39. Curtin (1975: 30–1) discusses another aspect of the tangled hierarchy. He talks of the threefold division of society as a hierarchy of rank, but that wealth and power did not line up in reality in the ranked order. Those who were better off in either of the lower groups, in terms of wealth, status and power, were better off than the lowest ranks of freemen. Elsewhere I have used the idea (Dilley 1984)

of a three-dimensional hierarchy in that the configuration of social ranks and categories could be conceived of as being arranged horizontally as well as vertically. Members of 'caste' groups were as much set to one side from the rank order as they were set within it as the middle rung.
40. See also Chapter 4 of *The Savage Mind* (Lévi-Strauss 1989 [1966]).
41. The power of the spoken word is contrasted locally with the power of the written word, and this topic will be dealt with in Chapter 7.

CHAPTER 4

1. I use the term 'ideology' in the sense of a social configuration of ideas within a culture or part of a culture. I do not intend it to mean necessarily a 'distorted or illusory form of thought which departs from a criterion of objectivity' (Macey 2000: 198), nor do I wish to divorce it from issues of power and domination. If culture comprises in part a set of competing ideologies that may contest one with another, then the way in which one set affects another brings into view relations of power and dominance.

   I also deploy below the concept of hegemony, derived from Gramsci, in the sense that when a conception of the world or an ideology becomes hegemonic it permeates all levels of society (see Gramsci 1971 and Macey 2000: 165–7). A potentially hegemonic group may set out to absorb, transform or accommodate the ideologies of other, even rival, groups. Such a group is represented by the clerics in the present ethnographic example and it is they who attempted, I argue, to set in train a form of ideological dominance in relation to Islamic powers and forms of knowledge.

   While Gramsci's distinction between the state or political society and the civil society may not be applicable outside European societies (whereby civil society reproduces spontaneously its consent to the social ideas of the ruling group), I do wish to emphasise, however, the partiality of hegemonic domination, and highlight the forms of dialogue and debate this attempt at dominance has set in train. (See Gramsci 1971: 245–6 and Macey 2000: 176–7.)

2. It is difficult to find a term to describe forms of practice and belief that may not have originated within Islam. I use the phrase 'traditional local religious practice' for want of a better description, but do not wish to imply the notion of static traditions or of discrete local practices. (See Soares (1999) for discussion of a similar point.) The situation is made more complex from an analytical point of view in that local Muslims are often making similar kinds of distinction between forms of religous thought and practice considered to be Islamic or non- or pre-Islamic. However, the reasons for doing so diverge from those of the analyst, and indeed the line between types of religious thought and practice might be drawn differently.

3. See for a discussion of a similar point Gilsenan (1982).

4. Arab writers before al-Bakri in the eleventh century were not manifestly interested in the region to the same extent that he was. They were full of scorn for the local populations, who were not yet Muslims and who still had not adopted Islamic ideas concerning modesty and clothing. Nudity – a relative concept – was a sign of paganism, therefore, and frequent references are made to this fact in evidence of the lack of religious faith (see Cuoq 1975: 16).

5. *Takruri*, the people of this empire on the Senegal, became known as a label to Middle Eastern writers and was synonymous with West African Muslims in general. Initially known from the pilgrimages made by the inhabitants of the original empire of Takrur, all black Muslims seen in the Hijaz were eventually

labelled as 'Takrurians'. The story of Mansa Musa, Lord of Mali being greeted as 'King of Takrur' illustrates this misconception. Mansa Musa made a pilgrimage to Mecca in 1324 as the ruler of the empire of Mali then at the height of its splendour. Mali had overtaken Takrur during the course of the thirteenth century as the supreme regional power. The Mansa en route to Mecca stopped off in Egypt, where he was introduced as the King of Takrur, much to his indignation, since now Takrur was only one of his many vassals. He preferred the title 'Lord of Mali' (Davidson 1967: 77).

6. See also Samb's account (1971) of Islam and the history of Senegal.
7. Johnson (1974) and Robinson (1975b) report that some of the late sixteenth-century and early seventeenth-century Deniyaŋke *satigis* practised a form of Islam, and that the conduct of some of them was pious and austere in their observance of Shari'a law; one member of the royal dynasty is reported to have gone on the Haj. The reputation the Deniyaŋke dynasty has gained for decadence and back-sliding in the faith can be partly accounted for as an outcome of the zealous proselytising efforts of Muslim reformers who became increasingly strident prior to their uprising. This image was also reinforced by the way the regime was protrayed in the Timbuktu chronicles (Robinson 1985: 48).
8. See, for example, Klein (1968), Curtin (1971), Robinson (1975a, 1975b, 1985), as well as Barry's account (1971) of the war of the marabouts in the late seventeenth century.
9. See the two case studies in Chapter 2.
10. Robinson states elsewhere that there is no evidence to suggest that Abdul Qadir Kan and the *toorobe* clerics belonged to the Qadiriyya, 'or if they did or some of them did ... this was not an important dimension of their movement' (1975b: 197, fn 32). Cruise O'Brien (1988a) adds that in the eighteenth century membership of a Sufi order was reserved for the learned elite and that, like a gentlemen's club, membership of more than one was possible. This was to change in the nineteenth century. See also Last (1988) on the shifting portrayal of the role of Sufi orders from the fourteenth century to the present-day in Nigeria.
11. *Toorobe* are associated with the province of Toro in Fuuta, known as the cradle of 'toorodism' (Robinson 1985: 83); however, others suggest that the label is derived from the idea of 'imploring Allah' (Wane 1969; Willis 1978).
12. Hilliard and Willis have both used and commented on Kamara's work as a source of insight into the social processes of the Almaamate period. See also Samb (1970) and Schmitz (1998) who cover similar ground.

    Kamara also considered the *toorobe* to be 'a people of the villages and cities so long as they can learn the Islamic sciences, whether their origin was from people of the desert who became sedentarised afterwards or the people living in a primitive state like the inhabitants of caves' (ibid.).
13. This idea again comes from Kamara (Hilliard 1997: 184) and is reworked by Willis (1978 and 1979).
14. Gaden reported the claim that this family had changed its patronym many times and their ancestors originally belonged to the Wan clan (in Soh 1913: 197).
15. Kamara is described by Willis as 'the single spark of illumination in an otherwise darkened corner' (1989: 60).

    Shaykh Musa Kamara (1864–1945) lived through an especially turbulent period of West African history, during which he saw the upheavals in Fuuta Toro caused by the aftermath of Al-Hajj Umar Taal's missions further east, particularly the return of partisans in the 1890s under the forced repatriation scheme organised by the French Officer Archinard (Schmitz 1998: 29). The period also witnessed, for example, confrontations between French colonial forces and the newly Islamised Wolof and Serer populations further south. Hilliard comments that Kamara had a 'critical sense uncommon among his African Muslim peers' (1997: 175), and he undertook a series of historical writings (see ibid.; Samb 1970; Kamara 1998; Schmitz 1992, 1998).

Born in Gouriki Samba Diom in Damnga province, Kamara studied Arabic and the Qur'an as a youth, and eventually moved on to develop his instruction under notable Qur'anic scholars of his day, especially under the famous Mauritanian, Shaykh Sa'ad Bu, who initiated him into the Qadiri *wird* and conferred upon him the title 'Shaykh'. Little is known about the social position and circumstances of his family, and he himself was silent about his background. Hilliard argues that 'the social circumstances of his life undoubtedly played a seminal role in producing the objectivity, sensitivity and insights with which he investigated the social history of the region', and that 'the missing elements in Kamara's biography relating to family history and social status are essential to understanding his writings' (1997: 180). The mystery surrounding Kamara's origins has given rise to conjectures that his parents were either of slave status or one generation removed from it. Not unconnected perhaps to this assumed humble status were two factors: that he was refused in marriage the hands of several women from noble Fulɓe families; his inclination to identify closely with European circles, where he could be acknowledged fully for his intellect and learning – attributes which could offer a route to social elevation. He had close ties to French administrators and was commissioned by Henri Gaden to produce the two-volume history of Fuuta Toro, *Zukûr al-basâtîn*... or *Florilège au jardin de l'histoire des noirs* ... (see Kamara 1998). Other works include in manuscript form *Al-Majmû'al-Nafis* ... or *The Precious Collection, Secret and Public, on some White and Black Notables*, which has been the focus of Hilliard's writing (1997), and his life of Al-Hajj Umar Taal, presented and translated by A. Samb (1970). See also Robinson's (1988) article on this Senegalese historian and anthropologist.

16. The transparency of the means by which the clerics established their position of pre-eminence is recalled in Fulɓe proverbs that evince the tensions that these political developments must have generated. While the *tooroɓe* poured scorn on pastoralism as a lowly way of life, the herders noted their views of cleric activities. They suggested that the cleric was 'God's beggar' who with his calabash outstretched sought alms from the local community. Indeed, the Pulaar phrase, no doubt coined by the *tooroɓe's* detractors, *nyaagotoodo Allah* evokes a pejorative sense associated with men-of-skill activities, for these latter too are called the *nyaagotooɓe*, 'scroungers'. Fulɓe also noted with disdain that the cleric was Allah's slave (*maccuɗo Allah*), or that 'a slave, if he alone merely studies, becomes a cleric; if a fisherman studies, he becomes a cleric; if a woodcarver studies he becomes a cleric' (Gaden 1931). While the *tooroɓe* generated a discourse of their own superiority and cultural exclusiveness, the Fulɓe provided their own commentary, recalled in proverbs and maxims, in a cultural dialogue with the cleric upstarts.

17. There is a saying in Pulaar that applies to such families: *wakhli diine wakhlaani yettoode* – change religion without changing patronym (see Wane 1969: 40).

18. Kamara gives us an illuminating case of a cleric of the Talla family who changed his identity in the opposite direction from *tooroɗo* to fisherman. The man had settled among fishermen in the area of Mbaany and had married one of their daughters. His parents eventually searched out the man and sought to bring him home on condition that he left his children with their mother, for they were considered to be of fisher stock. The man responded indignantly, ordering his

parents to leave, and stating that he would never return home nor any longer bear their patronym, but would henceforth be known by his wife's family name of 'Sih' (Kamara 1998: 284).
19. Kyburz cites the example of a contemporary individual, Ceerno Paté, who is of smith stock but has abandonned the craft to take up full-time Qur'anic study. He is held in great admiration by some sectors of the local population, and Kyburz concludes that: *Il est probable qu'un tel homme aurait pu quelques siècles plus tôt, rejoindre leurs rangs* [of the *toorobe*] *et ainsi être à l'origine d'une lignée de toorobbe Mbow* (Kyburz 1994: 152).
20. One exception to this is the griot praise-singers, who are thought to make particularly good muezzins, given their vocal abilities. It perhaps also mirrors the role of Bilal, Mohammed's black slave, who was allowed to call the faithful to prayer. See also Botte who details the position of slaves with respect to Haalpulaar Islam in Fuuta Jallon (1990).
21. See Brenner (1988). In addition, Willis notes that Timbuktu craftsmen were ineligible to become *alfas* (someone trained in Islamic sciences) no matter how scholarly their attainments (Willis 1979: 34, fn 90). Miner reports something similar for the contemporary period (1953).

The situation in Timbuktu closely parallels that in Fuuta Toro regarding the social position of specific craft groups. Miner describes the Gabibi – 'masters of black talk' – namely, masons, smiths and butchers who practise hereditary occupations. They have a reputation for controlling jinn conjured up by use of incantations, they wield the greatest supernatural power, and their techniques for controlling this power is secured from one's father or some other older relative. Miner also recounts a belief in how jealous competitors can afflict other masons by commanding a jinni to throw the victim from the house on which he is working (1953: 98–100). A mason's power is thought to increase with age, although some of this expertise is taught in the final stages of apprenticeship (1953: 57).
22. The Qur'an, 'The Chapter of the Inner Apartments', chapter XLIX, verse 10.
23. The idiom of different animal species to connote members of different social categories is widespread. See Gaden (1931) on a wide range of Haalpulaar proverbs and maxims that depict social difference in terms of distinctions between animal species.
24. In another earlier example taken from the Songhay kingdom further east, M. Kati reported in *Tarikh el Fettach* a discussion between the *askia* or king and his Muslim advisor, a shaykh, who was advising him as to the standing of children of mixed marriages between nobles and craftsmen, warning them against such unions (Kati 1964: 21). The same author recorded a myth in which it was claimed that the fall in dignity of the Songhay monarchy was due to an association between a specific king (*Askia* Mar-Bounkan-Kiria in the mid-sixteenth century) and the production of craftwork and the playing of drums (1964: 158).
25. Willis comments that artisans were deprived of all consideration to succession to the 'imâmiyya', as indeed 'the ranks of the Turudiyya had remained closed to them when they continued to pursue their tradtional crafts' (Willis 1979: 29). Botte relates an example of a recent dispute in Fuuta Jallon between a servile who had achieved a level of Islamic learning but who was denied the same Islamic title as his freeborn fellows (1990).
26. These two terms derive from the Arabic, the latter from the root *ruh*, 'of or relating to, the angels, the jinn or genii ... Among the angels are those who are termed *ruh* ... those who are created of light' (Lane 1968: book I, part 3, p. 1182).
27. Westermarck reported a similar distinction in Morocco among jinn, some being converted to Islam and others being regarded as the enemies of Allah (1933: 12).

28. Gibbal (1994) reported among the inhabitants of the banks of the Niger, far to the east of Fuuta Toro, that a similar ambiguity surrounds the idea of jinn. In addition, he noted that the word 'genii' is linked to the idea of a person's double, a notion also current in Fuuta Toro. See Westermarck too (1933: 20) for a discussion of the blurring of the distinction between jinn and saints in Morocco.
29. Lewis notes that Islam recognises the existence of heathen gods and spirits, and classifies them as demons, belonging to the category of disbelieving jinn (1980).
30. Westermarck (1933: 127) makes the intriguing suggestion that: 'The dangerous elements in *baraka* are in many cases personified in the shape of jinn.'
31. Kamara uses these two terms in the title one of his works (Hilliard 1997).
32. This work draws on L. Dumont's idea of 'hierarchical encompassment', the encompassing of the contrary (see Dumont 1970 and 1986).
33. This form of ideological distinction is known elsewhere in West Africa, for Trimingham reported the widespread use of black/white colour symbolism to denote different bodies of spiritual agent or forms of knowledge (1959: 54); Gibbal also observed a similar division among the peoples of the Niger bend (1994).
34. Sanneh (1989: 242) discusses the wide degree of tolerance within the Maliki school of Islamic law, the dominant school in West Africa, which extends to the assimilation of local customary practice (*urf* or *adah* in Arabic).
35. See, for details on Umar Taal, Robinson's magisterial work (1985), the writings of Willis (1970 and 1989), as well as Tyam's hagiography (1935) and Kamara's life of the Shaykh (Samb 1970).
36. F. Dumont casts Taal as the 'anti-Sultan', rejecting as too simple the image of him as a conquering cleric, the founder of a temporal empire (Dumont 1974). He was also a mystical warrior, an aspect of his career highlighted by Willis as the 'mystic shaykh' (1989).
37. Marone too notes that Tijani ideology advocates equality between believers, bringing upheaval in social relations in hierarchical societies (1970: 149).
38. Willis (1967) speculates on the possible influence of Wahhabism – a movement sweeping the length and breadth of the Arabian peninsula in the nineteenth century – on Taal's campaigns. Taal, perhaps coming into contact with these ideas while on pilgrimage to Mecca, did seem to espouse, Willis writes, 'the Wahhabi belief in the rigorous prosecution of the jihad as an instrument for achieving religious revival ... [and] of revolt against "syncretist" Muslim government' (1967: 400).
39. Willis, for example, reports that a slave named Mustafa was offered the post of amir or commander of Nioro, one of the seats of Taal's influence (1989: 72, fn 79).
40. See Robinson (1975a: 48 and 1985) for details of this depopulation of the river valley.
41. Known as Mohammadou Aliou Tyam in French literature, his work on Al-Hajj Umar Taal was presented in the form of a *qacida*, a type of Arabic poem but written in Pulaar. He chose this form, it is suggested, as a means to disseminate knowledge among a non-literate population, who learnt it by heart through songs sung by the blind, beggars and the poor (Gaden, in Tyam 1935: viii).

Caam, born *c*.1830 in Hayre or Aéré in Laaw province close to the town of Podor, left Fuuta Toro to join Umar Taal's mission as a disciple around 1846. He followed Taal for ten years, travelling from the Senegal to the Niger rivers, through countries that were being brought under the yolk of Taal's Tijaniyya. He took part in many of Taal's military campaigns, from the first at Hamdallahi, to those in Kaarta and Ségou. His fortunes were eventually linked to Ahmadu, Taal's son, who was commander of the Umarian forces at Hamdallahi. Caam went on to hold the garrison at Ségou-Sikoro, from where he started composing his *qacida*, a praise-poem for his Shaykh. He finished his work in 1890, when he was sixty years old, and returned to end his days in his natal village. He died there in 1911. (See Tyam 1935.)

42. The Shaykh indulged in the 'paradox of elevating the lowest orders of humanity to the highest offices of state', reports Willis (1989: 72).
43. Both Willis (1970) and Zebadia (1974) describe the correspondence from Al-Bakkai, in which he comments on the racial background of various parties. Zebadia passes over this without much comment, but Willis develops a line of argument that these passages betray Al-Bakkai's 'racist feelings towards the black Sudanese Muslims' (1970: 278). As a person by origin of nomadic stock from the desert margins, Al-Bakkai would have classed himself as 'white' (*al-bidan*) rather than black (*as-Sudan*). F. Dumont too notes the racism inherent in the writings of Arabic scholars in relation to Taal's mission (1974: x) and, if not all Arabs were exactly racist, they did, however, often consider black Muslims with a certain degree of condescension. This is what Monteil (1980) refers to a 'Bilalism', a reference to the descendants of Bilal, Mohammed's black Abyssinian slave and muezzin. These ideas shed light on some of the social attitudes that prevailed among Arab-Berber groups, and is also consistent with the view of caste prejudice as involving essential racial-like distinctions between one caste and another.

    Zebadia (1974) brings a nuanced historical perspective to bear on the whole range of correspondence between the Taal camp and the Kuntas, showing how over time the exchanges initially with Umar Taal and Al-Bakkai were polite and respectful; however, they slowly degenerated after it became apparent that a peaceful coexistence between the Qadiri Kuntas and Taal's Tijanis was not going to be agreed. The later correspondence between the Kunta Shaykh and the followers of Taal finds its expression in a style that is increasingly vitriolic and personally defamatory. (See also Samb 1970, chs 2 and 3 of Kamara's life of Umar Taal.)

44. Zebadia (1974: 550) gives an alternative English translation for this passage. See also Willis (1970) and Zebadia (1974) for other reasons for the Qadiri's flight.
45. I will return to this issue below, when I consider some of the more contemporary Islamic developments, particularly in the shape of Ceerno Bokar Taal, a direct descendent of the Shaykh.
46. This phrase is borrowed from F. Dumont's characterisation of Umar Taal as the 'mystical warrior' or *le guerrier mystique* (1974).
47. Robinson (1985) does, however, report a range of myths and legends associated with Umar Taal, as well as the some of the many miracles he is said to have performed.
48. See also Tall (1984) in which a Caam genealogy is given, although Adama is portrayed as a man. See also Robinson (1985: 69 and 349) on Taal's family ties.

    Adama is referred to as 'the purified who will never be sullied'; Sokhna is an honorific often given to the wives of marabouts.
49. This story is also recorded in Kane and Robinson's anthology of oral traditions (1984).
50. Kamara recounts a story of how Umar Taal had Tijani disciples among the jinn, especially one referred to as the 'old jinni of Colétek', who lived 800 metres outside the town of Hoorefonde, and he gave Umar his son to instruct in the faith (Samb 1970: 381).
51. See for an analogy on legitimacy that inheres in the breaking of rules that affect ordinary humans but which endow an extraordinary individual with authority, Arens (1989) on the Shilluk divine king.

52. See Brenner's account (1983a) of his life and mission, from which much of what follows has been taken.
53. Ceerno Bokar also retained connections with the Caam family – indeed he married into it – and it is Brenner's view that he was shunned by his fellow Haalpulaar'en because of these links with a family of reputedly caste origins (personal communication). His closest company comprised his brother-in-law, Tijani Caam, and a tailor-embroiderer called Bookar, and the three formed an inseparable group in Bandiagara. The wider Haalpulaar community in Mali refused to forget the Caam family origins and as a consequence Ceerno Bokar himself led something of an isolated existence from mainstream Futanke society. His attempt to integrate the still scorned Caam family into the dominant *toorobe* Islam failed, for it was unable to accept such a close association between high office in Islam and putative craftsmen origins. Moreover, Ceerno Bokar must have been further compromised in the eyes of this community by virtue of his close dealings with the Dogon and the association of such knowledge with his own mission. He died in 1940 an isolated, lonely man, cut off from the rest of the Islamic community.

Ceerno Bokar's funeral was described in terms that are also suggestive of 'black' connections with the bush. One witness described the event as miraculous: 'In the bush (surrounding the cemetary [*sic*]) there were many people, though one could not tell if they were human or not .... All the bush had become as people to attend his corpse' (Brenner 1983a: 138). In other words, the spirits of the bush, those whom he had learnt about through his contacts with Ancamba the Dogon, had turned out to pay their last respects to a mystic. Moreover, the isolation and marginalisation he suffered towards the end of his life bring to mind the image of a *bileejo*, a magician and curer, who are often similarly rejected by their communities. See Chapter 6 below.
54. A similar view on the relationship between the 'black' and the 'white' is reported by Gibbal in his account of a local commentator's views regarding a possession cult and the Muslim religion on the Niger bend: 'When black has left its path to go toward the white, it's no good. But if white goes toward black, it's no good either. White must work on its own side and black the same on its own' (Gibbal 1994: 136).
55. See, for example, Eickelman (1982), Gilsenan (1982), Asad (1986).
56. See, for example, Westermarck's work (1926 and 1933), whose aim was 'to discuss certain traces of pagan beliefs and practices that survive in the popular religion and magic of Mohammedan peoples' (1933: 1).
57. While Trimingham argued that craftsmen at best held only to a superficial Muslim faith, Bravmann talked of a 'Muslim domination of certain important technical and artistic expertise' and how the 'frontiers of Islam were also expanded through the dispersion of Muslim specialists', namely artisans such as ironworkers, goldsmiths, beadmakers and weavers (1974: 11). See also Lewis (1980 [1966]: 26) on a similar idea.
58. Marone articulates a similar idea: *Dans leurs faits et gestes quotidiens on constate chez les gens une étroite association de l'Islam et du culte de génie, à telle enseign que pour certains musulmans sénégalais, passer des prière islamiques à des pratiques animistes ne crée nullement un cas de conscience. Tout se déroule comme si l'Islam avait réussi à s'implanter mais en épousant, comme l'eau, la forme du recipient qui la recueille* (1970: 160).
59. This was linked also to a colonial policy in which *Islam maure* or Moorish Islam, a white Islam, was considered the religion of a more naturally Islamic race. (See Robinson and Triaud (1997) on this and the following point.)

236   ISLAMIC AND CASTE KNOWLEDGE PRACTICES

60. See Amselle (1998) on what he calls the problem of reaching 'degree-zero', an earlier pristine historical state in which uncontaminated social categories are detectable; this idea is relevant to the discussion of the possibility of a 'pristine pre-Islamic' situation in Fuuta Toro.
61. Cf. Coulon (1983) on his view of a dynamic of Islam within West Africa, one which he locates in the articulation of Islam and centralised political authority.
62. This phrase has been borrowed from Fardon (1988), who used it in another context.
63. Trimingham stated: 'Upon the elaborate [social] systems of the Wolof and Tukolor Islam has had no effect' (1959: 136). Kyburz also argues that the accession of the clerics to power in no way modified the hierarchical structure of society (1994: 419–20), a point iterated much earlier by Diagne, who talked of the continuity of social structure from the Deniyaŋke to Almaamate regimes (1967: 187). While Kyburz stresses the way in which the tooroɓe added nothing to the hierarchical system, he adds that they were promoters of an ideological unity around Islam, without ever analysing in depth the significance and consequences of this (1994: 421). Diagne again anticipated a fruitful line of argument when he argued that there were profound readjustments accompanying the emergence of the tooroɓe clerics, in particular that the inferiority of the men-of-skill was accentuated (1967: 216).

CHAPTER 5

1. This view contrasts with that of Lévi-Strauss (e.g. 1969) or Needham (1978 and 1980) who, according to Dumont (1979), failed to appreciate the concept of hierarchy and referred instead to complementary oppositions or 'diarchy'. Each element in a dualism or an opposition was not necessarily complementary in terms of value. Dumont defined hierarchy as 'the opposition between a set (and more particularly a whole) and an element of this set (or of this whole); the element is not necessarily simple, it can be a sub-set. This opposition is logically analyzable in two contradictory partial aspects: on the one hand, the element is identical to the set in that it forms part thereof ... on the other hand there is a difference or, more strictly, contrariety' (Dumont 1979: 809).
2. See Morris's critique of Dumont's analysis of the ideological totality of 'Universitas' (1991). He argues that it was not the only ideological formation or discourse available to folk in medieval Europe, but that it was given a broad currency by those in positions of authority and dominance, among whom was the Church. I hold a similar conception of the ideological discourse of accommodationist Islam, which was likewise an attempt at hegemonic domination and was also contested as such.
3. This might be likened to what Stirrat has called in another context the 'timeless' and the 'time-bound' aspects of the sacred (1984).
4. Peel (1968), Horton (1993). See Lewis (1980: 59) for a discussion of Muslim eschatology in contrast with the concerns of traditional African religion.
5. A maternal uncle (kaaw), like the paternal aunt (gorgol), is given an important role in many rites of passage. The mother's brother is especially singled out as a favoured relative. For taalibes, pupils or disciples of a marabout, sing about the day of resurrection: The eyes of the mother are red like the rising sun and the eyes of the father are red like the setting sun. Mother and father will not recognise their son. Only the mother's brother will speak up for his sister's son on the day of judgement. (See Bousso 1957.)
   Infants are also given pet-names, double-names or teknonyms (sowoore), that

are frequently used as a mark of affection by close kin and friends. Also, if a child shares the same name as his father, it is considered a matter of ill luck to use that name while the father is alive, and a double-name is used. (See Gaden (1912b).)

6. The Wolof and Mande practice of leaving the bodies of praise-singers in the forks of branches or in the trunk of the baobab tree seems not to have taken place in Haalpulaar territory (see Conrad and Frank 1995; Diouf 1983: 232). See the latter source for a reference to a case involving a French Catholic priest who allowed a praise-singer to be buried in a local cemetery and the outrage this provoked in the local community.
7. See for further details on male circumcision and initiation: Ba (1985–86); Bousso (1957); Diop (1965: 28–34); Kane (1935); Ly (1938); and Wane (1969: 27–9). On the position of women within West African Islam see, for example, Callaway and Creevy (1994) and Coulon (1988).
8. Verbs to indicate circumcising boys or excising girls are: *duunude*, *boornude* (also to castrate) and *hadaade*, to each of which is an associated substantive for the circumcisor: *duunoowo*, *boornoowo* and *kadinoowo* respectively. *Naattude*, 'to enter', is often used to refer to circumcision in a figurative sense of a boy entering manhood by submitting to the operation.
9. Diop (1965) states that the *fedde* bypasses forms of social organisation based upon blood or birth to constitute a fraternal and equal community, in which relations are marked by cooperation and not by dominance. Wane (1969) reiterates such sentiments, suggesting that 'real hierarchy' is found in 'castes' and not in the *fedde*.
10. Marriage it might be claimed is an exception to this, perhaps due to the fact that it is linked to the importance of family and inheritance law within Islam.
11. See Lewis (1980: 68) on the similar idea that Muslim practitioners attempted to exert control over circumcision rituals, often leaving initiation retreats in the hands of other religious officiants.
12. This phrase is derived from the Arabic *al-kaba'ir*, great or mortal sins, and contrasts with *al-sagha'ir*, small or venal sins. See Abun-Nasr (1965).
13. See Gibbal who provided a number of versions of the origins of Ghimbala possession cult, some of which developed a more pro-Islamic stance.
14. Kyburz proposes an explanation for the reframing of craft origins with reference to Islam by pointing out *la difficulté d'intégrer le forgeron dans un système de valeur propre aux Peuls* [not the more recent *toorobe* Muslims]' (1994: 399); or with regard to the praise-singers he adds: *l'islamisation du mythe pourrait donc obéir à des déterminations locales* (1994: 411). He finds no sense in the overall pattern of reinterpretation.
15. See Botte (1990) on the way in which domination through religious ideology was achieved by clerics in Fuuta Jallon.
16. Diabate (1985: frontispiece) makes the following observation about Malian praise-singers ('griots'): *Une assemblée de griots est aussi dangereuse qu'une confrontation des djinns. Chacun y vient, nanti de pouvoirs occulte.*
17. Arens and Karp (1989) talk of 'multiple centres' of power and authority, in an attempt to break the undifferentiated vision of 'centralised polities' with a single core. Last (1988) also invesitgates ethnographically the multiple sources of power in Kano.

CHAPTER 6

1. Schmitz (1985b) once used the French compound noun 'savoir-pouvoir' to describe Islamic knowledge. This term in French could be contrasted with 'savoir-faire', 'know-how' or an expertise in the sense of practical knowledge. Men-of-skill *gandal*, like that of the clerics too, embodies both these senses of knowledge-power and knowledge-practice, for one is predicated upon the other.
2. This account is based upon discussions with my two master weavers, Bomma and Seydou Guisse, during fieldwork in 1980–82 and 1995.
3. The term used here is *awooɓe*, denoting generally anyone who fishes without using the specialised *subalɓe* methods.
4. See Dilley (1991) for an analysis of the myth of the nine *maabuɓe* clan names (*jettoode jeynaayi*). The puzzle as to why only nine names are ever included in the myth, even though there are ten or eleven patronyms recognised as belonging almost exclusively to weavers, might be related to Islamic numerology. Brenner reports that the number nine 'represents imperfectible materiality because it cannot change. No matter what number is multiplied by nine, if one adds the digits of the resultant number they will always equal nine' (1983: 93). The number nine might, therefore, be seen as somehow appropriate for a myth that speaks of the origins of a social category through the consumption of hyena flesh – processes linked with the notion of materiality.
5. The phrase *asko ranewo*, a clear or pure pedigree, is derived from the root *ran* or *dan* that also translates as 'white'.
6. See Calame-Griaule (1986: 16–17) on the connection between weaving, the river and the power of language in Dogon mythical thought.
7. *Suudde* is the verb meaning 'to hide' or 'to hold a secret', and *suundde* is 'a hidden thing' or 'a secret' (cf. *sirru*, from Arabic).
8. See Dilley (1987c) for further details of this myth.
9. See Chapter 2 for an earlier discussion of this point.
10. Trimingham makes the same claim about possession: 'Its [Islam's] clergy are powerless when confronted with the phenomena of possession and though they regard these cults as illegitimate and cannot Islamize them they have been forced to recognize that they have a function to fill in society by their proved technique of healing' (1959: 110).
11. Tall (1984) presents an interesting 'Islamic' interpretation of the origins of witchcraft, and it might be understood in the context of the reinterpretations of craft origin myths considered in the last chapter. Mohammed had bled onto a cloth, and he requested that someone should dispose of it. The person who came to throw away the blooded cloth decided, on leaving Mohammed, that he would drink the blood rather than throw it away because it was the blood of the Prophet. He was later forced to admit to having drunk the blood as a mistaken gesture of admiration for the Prophet and was condemned for committing such a vile act. Henceforth, Mohammed decreed, all the descendants of the witch who had tasted human blood would be stigmatised as the 'drinkers of blood'. I am unsure who had recited this myth of origin of witchcraft to the ethnographer Tall, nor whose viewpoint it expresses.
12. Gaden (1931: 220) reports a case of witchcraft affecting a young man who complained of having pains in his stomach and imagined it as though snakes were biting him from the inside. A neighbour, with whom he had argued, was accused of bewitching him, and the victim later died in circumstances unknown to Gaden.
13. See Tall (1984) on this comparison, and see Schmitz (2000a), for example, on *relations propédeutiques-pédagogiques* among Muslim clerics.

14. See Gaden (1931: 110) for an account of this form of agency.
15. The word *marabout* was their pronunciation of the Portuguese word *marbuto*, a deformation of the Arabic *morâbit* or 'soldier-monk'.
16. The word *ɗuɗal* strictly refers to the nocturnal fire or hearth around which Qur'anic pupils (*almuɓe*) sit and recite verses at night, but is employed figuratively for the school itself. It is held that the renown of the school is measured by the height of the ashes in the hearth, under which protective talismans are buried. *Jaŋgirde* is another word which refers to 'school', and is associated with a semantic cluster of terms organised around the root *jaŋg*, from which is derived the verb 'to learn' or 'to read' or 'to follow the teachings of a master' (*jaŋgude*), and the nominative *jaŋguɓe*, 'those receiving instruction in Islam'.
17. See also Brenner (1983a: 74–5 and 2000c).
18. Little is known about the position of women regarding Qur'anic studies, although it is reported that a few female scholars have attained high levels of learning (Coulon 1988; Robinson 1997). Sanneh (1989: 165) states: 'Girls in Qurân schools seem to have been a rare phenomenon and nowhere in the sources are they given attention'.

    However, Botte has observed in Haalpulaar communities of Fuuta Jallon that if a woman completed the cycle of Qur'anic studies and graduated with the title *ceerno*, it was her husband rather than the woman herself on whom the qualification was conferred. She did not take part in the closing ceremony or graduation at which the title was bestowed. Botte states that everything happens as though it was the man himself who had finished the course of study, and it was he who received the *turban-diplôme*, a symbol of conferment of the title (Botte 1990: 47–8).

    See also Callaway and Creevey (1994: 48) on some comparisons between the religious education of women across different brotherhoods.
19. Most likely from the Arabic *fanna*, a branch of formal Islamic learning.
20. Evans-Pritchard (1937: 2) formulated the following description: 'The aim of Sufism has been to transcend the senses and to attain ... identification with God so complete that there is no longer a duality of "God" and "I", but there is only "God". This is brought about by asceticism, living apart from the world, contemplation, charity, and the performance of supernumerary religious exercises producing a state of ecstasy in which the soul, no longer conscious of its individuality, of its bodily prison, or of the external world, is for a while united with God.'
21. Gaden (1931: 258) provides the following Haalpulaar saying: *Khalwa ko gandal wonande seernaaɓe mawɓe, ko njogitaari wonande waliyaaɓe* – 'Khalwa is a form of knowledge particular to grand marabouts, a particular possession of saintly persons'. See also Triaud (1988) on the practice of *khalwa* in West Africa.
22. See for further details on sand divination Brenner (2000b).
23. See Gaden (1931) and Tall (1984), both of whom support not dissimilar claims. See Schmitz (2000a) who follows a line similar to the one developed here.
24. Gilsenan remarks that the memorising and reciting of Qur'anic texts is 'experienced on public occasions as rhythm and chanting' (1987: 91) – an oral and aural sensation. He goes on to add: 'A reading of the Qurân and the pattern of chanting bear little relation to terms such as sense or content as conventionally seen in the modern European tradition' (ibid.).
25. A term derived from the Arabic *aya* for 'verse'. I have adopted the translation 'script-potion' rather than the more literal 'verse-potion' in order to retain a sense of its written quality.
26. Brenner's notion of episteme is Foucauldian in conception, involving an implicit

world-view or structure of thought which informs social praxis and discursive practices. The esoteric episteme he defines as: 'a hierarchical conceptualization of knowledge, the highest "levels" of which are made available to only relatively few specialists. Knowledge is transmitted in an initiatic form and is closely related to devotional praxis. The acquisition of knowledge is progressively transformative: one must be properly prepared to receive any particular form of knowledge, the acquisition of which can provide the basis for a subsequent stage of personal transformation. Such transformative stages are explicitly expressed in the spiritual hierarchies of the Sufi orders, but they provide the basic framework for the transmission of all religious knowledge within an esoteric *episteme*' (2000d: 18).

27. Wilks (1968: 171) describes how elsewhere in West Africa it is customary for the student's family to make gifts to the Qur'anic teacher at intervals fixed not in time but with reference to the progress made.
28. Brenner makes an important point regarding the perception of the activities of marabouts and even *walis*, 'saints': the view from above is that miracles and marvels are seen as signs of a person's spiritual elevation and are not of their own making; from below, the person is seen to have spiritual power which they are able to employ as they wish (2000c). This distinction appears in another form here: namely the extent to which marabouts actively summon the presence of divine forces – the view from below – or passively prepare themselves in a state of purity and piousness to receive the divine word – the view from above.
29. Brenner reports that sand-writing, a form of Muslim geomancy (*khatt ar-raml*), taught through a series of initiatic stages, involves at the second stage a '"mystical marriage" which places the apprentice in contact with the occult forces which will "open the eyes" of the diviner' (2000b: 54) There is a comparison that could be developed with respect to *nyeŋgo* and also to the stages of craft apprenticeship analysed elsewhere (Dilley 1989b and 1999).
30. The *maabuɓe*, for instance, are often said by others, and this is indeed admitted by them, that they are 'close to the jinn' (*maabuɓe ina ɓadi jinneeje*), and this is a relationship that few ordinary Haalpulaar'en would purposefully seek out.
31. See Dilley (2004).
32. Hamès writes: '*l'islamisation de l'Afrique par la voie de la magie*' (1997: 22).
33. Marty's original words were: '... *c'est par l'écriture en effet que l'amulette musulmane a conquis l'admiration des Noirs*' (quoted by Hamès 1997: 37).

CHAPTER 7

1. See Gaden (1931).
2. Similar kinds of contradictoriness are expressed in relation to dreams, in a society in which dream divination is an important practice carried out by maraboutic specialists (*sirruyaŋkooɓe*), and dreams are an important medium of knowledge and inspiration in craftwork (Dilley (1992)). Allusions suggest that: 'the dream is nothing', *koydol ko fus*; or the more complex formulation: 'if the child of the dream is refused the hand in marriage of the offspring of divination, he is deprived of a wife' [for he will find one nowhere else and will have no offspring] (*so bii koydol yamoyii jibinaaɗo tiimgal haɗaama, waasi debbo mum*). The saying continues: 'they are both the children of a lie' (*kamɓe diɗo fuf ko ɓe ɓiɓɓe fenaade*). (See Gaden 1931.) This is a pretty strong condemnation and it sits ill at ease with the realities of Haalpulaar social life. One might expect on the basis of this 'proverb' that Pulaar speakers think of dreams as meaningless, empty illusions which have no social or cultural significance at all. Rather, such

sayings should be recognised as part of a cultural commentary on a central religious institution, namely dream divination. Moreover, this commentary embodies cultural ambiguities about certain practices that centre on the presence of maraboutic specialists (*sirruyaŋkooɓe*) whose exclusive expertise is esoteric and lies outside the everyday, beyond the ken of most people. For these reasons, the practice is called into question by claims that undermine the efficacy of dreams, and is another example of a specialist-spurning ethos (Gellner 1981).

3. Gaden reported (1914) the phrase *muumon Allaa*, in which *muumon* is a diminutive form suggesting the idea of 'little mutes of Allah', which is used to denote a class of animals – namely herbivores irrespective of their size, whether elephant, antelope, rabbit and so on. He contrasted this category of herbivores with the class composed of carnivores and serpents. This class is called *ŋati*, a term which is derived from the verb 'to bite' (*ŋatde*), and includes all those animals which bite and kill to live, such as the lion, leopard, hyena, crocodile and certain species of snake. I, however, could find no confirmation among contemporary Haalpulaar speakers of the significance Gaden attached to these two classes of animals, and indeed Niang (1997) refers only to 'insects' and 'bugs' under his entry for the term *ŋati*. Nonetheless, it is interesting to note that many of the animals that bite flesh or which kill prey for food to live (Gaden's *ŋati*) emit distinct sounds – they roar and cry with distinct 'voices' that are named in a rich Pulaar vocabulary.

4. A lion roars (*ubbude*) and has an *ubbaango*; the roar of a leopard is *hurɓaango* and its verbal form is *hurɓude*; 'to howl like a hyena' is *ŋuunyde*, giving the substantive *ŋuunyaali*, or 'to laugh like a hyena' is *waaktaade*, giving *waaktaango* or alternatively *goola* for a hyena's laugh, and so forth.

5. There are, however, Fulɓe (*jengelɓe*) who are considered to be masters in the art of interpreting animal language.

6. See also Sanneh (1979: 207) who reports something similar among the Jakhanke.

7. For example, in a weaver's song or *dillere* analysed elsewhere (see Dilley 1987b), the picture of the wet season with the river in flood can be alluded to by the use of three simple nouns, each invoking the images of rain and flood water. Also, the image of a tree clinging to the ground with its youthful roots in the face of rising floodwaters alludes to the qualities of great men endowed with power, potency and ability.

8. These pedigrees are given either in the form of *kaari jibini karri*, 'so-and-so begat so-and-so', or as a ascending list of names reaching back to an apical ancestor. This latter takes the form of, for example, Mamadou, Samba, Koda, Abdoulaye, Yerro and so on. In passages where a group of relatives with the same forefather is recalled, the performance often takes on a highly rhythmical style: for example, Yerro Ali, Bubu Ali, Bukar Ali, and so forth.

9. See Gaden's analysis (in Tyam 1935) of the structure of Mohammadou Tyam's (Caam's) *qacida* in praise of the life and deeds of Al-Hajj Umar Taal.

10. Brenner argues a similar point: '... prayer itself, of course, is believed to be possessed of spiritual power and therefore to provide inherent benefits' (1988: 35). But this power is dependent upon a number of factors, among them being the source of the prayer – namely from which Shaykh did it originate – and the chain of transmission of the prayer (*silsila*).

11. Gilsenan makes a suggestive comment that the reading or reciting of Qur'anic scripture 'constitutes a highly formalised aesthetic that controls and forms the experience of time ...' whereas 'the distinct and unchangeable types of calligraphy control and form the experience of space' (1987: 93).

12. See Brenner and Last (1985) on this connection, and on the use of Fulfulde as a language of instruction in West African Islam.
13. One of the few people I could find to help with the translation of a weaver's song (*dillere*) was a leading *toorodo* cleric from Dumga Rinjaow who had been initiated in the same age-set as the singer (see Dilley 1987b). He understood his use of language, his allusions and figures of speech from the secret codes they had developed as children in the same age-set (cf. Kyburz 1994: 241).
14. See Gaden (1914) and Delafosse (1922) who provide a range of examples of this kind.
15. Niang (1997) describes the stress patterns in Pulaar in the following rules:
    1. stress is not a distinctive feature in Pulaar;
    2. the last syllable of a word is never stressed;
    3. the first syllable carries the primary stress if there is no heavy syllable in the word (*a du na* = ^ ^ ^);
    4. the penultimate syllable is stressed if it is the only heavy syllable in the word (*ma laa do* = ^ – ^);
    5. when both the first and penultimate syllables have the same structure (CVC, CVV or CVVC) the primary stress falls on the first syllable (e.g. *baa waa do* = – ^ ^);
    6. when the first and penultimate syllables are heavy but carry different weight, the primary stress is placed on the heaviest syllable: CVVC is heavier than CVV > CVC > CV.
16. NB: an example of alternating consonants 's-c'.
17. See Malinowski (1935: vol. II) on a range of similar features of Trobriand magic, in which language plays an important role. He talked of the 'coefficient of weirdness' in magical language as against the 'coefficient of intelligibility' of ordinary speech. See also Tambiah (1969 and 1990) for discussions of some of these issues.
18. Malinowski (1935: vol. II) also analysed the prosody of Trobriand magical verse, and saw this too as linked to its intrinsic character, being sacred and set apart from ordinary language.
19. I was told by one expert in spoken verse that the formula *Bisimilaay Mohammadu, Arahamaani Mohammadu* might also be used to open an incantation.
20. On a recent trip back to Senegal, I met up again with Seydou, the master weaver, who had given me many of the verses included here, and we discussed which ones were appropriate to appear in a book. The ones of his that appear below do so with his consent.
21. Malinowski (1935) too concluded that this was a quality of Trobriand magical verse.
22. Again, Malinowski (1935) argued that a new 'context' had to be defined in order to elucidate the 'meaning' of untranslatable magical passages.
23. See also Hamès (1997) who quotes Marty favourably on the identity between word and thing in West African Islamic magic.
24. Cf. Gibbal who reported that Ghimbala priests on the Niger bend also referred to themselves as 'speakers', for writing was considered to be part of the magical arts of Islam: 'The marabouts write. We do not write, but we have everything in our head and our heart' (1994: 137).
25. See Soares (1997a) who uses the term to denote a type of Bambara religious object.
26. *Aaye* (sometimes called *safara*) comes from the Arabic *aya* for 'verse', and so could be translated by the compound 'verse-potion' or 'script-potion'; I prefer

the latter in this context in order to highlight its graphic quality compared to other forms of spoken verse. El-Tom (1985) choses 'erasure' as the translation of the local term among the Sudanese Berti.
27. For example, the science of letters (*ilm al-huruf*), the science of magic squares (*ilm al-awfaq*), and the esoteric interpretation of the verses of the Qur'an (*ilm al-ta'wil*) (see Brenner 1985). The word *haatumeere* comes from the Arabic *khâtem* for 'rectangle', 'seal' or 'stamp'.
28. See Hamès (1997: 112–18) for a fuller account.
29. See Cheikh A. Tall (1994).
30. I would like to thank Dr R. Kimber, University of St Andrews, for help with the translation from the Arabic of the text in this and the second talisman below.
31. See Sale's translation of *The Qur'an* (n.d. [1734]) for many of the details given here.
32. See Prussin (1986) on connections between *haatumere* design and features of West African architectural style. Recall also Gilsenan's point that the types of calligraphy used in Arabic control and form the experience of space (1987: 93), an idea derived from Ong's concept of the chirographic control of space.
33. Cf. Hamès who also argues that the Arabic alphabet *'est la matrice et le dictionnaire complet de la création et du pouvoir créateur. Sa présence dans les talismans actuellement confectionné indique la croyance à la potentialisation permanente de son action sur tout l'existant. Par la même occasion, on doit en déduire que dans la logique talismanique, seul ce qui est nommable existe ou peut être appelé à l'existence'* (1997: 173). And again: '*L'écriture en lettres séparées, un des procédés caracteristiques de l'art talismanique, est censée accroître la force de la chose écrite, non pas mot par mot mais lettre par lettre. Chaque lettre en effet est un monde, une entité en résonance avec les différentes structures du cosmos et en tant que telle ... de pouvoirs particuliers*' (1997: 203).
34. The original text is: '... *les lettres, tout comme les noms divins ou les sourates coraniques, ne "correspondent" pas seulement avec le restant du cosmos mais mettent en mouvement et font agir des "êtres" appelés "serviteurs" (hâdim, pl. huddâm) dont les pouvoirs sont mis à la disposition de ces lettres, noms, sourates lorsqu'on les écrit dans des conditions bien précises*'.
35. Cf. the explicit connections made in Dogon mythology between the word, weaving and the creation of the world, and the sense of the primordial mystical power of the word as the seed of creation (see Calame-Griaule 1986).
36. See Hamès who also suggests a parallel argument for the collapse of the oral-literate distinction when discussing these two elements of language in relation to Islamic talismans (1997: 229).
37. There is a secondary meaning to the verb *wiltude* ('to order the pages') which is 'to burgeon' or 'to grow again' (Gaden 1914) or 'to put forth leaves' (Niang 1997). This is suggestive of a semantic connection between the idea of natural vitality and increase and the order of the 'prose of the world'.
38. A topic for further research is the idea that forms of 'black' divination using cowrie shells and so forth constitute a form of inscription that leaves traces via the medium used by the divinatory technique. The diviner (*tiimoowo*) is the one who sees in these traces – the patterns of shells, sticks or whatever – signatures that are to be read and interpreted. The materials of divination comprise a system of signs, and it might be possible to consider it as a form of special 'writing' or inscription. The elements of iconic inscription in cowrie divination are suggestive of a particular kind of relationship between the 'language' of divination and the order of the world. As in the case of incantations and verses, the language of divination is transparent, the identity of the 'word' and the thing

are intimately linked, the signifier and signified being connected by means of a similitude that constitutes an iconic resemblance.

CHAPTER 8

1. It is named after Shaykh Muhammad b. Abd al-Wahhab, born in central Arabia in 1703. He entered into an alliance with the Emir of Dariya in Saudi Arabia, and this resulted in the establishment of the house of Saud. (See Clarke 1982: 216–17.)
2. The anti-Sufi Wahhabi movement was much stronger in Mali and Côte d'Ivoire (see, for example, Brenner 1983b and Soares 1999).
3. Adult illiteracy levels were over 70 per cent in the 1988 census, but had dipped below that figure in 1995, although it is doubtful whether literacy in Arabic would have been used as a criterion for exclusion from this statistic (*Africa South of the Sahara*, 1999).
4. Brenner and Last make the following comment regarding the situation in the neighbouring country of Mali, and it could well apply to Senegal: 'Educational reformers in Mali, through medersas, have virtually managed to establish themselves as a new dominant class of 'neo-'ulama'. They not only condemn the French educational system which, they claim, destroys Islamic values, but they have succeeded in portraying the traditional maraboutic and Sufi *'ulama* class as perpetrators of a form of popular Islam, that is, one which is semi-literate and doctrinally aberrant' (Brenner and Last 1985: 442).
5. See, for example, Evers Rosander (1997) and Gomez-Perez (1991) for a discussion of this issue.
6. See Loimeier (2000) on the 'two generations' of Islamic reform in Senegal, the first of which he dates as developing in the 1950s, the second from the 1970s onwards.
7. In Arabic this group was entitled '*Ittihad ath-Thaqafi al-Islami* (Loimeier 2000).
8. See Monteil (1980: 274) from whom the quotation is taken: '... *fétichisme religieux et l'exploitation dont est victime la masse sous le couvert d'un Islâm préfabriqué ... C'est en partie par une religion dévaluée que nos populations ont été intoxiquées et ce sera par une foi rénovée que la désintoxication se fera.*'
9. The account that follows draws heavily on Gomez-Perez (1991). See also Monteil (1980), Clarke (1982), Callaway and Creevy (1994), Evers Rosander and Westerlund (1997), Schmitz (2000b). Loimeier notes (2000) that post-independence, President Senghor managed to bring the UCM under state control by integrating its reformers into the political system and into certain professions.
10. The first title in Arabic is translated by Loimeier (2000) as the 'Society of the Servants of the Merciful', and the second slightly different transcription as 'a group of individuals recognising the supremacy of their creator and desirous of figuring among his servants' by Clark and Colvin Phillips (1994).
11. Cruise O'Brien (1988b) notes that in the period from 1945 to 1986 urbanisation among the Murid brotherhood was in the process of creating a dichotomy within the order: one represented by the merchants was a 'closed' version; the second, was an 'open' version which developed among the urban intelligentsia committed to Islamic reform. A power struggle between these two appeared to be imminent.
12. Given that the discussion here is also pertinent to members of similar social categories among neighbouring language groups, the gloss 'caste' provides a suitable generalised, non-ethnic-specific shortcut. Its use also reflects popular

usage by local speakers who use the term 'caste' interchangeably with 'race'. See Dilley (2000) for reflections on these terms.
13. The first Islamic brotherhood to be introduced into West Africa, the Qadiriyya traces its origin to a Muslim from Baghdad named Sidi Abd al-Qadir al-Jilani or Gilani (1079–1166). The order spread throughout the region in the late fifteenth century and early sixteenth centuries, and it is most probable that Abdul Qadir Kan, the founder of the Almaamate regime in Fuuta Toro in the late eighteenth century, was one of its leading figures in the area.
14. Of the three main Sufi brotherhoods in Senegal – Qadiriyya, Tijaniyya and Muridiyya (or Mouridiyya to adopt the Gallicised spelling) – the latter two represent something in the region of 47 per cent and 30 per cent respectively of the Muslim population, which itself constitutes around 85 per cent of the total number of seven million Senegalese (see *Recensement général*, 1988). The Qadiriyya is a much smaller order than the other two. The Murid brotherhood has its roots in the Qadiriyya, and the Tijaniyya embraces a number of offshoot sects such as: the Layeens of Cap Vert, the Nyasiyya of Kaolack and the Hamilliyya which developed in Mali.
15. See Cruise O'Brien (1971) and Diouf (1983). The former argues that the Murid order provided a new social framework for displaced Wolof populations, especially craftsmen and musicians who lost their means of patronage after the collapse of the leading families among the Wolof (1971: 15). He also notes that there were more artisans in Murid villages than in others (1971: 84).
16. Villalón states, for example, '... Islamic theology ... tends to be hostile to any distinction that is incompatible with the notion of the fundamental equality of all men before God' (1994: 57).

    Also, Ceerno Bokar Taal, the Haalpulaar cleric who settled in Mali, believed in the 'inevitability of the inequality in society, but also in the equality of all men before God' (Brenner 1983a: 17). This statement suggests different principles are appropriate to different domains of thought and different contexts of action – the secular and the sacred.
17. See Diop for a discussion on this issue among Wolof (1981: 94–104)
18. Panzacchi (1994) reports an interesting observation that among Praise-singer families the members of the generation 40–60 years old in the mid-1990s were more self-conscious about their social origins than their children tended to be. This younger generation has embraced the traditional occupation with a new zeal, offering at once a romanticisation of an unalienated and 'authentic' construction of the past, as well as a potentially lucrative career as modern musicians in Dakar and Europe.
19. Diouf (1983: 233), for example, states: '*De nombreux marabouts aujourd'hui encore ont été "blanchis" par l'islam*'.
20. The original paragraph in full is as follows: '*Il est permis d'affirmer donc que l'Islam n'a pas realisé dans la société de castes la révolution qu'on était en droit d'attendre de lui. Les marabouts se sont montrés conservateurs, devant la force des traditions qu'ils n'ont pas osé ou voulu bousculer, étant issus eux-mêmes, dans leur grande majorité, de la caste superieur. Ils ont justifié leur attitude en affirmant que "la religion ignore les castes mais ne s'oppose pas à elles". Ainsi, l'Islam s'est beaucoup plus adapté au système des castes que ce dernier ne s'est conformé à ses principes, surtout en ce qui concerne l'égalité et la fraternité des croyants*' (my translation, 1981: 98).
21. One of the problems of land development schemes, particularly irrigation systems, introduced in Fuuta Toro over the last twenty years or so has been the challenge they posed to the customary distribution of land among different caste groups in any village. Many schemes have insisted upon private ownership and

equal access to land by all members of a community irrespective of caste status, whereas those which have attempted to be more 'sensitive' to local conditions run the risk of maintaining the differential distribution of cultivable land (see Knight 1994 and Adams and So 1996).
22. See Callaway and Creevy (1994) for further discussion of the variations in the position of women in relation to different Sufi brotherhoods.
23. Callaway and Creevy suggest that paternalistic, maraboutic Sufism provides a check on the extremes of 'fundamentalism' that is spreading through a young and educated urban elite: 'So far, the continuing political power of the marabouts has acted as a buffer protecting Senegalese women against the extremes of seclusion, veiling, and withdrawal from many facets of public life, all of which the fundamentalists demand' (1994: 174).
24. See Ba (1985–86: 47); LeBlanc (1964) on restrictions of singing and dancing in the village of 'Amadou Ounaré'; Tall (1984: 190) on the strict regime of the Haalpulaar Muslim enclave Medina Gunass in southern Senegal.
25. See Panzacchi (1994) and McLaughlin (1997, 2000), who discuss some of these developments. The extent to which songs praising religious leaders represent the emergence of a 'new tradition' (McLaughlin 1997: 560) is perhaps a moot point. There are examples of praise-poems to religious leaders from the late nineteenth century – see Tyam's eulogy of Umar Taal (1935) for instance. As Gaden noted regarding this poem, being written in Pulaar, passages from it quickly became absorbed as common stock in many forms of popular song (see Gaden, in Tyam 1935: viii). What is important is that griots, conventionally shunned within Sufi orders, have found a new role, although McLaughlin makes the significant point that singers still retain a poetic licence to criticise the antics of marabouts.
26. A weaver informant reported to me in 1995 that weavers' songs or *dille* were no longer sung for they were evil. Many people would die the following morning as a result of singing such songs the previous night, he told me.
27. This account is based on a number of sources on the Nyas movement (sometimes spelt Niasse or Niass in the literature); see for example: Abun-Nasr (1965); Brenner (1983b); Clarke (1982); Diouf (1983); Gray (1988); O. Kane (1997); Klein (1968: 223–4); Marty (1915–16); Monteil (1980: 155–6); Morice (1982); Schmitz (2000b); Villalón (1995: 140–2).
28. Dates vary concerning his birth: for example, Gray gives 1840, Marty 1845, others 1844.
29. O. Kane (1997) estimates the number of disciples of the movement in West Africa to be in the order of millions, most notably in Mauritania, Niger, Nigeria, Togo, Guinée, Ghana, Burkina Faso and Chad.
30. It is known as *Zawiya al-Madinat al-Jadi* or 'Retreat of the New City'.
31. Schmitz (2000b: 129) reports that each year in the 1980s some 4–5,000 Nigerians, many of whom were rich Hausa traders, made their way to Kaolack, the town being connected to Kano by two flights per day, especially during the period of the annual celebrations.
32. See Villalón (1995: 141). He suggests that this form of succession and the inheritance of charisma by a son-in-law is unusual. Schmitz (2000a) has illustrated, however, that the favouring of a bright and gifted pupil, who is often given the hand of a daughter of a marabout, is one means by which religious authority and charisma in Sufi orders is passed on.
33. It is difficult to gain an accurate picture of the number of followers of the Nyasiyya in Senegal, for the figures that are available regarding religious affiliation usually embrace under the rubric of 'Tijani' an array of such offshoots. Villalón reports (1995) that in the town of Fatick, just fifty miles or so north-west

of Kaolack, the centre of the Nyas order, only one of the seventeen *dahira*s or urban cells of a Sufi order belongs to the Nyasiyya. This perhaps gives an indication of its minority status in the country. O. Kane (1997) notes that one family with the patronym Sakho are particularly associated with the order in Fuuta Toro, where it is particularly attractive with the young. Sakho is a patronym associated with the Fishermen social category.

34. For instance, Monteil, like other commentators, refers to Ibrahima Nyas as the 'son of a marabout, and grandson of a simple blacksmith' (1969: 104). See also Seesemann's recent study (n.d.) of Nyas's blacksmith origins and his relationship with the Tjiani shaykhs among the Idaw 'Alî of Mauritania.
35. Furthermore, the followers of Nyas pointed up his alleged Arab ancestry (see Seesemann, n.d.).
36. Villalón makes a similar observation: '... Abdoulaye Niasse [Nyas] was a blacksmith, and despite several generations of clerical careers the taint of caste seems to continue to play a role in limiting the family's capacity to draw followers from non-casted people. Perhaps partly as a result, the Niasse have been especially successful in developing a following outside Senegal, most notably in northern Nigeria' (1995: 68).
37. Kane's words in the original are: '*L'attrait de ce mouvement s'explique en grande partie par le fait qu'il prônait une plus grande démocratisation du sacré*' (1997: 316).

AFTERWORD

1. Cf. Jackson (1982).
2. Van Hoven (2000) has suggested a new Muslim order could emerge on the basis of a redefinition of charisma.

    The Nyasiyya suggests one possible line of development not yet exploited within the Islamic community. Perhaps if there are to be new forms of charismatic power and leadership that would break the mould of conventional cleric-dominated Sufism or Islamist reformism, they could be represented in the figure of women. The existence of female mystics and saints has been recognised in some orders (especially the Muridiyya and the Nyasiyya), and it might be to these potentially emerging figures of spiritual power and religious leadership to whom we should look. The position of women within Islam has been likened to that of the men-of-skill: both have been 'muted' within the Islamic community, and both were variously excluded from important religious offices. As the vehicles of specific spiritual forces within the 'traditional' pantheon of powers (such as witchcraft substance or the spirits of possession cults) that also lie outside the domain of Islam, women may represent the possibility of harnessing new combinations of spiritual potency to the carriage of Islamic religious culture.
3. Cruise O'Brien (1988a: 2) makes a distinction between sacred and secular approaches to brotherhoods: 'The actor's idiom is that of the sacred, but the approach taken below often emphasises the secular questions which are raised in the study of holy organisation.'
4. Launay states: 'The notion of an African Islam, an *Islam noir*, is *entirely* the product of European scholars and administrators. Virtually all Muslims in Africa would deny the very possibility of a specifically "African" Islam ...' (1992: 229, my emphasis). Amselle too is critical of the concept of *Islam noir*, and of the notion of ethnic specific religions, such as 'Bambara religion' (1998). However, Robinson argues, close to my own position, that West African Muslims were not necessarily resistant to the 'localisation' of religion, 'since they were interested in

strengthening and diversifying the roots of their own religious identity (1997: 563). If conceptions of religion are rooted in networks of social relations, then by definition some aspects of those conceptions will be localised.
5. See Coulon (1999) on the grand Magal in Touba, the annual pilgrimage of Murids to their spiritual home.

BIBLIOGRAPHY

Abun-Nasr, J. M. 1965. *The Tijaniyya: A Sufi Order in the Modern World*. London: Oxford University Press.
Adams, A. and J. So. 1996. *A Claim to Land by the River: A Household in Senegal 1720–1994*. Oxford: Oxford University Press.
Africa South of the Sahara, 28th edn. 1999. London: Europa Publication.
Al-Naqar, U. 1969. 'Takrur: the History of a Name', *Journal of African History* X (3): 365–74.
Amselle, J.-L. 1998. *Mestizo Logics: Anthropology of Identity in Africa and Elsewhere*. Stanford, CA: Stanford University Press.
Anderson, B. 1983. *Imagined Communities: Reflections on the Origin and Spread of Nationalism*. London: Verso.
Anonymous. 1960. *Les Hommes du Fouta Toro*, 5 vols, M.A.S. Bulletin No. 121. Saint Louis: Mission d'Amenagement du Sénégal.
Appia-Dabit, B. 1941. 'Quelques artisans noirs', *Bulletin de l'IFAN* (série B) III (14): 1–44.
Appiah, K. A. 1993. *In My Father's House: Africa in the Philosophy of Culture*. London: Methuen.
Ardener, E. 1989. *The Voice of Prophecy and Other Essays*, ed. M. Chapman. Oxford: Blackwell.
Arens, W. 1989. 'The power of incest', in W. Arens and I. Karp (eds), *Creativity of Power: Cosmology and Action in African Societies*. Washington, DC and London: Smithsonian Institution Press.
Arens, W. and I. Karp (eds). 1989. *Creativity of Power: Cosmology and Action in African Societies*. Washington, DC and London: Smithsonian Institution Press.
Asad, T. 1980. 'Ideology, class and the origin of the Islamic state', in *Economy and Society* 9 (4): 450–73.
Asad, T. 1986. *The Idea of an Anthropology of Islam*, Occasional Paper Series, Washington, DC: Center for Contemporary Arab Studies, Georgetown University.
Asad, T. 1993. *Genealogies of Religion: Discipline and Reasons of Power in Christianity and Islam*. Baltimore, MD and London: Johns Hopkins University Press.
Augé, M. 1975. *Théories des pouvoirs et idéologie: étude de cas en Côte d'Ivoire*. Paris: Hermann.
Augé, M. 1977. *Pouvoirs de vie, pouvoirs de mort: introduction à une anthropologie de la répression*. Paris: Flammarion.
Augé, M. 1989. 'L'ordre du récit et le pouvoir des mots', in *Graines de parole, puissance du verbe et traditions orales: textes offerts à G. Calame-Griaule*. Paris: Editions CNRS, pp. 39–43.
Azevedo, W. L. d'. 1973. 'Sources of Gola artistry', in W. L. d'Azevedo (ed.), *The Traditional Artist in African Societies*. Bloomington, IN and London: Indiana University Press, pp. 282–340.

Ba, Omar. 1985–86. *Le rôle des écoles islamiques dans le développement de la culture arabo-islamique dans le bassin du Fleuve Sénégal*. Thèse de doctorat de 3ième cycle, Université de Paris IV-Sorbonne.

Ba, Oumar. 1977. *Le Foûta Tôro au carrefour des Cultures*. Paris: L'Harmattan

Bacou, M. and B. Biebuyck. 1986. 'Editorial', in *Cahiers de littérature orale* (special issue entitled *Paroles tissées, paroles sculptées*) 19: 7–14.

Barber, K. and P. de Morias Farias (eds). 1989. *Discourse and its Disguises: Interpretation of African Oral Texts*, Birmingham University African Studies Series 1. Birmingham: West African Studies Centre.

Barnes, R. H., D. de Coppet and R. J. Parkin (eds). 1985. *Contexts and Levels: Anthropological Essays on Hierarchy*. Oxford: JASO.

Barry, B. 1971. 'La Guerre des marabouts dans la région du fleuve sénégalais 1673 à 1677', *Bulletin de l'IFAN* (série B) 33 (3): 564–89.

Beek, W. E. A. van. 1982. 'Eating like a blacksmith: symbols in Kapsiki ethnozoology', in P. E. de Josselin de Jong and E. Schwimmer (eds), *Symbolic Anthropology in the Netherlands*. The Hague: Martinus Nijhoff, pp. 114–24.

Beek, W. E. A. van. 1992. 'The dirty smith: smell as a social frontier among the Kapsiki/Higi of North Cameroon and North-Eastern Nigeria', *Africa* 62 (1): 38–58.

Behrman, L. Creevy. 1970. *Muslim Brotherhoods and Politics in Senegal*. Cambridge Mass: Harvard University Press.

Behrman, L. Creevy. 1977. 'Muslim politics and development in Senegal', *Journal of African Studies* 15 (2): 261–77.

Beteille, A. 1996. 'Caste', in A. Barnard and J. Spencer (eds), *Encyclopedia of Social and Cultural Anthropology*. London: Routledge, pp. 90–1.

Bloch, M. 1968. 'Astrology and writing in Madagascar', in J. Goody (ed.), *Literacy in Traditional Societies*. Cambridge: Cambridge University Press, pp. 278–97.

Bloch, M. 1977. 'The past and the present in the present', *Man* 12: 278–92.

Bloch, M. 1985. 'From cognition to ideology', in R. Fardon (ed.), *Power and Knowledge: Anthropological and Sociological Approaches*. Edinburgh: Scottish Academic Press, pp. 21–48.

Bocoum, I. C. 1957. 'Deux contes toucouleurs: la mort et la richesse suivi de l'hyène et les animaux de la brousse', *Bulletin de l'Enseignement de l'Afrique Occidentale Française* 41–2: 165–7.

Boser-Sarivaxévanis, R. 1972a. *Les tissus de l'Afrique Occidentale*. Basle: Pharos-Verlag.

Boser-Sarivaxévanis, R. 1972b. 'Les tissus de l'Afrique Occidentale à dessin réservé par froissage', *Ethnologische zeitschrift* 1: 53–9.

Boser-Sarivaxévanis, R. 1975. *Recherche sur l'histoire des textiles traditionnels tissés et teints de l'Afrique occidentale*. Basle: Birkhäuser AG.

Boser-Sarivaxévanis, R. 1983. 'Ariadne's thread through a west African textile labyrinth', *Swissair Gazette* November.

Botte, R. 1990. 'Pouvoir du livre, pouvoir des hommes: la religion comme critère de distinction', *Journal des Africanistes* 60 (2): 37–51.

Bouche, D. 1968. 'Autrefois, notre pays s'appelait La Gaule ... Remarques sur l'adaptation de l'enseignement au Sénégal de 1817 à 1960', *Cahiers d'Etudes Africaines* 8 (29): 110–22.

Bouche, D. 1974. 'L'Ecole française et les Musulmans au Sénégal de 1850 à 1900', *Revue Française d'Histoire d'Outre-Mer* 61 (223): 218–35.

Bourdieu, P. 1977. *Outline of a Theory of Practice*. Cambridge: Cambridge University Press.

Bousso, A. 1957. 'La famille toucouleur', *Bulletin de l'Enseignement de l'Afrique Occidentale Française* 39: 71–87.

Boutillier, J. C. 1962. *Le moyenne vallée du Sénégal (étude socio-économique)*. Paris: Ministère de la Coopération.
Boutillier, J. C. 1963. *Les rapports du système foncier toucouleur et l'organisation sociale et économique traditionelles: leur évolution actuelle*. London: African Agrarian Systems.
Boutillier, J. C., P. Cantrelle, J. Caussé, C. Laurent and Th. N'Doye. 1962. *La moyenne vallée du Sénégal (Etude socio-économique)*. Paris: Ministère de la Coopération.
Boyer, P. 1983. 'Le status des forgerons et ses justifications symboliques: une hypothèse cognitive', *Africa* 53 (1): 44–63.
Brain, R. 1980. *Art and Society in Africa*. London and New York: Longman.
Bravmann, R. A. 1974. *Islam and Tribal Art in West Africa*. London: Cambridge University Press.
Brenner, L. 1983a. *West African Sufi: The Religious Heritage and Spiritual Search of Cerno Bokar Salif Taal*. London: Hurst & Co.
Brenner, L. (ed.). 1983b. *Muslim Identity and Social Change in Sub-Saharan Africa*. London: Hurst & Co.
Brenner, L. 1985a. *Reflexions sur le savoir islamique en Afrique de l'ouest*. Bordeaux: Centre d'Etude d'Afrique Noire, Université de Bordeaux I.
Brenner, L. 1985b. 'The "esoteric sciences" in West Africa', in B. M. Toit and I. H. Abdalla (eds), *African Healing Strategies*. New York: Trado-Medic Books, pp. 20–8.
Brenner, L. 1988. 'Concepts of Tariqa in West Africa', in D. B. Cruise O'Brien and C. Coulon (eds), *Charisma and Brotherhood in African Islam*. Oxford: Clarendon Press, pp. 33–52.
Brenner, L. 1997. 'Becoming Muslim in Soudan français', in D. Robinson and J. L. Triaud (eds), *Le temps des marabouts: itinéraires et stratégies islamiques en Afrique occidental français v.1880–1960*. Paris: Editions Karthala. pp.467–92.
Brenner, L. 2000a. 'Histories of religion in Africa', *Journal of Religion in Africa* XXX (2): 143–67.
Brenner, L. 2000b. 'Muslim divination and the history of religion in Sub-Saharan Africa', in J. Pemberton (ed.), *Insight and Artistry: A Cross-Cultural Study of Divination in Central and West Africa*. Washington DC: Smithsonian Institute, pp. 45–59.
Brenner, L. 2000c. 'Sufism in Africa', in J. Olupona and C. Long (eds), *African Spirituality*. New York: Crossroads Publishing, pp. 324–49.
Brenner, L. 2000d. *Controlling Knowledge: Religion, Power and Schooling in a West African Muslim Society*. London: C. Hurst & Co.; Bloomington, IN: Indiana University Press.
Brenner, L. and M. Last. 1985. 'The role of language in West African Islam', *Africa* (special issue on *'Popular Islam' South of the Sahara*) 55, (4): 432–46.
Bruijn, M. de and H. van Dijk. 1995. *Arid Ways. Cultural Understandings of Insecurity in Fulbe Society, Central Mali*. Amsterdam: Thela Publishers.
Burnham, P. 1972. 'Racial classification and ideology in the Meiganga Region: North Cameroon', in P. Baxter and B. Sansom (eds), *Race and Social Difference: Selected Readings*. Harmondsworth: Penguin Books, pp. 301–18.
Burnham, P. 1980. *Opportunity and Constraint in a Savanna Society: The Gbaya of Meiganga, Cameroon*. London: Academic Press.
Burnham, P. 1996. *The Politics of Cultural Difference in Northern Cameroon*. Edinburgh: Edinburgh University Press for the International African Institute.
Burnham, P. and M. Last. 1994. 'From pastoralist to politician: the problem of a Fulɓe aristocracy', *Cahiers d'études africaines* XXXIV (1–3): 313–57.

Calame-Griaule, G. 1986. 'La parole qui est dans l'etoffe (Dogon, Mali)', *Cahiers de littérature orale* (special issue entitled *Paroles tissées, paroles sculptées*] 19: 15–27.
Callaway, B. and L. Creevey. 1994. *The Heritage of Islam: Women, Religion and Politics in West Africa*. Boulder, CO and London: Lynne Rienner.
Cham, M. B. 1985. 'Islam in Senegalese literature and film', in J. D. Y. Peel and C. C. Stewart (eds), *'Popular Islam' South of the Sahara*, special edition of *Africa* (in association with Manchester University Press) 55 (4): 447–64.
Chatty, D. and A. Rabo (eds). 1997. *Organising Women: Formal and Informal Women's Groups in the Middle East*. London: Berg (chapter by E. Evers Rosander on Senegal).
Clark, A. F. and L. Colvin Phillips. 1994. *Historical Dictionary of Senegal*, 2nd edn. Metuchen, NJ and London: Scarecrow Press.
Clarke, P. B. 1982. *West Africa and Islam: A Study of Religious Development from the 8th to the 20th Century*. London: Edward Arnold.
CNRS Equippe de Recherche. 1989. *Graines de parole, puissance du verbe et traditions orales: textes offerts à G. Calame-Griaule*. Paris: Editions CNRS.
Colin, R. 1980. *Systèmes d'éducation et mutations sociales: continuité et discontinuité dans les dynamiques socio-educatives. Le cas de Sénégal*. Paris: Librairie Honoré Champion.
Colvin, L. G. 1987. 'The Shaykh's Men: Religion and Power in Senegambia Islam', in N. Levtzion and H. J. Fisher (eds), *Rural and Urban Islam in West Africa*. Boulder, CO: Lynne Rienner, pp. 55–65.
Conrad, C. and B. E. Frank (eds). 1995. *Status and Identity in West Africa: Nyamakalaw of Mande*. Bloomington, IN: Indiana University Press.
Copans, J. 1980. *Les Marabouts de l'arachide: la confrérie mouride et les paysans du Sénégal*. Paris: Le Sycomore.
Copans, J. 1991. 'In the name of the Geer – the sociology of Senegal by Senegal (1950–90). Les noms du geer – essai de sociologie de la connaisance du Sénégal par lui-même', *Cahiers d'études africaines* XXXI Part 3 (123): 327.
Coulon, C. 1981. *Le Marabout et le prince*. Paris: Pedone.
Coulon, C. 1983. *Les Musulmans et le pouvoir en Afrique noire: religion et contre-culture*. Paris: Karthala.
Coulon, C. 1988. 'Women, Islam and Baraka', in D. B. Cruise O'Brien and C. Coulon (eds), *Charisma and Brotherhood in African Islam*. Oxford: Clarendon Press, pp. 113–34.
Coulon, C. 1999. 'The Grand Magal in Touba: a religious festival of the Mouride brotherhood in Senegal', *African Affairs* 98 (391): 195–210.
Coulon, C. and D. B. Cruise O'Brien. 1989. 'Senegal', in D. B. Cruise O'Brien, J. Dunn and R. Rathbone (eds), *Contemporary African States*. Cambridge: Cambridge University Press, pp. 145–64.
Creevey, L. E. 1979. 'Ahmad Bamba 1850–1927', in J. R. Willis (ed.), *Studies in West African Islam*. London: Frank Cass, pp. 278–307.
Crowder, M. 1962. *Senegal. A Study in French Assimilation Policy*. London and New York: Oxford University Press
Cruise O'Brien, D. 1971. *The Mourides of Senegal: The Political and Economic Organisation of an Islamic Brotherhood*. Oxford: Clarendon Press.
Cruise O'Brien, D. 1975. *Saints and Politicans: Essays in the Organisation of Senegalese Peasant Society*. London: Cambridge University Press.
Cruise O'Brien, D. B. 1988a. 'Introduction', in D. B. Cruise O'Brien and C. Coulon (eds), *Charisma and Brotherhood in African Islam*. Oxford: Clarendon Press, pp. 1–31.
Cruise O'Brien, D. B. 1988b. 'Charisma comes to town: Mouride urbanization

1945–86', in D. B. Cruise O'Brien and C. Coulon (eds), *Charisma and Brotherhood in African Islam*. Oxford: Clarendon Press, pp. 135–56.
Cruise O'Brien, D. B. and C. Coulon (eds). 1988. *Charisma and Brotherhood in African Islam*. Oxford: Clarendon Press.
Cultru, P. (ed.). 1913. *Premier voyage du Sieur de la Courbe fait à la coste d'Afrique en 1685*. Paris: Campion et Larousse.
Cuoq, J. M. 1975. *Receuil des sources arabes conçernant l'Afrique occidentale du VIIIe au XVIe siècle*. Paris: Editions de CNRS.
Curtin, P. D. 1971a. 'Pre-colonial trading networks and traders: the Diakhanké', in C. Meillassoux (ed.), *The Development of Indigenous Trade and Markets in West Africa*. London: Oxford University Press for the International African Institute, pp. 228–39.
Curtin, P. D. 1971b. 'Jihad in West Africa: early phases and inter-relations in Mauritania and Senegal', *Journal of African History* 12 (1): 11–24.
Curtin, P. D. 1974. 'Chronology of events and reigns in the Upper Senegal Valley', *Bulletin de l'IFAN* (série B) XXXVI: 525–58.
Curtin, P. D. 1975. *Economic Exchange in Pre-Colonial Africa: Senegambia in the Era of the Slave Trade*. Madison, WI: University of Winsconsin Press.
Davidson, B. 1967. *The African Past: Chronicles from Antiquity to Modern Times*. London: Longman.
Davis, J. 1991. *Times and Identities* (an inaugural lecture delivered on 1 May 1991). Oxford: Clarendon Press.
Davis, J. 1992. 'History and the people without Europe', in K. Hastrup (ed.), *Other Histories*. London: Routledge, pp. 14–28.
Delafosse, M. 1912. *Haut-Sénégal-Niger (Soudan français): le pays, les peuples, les langues, l'histoire, les civilisations*, 3 vols. Paris: Larousse.
Delafosse, M. (avec la collaboration de Henri Gaden). 1913. *Chroniques du Fouta sénégalais, traduites, de deux manuscrits arabes inédits de Siré-Abbâs Soh*. Paris: Leroux.
Delafosse, M. 1922. 'Langage secret et langage conventionnel dans l'Afrique Noire', *L'Anthropologie* XXI: 83–92.
Diabate, Massa M. 1985. *L'assemblée des djinns*. Dakar and Paris: Présence Africaine.
Diagne, P. 1967. *Pouvoir politique traditionnel en Afrique occidentale: Essais sur les institutions politiques précoloniales*. Paris: Présence Africaine.
Diagne, Y. 1982. *L'ordre de la tradition et les pouvoirs de la parole chez les Wolof du Sénégal, ou une approache anthropologique d'une culture orale*. Paris: Mémoire de l'EHESS.
Diallo, C. A. 1972. 'Contribution à une étude de l'enseignement privé coranique au Sénégal', *Revue Française d'Etudes Politiques Africaines* 76: 34–48.
Dieterlen, G. 1965. *Textes sacrés d'Afrique Noire* (Collection UNESCO D'Oeuvres Répresentatives, Série Africaine). Paris: Gallimard.
Dilley, R. M. 1984. 'Weavers among the Tukolor of the Senegal River Basin: A study of their Social Position and Economic Organisation'. Unpublished DPhil thesis, University of Oxford.
Dilley, R. M. 1986a. 'Itinerant Tukolor weavers: their economic niche and aspects of social identity', *Nomadic Peoples* 21/2: 117–33.
Dilley, R. M. 1986b. 'Tukolor weavers and the organization of their craft in village and town', *Africa* 56 (2): 123–47.
Dilley, R. M. 1987a. 'Myth and meaning and the Tukolor loom', *Man* 22 (2): 256–66.
Dilley, R. M. 1987b. 'Spirits, Islam and ideology: a study of a Tukolor weavers' song *(Dillere)*', in *Journal of Religion in Africa* XVII (3): 245–79.
Dilley, R. M. 1987c. 'Tukolor weaving origin myths: Islam and reinterpretation', in

A. Al-Shahi (ed.), *The Diversity of the Muslim Community*. London: Ithaca Press, pp. 70–9.

Dilley, R. M. 1988. 'Aspects of animal symbolism among the Tukulor of Senegal', in J. C. Stone (ed.), *The Exploitation of Animals in Africa*. Aberdeen: Aberdeen University Press, pp. 265–76.

Dilley, R. M. 1989a. 'Performance, ambiguity and power in Tukulor weavers' songs', in K. Barber and P. F. de Moraes Farias (eds), *Discourse and Its Disguises: Interpretation of African Oral Texts*. Birmingham: Centre for West African Studies, pp. 138–51.

Dilley, R. M. 1989b. 'Secrets and skills: apprenticeship among Tukolor weavers', in M. W. Coy (ed.), *Apprenticeship: From Theory to Method*. New York: SUNY Press, pp. 181–98.

Dilley, R. M. 1991. 'Interpreting Tukolor oral literature: the myth of origin of the nine Mabube clan names', in P. T. W. Baxter and Richard Fardon (eds), *Voice, Genre, Text: Anthropological Essays in Africa and Beyond* (special issue of *Bulletin of the John Rylands University Library of Manchester*) 73 (3): 25–36.

Dilley, R. M. 1992. 'Dreams, inspiration and craftwork among Tukolor weavers', in M. C. Jedrej and R. Shaw (eds), *Dreaming, Religion and Society in Africa*. Leiden: E. J. Brill, pp. 71–85.

Dilley, R. M. 1999. 'Ways of knowing, forms of power: aspects of apprenticeship among Tukulor mabuɓe weavers', *Cultural Dynamics* 11 (1): 33–55.

Dilley, R. M. 2000. 'The question of caste in West Africa, with special reference to Tukulor craftsmen', *Anthropos* 95: 149–65.

Dilley, R. M. 2004. 'Time-shapes and cultural agency among West African craft specialists', in W. James and D. Mills (eds), *The Qualities of Time: Temporal Dimensions of Social Form and Human Experience*. Oxford: Berg.

Diop, A. B. 1965. *Société toucouleur et migration. Enquête sur l'immigration toucouleur à Dakar*, Initiations Africaines No. XVIII. Dakar: IFAN.

Diop, A. B. 1981. *La société wolof: tradition et changement : les systèmes d'inégalité et de domination*. Paris: Karthala.

Diop, A. B. 1985. *La Famille Wolof: tradition et changement*. Paris: Karthala.

Diop, A. M. 1994. 'Les associations islamiques sénégalaises en France', *Islam et Sociétés au Sud du Sahara* 8: 7–15.

Diop, S. 1995. *The Oral History and Literature of the Wolof People of Waalo, Northern Senegal: the Master of the Word (Griot) in the Wolof Tradition*. Lewiston, NY: Edwin Mellen.

Diouf, M. B. 1981. 'Migration artisanale et solidarité villageoise: le cas de Kanen Njob, au Sénégal', *Cahiers d'études africaines* 21, Part 4 (84): 577–82.

Diouf, M. B. 1983. *Forgerons wolof du Kajoor; forgerons Sereer du Siin et du Jegem: de l'epoque précoloniale à nos jours*. Paris: Thèse de doctorat de 3ième cycle, EHESS.

Dumont, F. 1974. *L'anti-Sultan ou Al-Hajj Omar Tal du Fouta, combattant de la foi (1794–1864)*. Dakar and Abidjan: Les nouvelles éditions africaines.

Dumont, L. 1979. 'The anthropological community and ideology', *Social Science Information* 18 (6): 785–817.

Dumont, L. 1980 [1966]. *Homo Hierarchicus. The Caste System and Its Implications*. Chicago and London: University of Chicago Press.

Dumont, L. 1986. *Essays on Individualism: Modern Ideology in Anthropological Perspective*. Chicago: University of Chicago Press.

Durkheim, E. 1984. *The Division of Labour in Society*. Basingstoke: Macmillan.

Eickelman, D. F. 1982. 'The study of Islam in local contexts', *Contributions to Asian Studies* 17: 1–16.

Eickelman, D. F. and J. Piscatori (eds). 2000a. 'Social theory in the study of Muslim societies', in D. F. Eickleman and J. Piscatori (eds), *Muslim Travellers: Pilgrimage, Migration, and the Religious Imagination.* London and New York: Routledge, pp. 3–25.

Eickelman, D. F. and J. Piscatori (eds). 2000b [1990]. *Muslim Travellers: Pilgrimage, Migration, and the Religious Imagination.* London and New York: Routledge.

El-Tom, A. O. 1985. 'Drinking the Koran: the meaning of Koranic verses in Berti erasure', in J. D. Y. Peel and C. C. Stewart (eds), *'Popular Islam' South of the Sahara* (special edition of *Africa* in association with Manchester University Press) 55 (4): 414–31.

Evans-Pritchard, E. E. 1937. *Witchcraft, Oracles and Magic Among the Azande.* Oxford: Clarendon Press.

Evans-Pritchard, E. E. 1949. *The Sanusi of Cyrenaica.* Oxford: Clarendon Press.

Evans-Pritchard, E. E. 1964a. 'Anthropology and history', in *Social Anthropology and Other Essays.* New York: Free Press of Glencoe.

Evans-Pritchard, E. E. 1964b. 'Social anthropology: past and present' (The Marett Lecture 1950), in *Social Anthropology and Other Essays.* New York: Free Press of Glencoe.

Evers Rosander, E. 1997. 'Introduction: the Islamization of "tradition" and "modernity"', in E. Evers Rosander and D. Westerlund (eds), *African Islam and Islam in Africa: Encounters Between Sufis and Islamists.* London: Hurst & Co., pp. 1–27.

Evers Rosander, E. and D. Westerlund (eds). 1997. *African Islam and Islam in Africa: Encounters Between Sufis and Islamists.* London: Hurst & Co.

Fage, J. P. 1969. *A History of West Africa.* Cambridge: Cambridge University Press.

Fage, J. P. 1978. *A History of Africa.* London: Hutchinson.

Fahd, T. 1997 'Sihr', in C. E. Bosworth et al. (eds), *The Encyclopaedia of Islam.* Leiden: Brill, pp. 567–71.

Fairclough, N. 1992. *Discourse and Social Change.* Cambridge: Polity.

Fall, M. 1983. 'La question islamique au Sénégal. Le regain récent de l'Islam: un ménage pour l'etat?', in *Cultures et Développement* 15 (3): 443–54.

Fardon, R. (ed.) 1988. *Localizing Strategies: Regional Traditions of Ethnographic Writing.* Edinburgh: Scottish Academic Press.

Finnegan, R. 1996. 'Oral tradition', in D. Levinson and M. Ember (eds), *Encyclopedia of Cultural Anthropology.* New York: Henry Holt, pp. 887–91.

Fisher, A. G. B. and J. Humphrey. 1970. *Slavery and Muslim Society in Africa: The Institution in Saharan and Sudanic Africa and the Trans-Saharan Trade.* London: C. Hurst & Co.

Fisher, H. 1973. 'Conversion reconsidered: some historical aspects of religious conversion in Black Africa', *Africa* 43: 27–40.

Fisher, H. 1985. 'The Juggernaut's Apologica', *Africa* 55: 153–73.

Foucault, M. 1979. *Discipline and Punish: The Birth of the Prison.* London: Peregrine Books.

Foucault, M. 1984. *The Foucault Reader*, ed. P. Rabinow. Harmondsworth: Penguin.

Foucault, M. 1989 [1974]. *The Order of Things: An Archaeology of the Human Sciences.* London: Tavistock.

Gaden, H. 1912a. 'Légendes et coutumes sénégalaises: cahiers de Yoro Diaw', *Révue d'ethnographie et sociologie* I: 119–37 and 191–202.

Gaden, H. 1912b. 'Du nom chez les Toucouleurs et Peul islamisés du Fouta Sénégalais', *Révue d'ethnographie et sociologie* I: 50–6.

Gaden, H. 1914. *Le Poular, dialecte Peul du Fouta Sénégalais.* Paris: Leroux.

Gaden, H. 1931. *Proverbes et Maximes Peuls et Toucouleurs*, Paris: Institut d'Ethnologie.
Gaden, H. 1935. 'Du Régime des terres de la vallée du Sénégal au Fouta antérieurement à l'occupation française', *Bulletin du Comité des Etudes Historiques et Scientifiques de l'Afrique Occidentale Française* XVIII (4) 403–14.
Gaden, H. 1969. *Dictionnaire Peul–Français: Publication du fichier Gaden des manuscrits de l'I.F.A.N., enrichi par une équipe de chercheurs du Fuuta Tooro et du Fuuta Dyaloo*, Fascicule I. Dakar: IFAN.
Gell, A. 1992. 'The technology of enchantment and the enchantment of technology', in J. Coote and A. Shelton (eds), *Anthropology, Art and Aesthetics*. Oxford: Clarendon Press, pp. 40–63.
Gellar, S. 1995. *Senegal: An African Nation between Islam and the West*. Boulder, CO and Oxford: Westview Press.
Gellner, E. 1981. *Muslim Society*. Cambridge: Cambridge University Press.
Gennep, A. van. 1960. *The Rites of Passage*. Chicago: University of Chicago Press.
Gibb, H. A. R. 1980. *Islam: A Historical Survey*. Oxford: Oxford University Press.
Gibb, H. A. R. and J. H. Kramers. 1953. *Shorter Encyclopaedia of Islam*. London: Luzac.
Gibbal, J.-M. 1994. *Genii of the River Niger*. Chicago: University of Chicago Press.
Gilsenan, M. 1973. *Saint and Sufi in Modern Egypt: An Essay in the Sociology of Religion*. Oxford: Clarendon Press.
Gilsenan, M. 1982. *Recognising Islam: An Anthropologist's Introduction*. London and Canberra: Croom Helm.
Gilsenan, M. 1987. ' Sacred words', in A. Al-Shahi (ed.), *The Diversity of the Muslim Community*. London: Ithaca Press, pp. 92–8.
Gomez-Perez, M. 1991. 'Associations islamiques à Dakar', *Islam et Sociétés au Sud du Sahara* (5): 5–20.
Gomez-Perez, M. 1997. 'Un mouvement culturel vers l'independence: Le réformisme musulman au Sénégal (1956–1960)', in D. Robinson and J. L. Triaud (eds), *Le temps des marabouts: itinéraires et stratégies islamiques en Afrique occidental français, v.1880–1960*. Paris: Editions Karthala, pp. 521–38.
Goody, J. (ed.). 1968a. *Literacy in Traditional Societies*. Cambridge: Cambridge University Press.
Goody, J. 1968b. 'Introduction', in J. Goody (ed.), *Literacy in Traditional Societies*. Cambridge: Cambridge University Press, pp. 1–27.
Goody, J. 1968c. 'Restricted literacy in Northern Ghana', in J. Goody (ed.), *Literacy in Traditional Societies*. Cambridge: Cambridge University Press, pp. 199–264.
Goody, J. 1980. *Technology, Tradition and the State in Africa*. London: Hutchinson.
Goody, J. and I. Watt. 1968. 'The Consequences of Literacy', in J. Goody (ed.), *Literacy in Traditional Societies*. Cambridge: Cambridge University Press, pp. 27–68.
Gosselin, G. 1974. 'Ordres, castes et états en pays Sérèr (Sénégal): Essai d'interpretation d'un système politique en transition', *Canadian Journal of African Studies* 8 (1): 135–43.
Gramsci, A. 1971. *Selections from the Prison Notebooks of Antonio Gramsci*, ed. and trans. Q. Hoare and G. Nowell Smith. London: Lawrence & Wishart.
Gray, C. 1988. 'The rise of the Niassene Tijanniyya, 1875 to the present', *Islam et Sociétés au Sud du Sahara* 2: 34–60.
Griaule, M. 1965. *Conversations with Ogotemmeli: An Introduction to Dogon Religious Ideas*. Oxford: Oxford University Press for the International African Institute.
Hamès, C. 1997. *L'art talismanique en islam d'Afrique occidentale: personnes, supports, procédés, transmission. Analyse anthropologique et islamologique d'un corpus de talismans à écritures*. Doctoral thesis, Paris EPHE.

Hammond, P. B. 1966. *Yatenga: Technology in the Culture of a West African Kingdom*, London: Collier Macmillan.
Hanson, J. H. 1996. *Migration, Jihad and Muslim Authority in West Africa: The Futanke Colonies in Karta*. Bloomington, IN: Indiana University Press.
Hébert, J. C. 1961. 'Analyse structurale des géomancies comoriennes, malgaches et africaines', *Journal de la société des africainists* XXXI (2): 115–208.
Helms, M. W. 1993. *Craft and the Kingly Ideal: Art, Trade and Power*. Austin, TX: University of Texas Press.
Herbert, E. W. 1993. *Iron, Gender and Power: Rituals of Transformation in African Societies*. Bloomington, IN: Indiana University Press.
Hilliard, O. 1997. *'Al-Majû' al Nafîs*: perspectives on the origins of the Muslim torodbe of Senegal from the writings of Shaykh Musa Kamara', *Islam et Sociétés au Sud du Sahara* 11: 85–105.
Hiskett, M. 1982. *The History of Islam in West Africa*. London: Longman.
Hiskett, M. 1984. *The Development of Islam in West Africa*. London: Longman.
Hoffman, B. G. 1995. 'Power, Structure and Mande *Jeliw*', in C. Conrad, C. and B. E. Frank (eds), *Status and Identity in West Africa: Nyamakalaw of Mande*. Bloomington, IN: Indiana University Press, pp. 36–45.
Holy, L. 1991. *Religion and Custom in a Muslim Society: The Berti of Sudan*. Cambridge: Cambridge University Press.
Horton, R. 1993. *Patterns of Thought in Africa and the West: Selected Theoretical Papers in Magic, Religion, and Science*. Cambridge and New York: Cambridge University Press.
Hoven, E. van. 1996. 'Local tradition or Islamic precept? The notion of Zakat in Wuli (Eastern Senegal)', *Cahiers d'études africaines* XXXVI, Part 4 (144): 703–22.
Hoven, E. van. 2000. 'The nation turbaned? The construction of nationalist Muslim identities in Senegal', *Journal of Religion in Africa* XXX (2): 225–48.
Ingold, T. (ed.). 1996. *Key Debates in Anthropology*. London: Routledge.
Irvine, J. T. 1978. 'When is genealogy history? Wolof genealogies in comparative perspective', *American Ethnologist* 5 (4): 651–74.
Jackson. M. 1982. *Allegories of the Wilderness: Ethics and Ambiguity in Kuranko Narratives*. Bloomington, IN: Indiana University Press.
Jackson, M. 1989. *Paths Towards a Clearing: Radical Empiricism and Ethnographic Inquiry*. Chicago: University of Chicago Press.
Jackson, M. and I. Karp (eds). 1990. *Personhood and Agency: The Experience of Self and Other in African Cultures*. Uppsala: University of Uppsala Press.
Jacobson-Widding, A. 1991. *Body and Space: Symbolic Models of Unity and Division in African Cosmology and Experience*. Uppsala: University of Uppsala Press.
Jacobson-Widding, A. and W. van Beek (eds). 1990. *The Creative Communion: African Models of Fertility and the Regeneration of Life*. Uppsala: University of Uppsala Press.
Jedrej, M. C. and R. Shaw (eds). 1992. *Dreaming, Religion and Society in Africa*. Leiden: Brill.
Johnson, J. P. 1974. *The Almamate of Futa Toro, 1770–1836: A Political History*. PhD thesis, University of Wisconsin.
Johnson, J. W. 1986. *The Epic of Son-Jara: A West African Tradition*. Bloomington, IN: Indiana University Press.
Johnson, M. 1977. 'Cloth strips and history', *West African Journal of Archaeology* 7: 169–78.
Johnson, M. 1980. 'Cloth as money: the cloth strip currencies of Africa', in D. Idiens and K. G. Ponting (eds), *Textiles of Africa*. Bath: Pasold Research Fund, pp. 193–202.

Ka, T. n.d. *Ecole de Pir Saniokhor: Histoire, Enseignement et Culture arabo-islamiques au Sénégal du XVIIe au XXe siècle*. Publié avec le concours de la Fondation Cadi Amar Fall à Pir.
Kamara, Cheikh Moussa [Shaykh Muusa]. 1970. See under Samb, A. 1970.
Kamara, Shaykh Muusa. 1998. *Florilège au jardin de l'histoire des noirs. Zuhur al-Basatin. L'Aristocratie peule et la révolution des clercs musulmans (vallée du Sénégal)* (sous la direction de Jean Schmitz). Paris: CNRS Editions.
Kane, A. S. 1935. 'Du régime des terres chez les populations du Fouta sénégalais', *Bulletin du Comité des Etudes Historiques et Scientifiques de l'Afrique Occidentale Française* XVIII (4): 449–61.
Kane, I. 1932. 'L'enfant toucouleur, Cercle de Matam', *Bulletin de l'Enseignement de l'Afrique Occidentale Française* 79: 99–102.
Kane, I. 1937. 'Le circoncision chez les Toucouleurs', *Bulletin de l'Enseignement de l'Afrique Occidentale Française* 96: 42–7.
Kane, M. M. 1994. 'L'Empreinte de l'islam confrerique sur le paysage commercial sénégalais: islam et société en sénégambie', *Islam et Sociétés au Sud du Sahara* 8: 17–41.
Kane, M. and D. Robinson. 1984. *The Islamic Regime of Fuuta Tooro: An Anthology of Oral Tradition Transcribed in Pulaar and Translated into English*. Michigan: African Studies Center, Michigan State University.
Kane, O. 1974. 'Les Maures et le Futa-Toro au XVIIIe siècle', in *Cahiers d'études africaines* 14 (2): 237–52.
Kane, O. 1997. 'Shaikh al-Islam Al-Hajj Ibrahim Niasse', in D. Robinson and J. L. Triaud (eds), *Le temps des marabouts itinéraires et stratégies islamiques en Afrique occidentale française, v. 1880–1960*. Paris: Karthala, pp. 299–316.
Kane, O. and J.-L. Triaud (eds). 1998. *Islam et Islamismes au sud de Sahara*. Paris: Ireman-Karthala-MSH.
Kante, N. 1993. *Forgerons d'Afrique noire: transmission des savoirs traditionnels en pays malinké*. Paris: L'Harmattan.
Kati, M. 1964. *Tarikh el Fettach*, trans. O. Houdas and M. Delafosse. Paris: Adrien-Maisonneuve.
Klein, M. A. 1968. *Islam and Imperialism in Senegal: Sine-Saloum 1847–1914*. Edinburgh: Edinburgh University Press.
Klein, M. A. 1972. 'Social and economic factors in the Muslim revolution in Senegambia', *Journal of African History* XIII (3): 419–41.
Klein, M. A. (ed.). 1993. *Breaking the Chains: Slavery, Bondage and Emancipation in Modern African and Asia*. Madison, WI: University of Wisconsin Press.
Klein, M. A. 1998. *Slavery and Colonial Rule in French West Africa*. Cambridge: Cambridge University Press.
Knight, D. 1994. *A Burning Hunger*. London: Panos.
Koran, The. n.d. Trans. G. Sale, first published in 1734. London: Frederick Warne.
Kyburz, O. 1994. *Les hiérarchies sociales et leurs fondements idéologiques chez les Haalpulaar'en (Sénégal)*. Doctoral thesis, Université de Paris X.
Labouret, H. 1952. *La Langue des Peuls ou Foulbé. Lexique Français–Peul*, Mémoires de l'Institut Français d'Afrique Noire, No. 41. Dakar: IFAN.
Labutut, R. 1987. 'La parole à travers quelques proverbes peuls du Fouladou (Sénégal)', *Journal des Africanistes* 57 (1–2): 67–76.
Lagoutte, C. 1988. 'L'artisanat féminin dans la région du Fleuve, Sénégal', *Canadian Journal of African Studies* 22 (3): 448–71.
Lake, R. 1997. 'The making of a Mouride Mahdi: Serigne Abdoulaye Yakkine Diop of Thies', in E. Evers Rosander and D. Westerlund (eds), *African Islam and Islam in Africa: Encounters between Sufis and Islamists*. London: Hurst & Co., pp. 216–53.

Lambek, M. 1993. *Knowledge and Practice in Mayotte: Local Discourses of Islam, Sorcery and Spirit Possession.* London and Toronto: University of Toronto Press.
Lane, E. W. 1968. *Arabic–English Lexicon*, 8 Parts. Beirut: Librairie du Liban.
Last, M. 1967a. 'A note on attitudes to the supernatural in the Sokoto Jihad', *Journal of the Historical Society of Nigeria* IV (1): 3–13.
Last, M. 1967b. *The Sokoto Caliphate.* London: Longman.
Last, M. 1988. 'Charisma and medicine in Northern Nigeria', in D. B. Cruise O'Brien and C. Coulon (eds), *Charisma and Brotherhood in African Islam.* Oxford: Clarendon Press, pp. 183–204.
Launay, R. 1982. *Traders without Trade: Responses to Change in Two Dyula Communities.* Cambridge: Cambridge University Press.
Launay, R. 1992. *Beyond the Stream: Islam and Society in a West African Town.* Berkeley, CA: University of California Press.
Launay, R. 1997. 'Spirit media: the electronic media and Islam among the Dyula of Northern Ivory Coast', *Africa* 67 (3): 441–53.
Launay, R. 2000. 'Pedigrees and paradigms: scholarly credentials among the Dyula of the Northern Ivory Coast', in D. F. Eickelman and J. Piscatori (eds), *Muslim Travellers: Pilgrimage, Migration, and the Religious Imagination.* London and New York: Routledge, pp. 175–99.
Launay, R. and B. F. Soares. 1999. 'The formation of an "Islamic sphere" in French Colonial West Africa', *Economy and Society* 28 (4): 497–519.
Leach, E. 1970. *Political System of Highland Burma: A Study of Kachin Social Structure.* London: Athlone Press.
LeBlanc, C. 1964. 'Un village de la vallée du Sénégal: Amadi Ounaré', *Cahiers d'Outre-Mer* 66: 117–48.
Lévi-Strauss, C. 1969. *Totemism.* Harmondsworth: Penguin.
Lévi-Strauss, C. 1976 [1955]. *Tristes Tropiques.* Harmondsworth: Penguin.
Lévi-Strauss, C. 1989 [1966]. *The Savage Mind.* London: Weidenfeld & Nicolson.
Levtzion, N. 1977. 'The Western Maghrib and Sudan', in R. Oliver (ed.), *The Cambridge History of Africa*, Vol. 3, (c.1050–1600). Cambridge: Cambridge University Press.
Levtzion, N. 1978. 'The Sahara and the Sudan from the Arab conquest of the Maghrib to the rise of the Almoravids', in J. D. Fage (ed.), *The Cambridge History of Africa*, Vol. 2 (c.500 B.C.–A.D. 1050). Cambridge: Cambridge University Press.
Levtzion, N. 1979. ʻAbd Allah b. Yasin and the Almoravids', in J. R. Willis (ed.), *Studies in West African Islamic History: Volume I, the Cultivators of Islam.* London: Frank Cass.
Levtzion, N. 1987. 'Rural and urban Islam in West Africa: an introductory essay', in N. Levtzion and H. J. Fisher (eds), *Rural and Urban Islam in West Africa.* London: Lynne Rienner, pp. 1–20.
Lewis, I. M. 1980. 'Introduction', in I. M. Lewis (ed.), *Islam in Tropical Africa.* London: Oxford University Press for the International African Institute, pp. 1–98.
Leymarie, I. 1979. *The Role and Functions of the Griots among the Wolof of Senegal.* PhD thesis, Columbia University.
Lienhardt, G. 1963. 'On modes of thought', in E. Evans-Pritchard (ed.), *Institutions of Primitive Society: A Series of Broadcast Talks.* Oxford: Blackwell.
Lienhardt, P. A. (ed. and trans.) 1968. *The Medicine Man: Swifa Ya Nguvumali.* Oxford: Clarendon Press.
Lienhardt, P. A. 1987. 'Disorientations', in A. Al-Shahi (ed.), *The Diversity of the Muslim Community: Anthropological Essays in Memory of Peter Lienhardt.*

London: Ithaca Press, pp. 7–27.
Loimeier, R. 1994. 'Cheikh Toure: Du reformise à l'islamisme, un musulman sénégalais dans le siècle', *Islam et Sociétés au Sud du Sahara* 8: 55–66.
Loimeier, R. 2000. 'L'Islam ne se vend plus: the Islamic Reform Movement and the State in Senegal', *Journal of Religion in Africa* XXX (2): 168–90.
Ly, B. 1967. 'L'honneur dans les sociétés Oulof et Toucouleur du Sénégal', *Presence Africaine* 61: 32–67.
Ly, D. 1938. 'Coutumes et contes des toucouleurs du Fouta Toro', *Bulletin du Comité des Etudes Historiques et Scientifiques de l'Afrique Occidentale Française* XXI (2): 304–26.
Macey, D. 2000. *The Penguin Dictionary of Critical Theory*. Harmondsworth: Penguin.
McLaughlin, F. 1997. 'Islam and popular music in Senegal: the emergence of a new tradition', *Africa* 67 (4): 560–81.
McLaughlin, F. 2000. '"In the Name of God I Will Sing Again, Mawdo Malik the Good": popular music and the Senegalese Sufi Tariqas', *Journal of Religion in Africa* XXX (2): 191–207.
McNaughton, P. R. 1988a. *The Mande Blacksmiths: Knowledge, Power, and Art in West Africa*. Bloomington, IN: Indiana University Press.
McNaughton, P. R. 1988b. 'The semantics of *Jugu*: blacksmiths, lore and who's bad in Mande', *Anthropological Linguistics* 30 (2): 150–65.
McNaughton, P. R. 1995. 'The semantics of *Jugu*: blacksmiths, lore and "who's bad" in Mande', in C. Conrad and B. E. Frank (eds), *Status and Identity in West Africa: Nyamakalaw of Mande*. Bloomington, IN: Indiana University Press, pp. 46–60.
Magassouba, M. 1985. *L'Islam au Sénégal: Demain les mollahs?* Paris: Karthala.
Malinowski, B. 1935. *Coral Gardens and Their Magic: A Study of the Methods of Tilling the Soil and of Agricultural Rites in the Trobriand Islands*, 2 vols. London: George Allen & Unwin.
Markovitz, I. L. 1970. 'Traditional social structure, the Islamic brotherhoods and political development in Senegal', *Journal of Modern African Studies* 8 (1): 73–96.
Marone, I. 1970. 'Le Tidjanisme au Sénégal', *Bulletin de l'IFAN* (série B) 32 (1): 136–215.
Marty, P. 1915–16. *L'Islam en Mauritanie at au Sénégal* [*Revue du Monde Musulman*, vol. 31]. Paris: E. Leroux.
Marty, P. 1917. *Etudes sur l'Islam au Sénégal: Vol. I, Les Personnes; Vol. II, Les doctrines et les institutions*. Paris: Leroux.
Mauny, R. 1961. *Tableau géographique de l'ouest africain au Moyen Age*, Mémoire de l'IFAN, No. 61. Dakar: IFAN.
Mauss, M. 1990. *The Gift: the Form and Reason for Exchange in Archaic Societies*. London: Routledge.
Meillassoux, C. (ed.). 1971. 'Introduction', in C. Meillassoux (ed.), *The Development of Indigenous Trade and Markets in West Africa*. London: Oxford University Press for the International African Institute.
Meillassoux, C. 1975. *L'Esclavage en Afrique précoloniale*. Paris: Maspero.
Meillassoux, C. 1986. *Anthropologie de l'esclavage: le ventre de fer et d'argent*. Paris: Presse Universitaire de France.
Meyer, G. 1991. *Récits épiques toucouleurs*. Paris: Karthala.
Miner, H. 1953. *The Primitive City of Timbuctoo*. Princeton, NJ: Princeton University Press.
Mollien, G. T. [1820] 1967. *Travels in the Interior of Africa to the Sources of the Senegal and Gambia*, ed. T. E. Bowdich. London: Frank Cass.

Monteil, C. 1926. 'Le coton chez les noirs', *Bulletin du Comité des Etudes Historiques et Scientifiques de l'Afrique Occidentale Française* IX (4): 585–684.
Monteil, C. 1939. 'Le Tékrour et la Guinée', *Outre-Mer* 3: 387–405.
Monteil, C. 1965. 'Notes sur le Tarikh es Soudan', *Bulletin de l'IFAN* (série B) XXVII: 479–530.
Monteil, V. 1968. 'Al-Bakri; (Cordoe 1068), Routier de l'Afrique blanche et noire du Nord-Ouest', *Bulletin de l'IFAN* (série B) XXX: 39–116.
Monteil, V. 1969. 'Marabouts', in J. Kritzeck and W. H. Lewis (eds), *Islam in Africa*. New York: Van Nostrand-Reinhold, pp. 87–109.
Monteil, V. 1980. *L'Islam noir: une religion à la conquête de l'Afrique*. Paris: Editions du Seuil.
Morice, A. 1982. *Les forgerons de Kaolack: travail non salarié et déploiement d'une caste au Sénégal*. Paris: Thèse de doctorat de 3ième cycle.
Morris, B. 1991. *Western Conceptions of the Individual*. London: Berg.
Needham, R. 1978. 'Introduction', in R. Needham (ed.), *Right and Left: Essays on Dual Symbolic Classification*. Chicago: University of Chicago Press.
Needham, R. 1980. *Reconnaissances*. Toronto: University of Toronto Press.
Niang, M. 1997. *Pulaar–English/English–Pulaar Standard Dictionary*. New York: Hippocrene Books.
Panzacchi, C. 1994. 'The livelihoods of traditional griots in modern Senegal', *Africa* 64 (2): 190–210.
Parkin, D. (ed.). 1982. *Semantic Anthropology*. London: Athlone Press.
Paulme, D. 1939. 'Parenté à plaisanteries et alliance par le sang en Afrique occidentale', *Africa* 12, (4): 433–44.
Peel, J. D. Y. 1968. *Aladura: A Religious Movement among the Yoruba*. Published for the International African Institute by Oxford University Press.
Peel, J. D. Y. and C. C. Stewart (eds). 1985. *'Popular Islam' South of the Sahara* (special edition of *Africa* in association with Manchester University Press) 55 (4).
Pitt-Rivers, J. 1971. 'On the word "caste"', in T. O. Beidelman (ed.), *The Translation of Culture*. London: Tavistock, pp. 231–56.
Prussin, L. 1986. *Hatumere: Islamic Design in West Africa*. Berkeley, CA: University of California Press.
Quigley, D. 1995. *The Interpretation of Caste*. Oxford: Clarendon Press.
Rasmussen, S. J. 1992. 'Ritual specialists, ambiguity and power in Tuareg society', *Man* 27: 105–28.
Rattray, R. S. 1927. *Religion and Art in Ashanti*. London: Oxford University Press.
Ravault, F. 1964. 'Kanel. L'exode rural dans un village de la vallée du Sénégal', *Les Cahiers d'Outre-Mer* 17: 58–80.
Recensement général de la population. 1976 [1982] and 1988 [c.1992]. Dakar: Bureau National du Recensement.
Richter, D. 1980. 'Further considerations of caste in West Africa: the Senufo', *Africa* 50 (1): 37–54.
Ritchie, C. I. A. 1968. 'Deux textes sur le Sénégal', *Bulletin de l'IFAN* (série B) XXX: 289–353.
Rivière, C. 1969. 'Guinée: La difficile émergence d'un artisanat casté', *Cahiers d'études africaines* IX (36): 600–25.
Robin, J. 1947. 'L'Evolution du mariage coutumier chez les musulmans du Sénégal', *Africa* XVII: 192–201.
Robinson, D. 1975a. *Chiefs and Clerics: Abdul Bokar Kan and Futa Toro 1853–1891*. Oxford: Clarendon Press.
Robinson, D. 1975b. 'The Islamic revolution in Futa Toro', *International Journal of African Historical Studies* 3 (2): 185–221.

Robinson, D. 1985. *The Holy War of Umar Tal: The Western Sudan in the Mid-Nineteenth Century*. Oxford: Clarendon Press.
Robinson, D. 1988. 'Un historien et anthropologue sénégalais: Shaikh Musa Kamara', *Cahiers d'études africaines* 28 (1): 89–116.
Robinson, D. 1997. 'Muslim societies in secular space', in D. Robinson and J. L. Triaud (eds), *Le temps des marabouts: itinéraires et stratégies islamiques en Afrique occidental français, v.1880–1960*. Paris: Editions Karthala, pp. 559–75.
Robinson, D. and J. L. Triaud (eds). 1997. *Le temps des marabouts: itinéraires et stratégies islamiques en Afrique occidental français, v.1880–1960*. Paris: Editions Karthala.
Robinson, D., P. Curtin and J. Johnson. 1972. 'A tentative chronology of Futa Toro from the sixteenth century through the nineteenth century', *Cahiers d'études africains* XII (48): 555–92.
Ryan, P. J. 2000. 'The mystical theology of Tijani Sufism and its social significance in West Africa', *Journal of Religion in Africa* XXX (2): 208–224.
Said, E. W. 1978. *Orientalism*. Harmondsworth: Penguin.
Samb, A. 1970. 'La vie d'El-Hadji Omar' by Cheikh Moussa Kamara, trans. and ed. A. Samb, *Bulletin de l'IFAN* (série B) 32: 44–135, 370–411, 770–818.
Samb, A. 1971. 'L'Islam et l'histoire du Sénégal', *Bulletin de l'IFAN* (série B) 33 (3): 461 507.
Sanneh, L. O. 1979. *The Jakhanke: The History of an Islamic Clerical People of the Senegambia*. London: International Africa Institute.
Sanneh, L. O. 1987. 'Tcherno Aliou, the Walî of Goumba: Islam, colonialism and the rural factor in Futa Jallon 1867–1912', in N. Levtzion and H. J. Fisher (eds), *Rural and Urban Islam in West Africa*. London: Lynne Rienner.
Sanneh, L. 1989. *The Jakhanke Muslim Clerics: A Religious and Historical Study*. Lanham, MD and London: University Press of America.
Sanneh, L. 1997. *The Turban and the Crown: Muslims and West African Pluralism*. Boulder, CO and Oxford: Westview Press.
Savishinsky, N. J. 1994. 'The Baye Faal of Senegambia: Muslim Rastas in the promised land?', *Africa* 64 (2): 211–19.
Schmitz, J. 1983a. *Les Toorobbe du Fuuta Tooro: formation d'une classe cléricale et dispersion en Afrique de l'ouest*. Paper presented at 'La Table ronde: Les agents religieux islamiques en Afrique tropicale', Paris.
Schmitz, J. 1983b. 'Un politologue chez les marabouts', *Cahiers d'études africaines* XXIII, Part 3 (91): 329–51.
Schmitz, J. 1985a. 'Le féminine devient masculin: politique matrimoniale des Halpulaar', *Journal des Africanistes* 55 (1–2): 105–25.
Schmitz, J. 1985b. 'Autour d'al-Hajj Umar Taal. Guerre sainte et Tijaniyya en Afrique de l'ouest', *Cahiers d'études africaines* XXV, Part 4 (100): 555–65.
Schmitz, J. 1986. 'L'Etat géomètre: les *leydi* des Peuls du Fuuta Tooro (Sénégal) et du Maasina (Mali)', *Cahiers d'études africaines* XXVI, Part 3 (103): 349–94.
Schmitz, J. 1988. 'Rhétorique et géolitique [sic – géopolitique] du *jihâd* d'al-Hajj Umar Taal', *Cahiers d'études africaines* XXXVIII, Part 1 (109): 123–33.
Schmitz, J. 1990. 'Histoire savante et formes spatio-généalogiques de la mémoire (Haalpulaar de la vallée du Sénégal)', *Cahiers des sciences humaines* 26 (4): 531–52.
Schmitz, J. 1992. 'Florilège au jardin des opprimés ...: Une traduction de la monumentale histoire des Noirs de Shaykh Musa Kamara', *Islam et Sociétés au Sud du Sahara* 6: 81–94.
Schmitz, J. 1993. 'Anthropologie des conflits fonciers et hydropolitique du fleuve Sénégal (1975–1991)', *Cahiers des sciences humaines* 29 (4): 591–624.
Schmitz, J. 1994. 'Cités noires: les republiques villageoises du Fuuta Tooro (Vallée

du Fleuve, Sénégal)', *Cahiers d'études africaines* XXXIV (1–3): 419–60.
Schmitz, J. 1998. 'Introduction' to Shaykh Muusa Kamara, *Florilège au jardin de l'histoire des noirs. Zuhur al-Basatin. L'Aristocratie peule et la révolution des clercs musulmans (vallée du Sénégal)*, ed. Jean Schmitz. Paris: CNRS Editions, pp. 9–91.
Schmitz, J. 2000a. 'Le souffle de la parenté: mariage et transmission de la baraka chez des clercs musulmans de la vallée du Sénégal', *L'Homme* 154: 241–78.
Schmitz, J. 2000b. 'L'islam en Afrique de l'Ouest: les méridiens et les parallèles, *Autrepart* 16 (special issue, eds E. Grégoire et J. Schmitz, *Afrique noire et monde arabe: continuités et ruptures*): 117–37.
Schmitz, J. and R. Botte (eds). 1994. *L'Archipel Peul*. Paris: Ecole des Hautes Etudes en Sciences Sociales.
Searing, J. 1993. *West African Slavery and Atlantic Commerce: The Senegal River Valley 1700–1860*. Cambridge: Cambridge University Press.
Seesemann, R. n.d. 'The *Shurafâ*' and the blacksmith: the role of the Idaw 'Alî of Mauritania in the career of the Senegalese Tijânî Shaykh Ibrâhîm Niasse (1900–75)'. Unpublished paper.
Seydou, C. 1987. 'La notion de parole dans le dialecte peul du Massina (Mali)', *Journal des Africanistes* 57 (1–2): 48–66.
Seymour, S. 1996. 'Caste', in D. Levinson and M. Ember (eds), *Encyclopedia of Cultural Anthropology*. New York: Henry Holt, pp. 177–81.
Shaw, T. M. 1993. *The Fulani Matrix of Beauty and Art*. Lewiston, NY: Edwin Mellen Press.
Silla, O. 1966. 'Persistence des castes dans la société wolof contemporaine', *Bulletin de l'IFAN* (série B) XXVIII (3–4): 731–70.
Sirriyeh, E. 2000. 'Editorial', *Journal of Religion in Africa* XXX (2): 141–2.
Skinner, E. P. 1964. *The Mossi of the Upper Volta: the Political Development of a Sudanese People*. Stanford, CA: Stanford University Press.
Skinner, E. P. 1974. 'West African economic systems', in M. J. Herskovits and M. Harwitz (eds), *Economic Transition in Africa*. London: Routledge & Kegan Paul, pp. 77–98.
Soares, B. F. 1996. 'The prayer economy in a Malian town', *Cahiers d'études africaines* XXXVI, Part 4 (144): 739–53.
Soares, B. F. 1997a. *The Spiritual Economy of Nioro du Sahel: Islamic Discourses and Practices in a Malian Religious Center*. PhD dissertation, Northwestern University.
Soares, B. F. 1997b. 'The Fulbe Shaykh and the Bambara pagans', in Mirjam de Bruijn and Han van Dijk (eds), *Peuls et Mandingues: dialectique des constructions identitaires*. Paris: Karthala, pp. 267–80.
Soares, B. F. 1999. 'Muslim proselytization as purification: religious pluralism and conflict in contemporary Mali', in Abdullahi Ahmed An-Na'im (ed.), *Proselytization and Communal Self-Determination in Africa*. New York: Orbis Books, pp. 228–45.
Soh, S. A. 1913. *Chroniques du Fouta sénégalais*, trans. M. Delafosse and H. Gaden. Paris: Leroux.
Sterner, J. and N. David, 1990. 'Gender and caste in the Mandara Highlands: Northeastern Nigeria and Northern Cameroon', *Ethnology* 30: 355–69.
Stewart, C. C. 1973. *Islam and Social Order in Mauritania: A Case Study from the Nineteenth Century*. Oxford: Clarendon Press.
Stewart, C. C. 1985. 'Introduction: popular Islam in twentieth-century Africa', in J. D. Y. Peel and C. C. Stewart (eds), *'Popular Islam' South of the Sahara* (special edition of *Africa* in association with Manchester University Press) 55 (4): 364–68.
Stirrat, R. L. 1984. 'Sacred models', *Man* 19 (2): 199–215.

Stoller, P. 1987. *In Sorcery's Shadow: A Memoir of Apprenticeship among the Songhay of Niger*. Chicago: University of Chicago Press.
Stoller, P. 1992. *The Taste of Ethnographic Things*. Philadelphia: University of Pennsylvania Press.
Stoller, P. 1995. *Embodying Colonial Memories: Spirit Possession, Power and the Hauka in West Africa*. London: Routledge.
Sy, Cheikh Tidiane. 1969. *La Confrérie sénégalaise des Mourides*. Paris: Présence Africaine.
Sylla, Y. 1982. *Grammaire moderne du Pulaar*. Dakar: Les Nouvelles Editions Africaines.
Tall, Cheikh A. 1994. *Niche des Secrets*. Dakar, Fann (Sénégal).
Tall, E. K. 1984. *Guérir à Cubalel: interprétation de la maladie et pratiques thérapeutiques chez les Haalpulaar'en dans la vallée du Fleuve Sénégal*. Thèse du 3ième cycle, Paris: EHESS.
Tamari, T. 1991. 'The development of caste systems in West Africa', *Journal of African History* 32: 221–50.
Tamari, T. 1995. 'Linguistic evidence for the history of West African castes', in C. Conrad and B. E. Frank (eds), *Status and Identity in West Africa: Nyamakalaw of Mande*. Bloomington, IN: Indiana University Press, pp. 61–85.
Tamari, T. 1997. *Les castes de l'Afrique occidentale*. Paris: Société d'Ethnologie.
Tambiah, S. 1969. 'The magical power of words', *Man* 3 (2): 175–208.
Tambiah, S. 1990. *Magic, Science, Religion and the Scope of Rationality*. Cambridge: Cambridge University Press.
Taylor, F. W. [1932] 1995. *Fulani–English Dictionary*. New York: Hippocrene Books.
Thomas, N. 1996. 'History and anthropology', in A. Barnard and J. Spencer (eds), *Encyclopedia of Social and Cultural Anthropology*. London: Routledge, pp. 272–7.
Thurnwald, R. [1932] 1965. *Economics in Primitive Communities*. London: Oxford University Press.
Todd, D. M. 1977. 'Caste in Africa?', *Africa* 47 (4): 398–412.
Triaud, J.-L. 1988. 'Khalwa and the career of sainthood: an interpretative essay', in D. B. Cruise O'Brien and C. Coulon (eds), *Charisma and Brotherhood in African Islam*. Oxford: Clarendon Press, pp. 53–66.
Triaud, J.-L. 1997. 'Introduction', in D. Robinson and J. L. Triaud (eds), *Le temps des marabouts: itinéraires et stratégies islamiques en Afrique occidental français, v.1880–1960*. Paris: Editions Karthala, pp. 11–29.
Trimingham, J. S. 1959. *Islam in West Africa*. Oxford: Clarendon Press.
Trimingham, J. S. 1962. *A History of Islam in West Africa*. London: Oxford University Press.
Tuden, A. and L. Plotnicov (eds). 1970. *Social Stratification in Africa*. New York: Free Press.
Tyam, M. A. 1935. *La vie d'El Hajj Omar, qacida en Poular*, transcription, trans, notes and glossary Henri Gaden. Paris: Institut d'Ethnologie.
Vaughan, J. H. Jr. 1970. 'Caste systems in the Western Sudan', in A. Tuden and L. Plotnicov (eds), *Social Stratification in Africa*. New York: Free Press, pp. 52–92.
Vaughan, J. H. 1973. '@ŋkyagu as artists in Marghi society', in W. L. d'Azevedo (ed.), *The Traditional Artist in West African Societies*. Bloomington, IN: Indiana University Press, pp. 162–93.
Vidal, M. 1935. 'Etude sur la tenure des terres indigènes au Fouta', *Bulletin du Comité des Etudes Historiques et Scientifiques de l'Afrique Occidentale Française* XVIII (4): 415–48.
Villalón, L. A. 1993. 'Charisma and ethnicity in political context: a case study in the establishment of a Senegalese religious clientele', *Africa* 63 (1): 80–101.

Villalón, L. A. 1994. 'Sufi rituals as rallies: religious ceremonies in the politics of Senegalese state–society relations', *Comparative Politics* 26 (4): 415–38.
Villalón, L. A. 1995. *Islamic Society and State Power in Senegal: Disciples and Citizens in Fatick*. Cambridge: Cambridge University Press.
Wane, Y. 1969. *Les Toucouleurs du Fouta Tooro (Sénégal). Stratification sociale et structure familiale*. Dakar: IFAN.
Westermarck, E. 1926. *Ritual and Belief in Morocco*, 2 vols. London: Macmillan.
Westermarck, E. 1933. *Pagan Survivals in Mohammedan Civilisation*. London: Macmillan.
White, H. 1973. 'Foucault decoded: notes from underground', *History and Theory* 12: 23–54.
Wilks, I. 1968. 'The transmission of Islamic learning in the Western Sudan', in J. Goody (ed.), *Literacy in Traditional Societies*. Cambridge: Cambridge University Press. pp. 162–97.
Willis, J. R. 1967. '*Jihad fi sabîl Allâh*: its doctrinal basis in Islam and some aspects of its evolution in 19th century West Africa', *Journal of African History* 3: 395–415.
Willis, J. R. 1970. *Al-Hâjj 'Umar b. Sa'îd al-Fûtî al-Tûri (c. 1794–1864) and the Doctrinal Basis of his Islamic Reformist Movement in the Western Sudan*. PhD thesis, SOAS, University of London.
Willis, J. R. 1978. 'The Torodbe clerisy: a social view', *Journal of African History* XIX (2) 195–212.
Willis, J. R. 1979. 'Introduction: reflections on the diffusion of Islam in West Africa', in J. R. Willis (ed.), *Studies in West African Islamic History: The Cultivators of Islam*. London: Frank Cass, pp. 1–39.
Willis, J. R. 1989. *In the Path of Allah: The Passion of Al-Hajj 'Umar. An Essay into the Nature of Charisma in Islam*. London: Frank Cass.
Willis, R. 1996. 'Magic', in A. Barnard and J. Spencer (eds), *Encyclopedia of Social and Cultural Anthropology*. London: Routledge, pp. 340–2.
Wright, B. 1989. 'The power of articulation' in W. Arens and I. Karp (eds), *Creativity of Power: Cosmology and Action in African Societies*. Washington, DC: Smithsonian Institution.
Zebadia, Abdel Kader. 1974. *The Career and Correspondence of Ahmad al-Bekkay of Timbuktu, from 1847–1866*. PhD thesis, SOAS, University of London.
Zebadia, Abdel Kader. 1975. 'The career of Ahmad al-Bekkay in the oral evidence and recorded documents', *Revue d'Histoire Maghrebine* 3: 75–83.
el-Zein, Abdel Hamid, 1977. 'Beyond ideology and theology: the search for an anthropology of Islam', *Annual Review of Anthropology* 6: 227–54.

INDEX

Acc (family), 51, 52
age-set, 21, 104, 119
agriculture, 11, 15, 29, 46–7, 54, 55–6, 80–2
al-Bakkai, Ahmad, 105, 234n
al-Bakri, 60, 91, 226n
al-Idrissi, 60, 91, 225n
Allah, 69, 99, 107, 116, 136, 148, 150, 151, 168
　names of, 12, 132–3, 144, 151, 166, 188
Almaamate regime, 1, 6, 14, 16, 19, 50, 51, 52, 53, 57, 83, 89, 91, 94, 97, 101, 105, 112, 114, 126, 214
Almaamy, office of, 36–7, 55, 93, 94, 96, 97, 99
Almoravids, 91
Amadu Bamba, 20, 200
Amselle, J-L., 236n
amulets, 52, 70, 74, 117, 135, 151, 194
Anderson, B., 19
angels, 99, 127, 150, 165, 177, 185
animal 'voices', 162–3
　of birds, 176
apprenticeship, 95, 118, 135, 143, 148, 150, 155, 196, 197
Arabic (language), 20, 58, 94, 95, 96, 109, 148, 158, 172, 174, 180, 184, 185, 196, 225n, 232n
archaeology, Foucault's concept of, 2, 84, 220n
Ardener, E., 22
Asad, T., 7, 111, 221n
authority, forms of, 9, 10, 54, 77, 84, 85, 88, 89, 98, 108, 109, 133, 192, 193, 207, 212, 213, 215, 217

Ba, Omar, 140, 149, 205
Baal, Suleyman, 36, 92

Bakel, 14, 15, 16, 50
baraka, 10, 13, 24, 95, 102, 109, 150, 180, 207
Barber, K., 160
Bello, Muhammed, 12, 102
Berti, 131
bondsmen/women, 28, 29, 30, 33, 37, 46–8, 55, 77–9, 162; *see also* slaves
bondswomen, 45
Borno, 102
Botte, R., 118, 237n
Brenner, L., 14, 22, 109, 150, 152, 154, 195, 196, 197, 235n, 239–40n, 241n, 244n
bridewealth, 51, 96, 198
brotherhoods, Sufi, 2, 3, 10, 21, 93, 152, 169, 196, 199, 201, 203, 206–11, 216–18, 245n; *see also* Murids, Nyasiyya, Qadiriyya, Tijaniyya

Ca da Mosto, 60, 227n
Caam, Mamadu Aliyu, 103–5, 233–4n
caste
　anthropology of, 1, 43–5
　conceptions of, 6, 60, 78, 82, 84
　Indian system of, 27, 45
　inequality, 98, 200–4
cattle-herding, 31–2, 73, 96, 134, 221n
chief
　of territory, 29, 36, 50
　of village, 35–6
circumcision, 114, 118–22
　female, 38, 74, 118
　male, 71, 74, 104
clerics, 220n
cosmology, 23, 71, 88, 90, 99, 101, 114, 115, 128, 139
cotton cloth, 59–60, 224n, 226n
Coulon, C., 3, 220n, 236n

INDEX

crocodile, 67, 68, 69, 164
Cruise O'Brien, D., 5, 194, 216, 230n, 244n, 245n, 247n
cultivation rights, 29, 46–7, 53
Curtin, P., 228n

Dagana, 14, 15
dancing, 38
Davis, J., 227–8n
Delafosse, M., 225n
Deniyaŋke regime, 14, 31, 33, 40, 50, 62, 63, 64, 66, 78, 91, 92, 93, 98, 112, 222n
Diop, A. B., 202, 237n
divination, 9, 12, 135, 139, 149, 152, 180–1, 211, 243–4n
  by dreams, 34, 151, 240n
division of labour, 15, 27, 30, 54, 55, 82, 86, 136, 138, 139, 151, 152, 162
Dogon, 109, 212
dualism, 90, 110, 111, 115
Dumga Rinjaow, 51–3
Dumont, F., 233n, 234n
Dumont, L., 115, 222n, 233n, 236n
Durkheim, E., 138
Dyula, 7, 9, 11, 12, 193

education, 195–7
Eickelman, D., 8
el-Zein, A., 220n
episteme, 191, 220n, 239–40n
  esoteric, 154, 195, 196, 240n
estates see also social ranks
Evans-Pritchard, E. E., x, 141, 239n
  Lectures, xiii

Faidherbe, Louis, 195
Fairclough, N., 112
family code, 203, 218
fetishisation, 85–8
Fez, 35, 193
Fisher, H., 112
fishing, 67–9, 96
Foucault, M., 84, 177, 190, 191, 220n
freeborn, 27, 29, 30, 37, 54–5, 64, 66, 77–9, 162, 201, 208
Fulani, 11, 221n
Fuuta Jallon (Guinée), 17, 19, 20, 102, 118, 141, 149
Fuuta Toro, xi, 22
  description of, 15–16

Gaden, H., 107, 129, 174, 189, 190, 225n, 227n, 230n, 231n, 238n, 239n, 241n, 246n
gandal, 131–5; see also knowledge-power, lore
Gellner, E., 98, 162
genealogy
  Foucault's concept of, 1, 84, 220n
  of power, 57, 67, 84
Ghimbala cult, 25
Gibbal, J. M., 25–6, 233n, 235n, 237n, 242n
Gilsenan, M., 160, 239n, 241n, 243n
Gisse (family), 53, 136, 157, 211
Goody, J., 23, 160, 186, 188, 193, 222n
Gramsci, A., 129, 225–6n, 229n
griot, 5, 40, 205

Hadith, 7, 80, 96, 149
Hamadi Ounare, 28, 50–1, 53
Hamès, C., 158, 180, 187, 188, 194, 243n
healing, 152–5
hegemony, 229n
Helms, M., 54, 85, 87
hierarchy, 30, 45, 49–50, 83–5, 99, 100, 108, 112, 115, 122, 157
Hilliard, O., 230n, 231n
hippopotamus, 67, 68, 137, 165, 166
history
  and anthropology, x, 225n
  oral, 63–7
  sources of, 57–9
Horton, R., 116
Hoven, E. van, 219, 247n
hyena, 69, 74, 138

Ibn Khaldun, 13
ideology, 89–90, 98, 104, 114, 129, 159, 214, 233n
  definition of, 229n
  distinctions within, 100, 233n
  dominance by means of, 113
  Islamic, 99–101, 201
incantations, 23, 67, 68, 69–70, 71, 73, 74, 79, 86, 116, 137, 141, 144, 149, 151, 153, 164, 169, 171–5
Islam
  accommodationist, 23, 99, 108, 110, 112, 114–17, 121, 122, 129, 139, 157, 195, 201, 212, 214
  anthropology of, 1, 7

conceptions of, 7–9, 93, 99, 100, 103, 108, 192, 213, 214
in Senegal, 3–4, 90–3
integrationist, 108, 112, 113, 212, 214
multiple, 220n
noir, 110, 217, 221n
popular, 4–5, 197
reform of, 197–200
Sufism, 151, 152, 154, 212, 239n
Islamists, 2, 23, 124, 192, 198, 203, 207, 212, 213, 216, 217, 218

Jackson, M., 24, 82
Jahkanke, 25, 223n
jama'a (Muslim community), 2, 21, 22, 98, 99, 101, 104, 105, 106, 110, 129, 192, 200, 205
jinn (spirits), 13, 24, 25, 52, 59, 63, 67, 71, 73, 79, 99, 107, 114, 115, 123, 126, 141, 147, 150, 155, 156, 165, 177, 215–16, 234n
Johnson, J. P., 9, 230n

Kamara, Shaykh Musa, 51, 94, 95, 96, 102, 224fn, 230–1n, 234n
Kan, Abdul Qadir, 36, 37, 50, 52, 93, 102, 208, 224n
Kane, Cheikh Hamidou, 125
Kane, O., 246n, 247n
Kano, 207, 214
Klein, M., 7, 103
knowledge, 9, 110, 132–5, 193
  acquisition of, 9, 95, 112, 155
  esoteric, 150, 151, 154, 192, 212
  Islamic, 9, 95, 96, 97, 99, 102, 116, 147–51, 179–88, 207
  social division of, 57, 67, 84
  transmission of, 9, 88, 101, 150, 192, 207, 239n
  see also lore
knowledge-power, 4, 10, 13, 14, 62, 132, 133, 134, 154, 156, 157, 158, 213, 214; *see also gandal*, lore
Kyburz, O., 62, 63, 76, 96, 125, 126, 236n, 237n

Labutut, R., 160, 161
language, 161–4, 166–7, 169–71, 176–8, 189–91
  of spirits, 171, 172, 173

potency of, 164, 169, 189
secret, 120, 169
Last, M., 13, 197, 214, 217, 237n, 244n
Launay, R., 7, 8–9, 12, 193, 217, 247n
leatherworking, 73–4, 96
LeBlanc, C., 224n
Lévi-Strauss, C., 85, 186, 236n
Lewis, I. M., 113, 129, 216, 223n, 233n, 237n
Lienhardt, P., ix, 111, 146
Loimeier, R., 218, 244n
lore, 4, 56, 62, 69, 78, 79–82, 84, 86, 89–90, 95, 99, 100, 108, 111, 113, 114, 132, 156, 190, 212
  white and black, 89–113, 114–17, 131–2, 171, 202, 211
  see also gandal, knowledge-power

Ma Ba Diakhou, 20
Magassouba, M., 217
Maghreb, 16, 35, 90, 196
magic, 9, 24, 68, 79, 137, 139, 144, 147, 153, 158, 175–6, 177, 189
  Islamic, 12–14, 147
  nyengo, 155–7, 211
  of the book, 161, 192, 193–5, 197
  oral, 151, 175–8, 176–8
  written, 151, 179–80, 182–8
  see also power-practices, *sihr*
Mali, Empire of, 16
Maliki law, 11, 127, 223n, 233n
Malinowski, B., 171, 176, 187, 242n
Mande, 61, 62, 171, 174, 220n, 227n
marabouts
  derivation of term, 222n
  education of, 147–50
  role of, 34–5, 117–18, 124, 152–5, 178
Marone, I., 233n, 235n
Marty, P., 4, 158
Masina (Mali), 17, 25, 60, 98, 102
Matam, 50, 204
Mauritania, 14, 16, 35, 51, 93, 143, 207
medersa schools, 196, 197, 203
men-of-skill, 28, 29, 30, 37, 38–46, 54–5, 59–67, 77–9, 102, 105, 106, 108, 109, 112, 114, 118–22, 125, 128–30, 133, 134, 151, 154, 156, 164, 170, 211, 215–16
Miner, H., 232n

miracle, 12, 13
mode of accountability, 86
Monteil, C., 226n
Monteil, V., 17, 110, 204, 221n, 234n
Moors, 16, 19, 65, 92, 100
Morice, A., 202, 208
Morris, B., 236n
mosque, 21, 24, 52, 130, 146, 153, 154, 213, 214, 215
Murids, 3, 5, 10, 20, 21, 200, 201, 245n
musicians, 75, 204–5
muted groups, 22, 58; *see also* subaltern groups
myths of origin, 125–8

names, 164–7
Nasir al Din, 91, 92
Niang, M., 242n
noun classes, 80
Nyas family, 206–11
    Abdoulaye Nyas, 206
    Ibrahima Nyas, 207–9
Nyasiyya, 206–11
    legitimacy of, 210

Panzacchi, C., 205, 245n, 246n
parallelism *see* dualism
patronyms, 48–9, 72, 95, 96, 136, 138, 231n
pedigrees, 57, 58, 63, 67, 69, 75, 82, 94, 167, 192
Peel, J. D. Y., 4, 116
Pir Sagnakhor, 9, 94, 95, 149, 222n
plants, 80
poetry, 84, 149, 167–8, 177
political economy, 2, 15, 27, 45, 48, 49–50, 53–6
pottery, 70
power
    charismatic, 12, 24, 57, 80, 108, 194, 204, 213, 214
    domains of, 106, 153, 189
    indigenous theory of, 83, 214
    of spoken word, 75, 152, 158, 160–1, 166–7, 188
    of written word, 152, 158, 160–1, 178–80, 188
    sources of, 79, 83, 85, 86, 212
power-practices, 88, 133, 148, 150, 151, 153, 155, 157, 161, 175, 178, 180, 190; *see also* magic

praise-singing, 5, 75–7, 96
    origin myth of, 127–8; *see also* griot
prayer, 13, 21, 168–9, 187
    power of, 152
pre-Islam, 13, 23, 66, 83, 89–90, 100, 109, 110, 131, 144, 151, 158, 200
production, 54, 85–8

Qadiriyya, 3, 8, 20, 35, 93, 95, 98, 101, 102, 103, 105, 200, 245n
Qur'an, 7, 71, 95, 97, 101, 115, 118, 143, 149, 160, 168, 186, 187
Qur'anic schools, 9, 11, 52, 93, 95, 148, 169, 195

race, 18, 43, 65–7, 69, 83, 221n, 226n, 228n, 234n
rites of passage, 117–22
Robinson, D., 4, 94, 101, 102, 104, 216, 230n, 234n, 247n

saints, 24, 148, 177
Sanneh, L., 223n, 233n
Sanusi (of Cyrenaica), x
Schmitz, J., 4, 5, 36, 95, 197, 208, 222n, 238n, 246n
script-potions, 144, 151, 154, 156, 179, 194
secrets *see also* knowledge, esoteric
Shari'a, 10, 45, 55, 193, 195, 198, 205, 216, 218
shirk, 106, 123, 125, 128, 144, 147, 195
Shurr Bubba, 92
sihr, 12–13, 106, 123, 147, 175, 195, 205; *see also* magic
slaves, 11, 28, 46, 48, 91, 97, 106, 113, 223n, 232n, 233n
smithing, 70–3, 96, 135
snake, 68, 155, 156, 164, 165
social categories, 30–1
social ranks, 27–30, 45, 77–9
Soh, Siré Abbâs, 225n
Sokoto, 11, 12, 102
songs, 23–4, 167, 177, 204–5
Soninke, 17, 43, 50, 61, 64, 66, 95, 171
sorcery, 24, 68, 139, 140, 189
Stewart, C., 4, 92
Stirrat, R., 236n
subaltern groups, 3, 22, 58, 78, 129, 225–6n
Sufism *see also* Islam, Sufism

Sy, Malik (1640–1700), 19, 126, 127
syncretism, 110, 112

Taal, Al Hajj Umar, 20, 23, 37, 64, 72, 93, 97, 101–10, 150, 192, 200, 206, 208, 212
Taal, Ceerno Bokar, 109–10, 206, 212, 235n
Takrur, 14, 16, 60, 91
talismans, 151, 153, 154, 156, 179–80, 182–8, 190, 194
Tall, E. K., 68, 143, 144, 153, 238n
Tall, Saidou Nourou, 20
Tamari, T., 6, 61
Tambiah, S., 175, 176, 242n
technologies of power, 13, 14, 24
termite mound, 24, 71, 99, 130, 146, 153, 154, 213, 214, 215
Tijaniyya, 3, 8, 20, 35, 93, 98, 102, 103, 104, 106, 109, 168, 192, 200, 206, 208, 245n
Timbuktu, 35, 103
Triaud, J-L., 4, 218
tribunals, customary, 202
Trimingham, J. S., 83, 100, 110, 141, 223n, 233n, 235n, 236n, 238n
Touré, Cheikh, 198, 199
Tukulor, 16, 19
Tyam, Mohammadou Allou *see also* Caam, M. A.

ulema, 9, 10
umma, 20, 22, 160

Villalón, L., 212, 245n, 246n, 247n

Wahhabism, 193, 196, 199, 233n, 244n
Wane, Y., 5, 27, 64, 71, 72, 84, 237n
weaving, 69–70, 96, 223n, 228n
  lore of, 136–9
  origins of, 126–7
Westermarck, E., 232n, 235n
White, H., 190
Willis, J. R., 94, 104, 113, 232n, 233n, 234n
witchcraft, 24, 68, 74, 117, 128, 139, 141–3, 147, 157
witch-hunters (*wileebe* or *bileejo*, sing.), 116, 120, 121, 122, 123, 135, 140–7, 149, 151, 152–5, 164, 178, 180, 189, 190
Wolof, 16, 17, 61, 62, 63, 65, 92, 95, 220n
women, marginalised position of, 203–4, 247n
woodcarving, 73
word
  spoken, 160–1, 167
  written, 160–1, 178–80
  see also language, magic, power

zawıya (lodge), x, 16, 35, 207, 215
Zebadia, A. K., 105, 234n